THE STELLAR SIX OF GINGACHO™

Volume 1
Yuuki Fujimoto

HAMBURG // LONDON // LOS ANGELES // TOKYO

The Stellar Six of Gingacho Volume 1
Created by Yuuki Fujimoto

Translation - Adrienne Beck
Script Editor - Jill Bentley
Copy Editor - Tim Leavey
Retouch and Lettering - Star Print Brokers
Production Artist - Rui Kyo
Graphic Designer - Kenneth Chan

Editor - Cindy Suzuki
Print Production Manager - Lucas Rivera
Managing Editor - Vy Nguyen
Senior Designer - Louis Csontos
Art Director - Al-Insan Lashley
Director of Sales and Manufacturing - Allyson De Simone
Associate Publisher - Marco F. Pavia
President and C.O.O. - John Parker
C.E.O. and Chief Creative Officer - Stu Levy

A  Manga

TOKYOPOP Inc.
5900 Wilshire Blvd. Suite 2000
Los Angeles, CA 90036

E-mail: info@TOKYOPOP.com
Come visit us online at www.TOKYOPOP.com

KIRAMEKI☆GINGACHO SHOTENGAI by Yuuki Fujimoto
© 2006 by Yuuki Fujimoto All rights reserved.
First published in Japan in 2006
by HAKUSENSHA, INC., Tokyo
English language translation rights in the United States of
America and Canada arranged with HAKUSENSHA, INC.,
Tokyo through Tuttle-Mori Agency Inc., Tokyo
English text copyright © 2010 TOKYOPOP Inc.

ISBN: 978-1-4278-0678-9

First TOKYOPOP printing: November 2010
10 9 8 7 6 5 4 3 2 1
Printed in the USA

THE STELLAR SIX OF GINGACHO

Volume 1

Yuuki Fujimoto

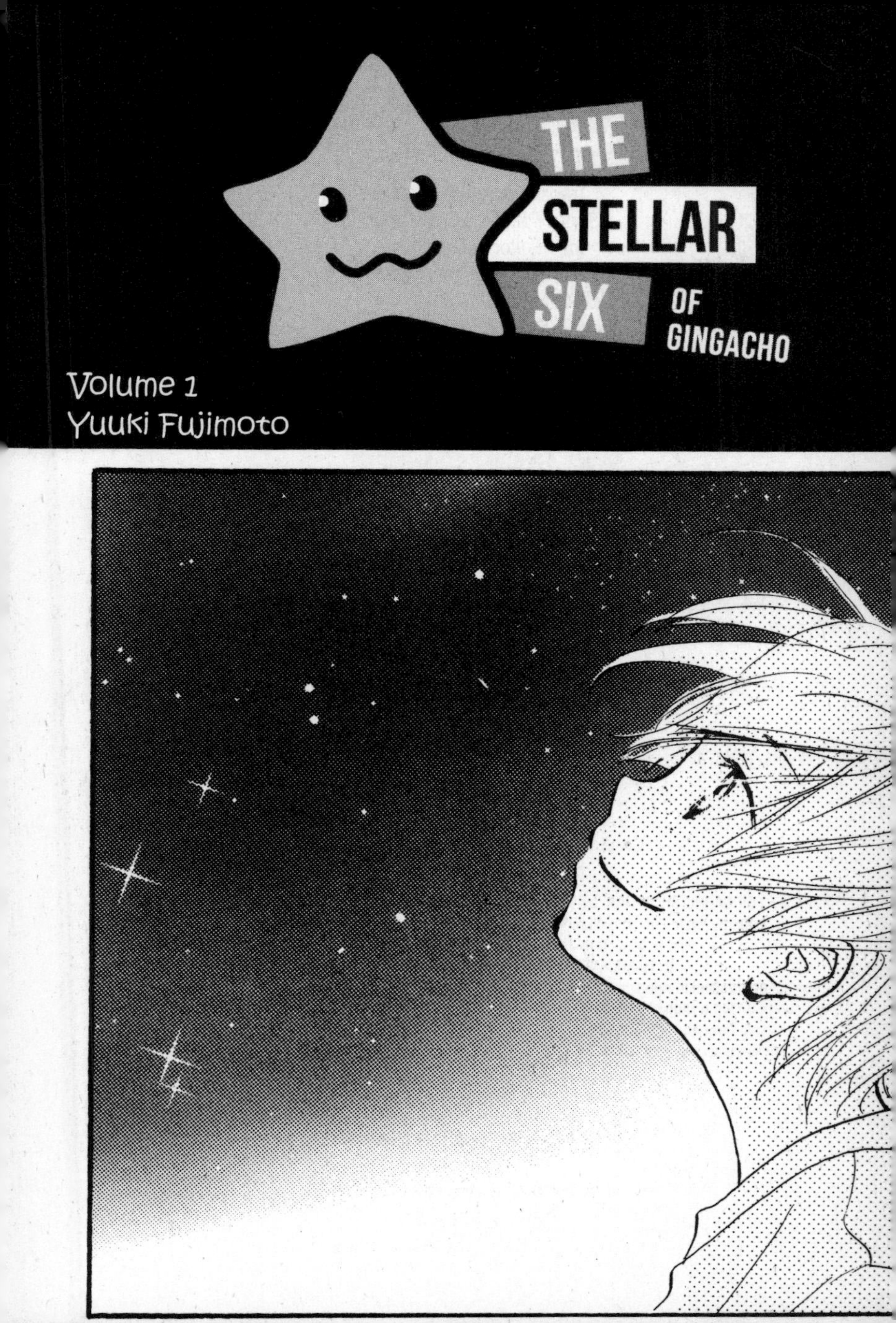

CONTENTS

The Stellar Six of Gingacho

~Chapter 1~ 5

~Chapter 2~ 83

~Chapter 3~ 143

~Bonus~ 203

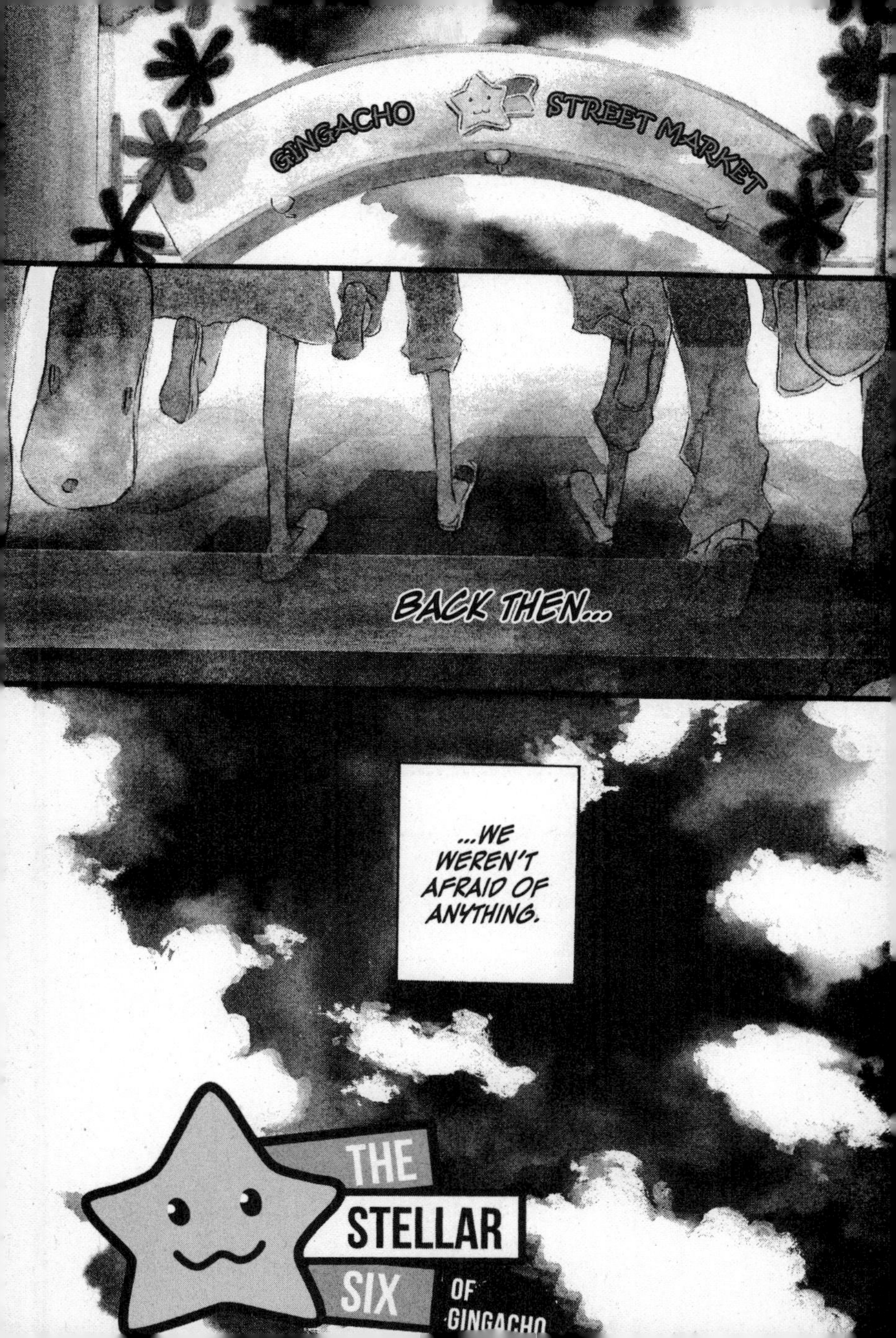
GINGACHO STREET MARKET
BACK THEN...
...WE WEREN'T AFRAID OF ANYTHING.
THE STELLAR SIX OF GINGACHO

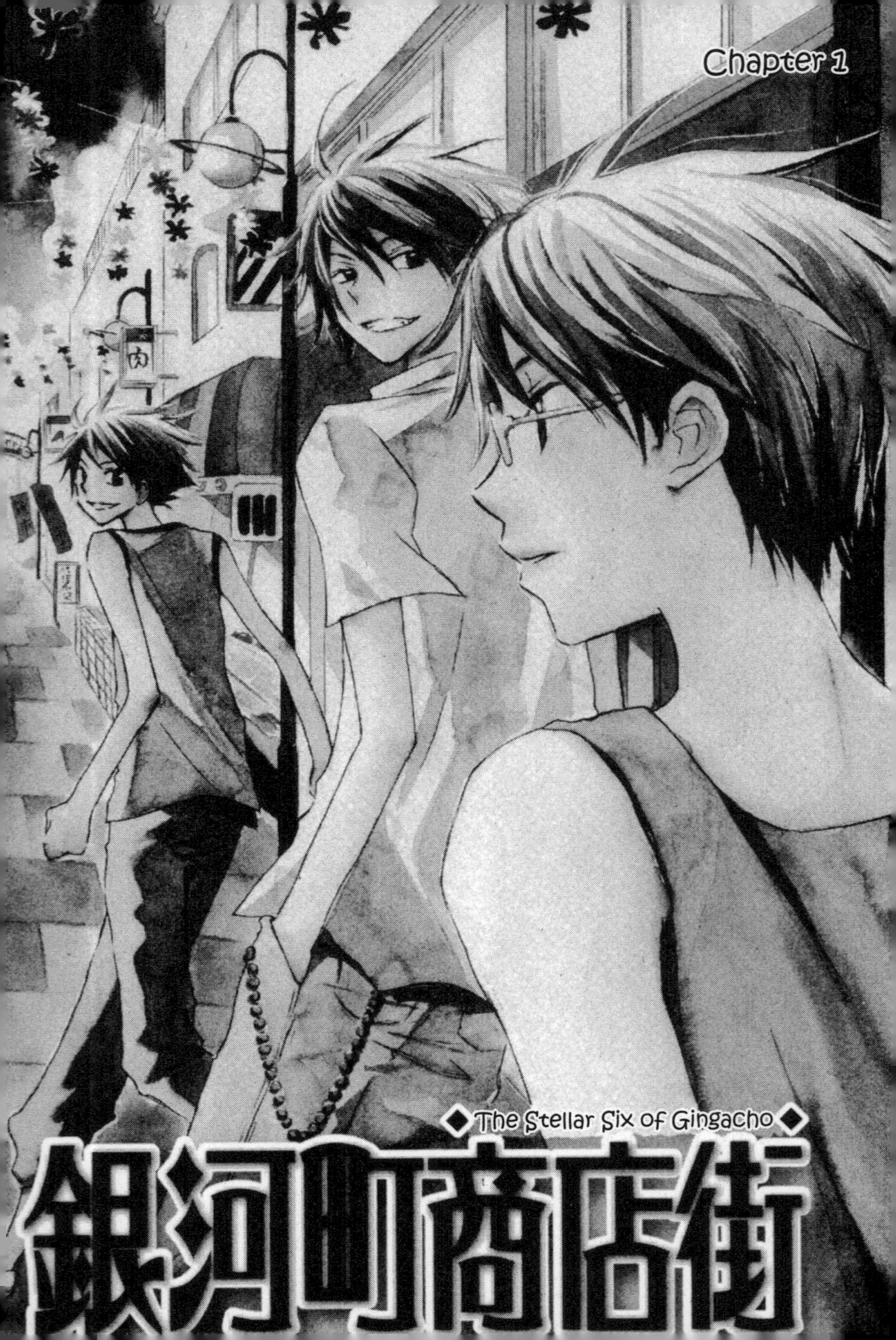
Chapter 1
肉
◆The Stellar Six of Gingacho◆
銀河町商店街

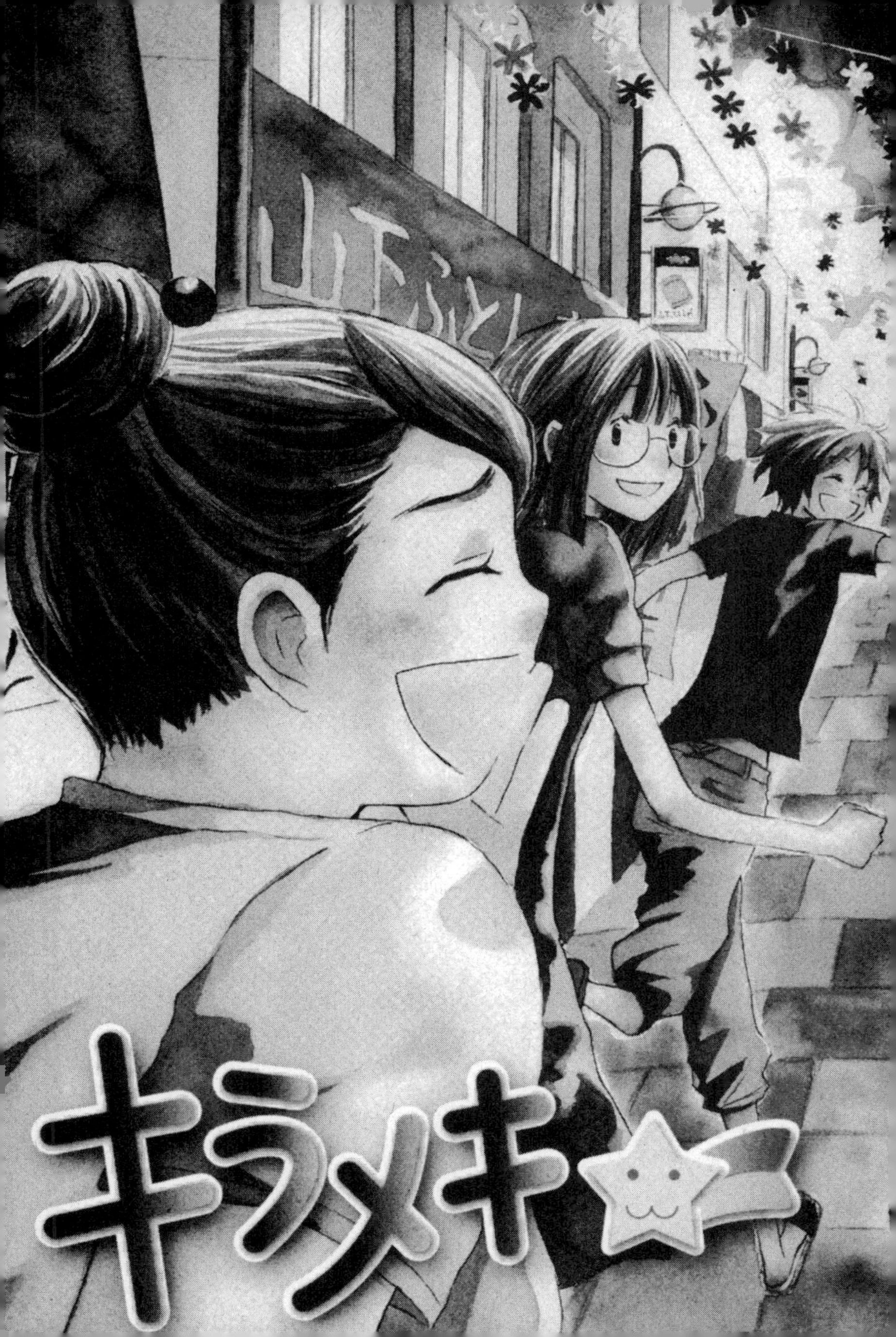
キラメキ☆

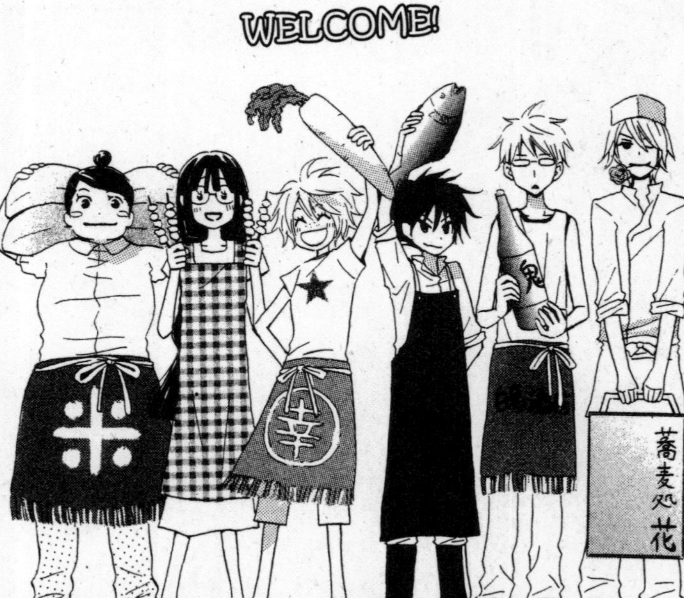
WELCOME!
蕎麦処花

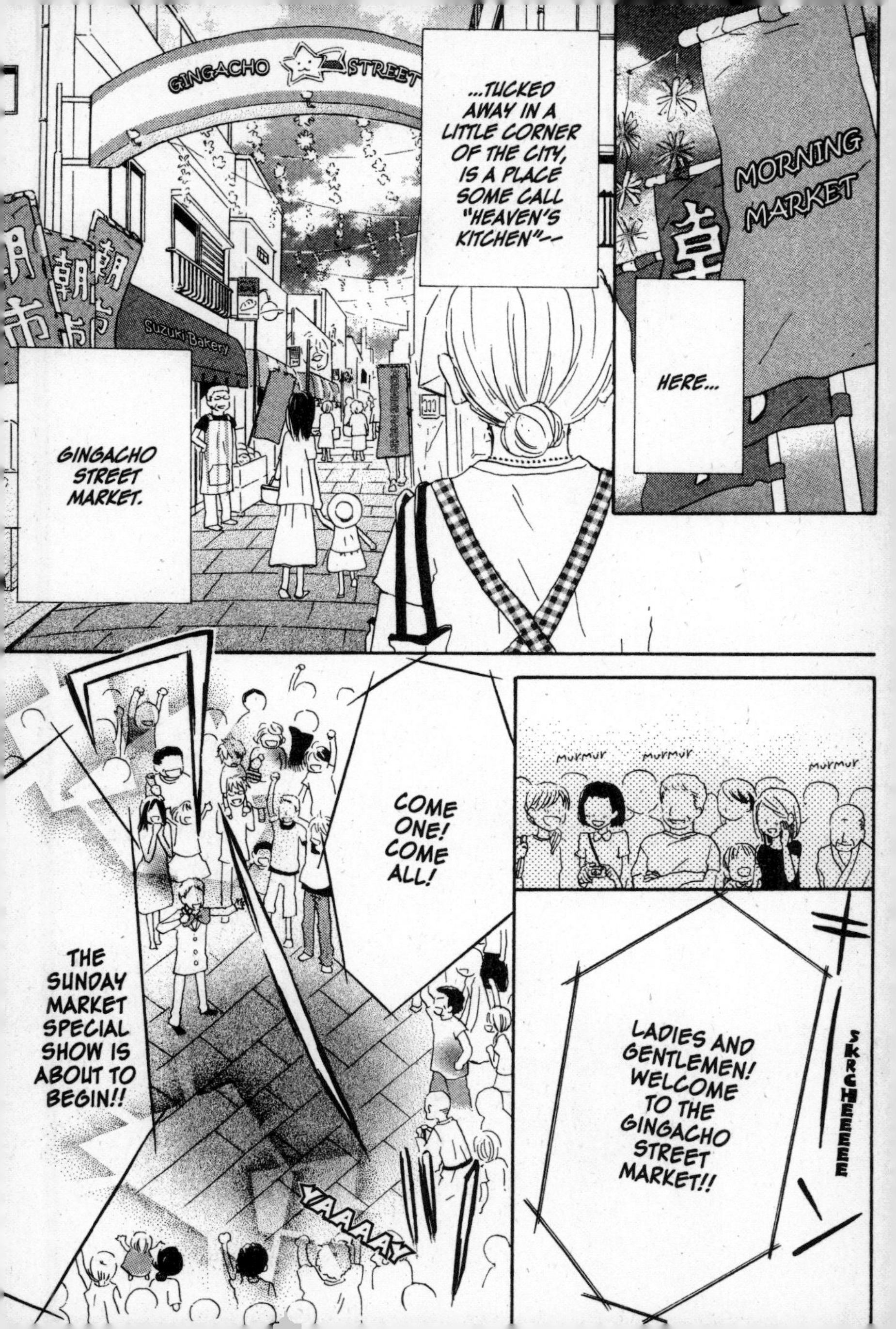
MORNING MARKET
HERE...
...TUCKED AWAY IN A LITTLE CORNER OF THE CITY, IS A PLACE SOME CALL "HEAVEN'S KITCHEN"--
GINGACHO STREET
SUZUKI BAKERY
GINGACHO STREET MARKET.
MURMUR
MURMUR
MURMUR
LADIES AND GENTLEMEN! WELCOME TO THE GINGACHO STREET MARKET!!
SKRCHEEEEE
COME ONE! COME ALL!
THE SUNDAY MARKET SPECIAL SHOW IS ABOUT TO BEGIN!!
YAAAAAY

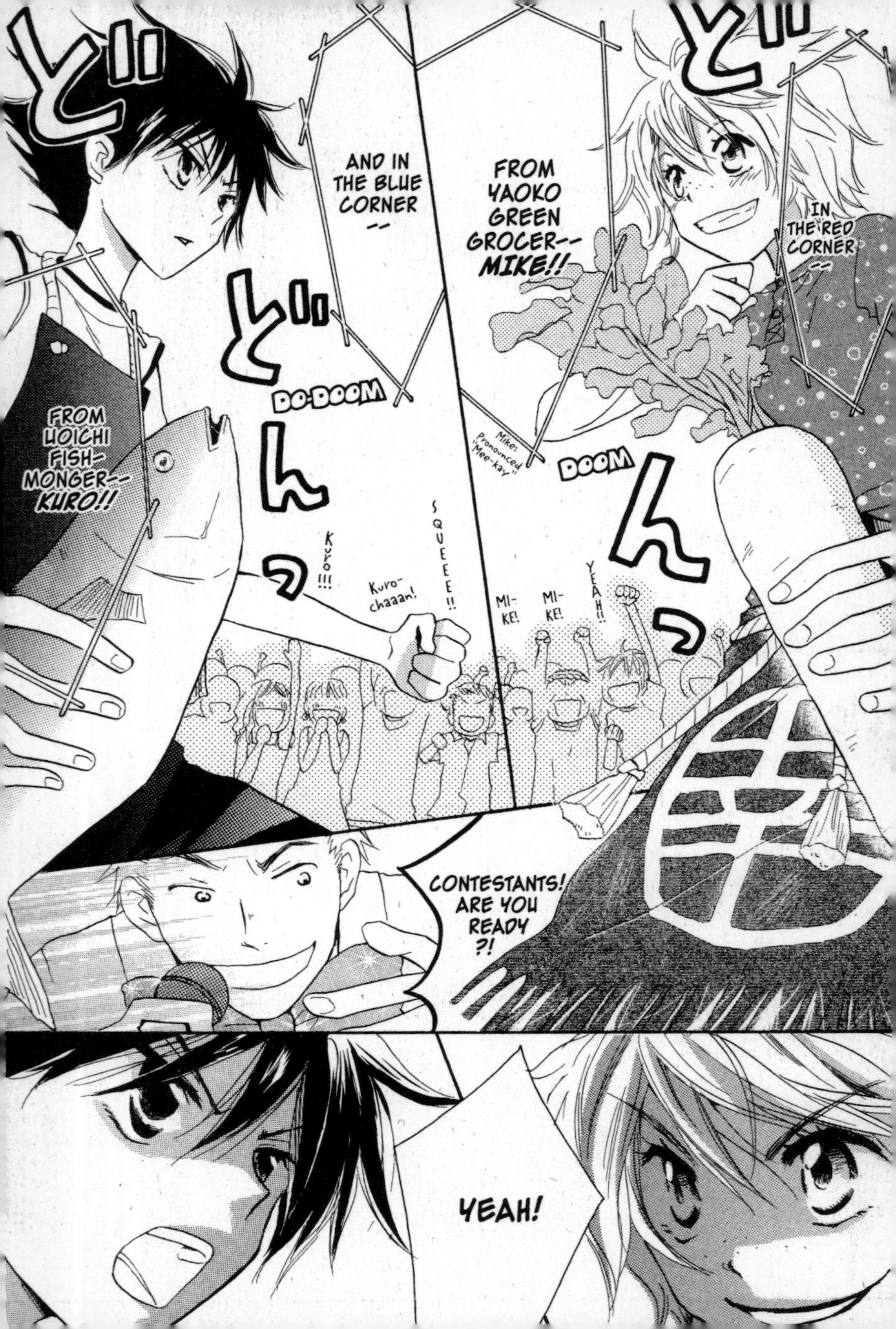

IN THE RED CORNER --
FROM YAOKO GREEN GROCER-- MIKE!!
どんっ
DOOM
Mike: Pronounced "Mee-kay"
YEAH!!
MI-KE!
MI-KE!
AND IN THE BLUE CORNER --
FROM UOICHI FISH-MONGER-- KURO!!
どどんっ
DO-DOOM
SQUEEEE!!
Kuro-chaaan!
Kuro!!!
CONTESTANTS! ARE YOU READY ?!
YEAH!

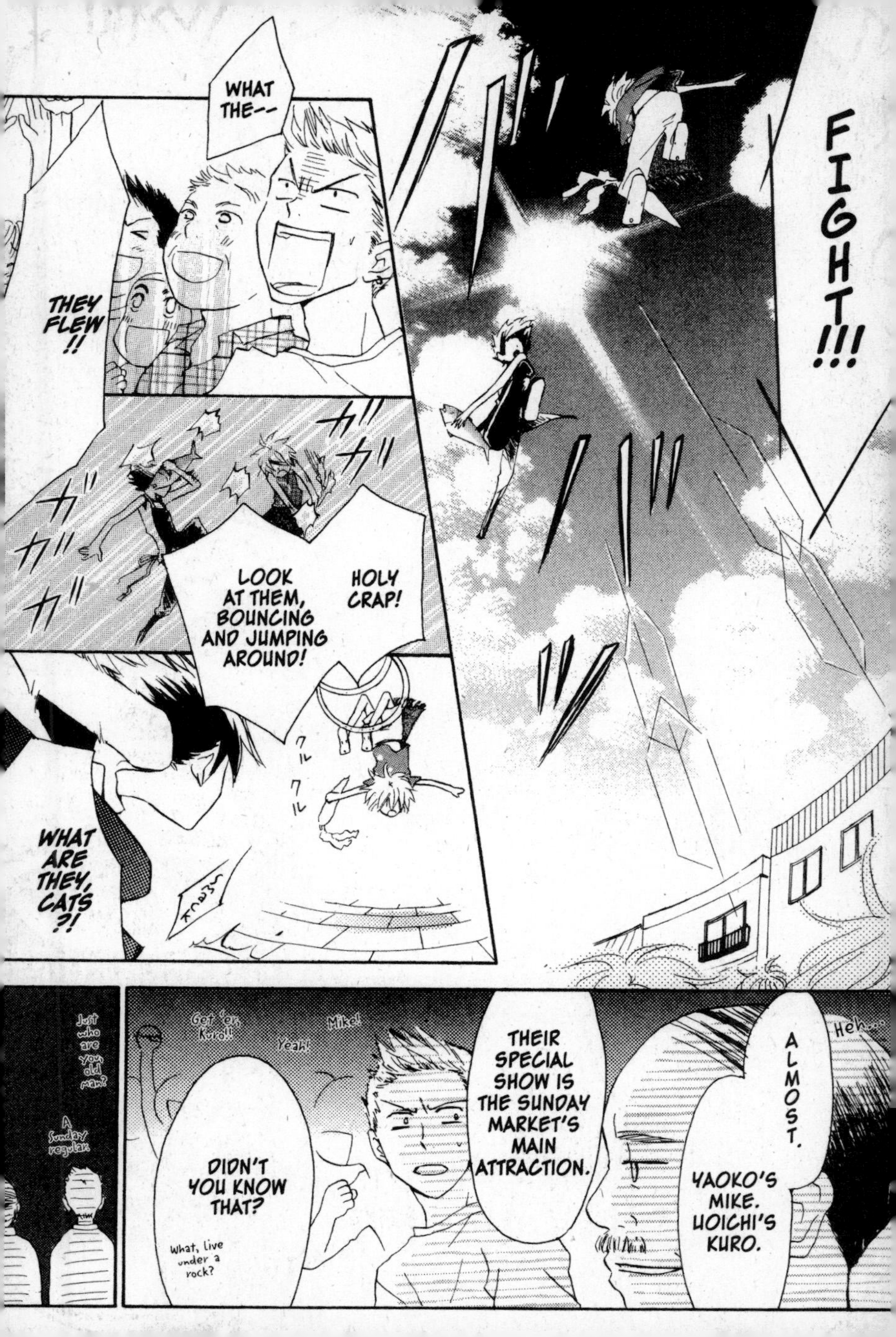
FIGHT!!!
WHAT THE--
THEY FLEW!!
HOLY CRAP!
LOOK AT THEM, BOUNCING AND JUMPING AROUND!
WHAT ARE THEY, CATS?!
Heh...
ALMOST.
YAOKO'S MIKE. UOICHI'S KURO.
THEIR SPECIAL SHOW IS THE SUNDAY MARKET'S MAIN ATTRACTION.
DIDN'T YOU KNOW THAT?
What, live under a rock?
Mike!
Yeah!
Get 'er, Kuro!!
Just who are you, old man?
A Sunday regular.

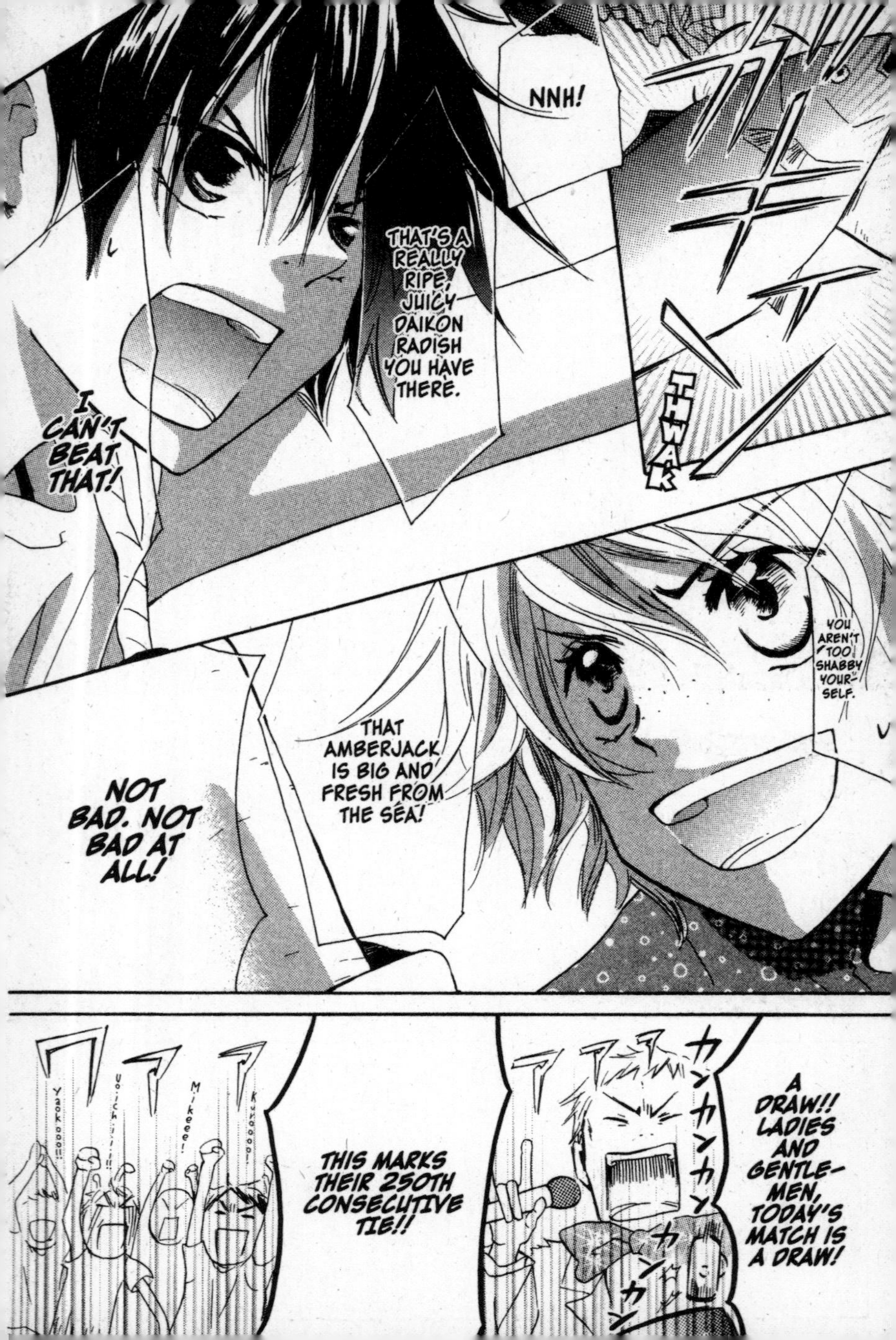
NNH!
THWAK
THAT'S A REALLY RIPE, JUICY DAIKON RADISH YOU HAVE THERE.
I CAN'T BEAT THAT!
YOU AREN'T TOO SHABBY YOURSELF.
THAT AMBERJACK IS BIG AND FRESH FROM THE SEA!
NOT BAD. NOT BAD AT ALL!
A DRAW!! LADIES AND GENTLEMEN, TODAY'S MATCH IS A DRAW!
THIS MARKS THEIR 250TH CONSECUTIVE TIE!!
Kukoooo!
Mikeee!
Uoichiii!!
Yaokooo!!

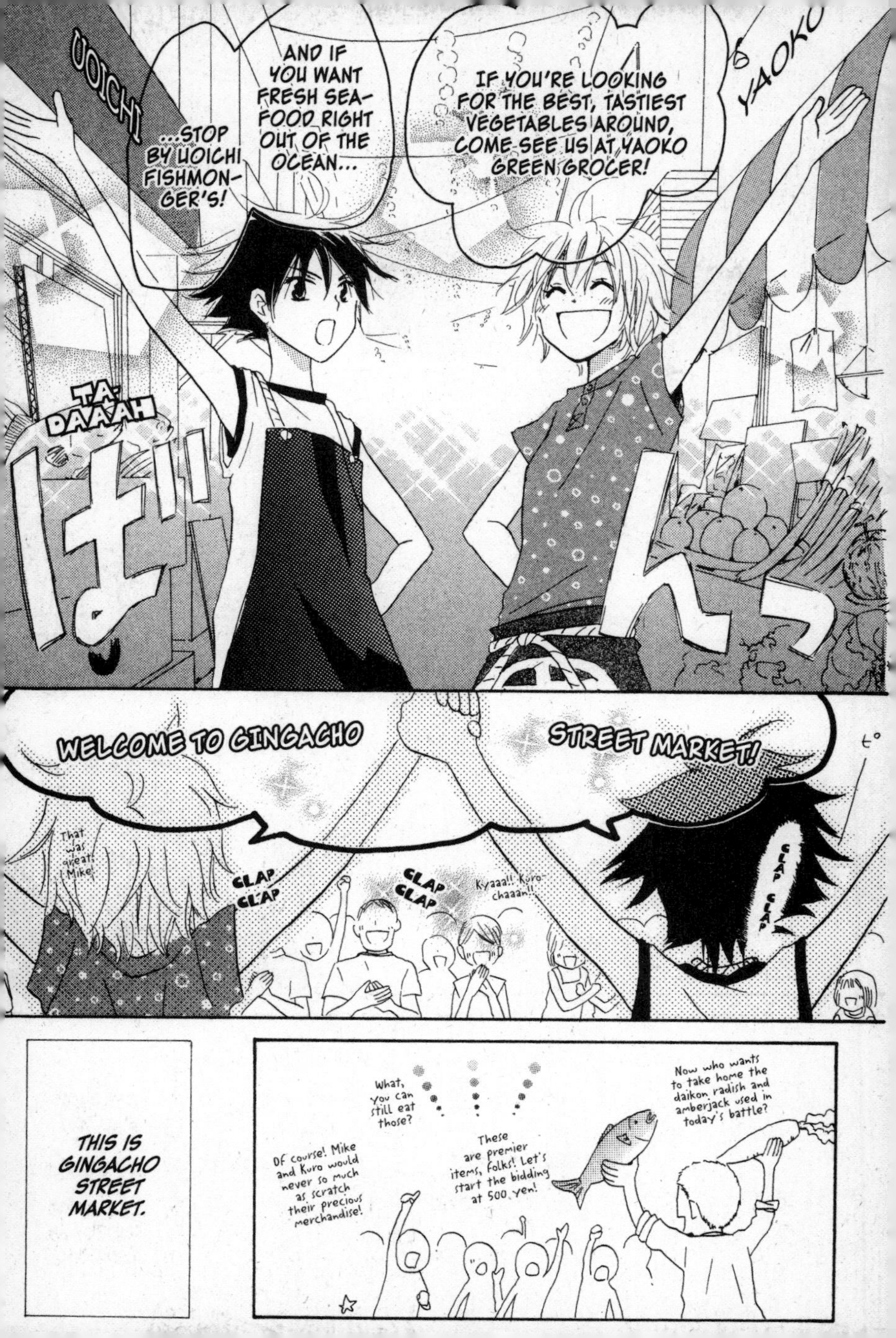
YAOKO
IF YOU'RE LOOKING FOR THE BEST, TASTIEST VEGETABLES AROUND, COME SEE US AT YAOKO GREEN GROCER!
AND IF YOU WANT FRESH SEA-FOOD RIGHT OUT OF THE OCEAN...
...STOP BY UOICHI FISHMON-GER'S!
UOICHI
TA-DAAAAH
WELCOME TO GINGACHO STREET MARKET!
CLAP CLAP
Kyaaa!! Kuro-chaaan!!
CLAP CLAP
CLAP CLAP
That was great, Mike!
Now who wants to take home the daikon radish and amberjack used in today's battle?
What, you can still eat those?
These are premier items, folks! Let's start the bidding at 500 yen!
Of course! Mike and Kuro would never so much as scratch their precious merchandise!
THIS IS GINGACHO STREET MARKET.

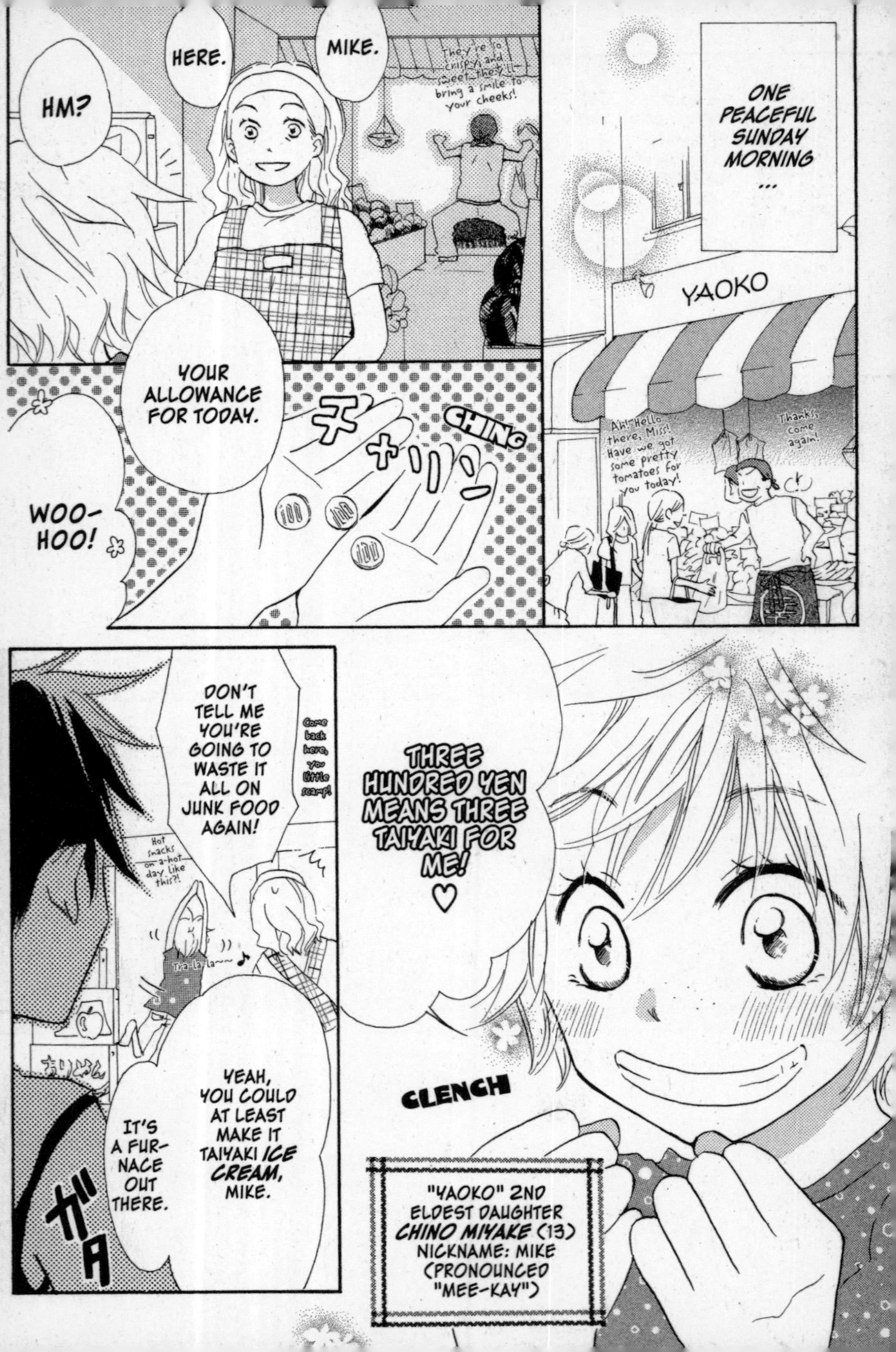
ONE PEACEFUL SUNDAY MORNING ...
YAOKO
Ah! Hello there, Miss! Have we got some pretty tomatoes for you today!
Thanks, come again!
MIKE.
HERE.
HM?
They're so crispy and sweet they'll bring a smile to your cheeks!
YOUR ALLOWANCE FOR TODAY.
チャリン
CHING
WOO-HOO!
THREE HUNDRED YEN MEANS THREE TAIYAKI FOR ME! ♡
CLENCH
"YAOKO" 2ND ELDEST DAUGHTER CHINO MIYAKE (13) NICKNAME: MIKE (PRONOUNCED "MEE-KAY")
DON'T TELL ME YOU'RE GOING TO WASTE IT ALL ON JUNK FOOD AGAIN!
Come back here, you little scamp!
Hot snacks on a hot day like this?!
Tra-la-la~~
YEAH, YOU COULD AT LEAST MAKE IT TAIYAKI ICE CREAM, MIKE.
IT'S A FURNACE OUT THERE.
ガタ

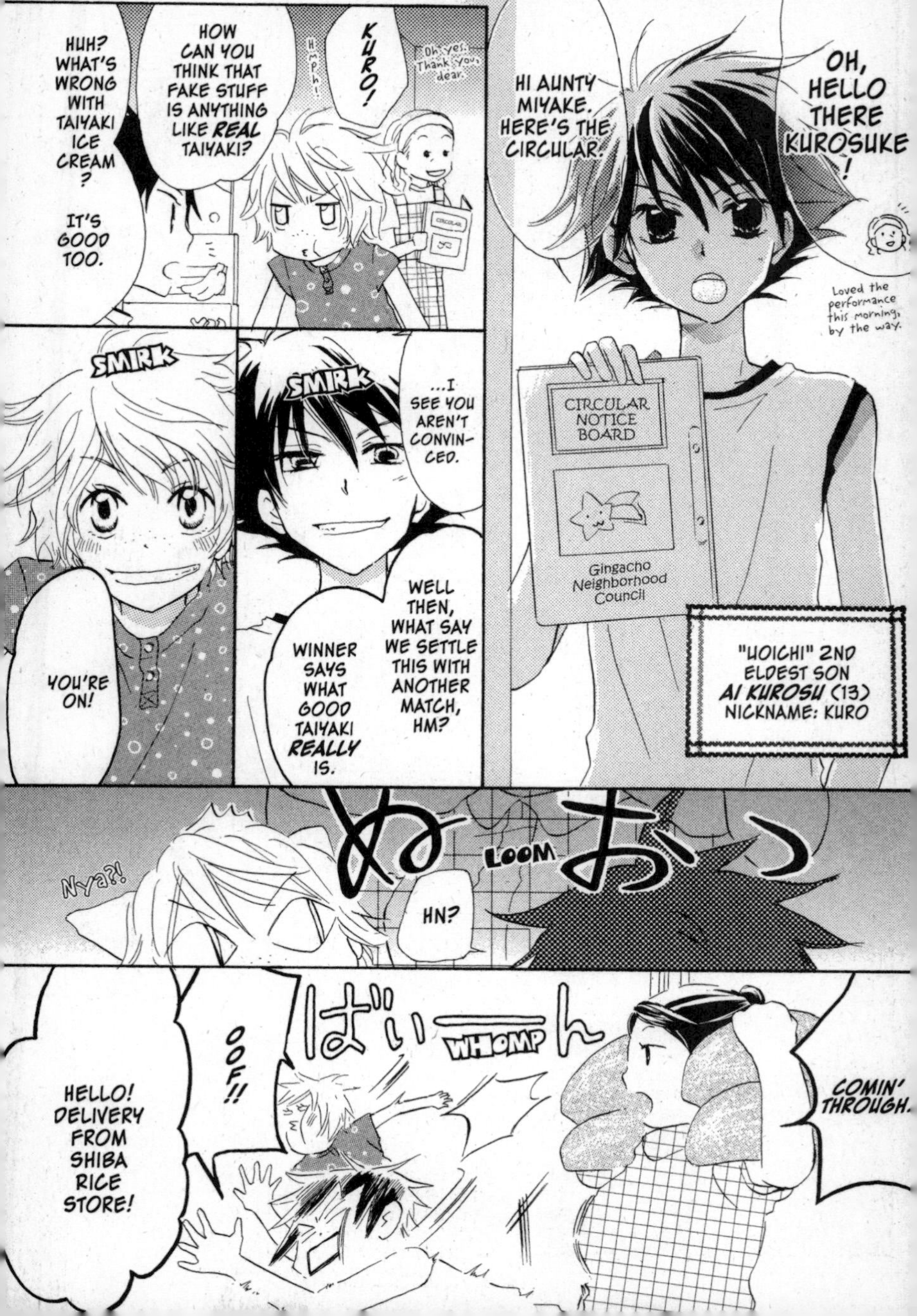

OH, HELLO THERE KUROSUKE!
HI AUNTY MIYAKE. HERE'S THE CIRCULAR.
Loved the performance this morning, by the way.
CIRCULAR NOTICE BOARD
Gingacho Neighborhood Council
"YOICHI" 2ND ELDEST SON AI KUROSU (13) NICKNAME: KURO
KURO!
Oh yes. Thank you, dear.
Hmph!
HOW CAN YOU THINK THAT FAKE STUFF IS ANYTHING LIKE REAL TAIYAKI?
HUH? WHAT'S WRONG WITH TAIYAKI ICE CREAM?
IT'S GOOD TOO.
SMIRK
...I SEE YOU AREN'T CONVIN-CED.
WELL THEN, WHAT SAY WE SETTLE THIS WITH ANOTHER MATCH, HM?
WINNER SAYS WHAT GOOD TAIYAKI REALLY IS.
SMIRK
YOU'RE ON!
ぬおっ
LOOM
HN?
Nya?!
COMIN' THROUGH.
ばいーん
WHOMP
OOF!!
HELLO! DELIVERY FROM SHIBA RICE STORE!

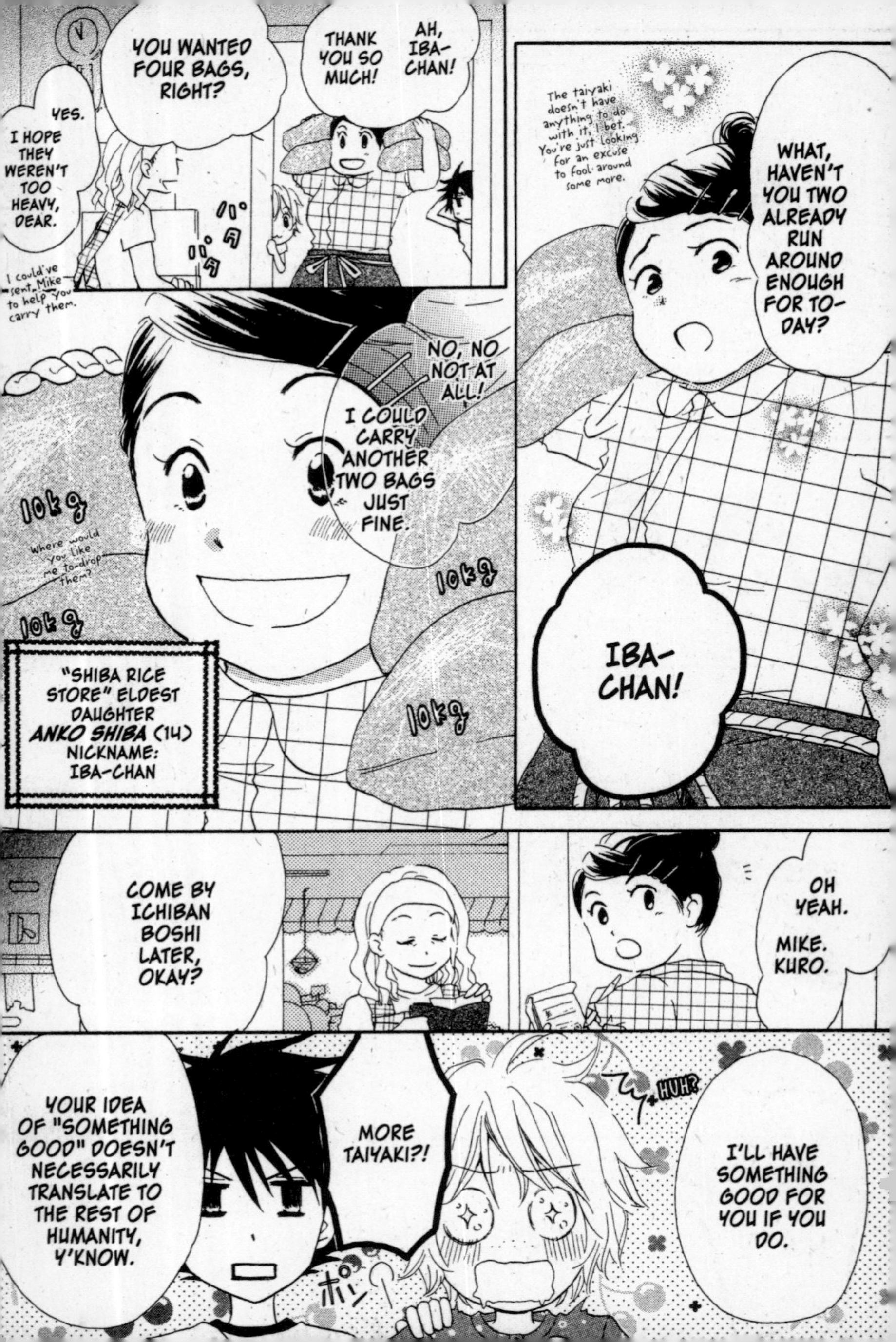

WHAT, HAVEN'T YOU TWO ALREADY RUN AROUND ENOUGH FOR TO-DAY?
The taiyaki doesn't have anything to do with it, I bet. You're just looking for an excuse to fool around some more.
IBA-CHAN!
AH, IBA-CHAN!
THANK YOU SO MUCH!
YOU WANTED FOUR BAGS, RIGHT?
YES. I HOPE THEY WEREN'T TOO HEAVY, DEAR.
I could've sent Mike to help you carry them.
NO, NO NOT AT ALL!
I COULD CARRY ANOTHER TWO BAGS JUST FINE.
10kg
10kg
Where would you like me to drop them?
10kg
10kg
"SHIBA RICE STORE" ELDEST DAUGHTER ANKO SHIBA (14) NICKNAME: IBA-CHAN
OH YEAH. MIKE. KURO.
COME BY ICHIBAN BOSHI LATER, OKAY?
I'LL HAVE SOMETHING GOOD FOR YOU IF YOU DO.
HUH?
MORE TAIYAKI?!
YOUR IDEA OF "SOMETHING GOOD" DOESN'T NECESSARILY TRANSLATE TO THE REST OF HUMANITY, Y'KNOW.

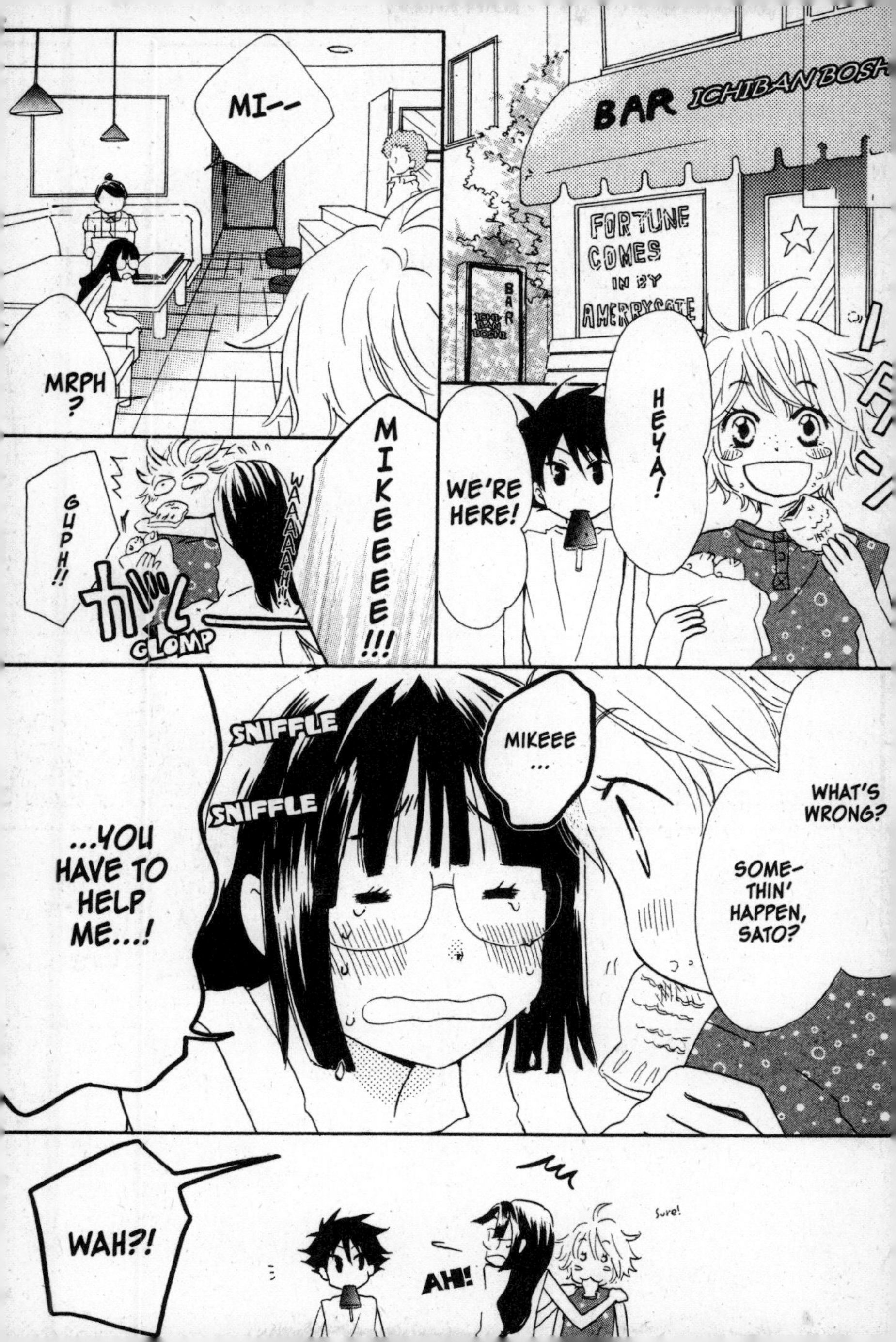
BAR ICHIBAN BOSH
FORTUNE COMES IN BY AMERRYGATE
BAR ICHI BAN BOSHI
MI--
MRPH?
HEYA!
WE'RE HERE!
MIKEEEEE!!!
WAAAAAAH
GUPH!!
GLOMP
MIKEEE ...
WHAT'S WRONG?
SOME-THIN' HAPPEN, SATO?
SNIFFLE
SNIFFLE
...YOU HAVE TO HELP ME...!
Sure!
AH!
WAH?!

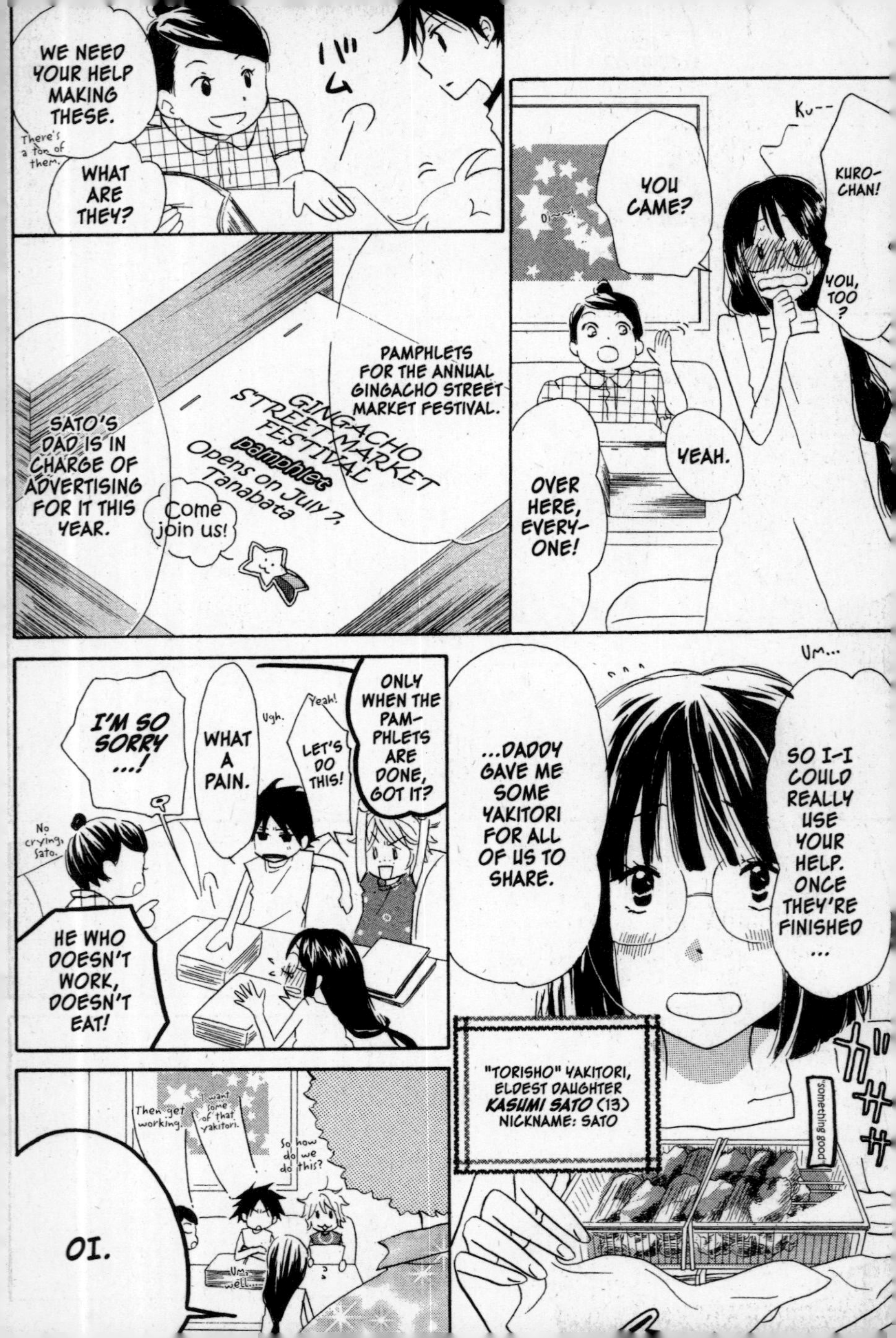

Ku--
KURO-CHAN!
YOU CAME?
YOU, TOO?
YEAH.
OVER HERE, EVERY-ONE!
WE NEED YOUR HELP MAKING THESE.
There's a ton of them.
WHAT ARE THEY?
PAMPHLETS FOR THE ANNUAL GINGACHO STREET MARKET FESTIVAL.
GINGACHO STREET MARKET FESTIVAL pamphlet
Opens on July 7, Tanabata
Come join us!
SATO'S DAD IS IN CHARGE OF ADVERTISING FOR IT THIS YEAR.
UM...
SO I-I COULD REALLY USE YOUR HELP. ONCE THEY'RE FINISHED ...
...DADDY GAVE ME SOME YAKITORI FOR ALL OF US TO SHARE.
"something good"
"TORISHO" YAKITORI, ELDEST DAUGHTER KASUMI SATO (13) NICKNAME: SATO
ONLY WHEN THE PAM-PHLETS ARE DONE, GOT IT?
Yeah!
LET'S DO THIS!
Ugh.
WHAT A PAIN.
I'M SO SORRY ...!
No crying, Sato.
HE WHO DOESN'T WORK, DOESN'T EAT!
I want some of that yakitori.
Then get working.
So how do we do this?
Um... well...
OI.

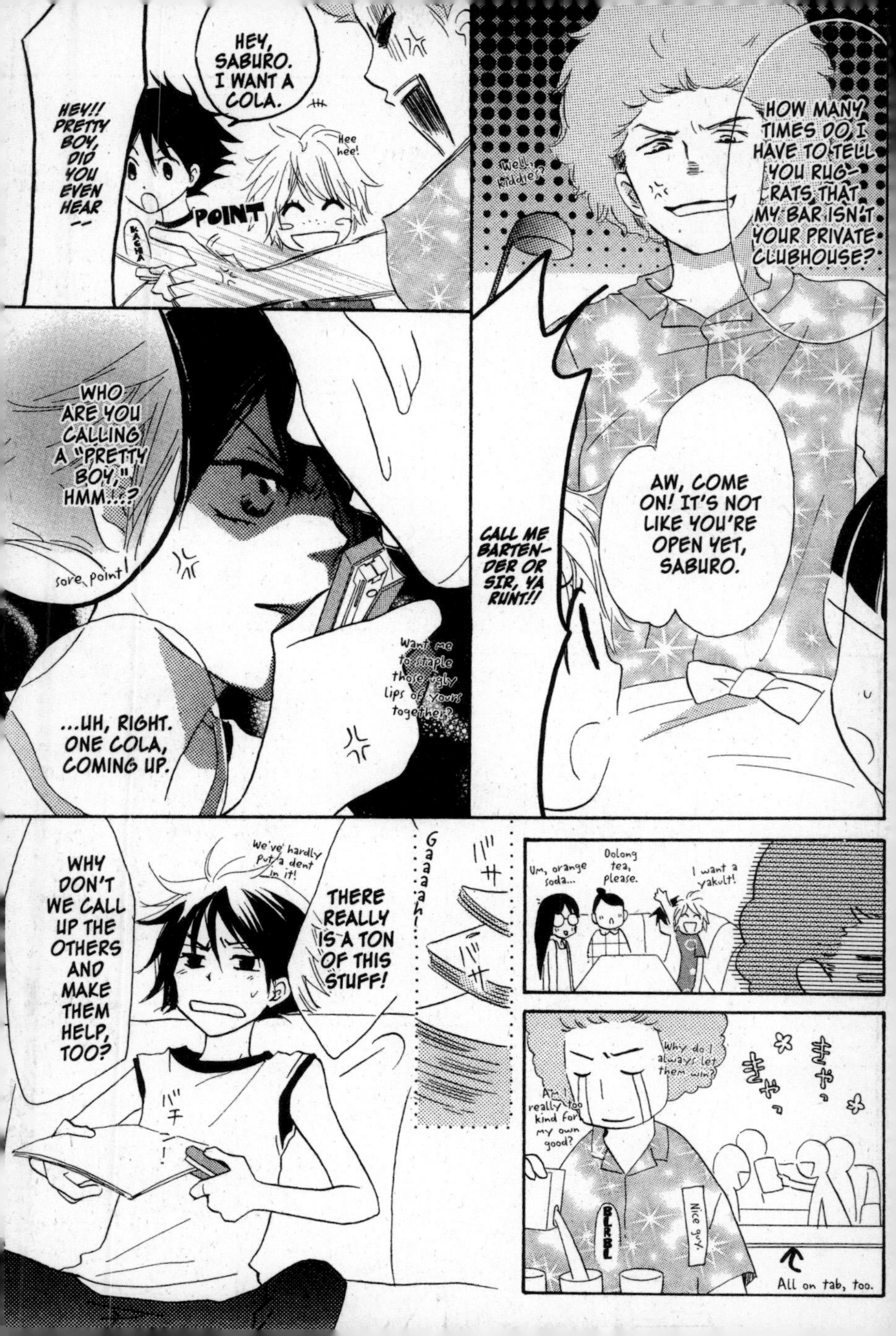
HOW MANY TIMES DO I HAVE TO TELL YOU RUG-RATS THAT MY BAR ISN'T YOUR PRIVATE CLUBHOUSE?
Well, kiddie?
AW, COME ON! IT'S NOT LIKE YOU'RE OPEN YET, SABURO.
CALL ME BARTENDER OR SIR, YA RUNT!!
HEY, SABURO. I WANT A COLA.
Hee hee!
HEY!! PRETTY BOY, DID YOU EVEN HEAR—
POINT
KACHA
WHO ARE YOU CALLING A "PRETTY BOY," HMM...?
sore point
Want me to staple those ugly lips of yours together?
...UH, RIGHT. ONE COLA, COMING UP.
I want a yakult!
Oolong tea, please.
Um, orange soda...
Why do I always let them win?
Am I really too kind for my own good?
Nice guy.
All on tab, too.
Gaaaaah!
THERE REALLY IS A TON OF THIS STUFF!
We've hardly put a dent in it!
WHY DON'T WE CALL UP THE OTHERS AND MAKE THEM HELP, TOO?

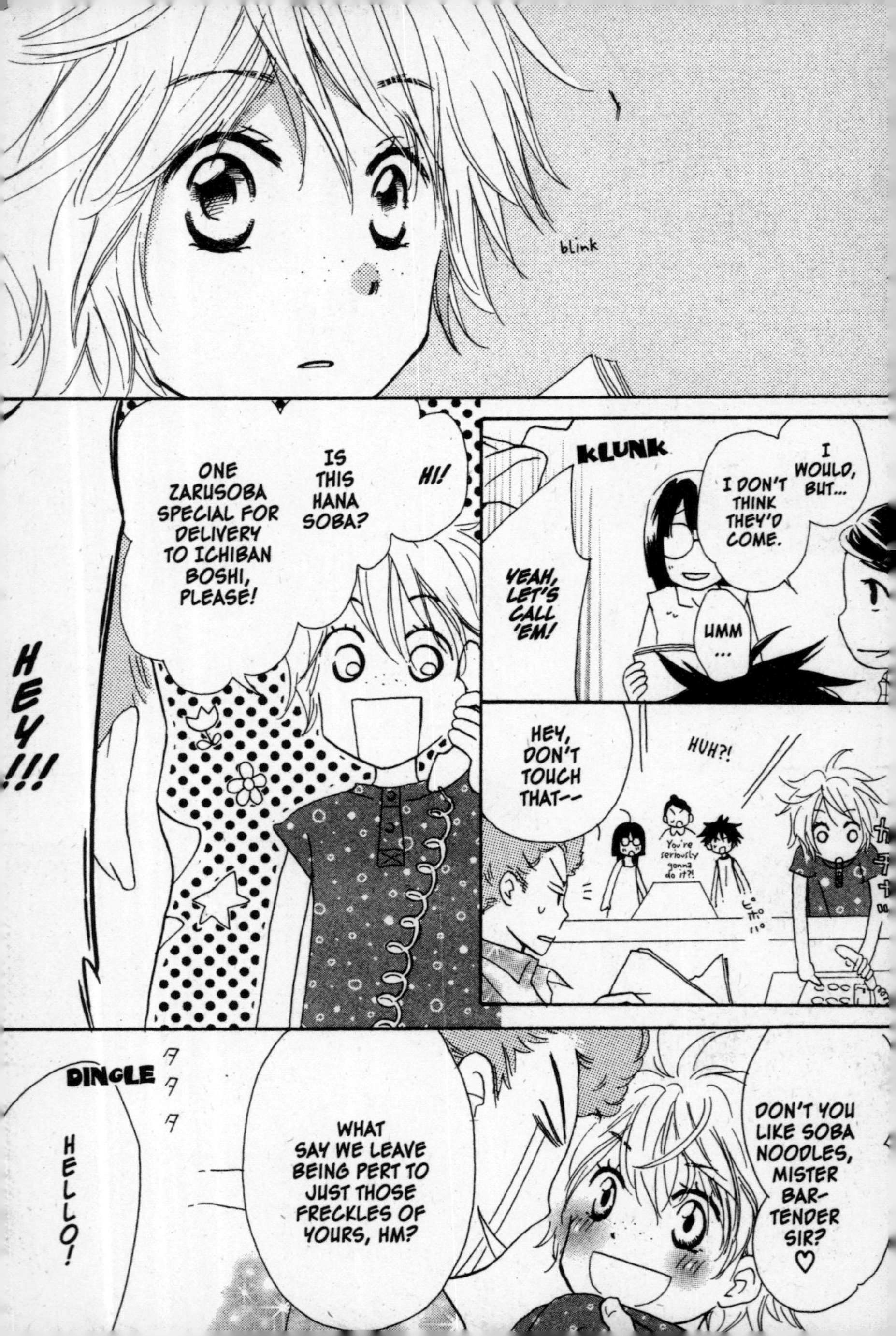
blink
I WOULD, BUT...
I DON'T THINK THEY'D COME.
KLUNK
UMM ...
YEAH, LET'S CALL 'EM!
HUH?!
HEY, DON'T TOUCH THAT--
You're seriously gonna do it?!
HI!
IS THIS HANA SOBA?
ONE ZARUSOBA SPECIAL FOR DELIVERY TO ICHIBAN BOSHI, PLEASE!
HEY!!!
DON'T YOU LIKE SOBA NOODLES, MISTER BAR-TENDER SIR? ♡
WHAT SAY WE LEAVE BEING PERT TO JUST THOSE FRECKLES OF YOURS, HM?
DINGLE
HELLO!

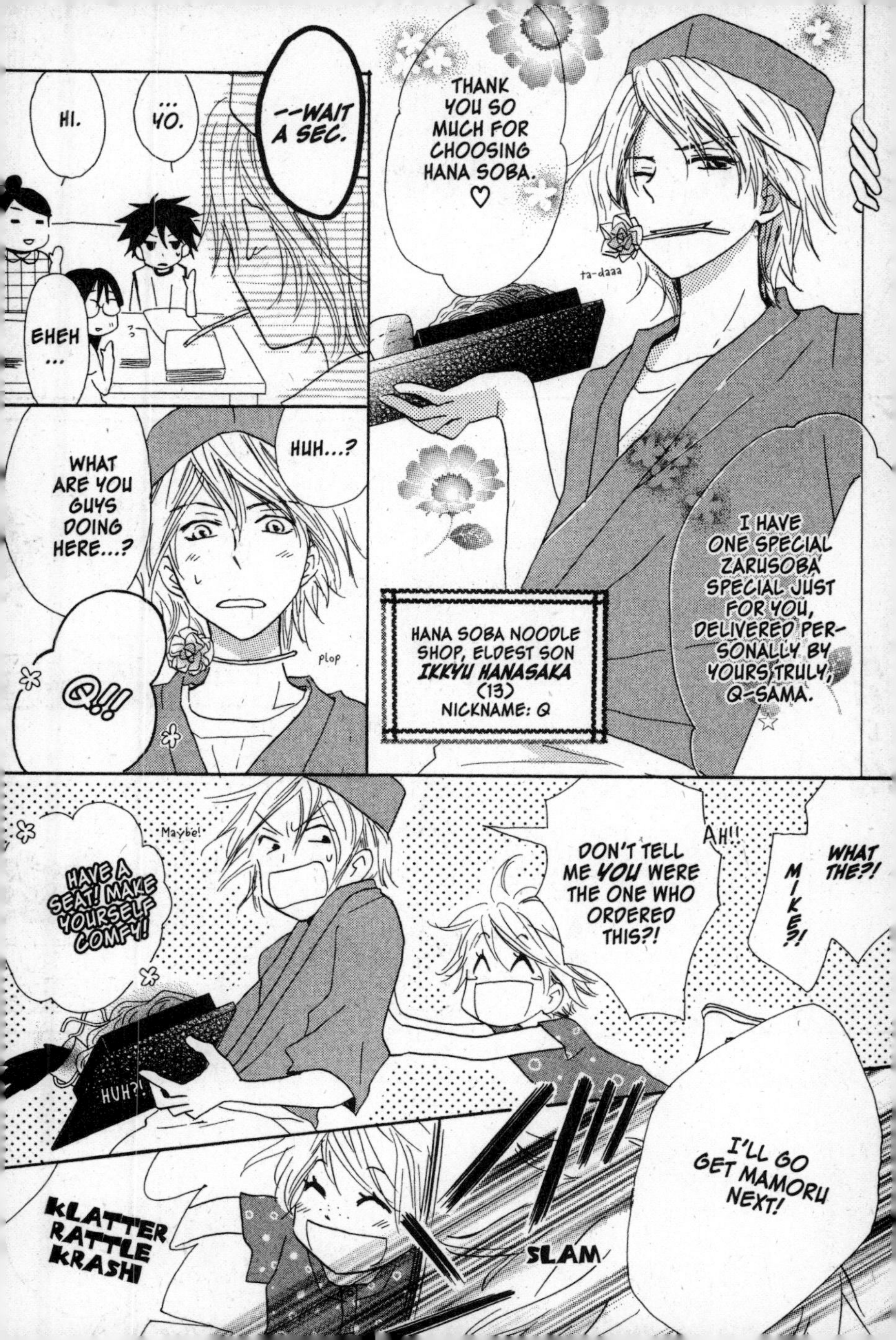
THANK YOU SO MUCH FOR CHOOSING HANA SOBA. ♡
ta-daaa
I HAVE ONE SPECIAL ZARUSOBA SPECIAL JUST FOR YOU, DELIVERED PERSONALLY BY YOURS TRULY, Q-SAMA.
HANA SOBA NOODLE SHOP, ELDEST SON
IKKYU HANASAKA
(13)
NICKNAME: Q
--WAIT A SEC.
... YO.
HI.
EHEH ...
HUH...?
WHAT ARE YOU GUYS DOING HERE...?
plop
Q!!!
WHAT THE?!
MIKE?!
AH!!
DON'T TELL ME YOU WERE THE ONE WHO ORDERED THIS?!
Maybe!
HAVE A SEAT! MAKE YOURSELF COMFY!
HUH?!
I'LL GO GET MAMORU NEXT!
SLAM
KLATTER RATTLE KRASH!

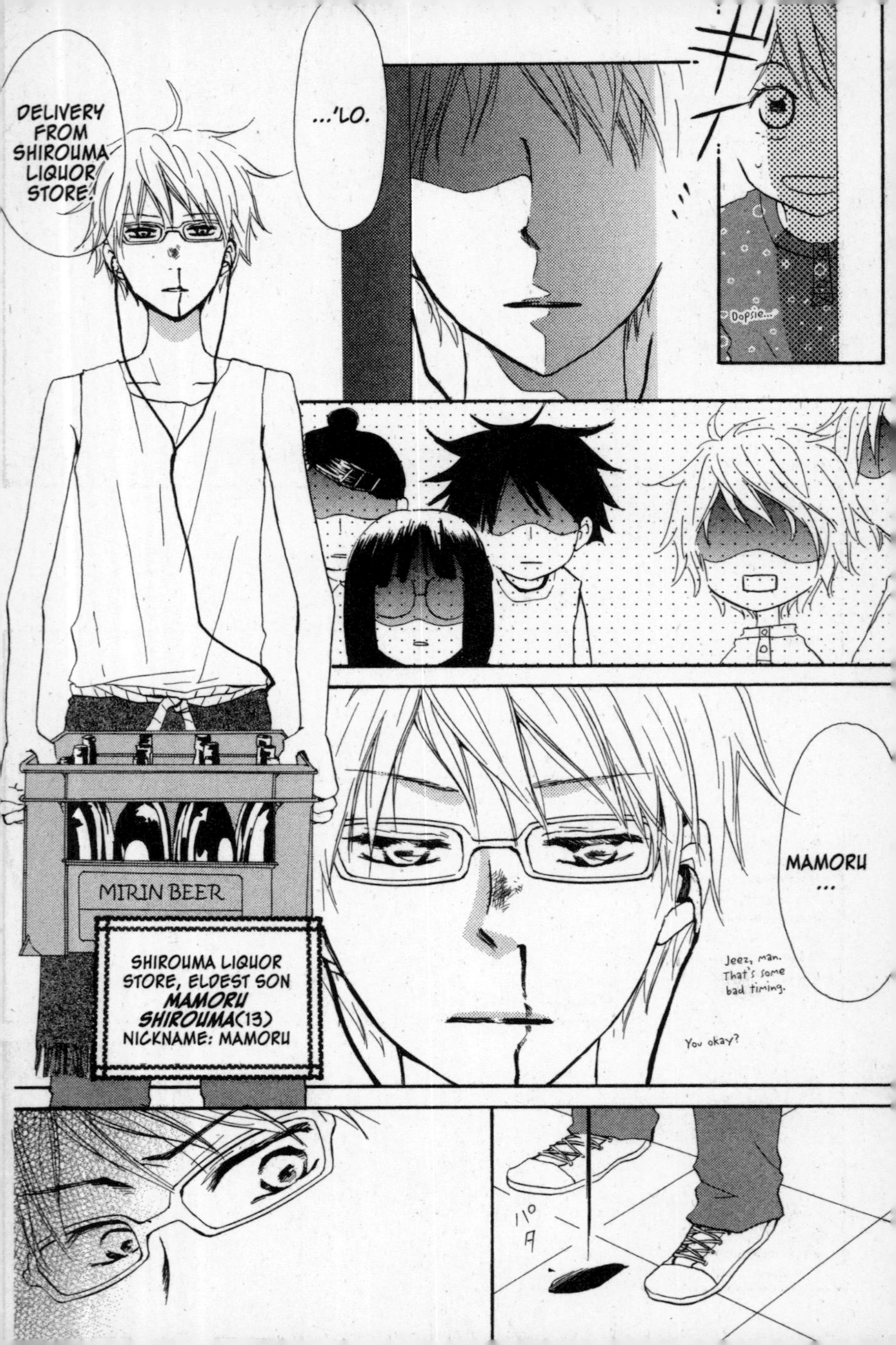
Oopsie...
...'LO.
MAMORU ...
Jeez, man. That's some bad timing.
You okay?
DELIVERY FROM SHIROUMA LIQUOR STORE!
MIRIN BEER
SHIROUMA LIQUOR STORE, ELDEST SON
MAMORU SHIROUMA(13)
NICKNAME: MAMORU
パタ

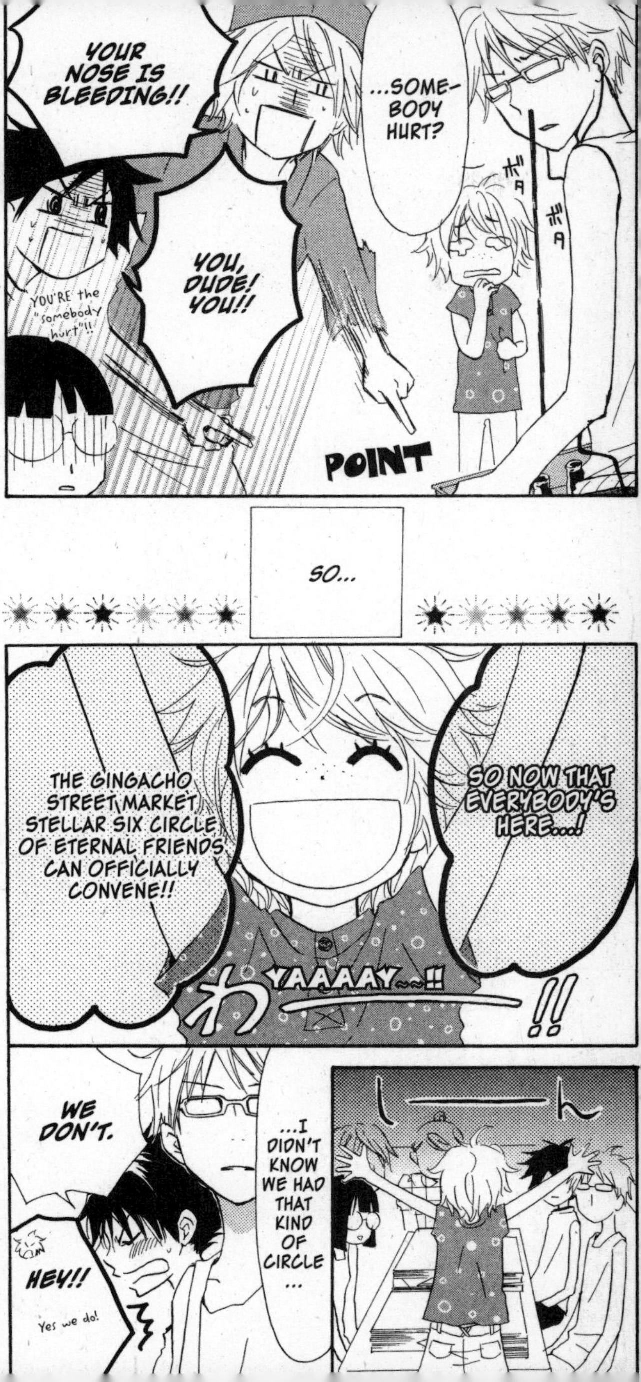
...SOME-BODY HURT?
ボタ
ボタ
YOUR NOSE IS BLEEDING!!
YOU, DUDE! YOU!!
YOU'RE the "somebody hurt"!!
POINT
SO...
SO NOW THAT EVERYBODY'S HERE...!
THE GINGACHO STREET MARKET STELLAR SIX CIRCLE OF ETERNAL FRIENDS CAN OFFICIALLY CONVENE!!
わ
YAAAAY~~!!
!!
し——ん
...I DIDN'T KNOW WE HAD THAT KIND OF CIRCLE ...
WE DON'T.
HEY!!
Yes we do!

1

Hello, everyone! I'm Fujimoto, and this first volume of The Stellar Six of Gingacho will be my third published tankoubon volume. Thanks to the kindness and help of the wonderful people around me and everyone who supports my work, I was able to produce this book. It's only the very beginning of the first volume but I... I'm tearing up--

Thank you so much, everyone!!

waaah!

Oi, oi, this is only the beginning. We've just barely met. We don't even know you. ...is what some of you may be thinking, I'm sure. :-) Anyway, I hope you have an enjoyable read.

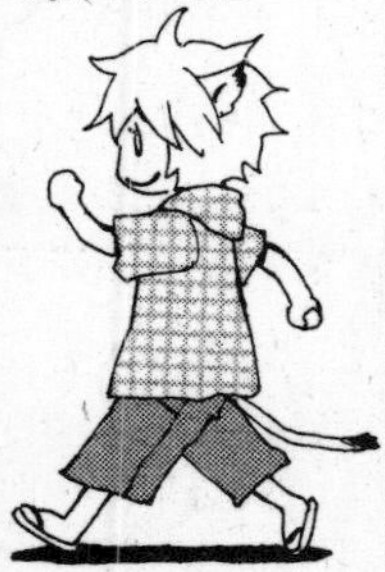

1/4 Theater Let's play with Kuro!

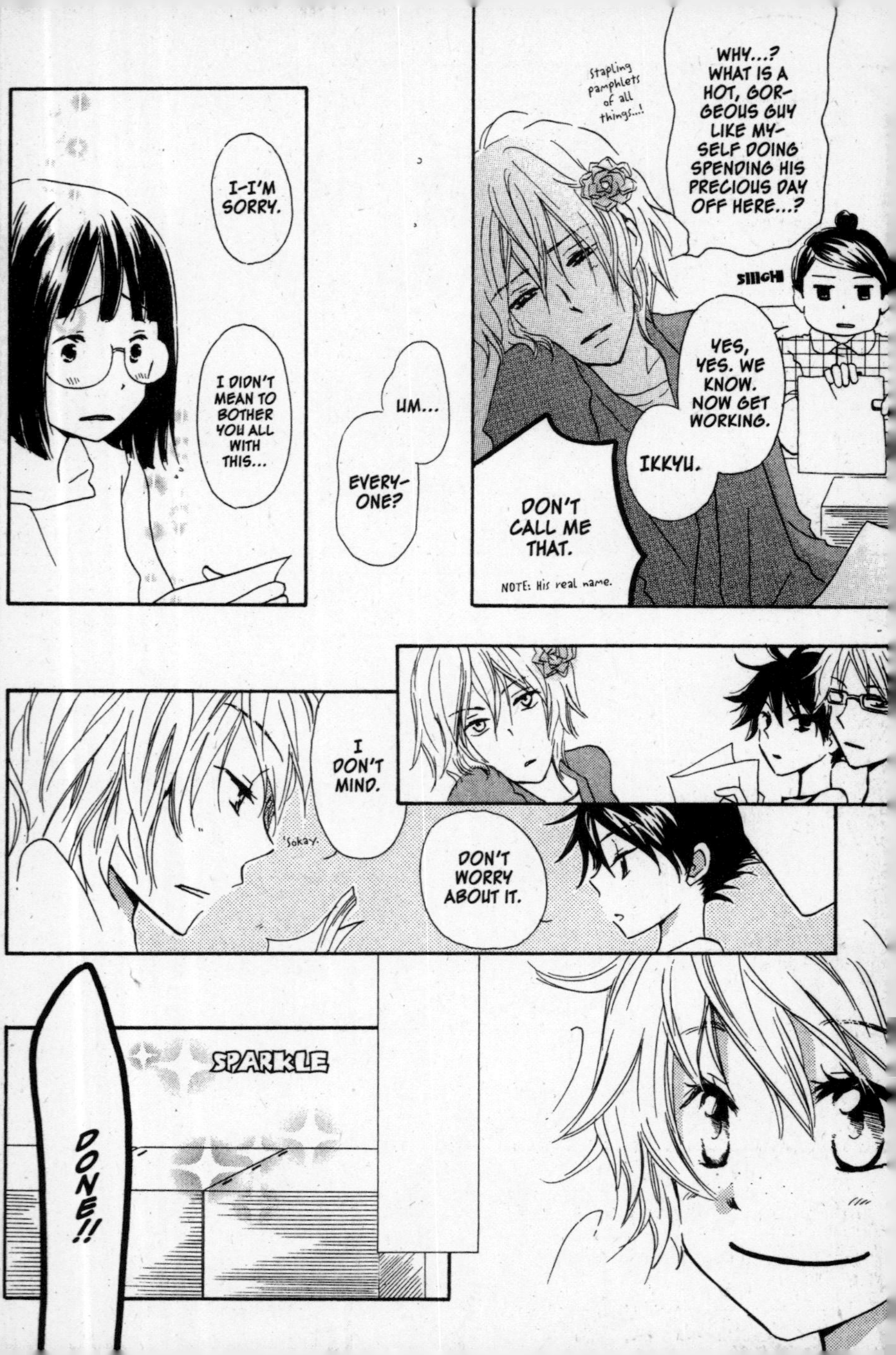
Stapling pamphlets of all things...!
WHY...? WHAT IS A HOT, GORGEOUS GUY LIKE MYSELF DOING SPENDING HIS PRECIOUS DAY OFF HERE...?
SIIIGH
YES, YES. WE KNOW. NOW GET WORKING.
IKKYU.
DON'T CALL ME THAT.
NOTE: His real name.
UM...
EVERYONE?
I-I'M SORRY.
I DIDN'T MEAN TO BOTHER YOU ALL WITH THIS...
DON'T WORRY ABOUT IT.
I DON'T MIND.
'Sokay.
SPARKLE
DONE!!

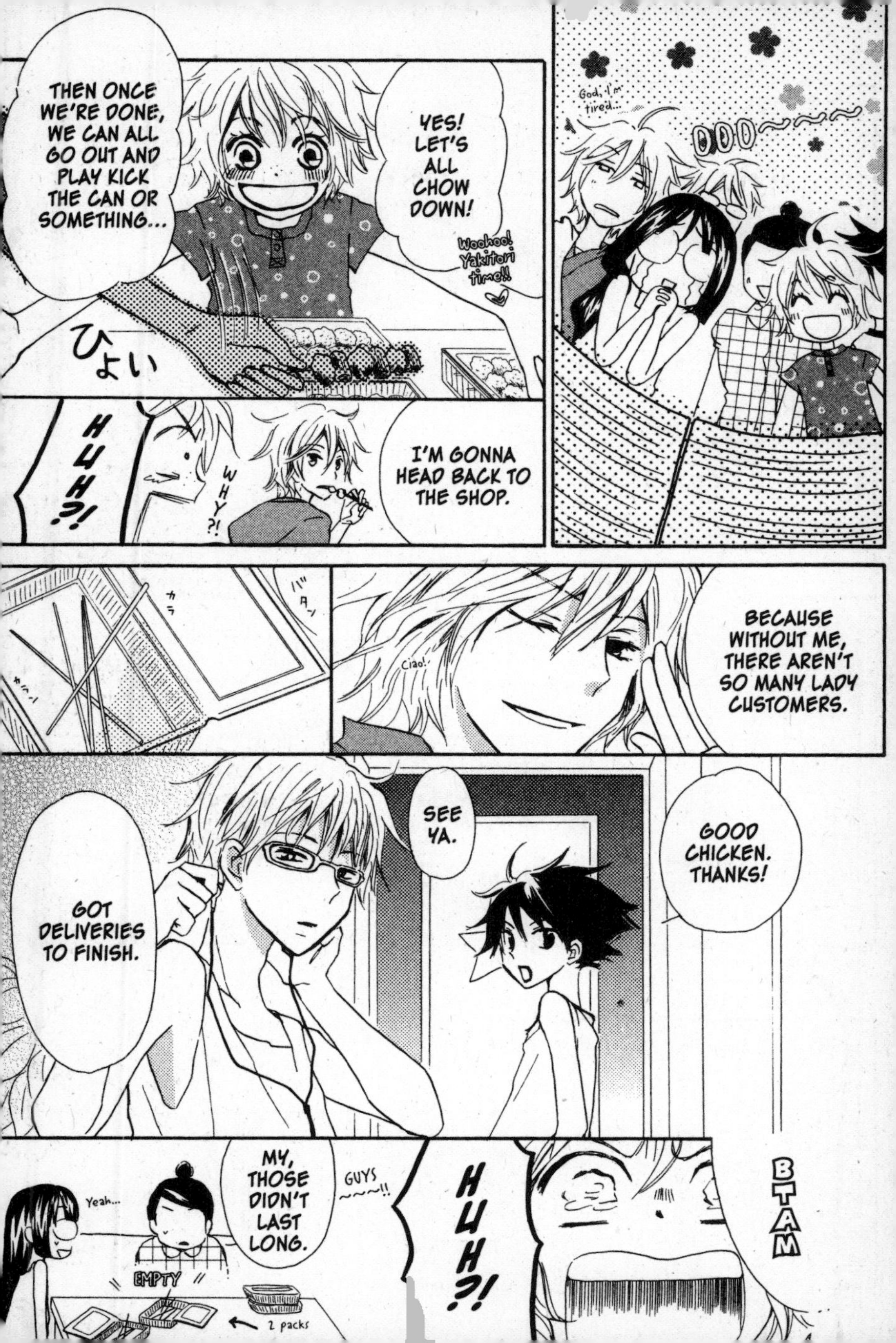
DOO~~~
God, I'm tired...
YES! LET'S ALL CHOW DOWN!
Woohoo! Yakitori time!!
THEN ONCE WE'RE DONE, WE CAN ALL GO OUT AND PLAY KICK THE CAN OR SOMETHING...
ひょい
I'M GONNA HEAD BACK TO THE SHOP.
WHY?!
HUHH?!
BECAUSE WITHOUT ME, THERE AREN'T SO MANY LADY CUSTOMERS.
Ciao!
バタン
カラ
カラン
GOOD CHICKEN. THANKS!
SEE YA.
GOT DELIVERIES TO FINISH.
BTAM
HUHH?!
GUYS ~~~!!
MY, THOSE DIDN'T LAST LONG.
Yeah...
EMPTY
2 packs

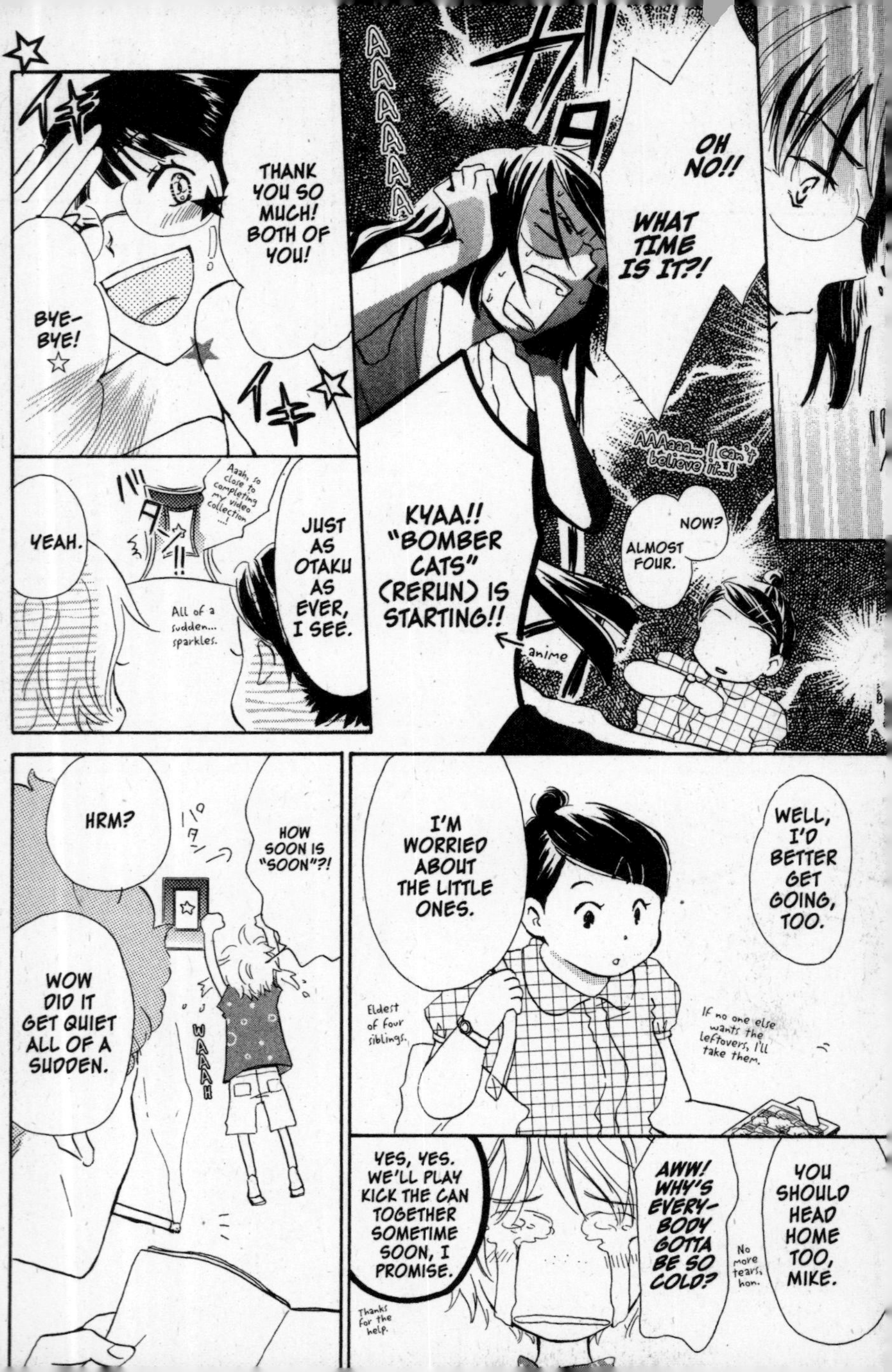
AAAAAAA
OH NO!!
WHAT TIME IS IT?!
AAAaaa... I can't believe it...!
NOW?
ALMOST FOUR.
KYAA!! "BOMBER CATS" (RERUN) IS STARTING!!
anime
THANK YOU SO MUCH! BOTH OF YOU!
BYE-BYE!
JUST AS OTAKU AS EVER, I SEE.
Aaah, so close to completing my video collection...!
YEAH.
All of a sudden... sparkles.
WELL, I'D BETTER GET GOING, TOO.
If no one else wants the leftovers, I'll take them.
I'M WORRIED ABOUT THE LITTLE ONES.
Eldest of four siblings.
YOU SHOULD HEAD HOME TOO, MIKE.
No more tears, hon.
AWW! WHY'S EVERY-BODY GOTTA BE SO COLD?
YES, YES. WE'LL PLAY KICK THE CAN TOGETHER SOMETIME SOON, I PROMISE.
Thanks for the help.
HOW SOON IS "SOON"?!
HRM?
WOW DID IT GET QUIET ALL OF A SUDDEN.
WAAAH

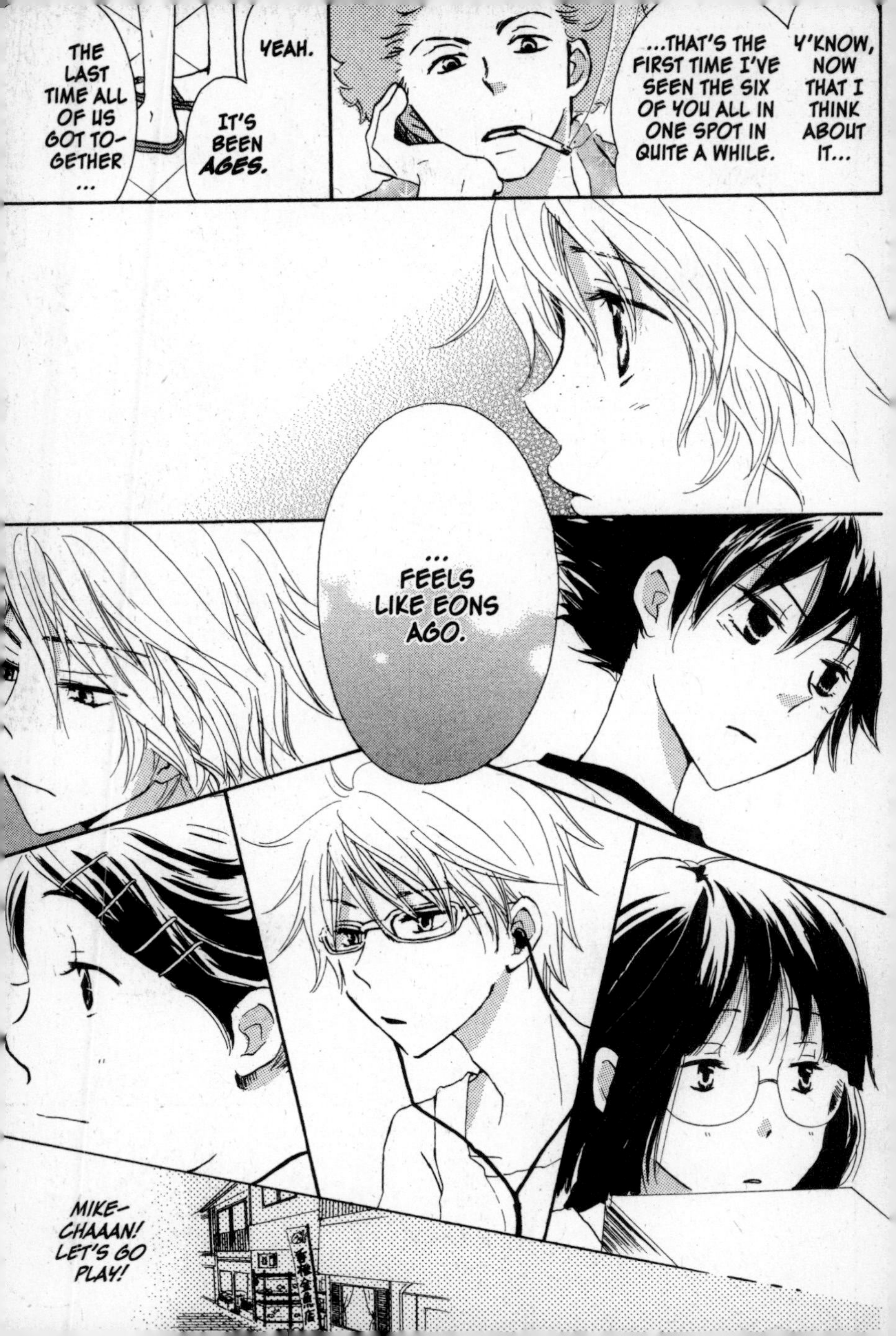
Y'KNOW, NOW THAT I THINK ABOUT IT...
...THAT'S THE FIRST TIME I'VE SEEN THE SIX OF YOU ALL IN ONE SPOT IN QUITE A WHILE.
YEAH.
IT'S BEEN AGES.
THE LAST TIME ALL OF US GOT TOGETHER ...
... FEELS LIKE EONS AGO.
MIKE-CHAAAN! LET'S GO PLAY!

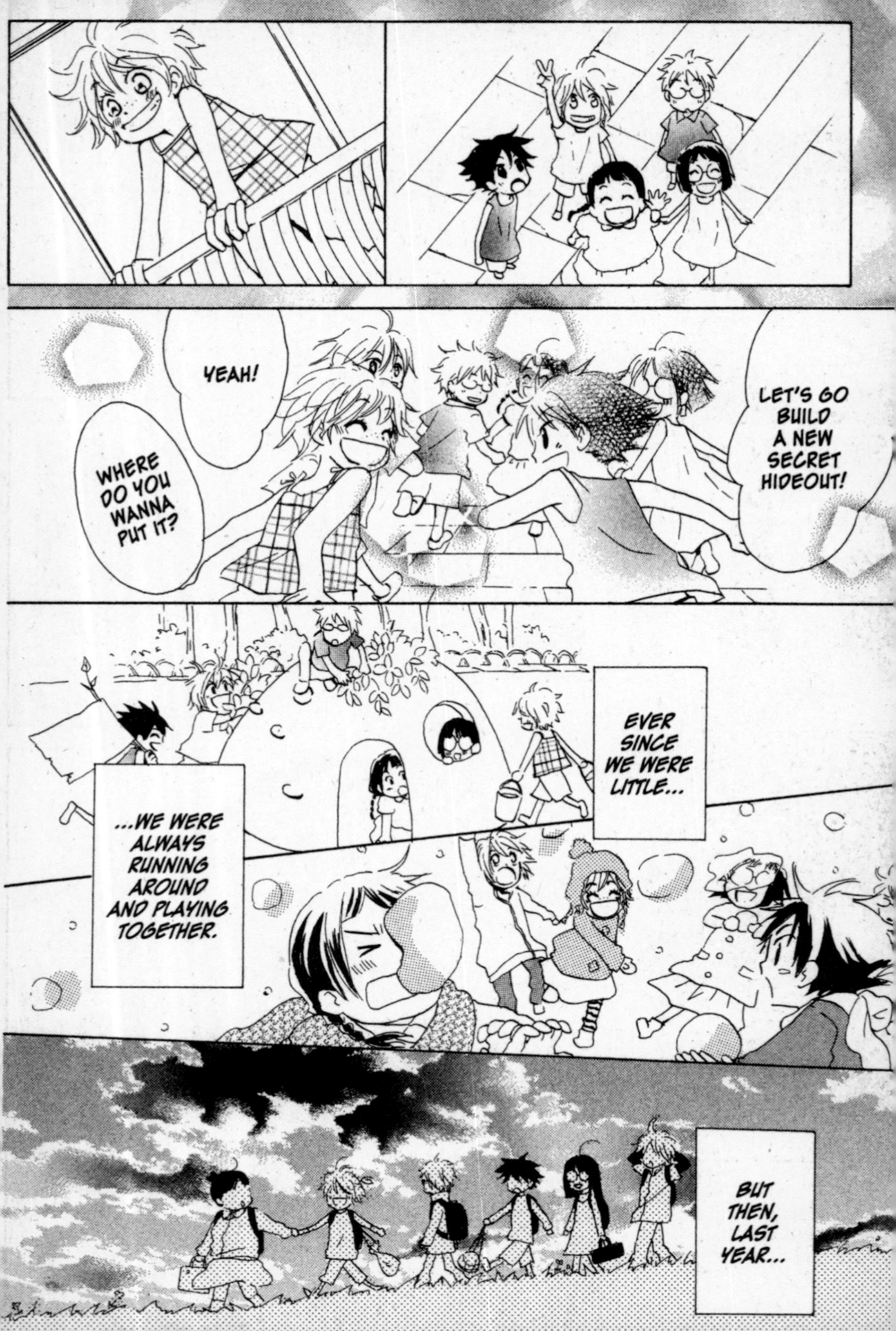
LET'S GO BUILD A NEW SECRET HIDEOUT!
YEAH!
WHERE DO YOU WANNA PUT IT?
EVER SINCE WE WERE LITTLE...
...WE WERE ALWAYS RUNNING AROUND AND PLAYING TOGETHER.
BUT THEN, LAST YEAR...

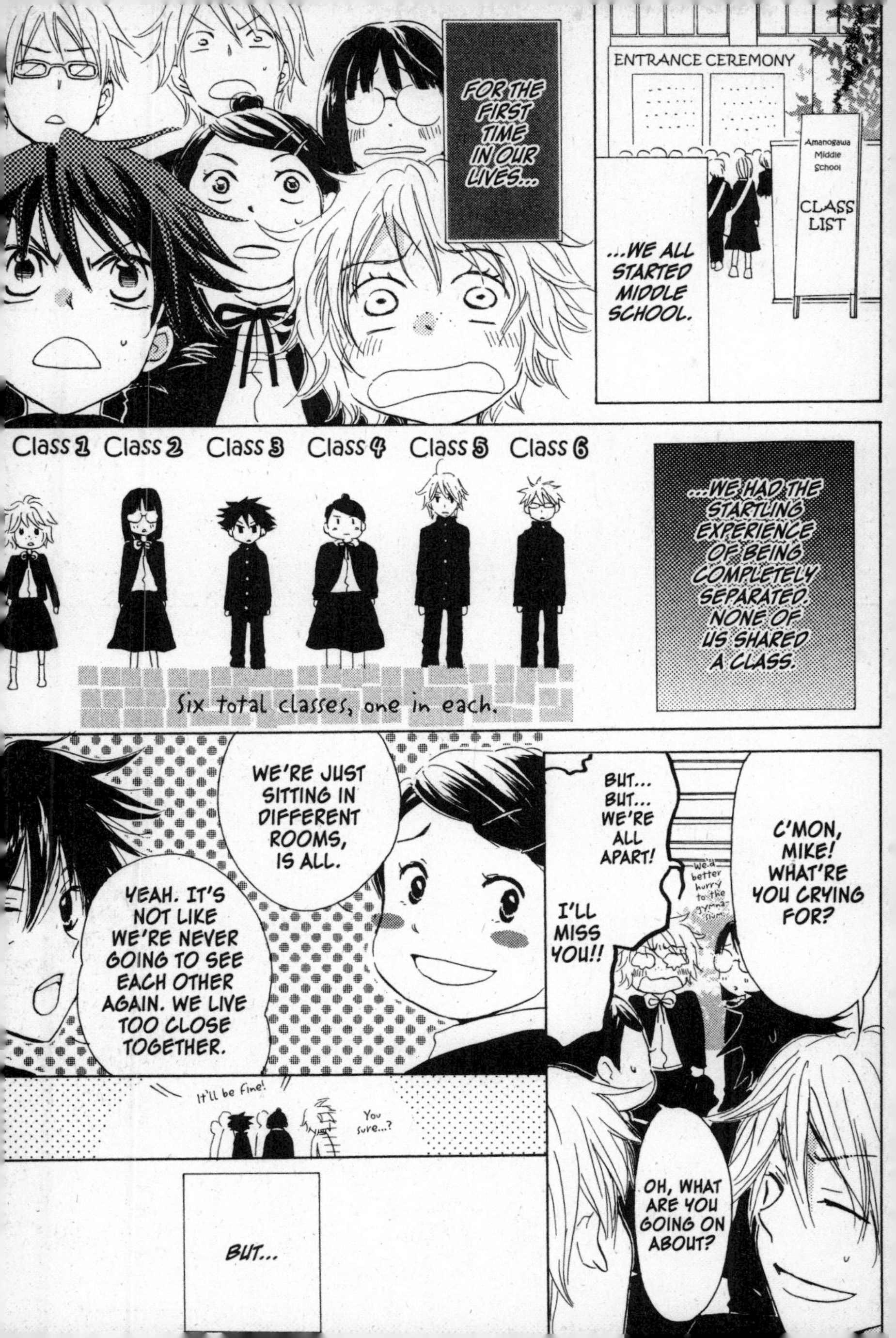
ENTRANCE CEREMONY
Amanogawa Middle School
CLASS LIST
...WE ALL STARTED MIDDLE SCHOOL.
FOR THE FIRST TIME IN OUR LIVES...
...WE HAD THE STARTLING EXPERIENCE OF BEING COMPLETELY SEPARATED. NONE OF US SHARED A CLASS.
Class 1
Class 2
Class 3
Class 4
Class 5
Class 6
Six total classes, one in each.
C'MON, MIKE! WHAT'RE YOU CRYING FOR?
BUT... BUT... WE'RE ALL APART!
I'LL MISS YOU!!
We'd better hurry to the gymnasium.
OH, WHAT ARE YOU GOING ON ABOUT?
WE'RE JUST SITTING IN DIFFERENT ROOMS, IS ALL.
YEAH. IT'S NOT LIKE WE'RE NEVER GOING TO SEE EACH OTHER AGAIN. WE LIVE TOO CLOSE TOGETHER.
It'll be fine!
You sure...?
BUT...

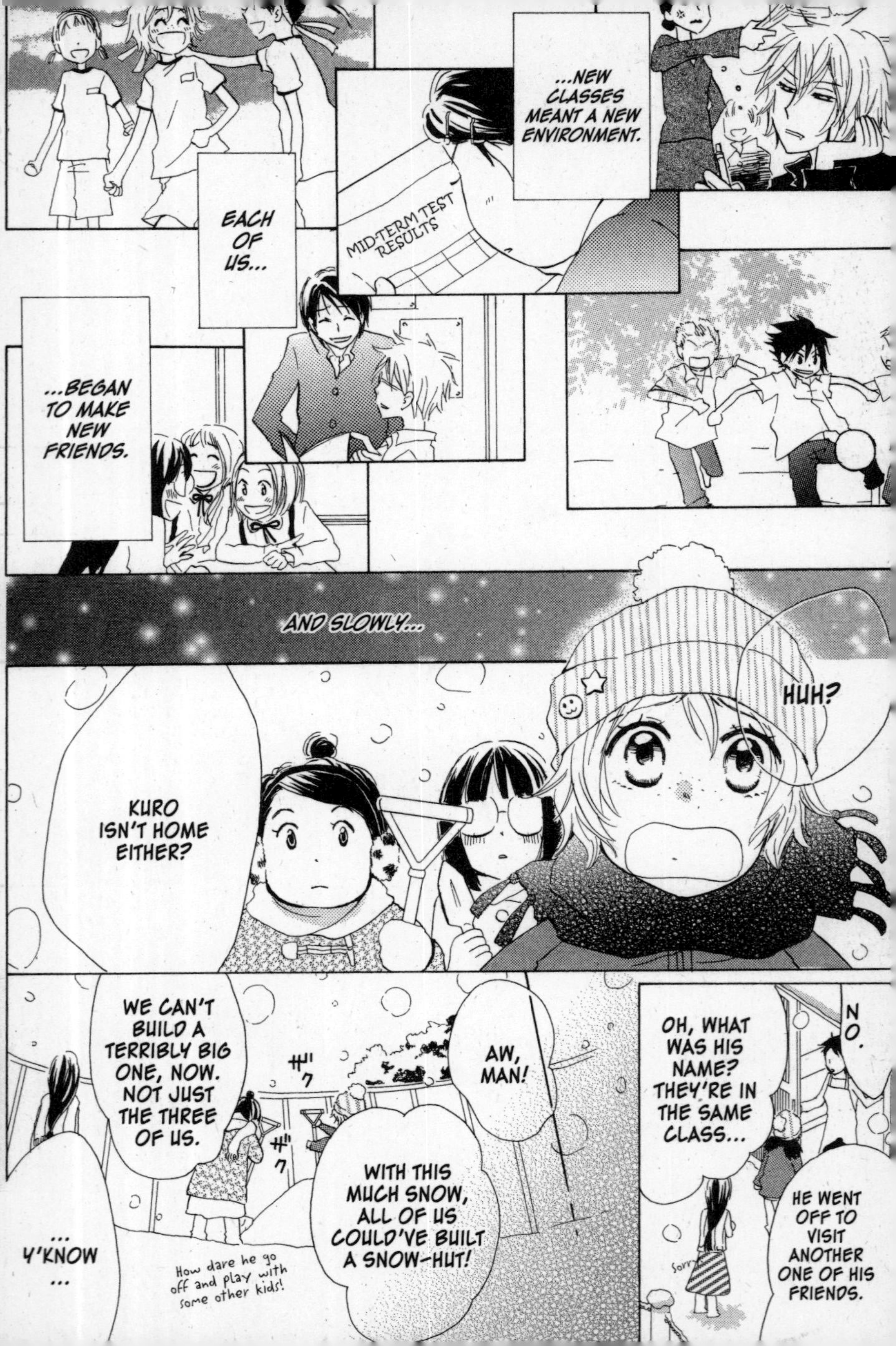
...NEW CLASSES MEANT A NEW ENVIRONMENT.
MID-TERM TEST RESULTS
EACH OF US...
...BEGAN TO MAKE NEW FRIENDS.
AND SLOWLY...
HUH?
KURO ISN'T HOME EITHER?
NO.
OH, WHAT WAS HIS NAME? THEY'RE IN THE SAME CLASS...
HE WENT OFF TO VISIT ANOTHER ONE OF HIS FRIENDS.
AW, MAN!
WITH THIS MUCH SNOW, ALL OF US COULD'VE BUILT A SNOW-HUT!
WE CAN'T BUILD A TERRIBLY BIG ONE, NOW. NOT JUST THE THREE OF US.
ザク
ザク
How dare he go off and play with some other kids!
...Y'KNOW...

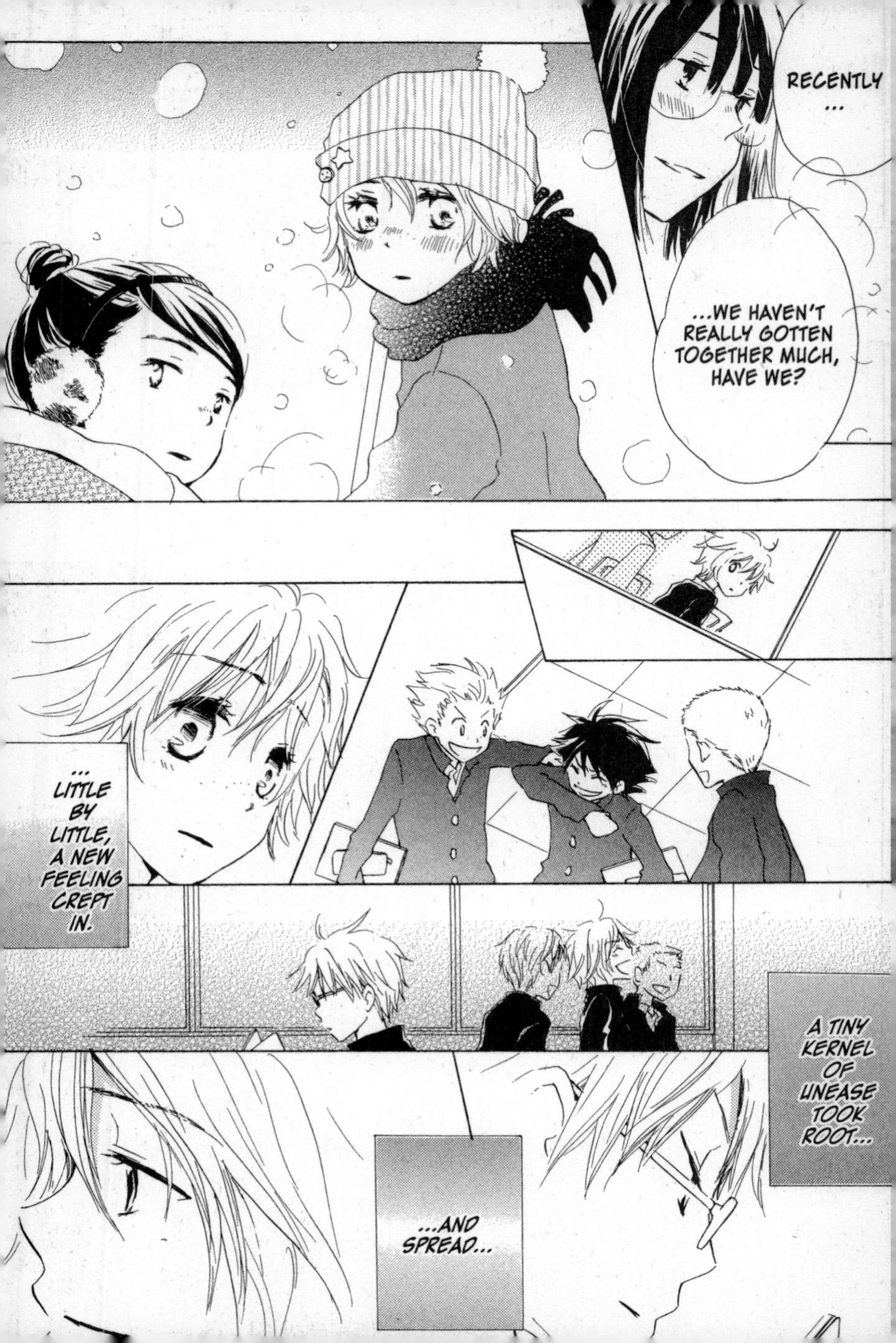
RECENTLY ...
...WE HAVEN'T REALLY GOTTEN TOGETHER MUCH, HAVE WE?
... LITTLE BY LITTLE, A NEW FEELING CREPT IN.
A TINY KERNEL OF UNEASE TOOK ROOT...
...AND SPREAD...

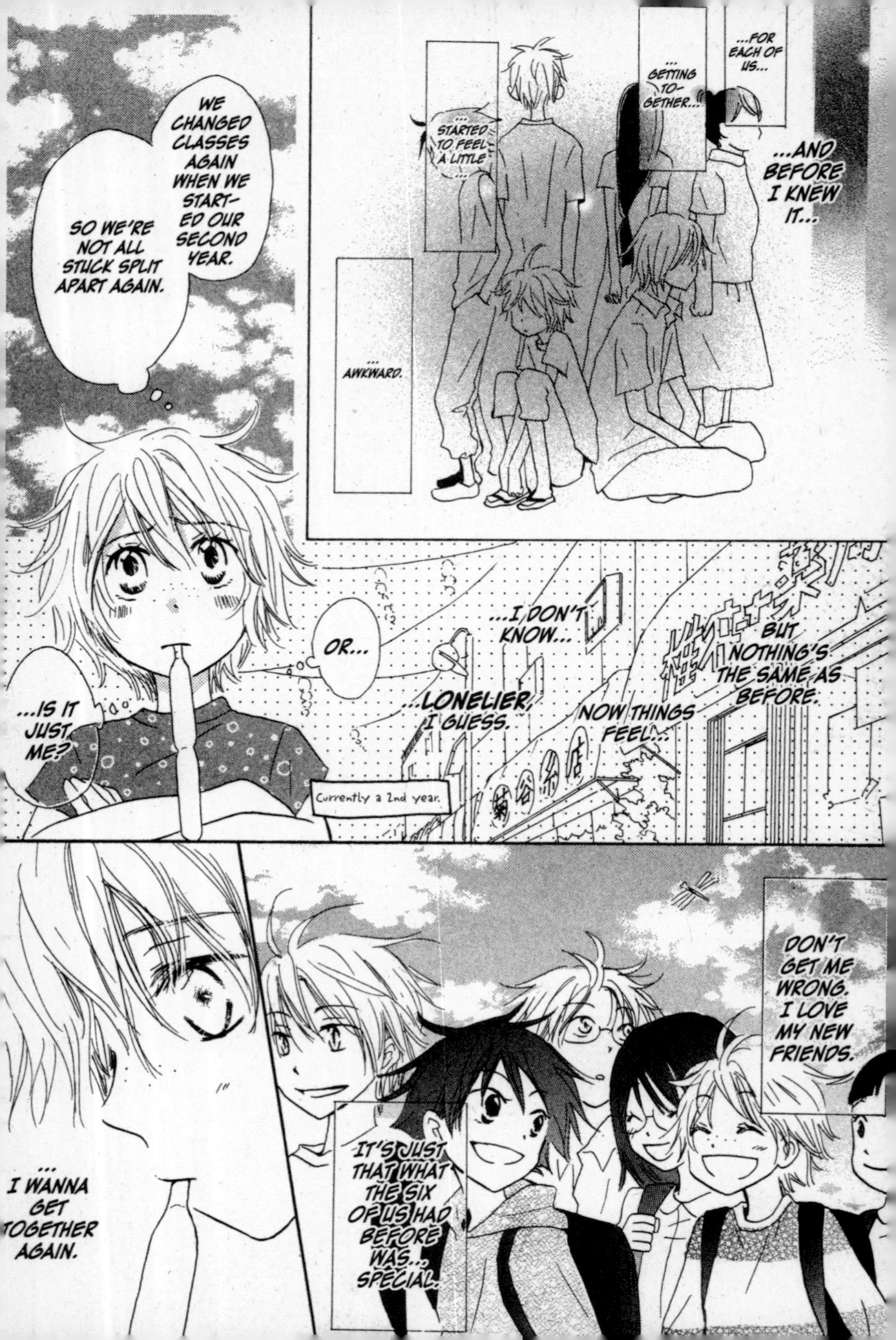

...FOR EACH OF US...
...AND BEFORE I KNEW IT...
...GETTING TO-GETHER...
...STARTED TO FEEL A LITTLE...
...AWKWARD.
WE CHANGED CLASSES AGAIN WHEN WE START-ED OUR SECOND YEAR.
SO WE'RE NOT ALL STUCK SPLIT APART AGAIN.
BUT NOTHING'S THE SAME AS BEFORE.
NOW THINGS FEEL...
...I DON'T KNOW...
...LONELIER, I GUESS.
OR...
...IS IT JUST ME?
Currently a 2nd year.
DON'T GET ME WRONG. I LOVE MY NEW FRIENDS.
IT'S JUST THAT WHAT THE SIX OF US HAD BEFORE WAS... SPECIAL.
... I WANNA GET TOGETHER AGAIN.

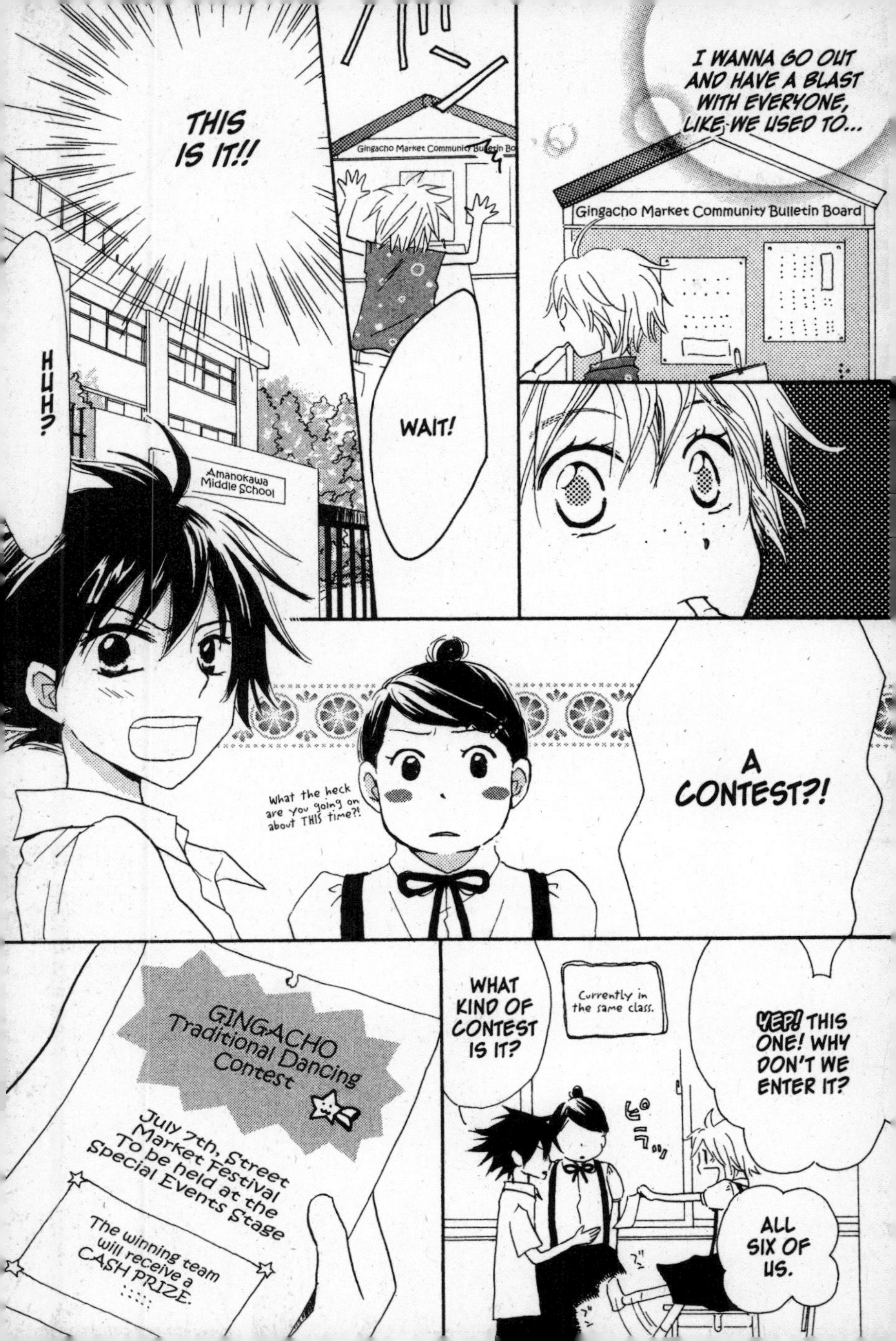

I WANNA GO OUT AND HAVE A BLAST WITH EVERYONE, LIKE WE USED TO...
Gingacho Market Community Bulletin Board
Gingacho Market Community Bulletin Bo
WAIT!
THIS IS IT!!
HUH?
Amanokawa Middle School
A CONTEST?!
What the heck are you going on about THIS time?!
YEP! THIS ONE! WHY DON'T WE ENTER IT?
WHAT KIND OF CONTEST IS IT?
Currently in the same class.
ALL SIX OF US.
GINGACHO Traditional Dancing Contest
July 7th, Street Market Festival
To be held at the Special Events Stage
The winning team will receive a CASH PRIZE.

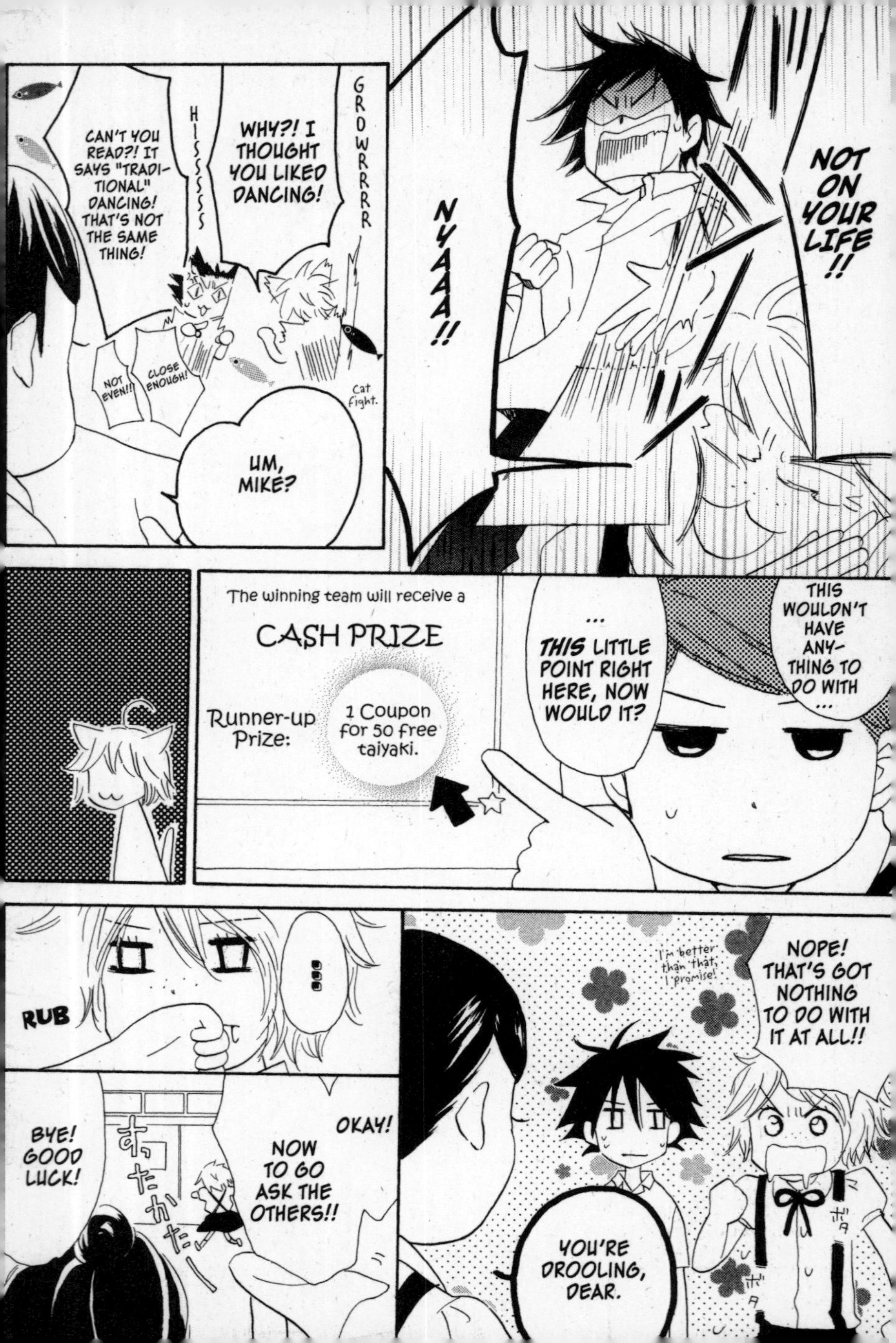
NOT ON YOUR LIFE!!
NYAAAA!!
WHY?! I THOUGHT YOU LIKED DANCING!
GROWRRRR
HISSSSSS
CAN'T YOU READ?! IT SAYS "TRADITIONAL" DANCING! THAT'S NOT THE SAME THING!
CLOSE ENOUGH!
NOT EVEN!!
Cat fight.
UM, MIKE?
THIS WOULDN'T HAVE ANYTHING TO DO WITH ...
... THIS LITTLE POINT RIGHT HERE, NOW WOULD IT?
The winning team will receive a
CASH PRIZE
Runner-up Prize:
1 Coupon for 50 free taiyaki.
NOPE! THAT'S GOT NOTHING TO DO WITH IT AT ALL!!
I'm better than that, I promise!
YOU'RE DROOLING, DEAR.
...
RUB
OKAY!
NOW TO GO ASK THE OTHERS!!
BYE! GOOD LUCK!

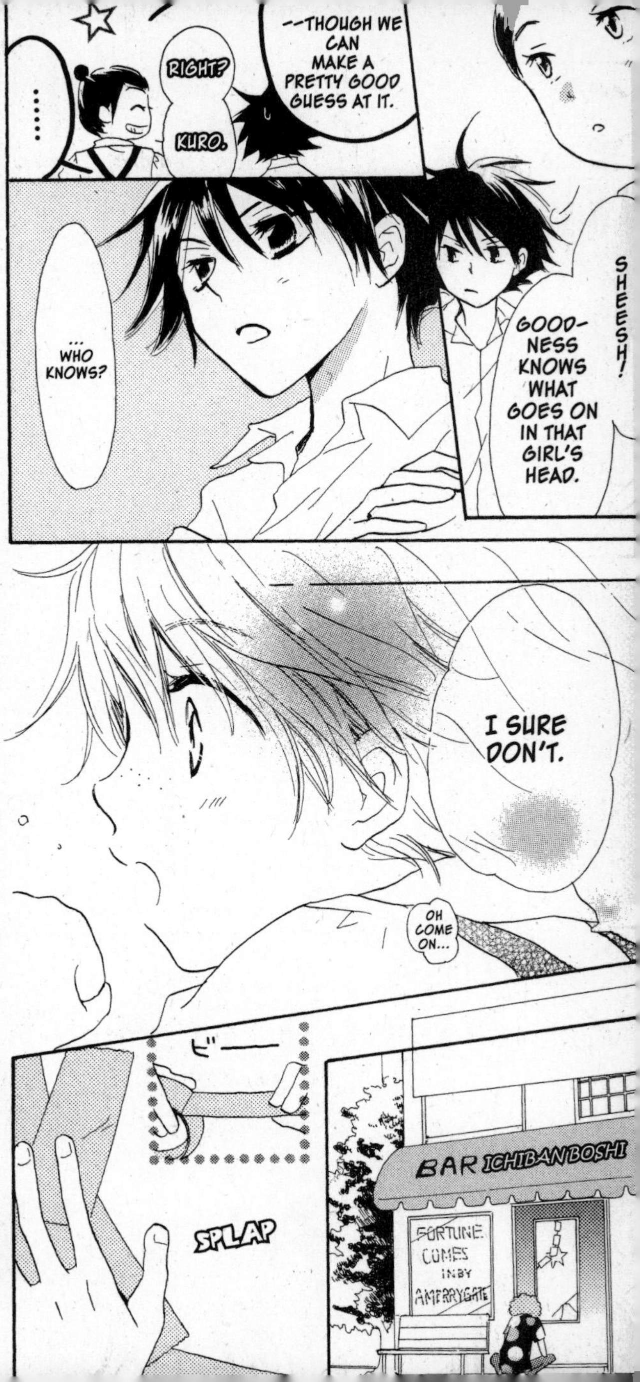
--THOUGH WE CAN MAKE A PRETTY GOOD GUESS AT IT.
RIGHT?
KURO.
......
SHEESH!
GOODNESS KNOWS WHAT GOES ON IN THAT GIRL'S HEAD.
... WHO KNOWS?
I SURE DON'T.
OH COME ON...
BAR ICHIBANBOSHI
FORTUNE
COMES
INBY
AMERRYGATE
ビーー
SPLAP

2

To all the people who send me fan mail and fan art and handmade trinkets and knickknacks... thank you!! I always appreciate receiving them. They help inspire me a lot! Just the thought that someone took the time to sit at their desk, take up a pen and create something just for me is an incredible joy. It's like they're right there, talking with me, even though we've never met. I love it! Thank you! My replies are really, really late, though. I'm so sorry! And you really don't need to send return postage along, honest!

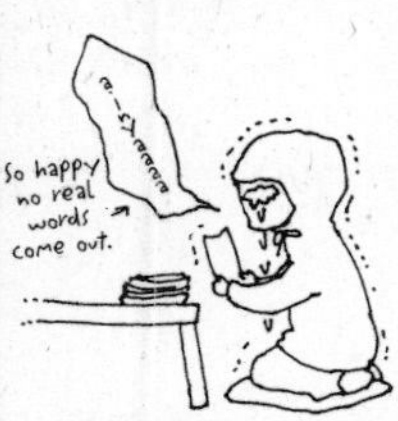
So happy no real words come out.

I always read them when seated properly.

Feels more appropriate that way...

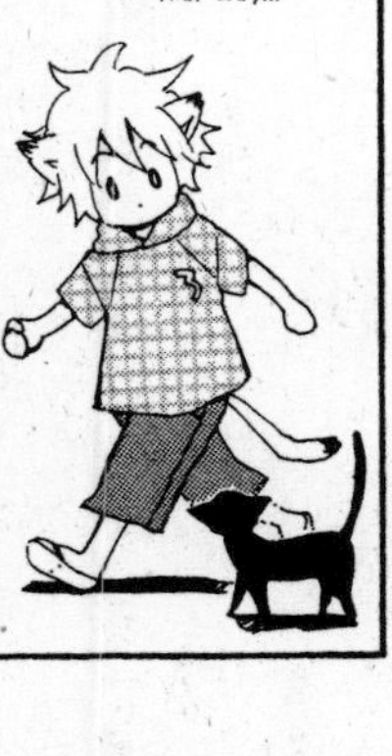

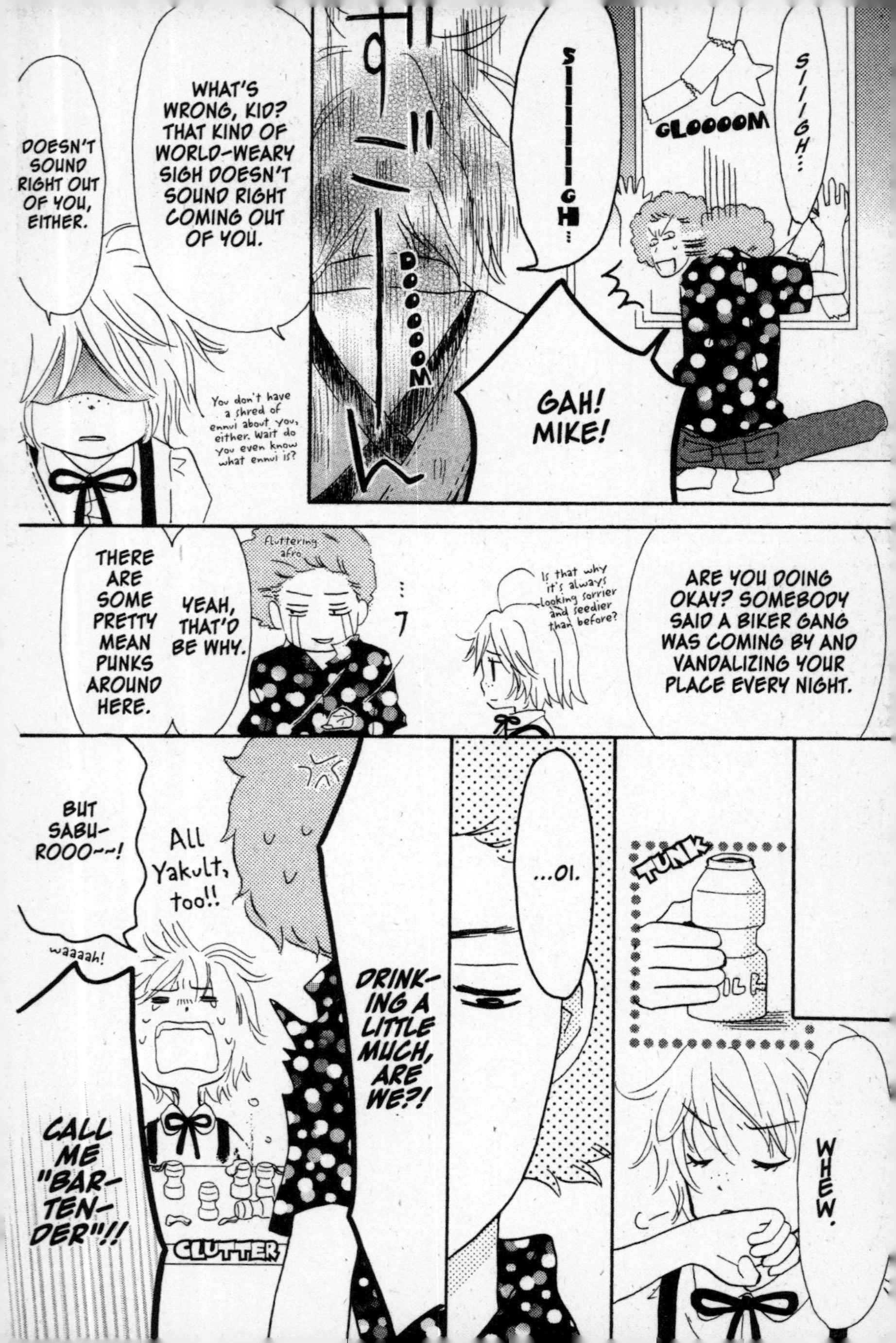
SIIIGH...
GLOOOOM
GAH! MIKE!
SIIIIIGH...
DOOOOOOM
WHAT'S WRONG, KID? THAT KIND OF WORLD-WEARY SIGH DOESN'T SOUND RIGHT COMING OUT OF YOU.
DOESN'T SOUND RIGHT OUT OF YOU, EITHER.
You don't have a shred of ennui about you, either. Wait do you even know what ennui is?
ARE YOU DOING OKAY? SOMEBODY SAID A BIKER GANG WAS COMING BY AND VANDALIZING YOUR PLACE EVERY NIGHT.
Is that why it's always looking sorrier and seedier than before?
Fluttering afro.
YEAH, THAT'D BE WHY.
THERE ARE SOME PRETTY MEAN PUNKS AROUND HERE.
WHEW.
TUNK
...OI.
DRINKING A LITTLE MUCH, ARE WE?!
All Yakult, too!!
BUT SABU-ROOO~~!
waaaah!
CALL ME "BARTENDER"!!
CLUTTER

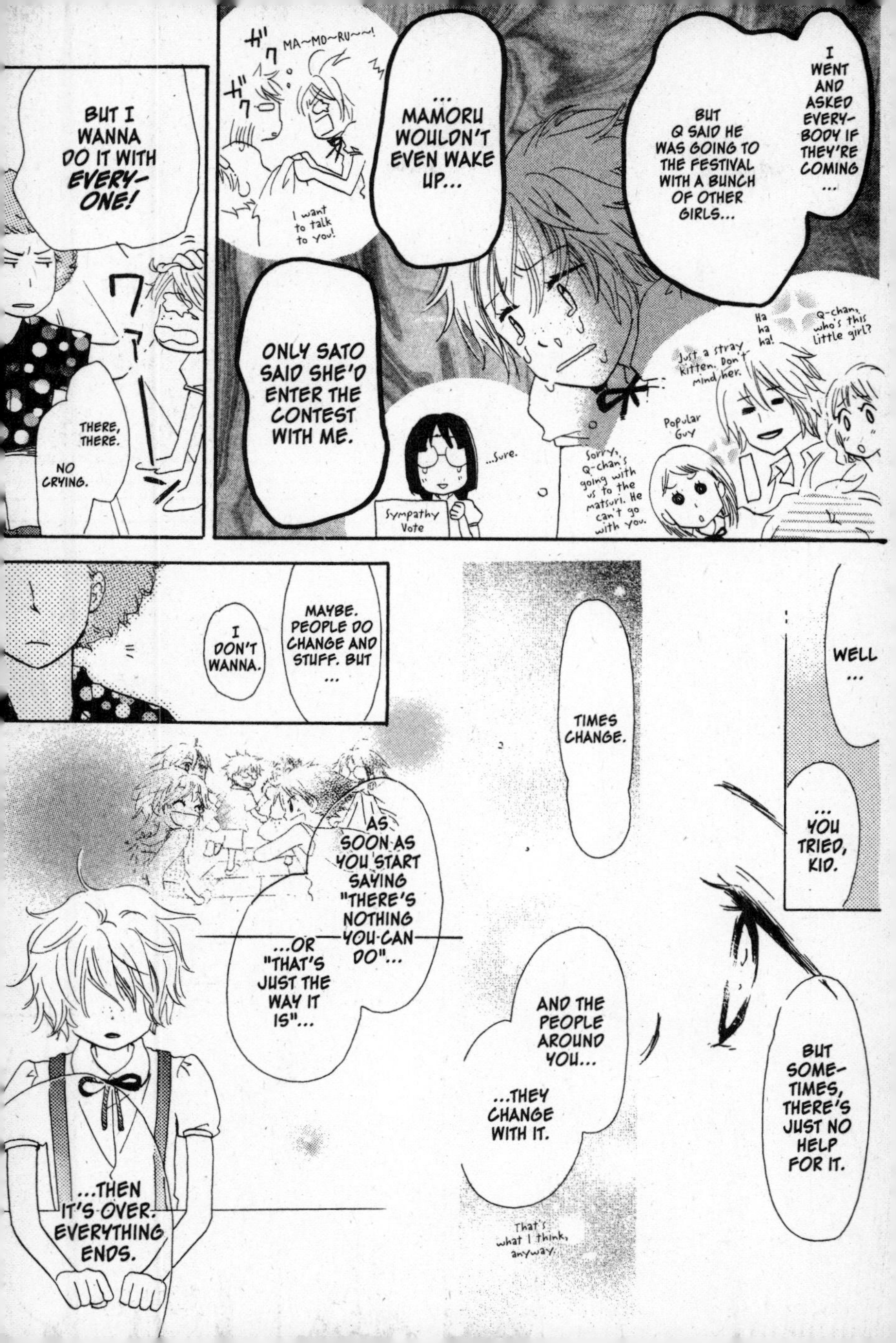
I WENT AND ASKED EVERYBODY IF THEY'RE COMING...
BUT Q SAID HE WAS GOING TO THE FESTIVAL WITH A BUNCH OF OTHER GIRLS...
Q-chan, who's this little girl?
Ha ha ha!
Just a stray kitten. Don't mind her.
Popular Guy
Sorry, Q-chan's going with us to the matsuri. He can't go with you.
...MAMORU WOULDN'T EVEN WAKE UP...
MA~MO~RU~~!
I want to talk to you!
ONLY SATO SAID SHE'D ENTER THE CONTEST WITH ME.
...Sure.
Sympathy Vote
BUT I WANNA DO IT WITH EVERYONE!
THERE, THERE.
NO CRYING.
WELL...
...YOU TRIED, KID.
BUT SOMETIMES, THERE'S JUST NO HELP FOR IT.
TIMES CHANGE.
AND THE PEOPLE AROUND YOU...
...THEY CHANGE WITH IT.
That's what I think, anyway.
MAYBE. PEOPLE DO CHANGE AND STUFF. BUT...
I DON'T WANNA.
AS SOON AS YOU START SAYING "THERE'S NOTHING YOU CAN DO"...
...OR "THAT'S JUST THE WAY IT IS"...
...THEN IT'S OVER. EVERYTHING ENDS.

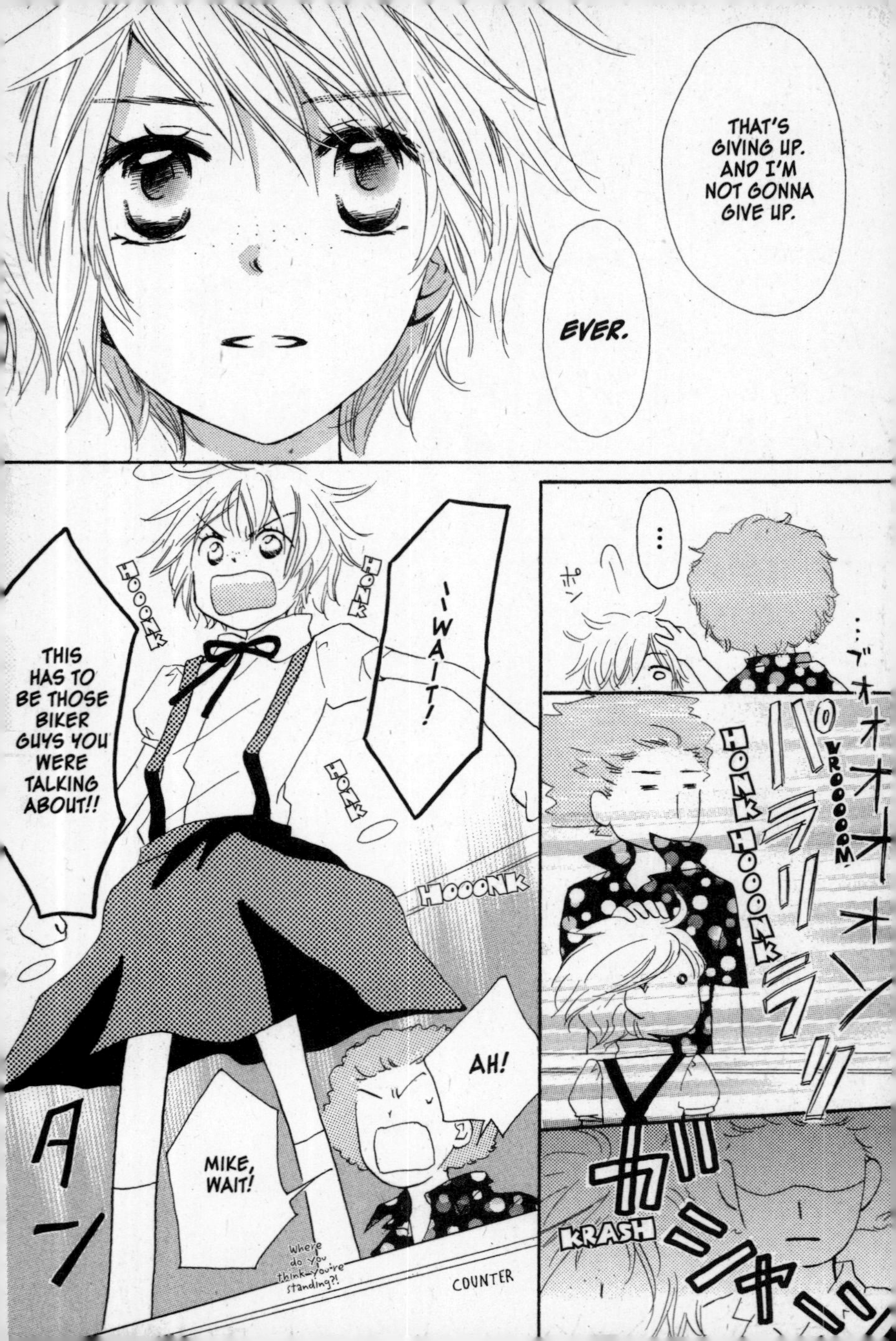
THAT'S GIVING UP. AND I'M NOT GONNA GIVE UP.
EVER.
...
ポン
VROOOOOOM
HONK HOOOONK
KRASH
I-I WAIT!
HONK
HOOOONK
THIS HAS TO BE THOSE BIKER GUYS YOU WERE TALKING ABOUT!!
HONK
HOOONK
AH!
MIKE, WAIT!
Where do you think you're standing?!
COUNTER
ダーン

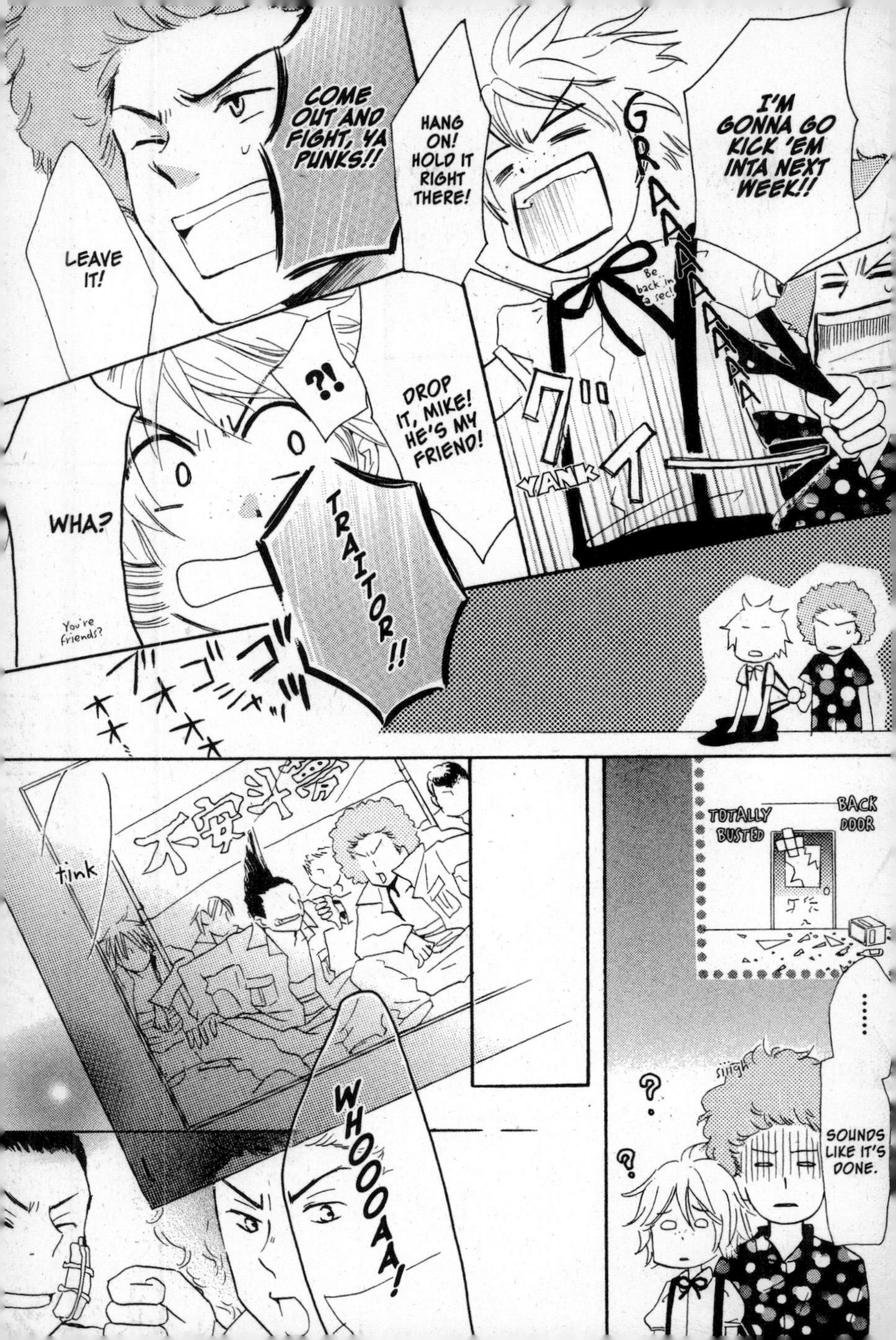
I'M GONNA GO KICK 'EM INTA NEXT WEEK!!
GRAAAAAAAAA
Be back in a sec!
HANG ON! HOLD IT RIGHT THERE!
COME OUT AND FIGHT, YA PUNKS!!
LEAVE IT!
YANK
DROP IT, MIKE! HE'S MY FRIEND!
?!
TRAITOR!!
WHA?
You're friends?
BACK DOOR
TOTALLY BUSTED
......
sigh
SOUNDS LIKE IT'S DONE.
?
?
tink
WHOOOAA!

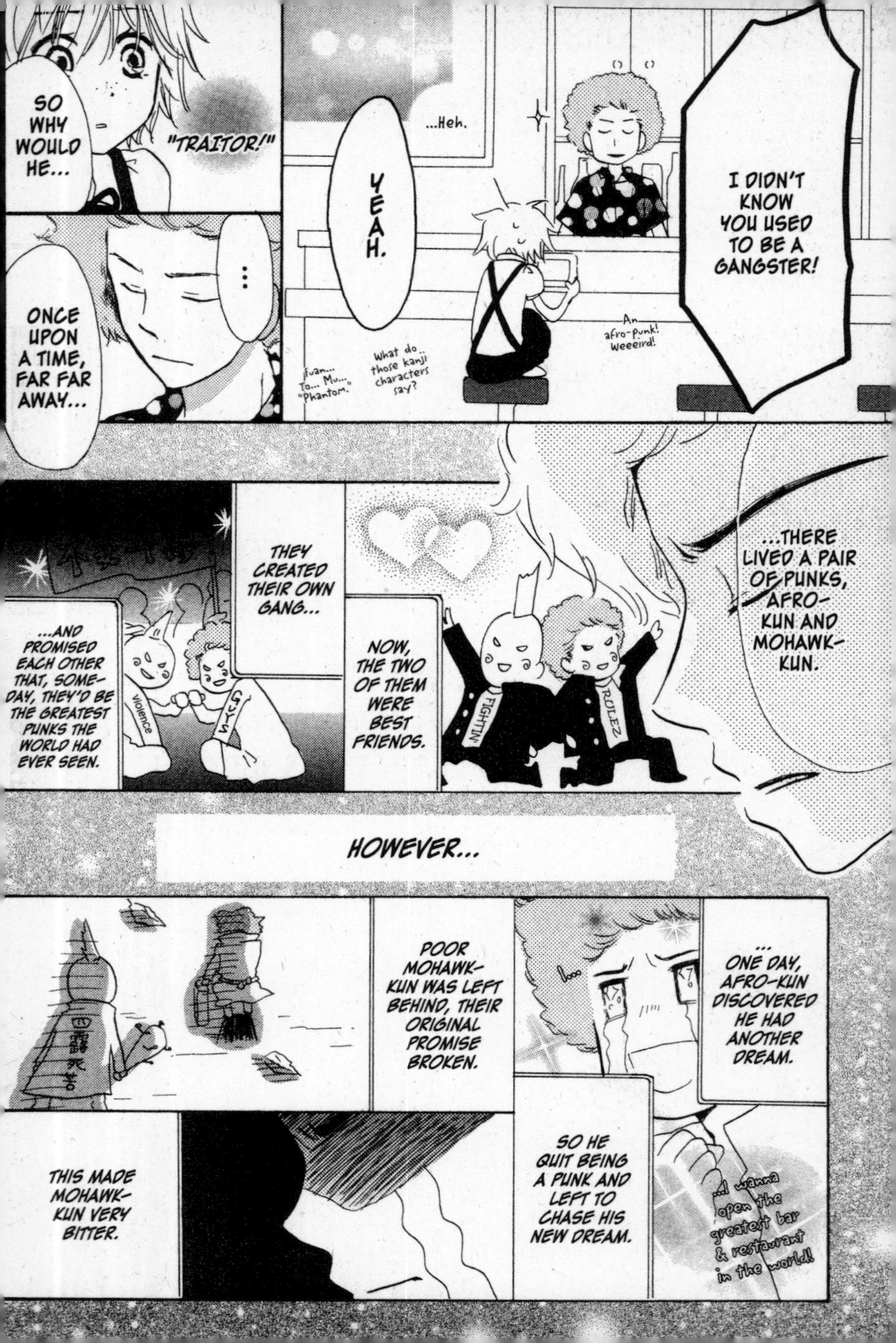
I DIDN'T KNOW YOU USED TO BE A GANGSTER!
...Heh.
YEAH.
An afro-punk! Weeeird!
What do those kanji characters say?
Fuan... To... Mu... "Phantom."
SO WHY WOULD HE...
"TRAITOR!"
...
ONCE UPON A TIME, FAR FAR AWAY...
...THERE LIVED A PAIR OF PUNKS, AFRO-KUN AND MOHAWK-KUN.
THEY CREATED THEIR OWN GANG...
NOW, THE TWO OF THEM WERE BEST FRIENDS.
RULEZ
FIGHTIN'
...AND PROMISED EACH OTHER THAT, SOME-DAY, THEY'D BE THE GREATEST PUNKS THE WORLD HAD EVER SEEN.
GUYS
violence
HOWEVER...
... ONE DAY, AFRO-KUN DISCOVERED HE HAD ANOTHER DREAM.
...I wanna open the greatest bar & restaurant in the world!
SO HE QUIT BEING A PUNK AND LEFT TO CHASE HIS NEW DREAM.
POOR MOHAWK-KUN WAS LEFT BEHIND, THEIR ORIGINAL PROMISE BROKEN.
THIS MADE MOHAWK-KUN VERY BITTER.

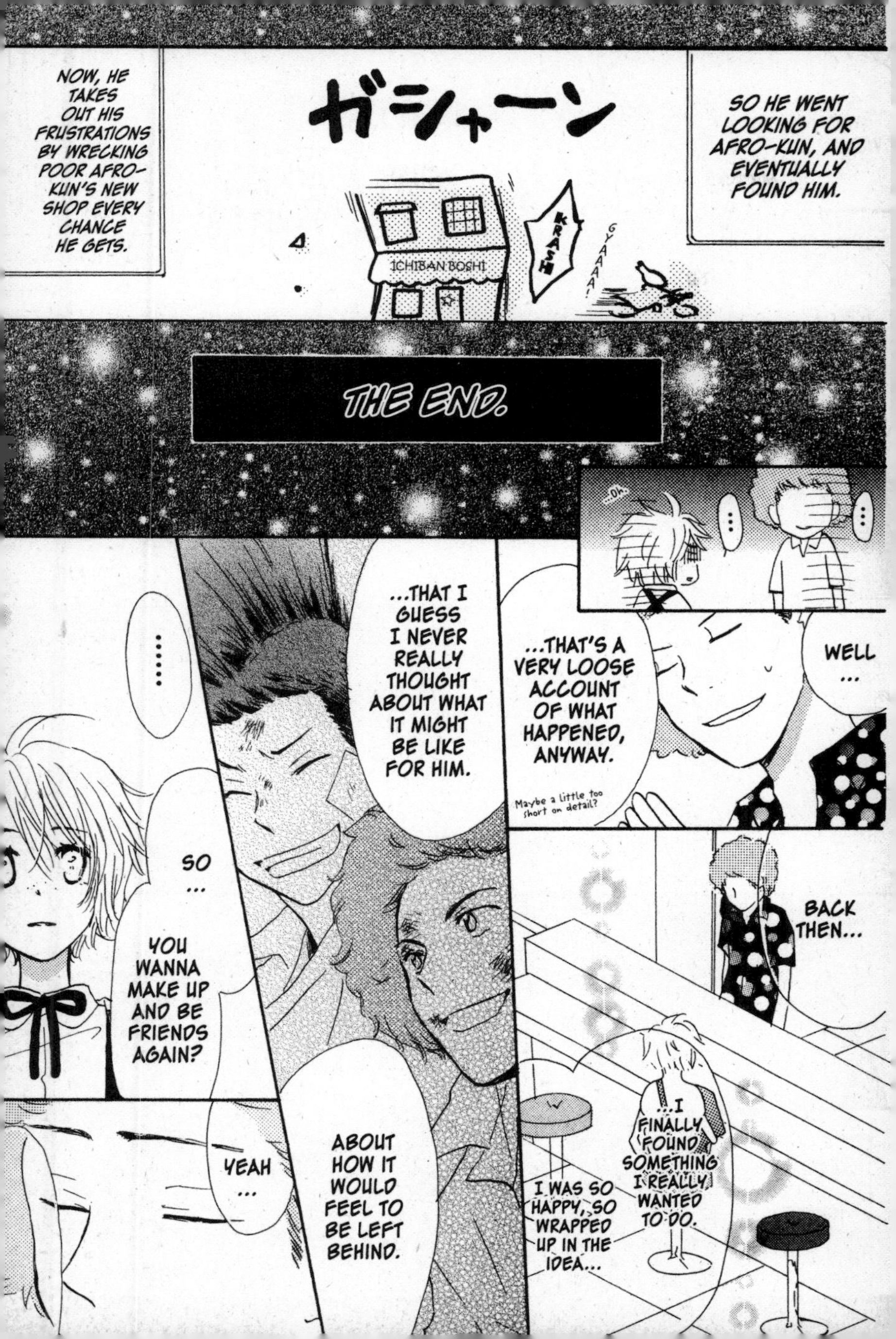

SO HE WENT LOOKING FOR AFRO-KUN, AND EVENTUALLY FOUND HIM.
ガシャーン
KRASH
GYAAAA!
ICHIBAN BOSHI
NOW, HE TAKES OUT HIS FRUSTRATIONS BY WRECKING POOR AFRO-KUN'S NEW SHOP EVERY CHANCE HE GETS.
THE END.
...Oh
...
...
WELL ...
...THAT'S A VERY LOOSE ACCOUNT OF WHAT HAPPENED, ANYWAY.
Maybe a little too short on detail?
BACK THEN...
...I FINALLY FOUND SOMETHING I REALLY WANTED TO DO.
I WAS SO HAPPY, SO WRAPPED UP IN THE IDEA...
...THAT I GUESS I NEVER REALLY THOUGHT ABOUT WHAT IT MIGHT BE LIKE FOR HIM.
ABOUT HOW IT WOULD FEEL TO BE LEFT BEHIND.
......
SO ...
YOU WANNA MAKE UP AND BE FRIENDS AGAIN?
YEAH ...

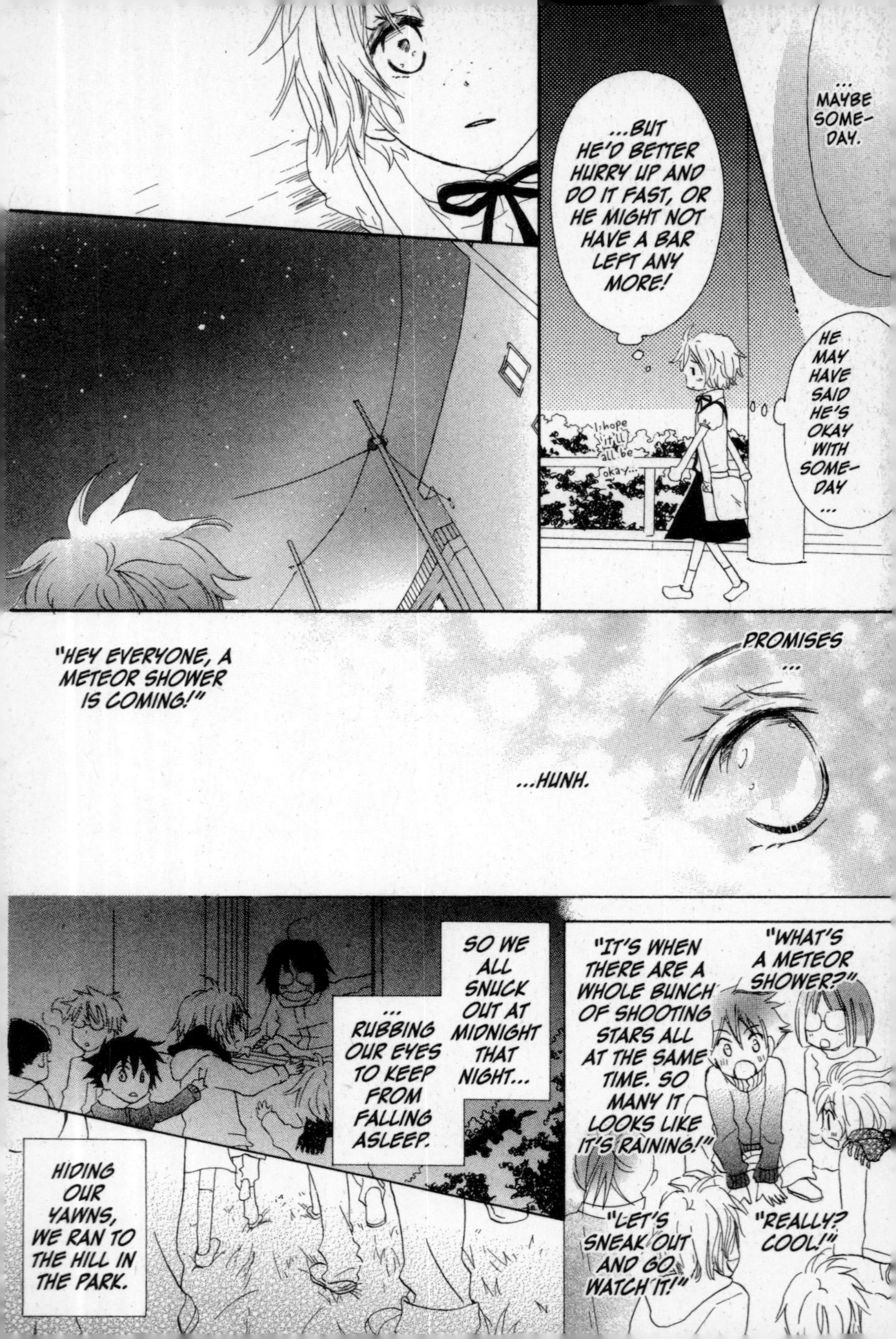
...MAYBE SOMEDAY.
HE MAY HAVE SAID HE'S OKAY WITH SOMEDAY...
...BUT HE'D BETTER HURRY UP AND DO IT FAST, OR HE MIGHT NOT HAVE A BAR LEFT ANY MORE!
I hope it'll all be okay...
PROMISES...
...HUNH.
"HEY EVERYONE, A METEOR SHOWER IS COMING!"
"WHAT'S A METEOR SHOWER?"
"IT'S WHEN THERE ARE A WHOLE BUNCH OF SHOOTING STARS ALL AT THE SAME TIME. SO MANY IT LOOKS LIKE IT'S RAINING!"
"REALLY? COOL!"
"LET'S SNEAK OUT AND GO WATCH IT!"
SO WE ALL SNUCK OUT AT MIDNIGHT THAT NIGHT...
...RUBBING OUR EYES TO KEEP FROM FALLING ASLEEP.
HIDING OUR YAWNS, WE RAN TO THE HILL IN THE PARK.

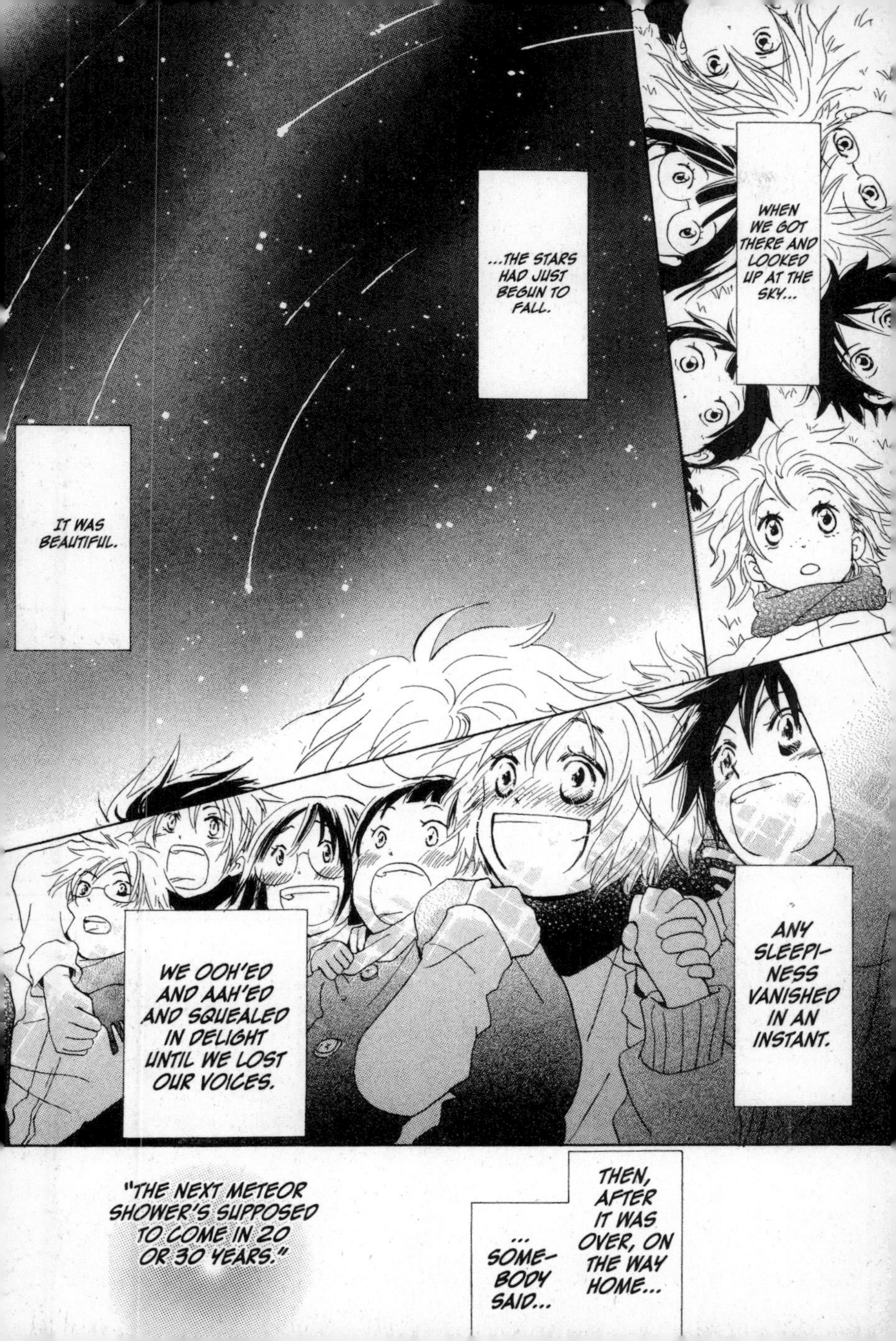
WHEN WE GOT THERE AND LOOKED UP AT THE SKY...
...THE STARS HAD JUST BEGUN TO FALL.
IT WAS BEAUTIFUL.
ANY SLEEPINESS VANISHED IN AN INSTANT.
WE OOH'ED AND AAH'ED AND SQUEALED IN DELIGHT UNTIL WE LOST OUR VOICES.
THEN, AFTER IT WAS OVER, ON THE WAY HOME...
...SOMEBODY SAID...
"THE NEXT METEOR SHOWER'S SUPPOSED TO COME IN 20 OR 30 YEARS."

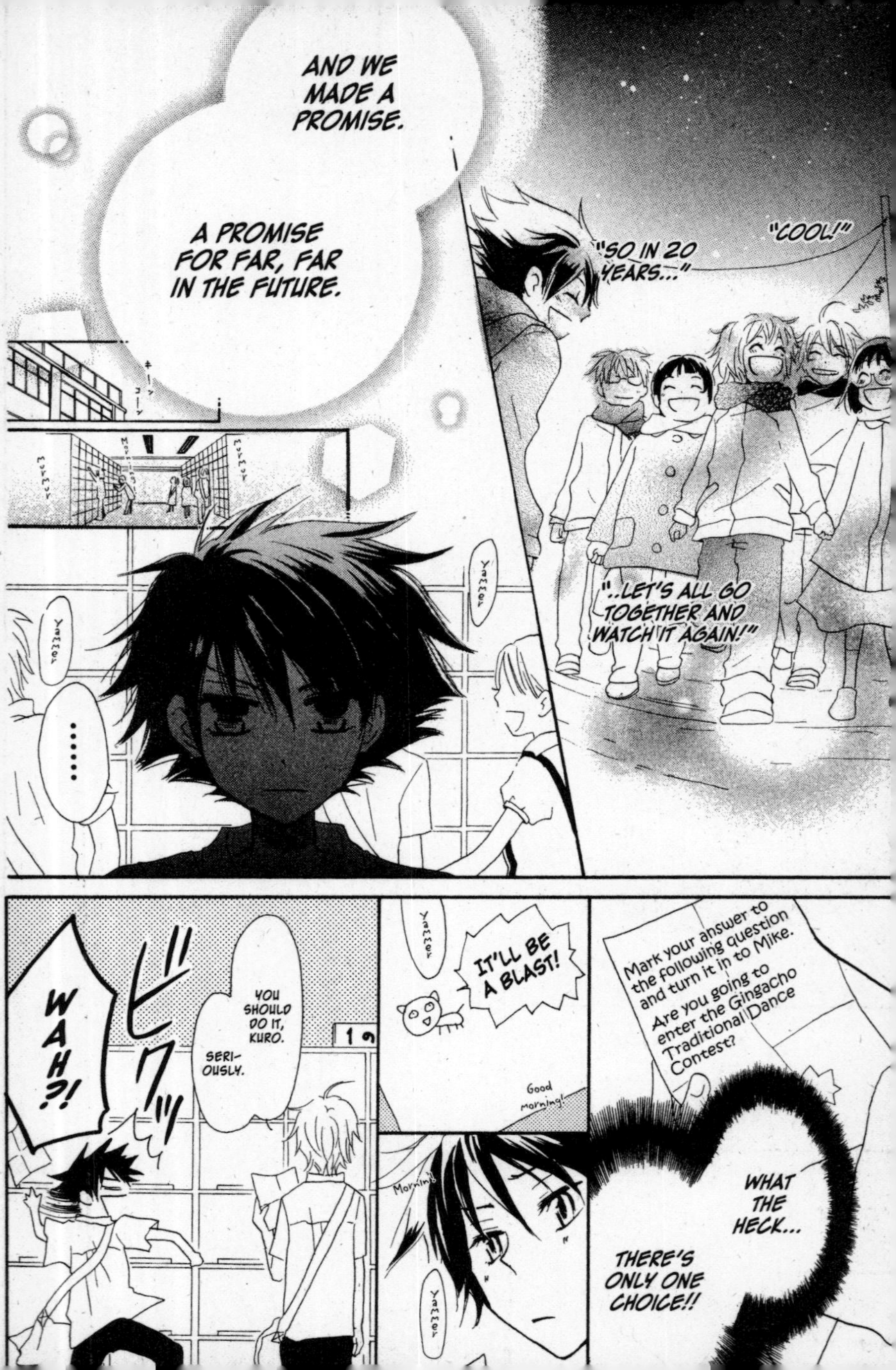
AND WE MADE A PROMISE.
A PROMISE FOR FAR, FAR IN THE FUTURE.
"COOL!"
"SO IN 20 YEARS..."
"..LET'S ALL GO TOGETHER AND WATCH IT AGAIN!"
キーンコーン
Murmur
Murmur
Murmur
Yammer
Yammer
......
Mark your answer to the following question and turn it in to Mike.
Are you going to enter the Gingacho Traditional Dance Contest?
WHAT THE HECK...
THERE'S ONLY ONE CHOICE!!
Yammer
IT'LL BE A BLAST!
Good morning!
Mornin'!
Yammer
YOU SHOULD DO IT, KURO.
SERI-OUSLY.
ビクッ
WAH?!

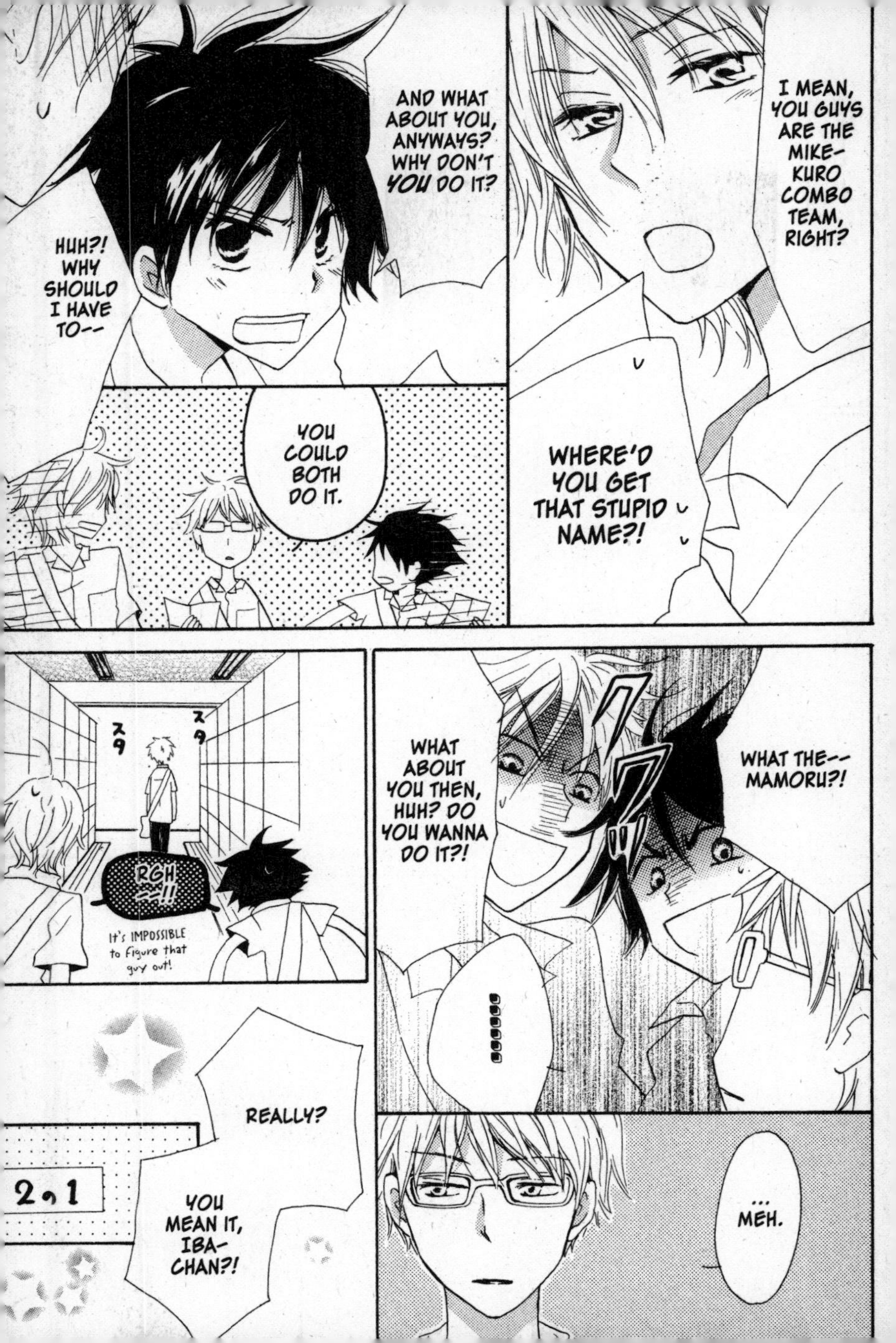
I MEAN, YOU GUYS ARE THE MIKE-KURO COMBO TEAM, RIGHT?
WHERE'D YOU GET THAT STUPID NAME?!
AND WHAT ABOUT YOU, ANYWAYS? WHY DON'T YOU DO IT?
HUH?! WHY SHOULD I HAVE TO--
YOU COULD BOTH DO IT.
WHAT THE-- MAMORU?!
WHAT ABOUT YOU THEN, HUH? DO YOU WANNA DO IT?!
......
... MEH.
スタ
スタ
RGH ~~!!
It's IMPOSSIBLE to figure that guy out!
REALLY?
YOU MEAN IT, IBA-CHAN?!
2の1

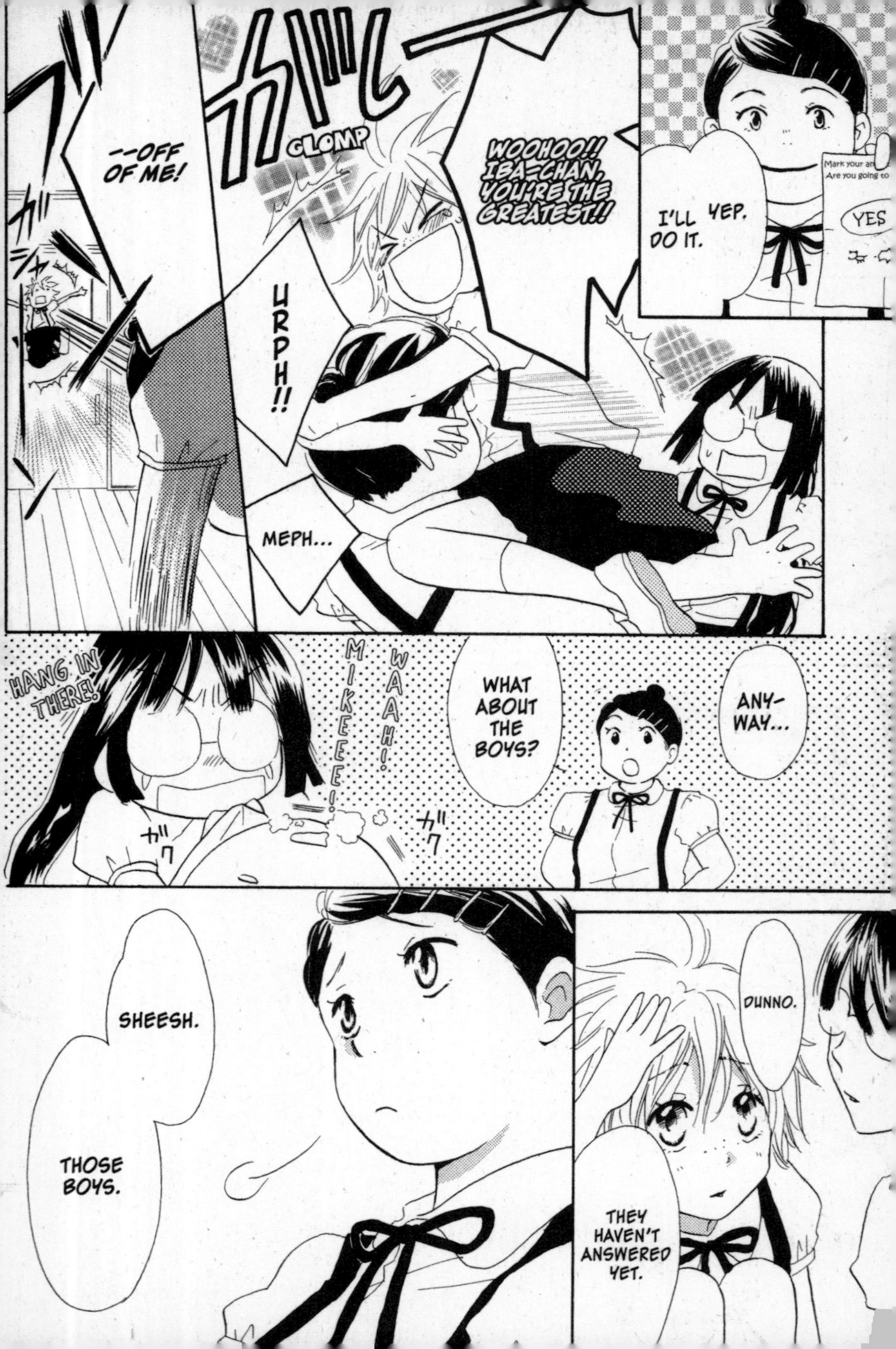
Mark your an
Are you going to
YES
YEP.
I'LL DO IT.
WOOHOO!! IBA-CHAN, YOU'RE THE GREATEST!!
GLOMP
URPH!!
MEPH...
--OFF OF ME!
ANY-WAY...
WHAT ABOUT THE BOYS?
WAAAH!
MIKEEEE!
HANG IN THERE!
DUNNO.
THEY HAVEN'T ANSWERED YET.
SHEESH.
THOSE BOYS.

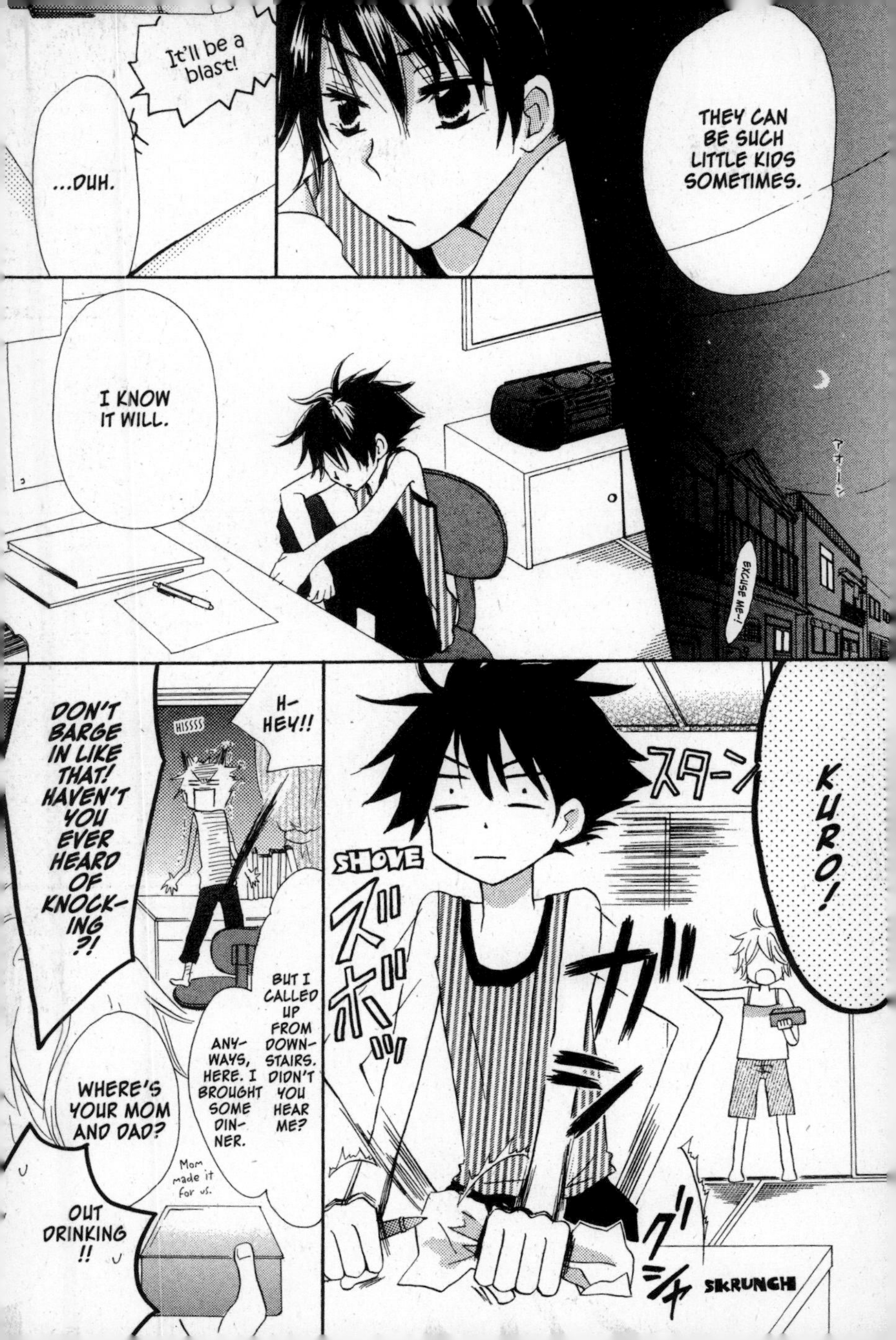
THEY CAN BE SUCH LITTLE KIDS SOMETIMES.
It'll be a blast!
...DUH.
アオーン
EXCUSE ME--!
I KNOW IT WILL.
KURO!
スターン
SHOVE
ズボッ
ガッ
グシャ
SKRUNCH
H-HEY!!
HISSSS
DON'T BARGE IN LIKE THAT! HAVEN'T YOU EVER HEARD OF KNOCKING?!
BUT I CALLED UP FROM DOWNSTAIRS. DIDN'T YOU HEAR ME?
ANYWAYS, HERE. I BROUGHT SOME DINNER.
Mom made it for us.
WHERE'S YOUR MOM AND DAD?
OUT DRINKING!!

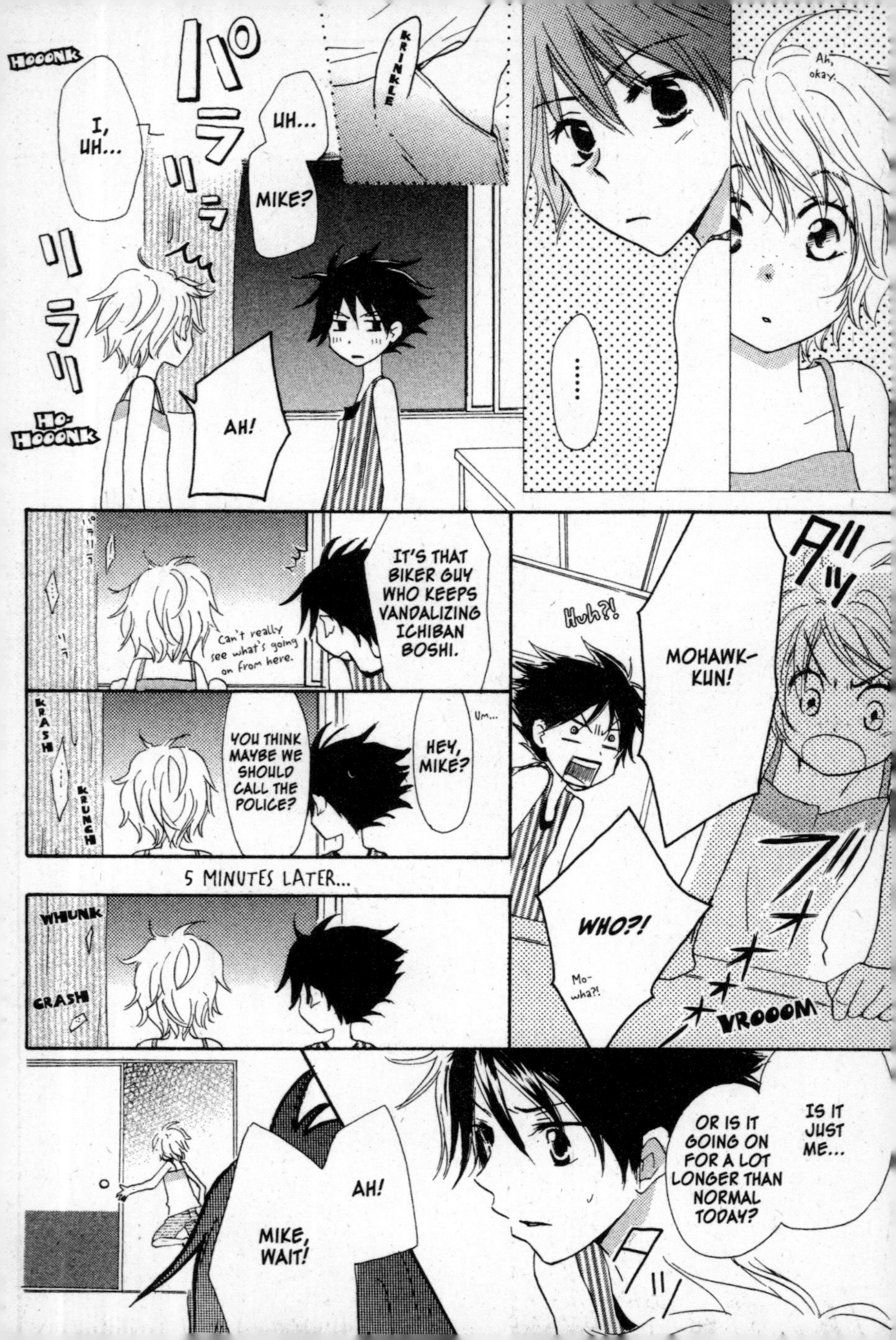

Ah, okay.
......
KRINKLE
UH...
MIKE?
HOOONK
I, UH...
AH!
HO-HOOONK
Huh?!
MOHAWK-KUN!
WHO?!
Mo-wha?!
VROOOM
IT'S THAT BIKER GUY WHO KEEPS VANDALIZING ICHIBAN BOSHI.
Can't really see what's going on from here.
Um...
HEY, MIKE?
YOU THINK MAYBE WE SHOULD CALL THE POLICE?
KRASH
KRUNCH
5 MINUTES LATER...
WHUNK
CRASH
IS IT JUST ME...
OR IS IT GOING ON FOR A LOT LONGER THAN NORMAL TODAY?
AH!
MIKE, WAIT!

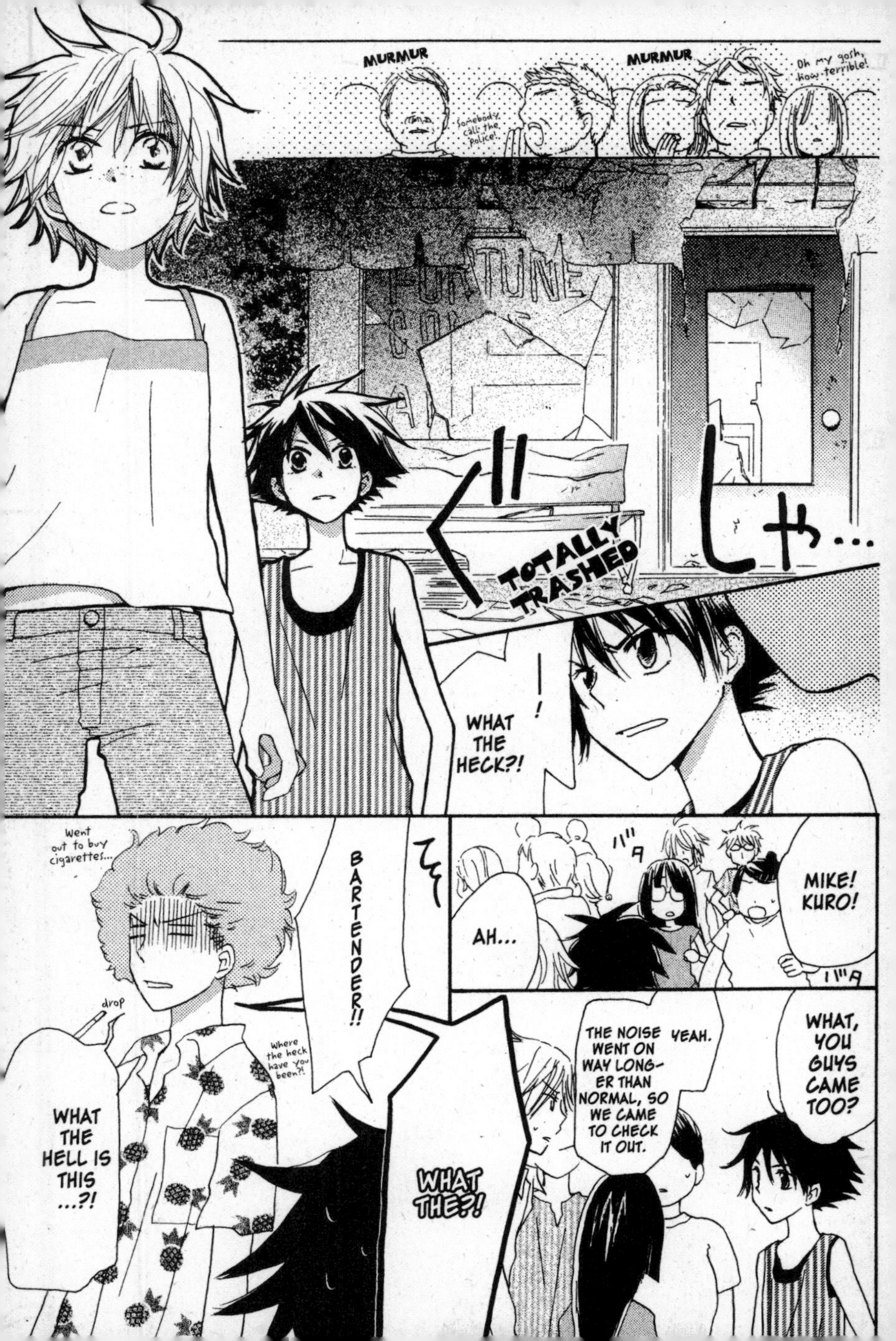
Oh my gosh, how terrible!
MURMUR
Somebody call the police!
MURMUR
ぐしゃ…
TOTALLY TRASHED
!
WHAT THE HECK?!
MIKE! KURO!
バタ
バタ
AH...
WHAT, YOU GUYS CAME TOO?
YEAH.
THE NOISE WENT ON WAY LONGER THAN NORMAL, SO WE CAME TO CHECK IT OUT.
WHAT THE?!
BARTENDER!!
Went out to buy cigarettes...
Where the heck have you been?!
drop
WHAT THE HELL IS THIS ...?!

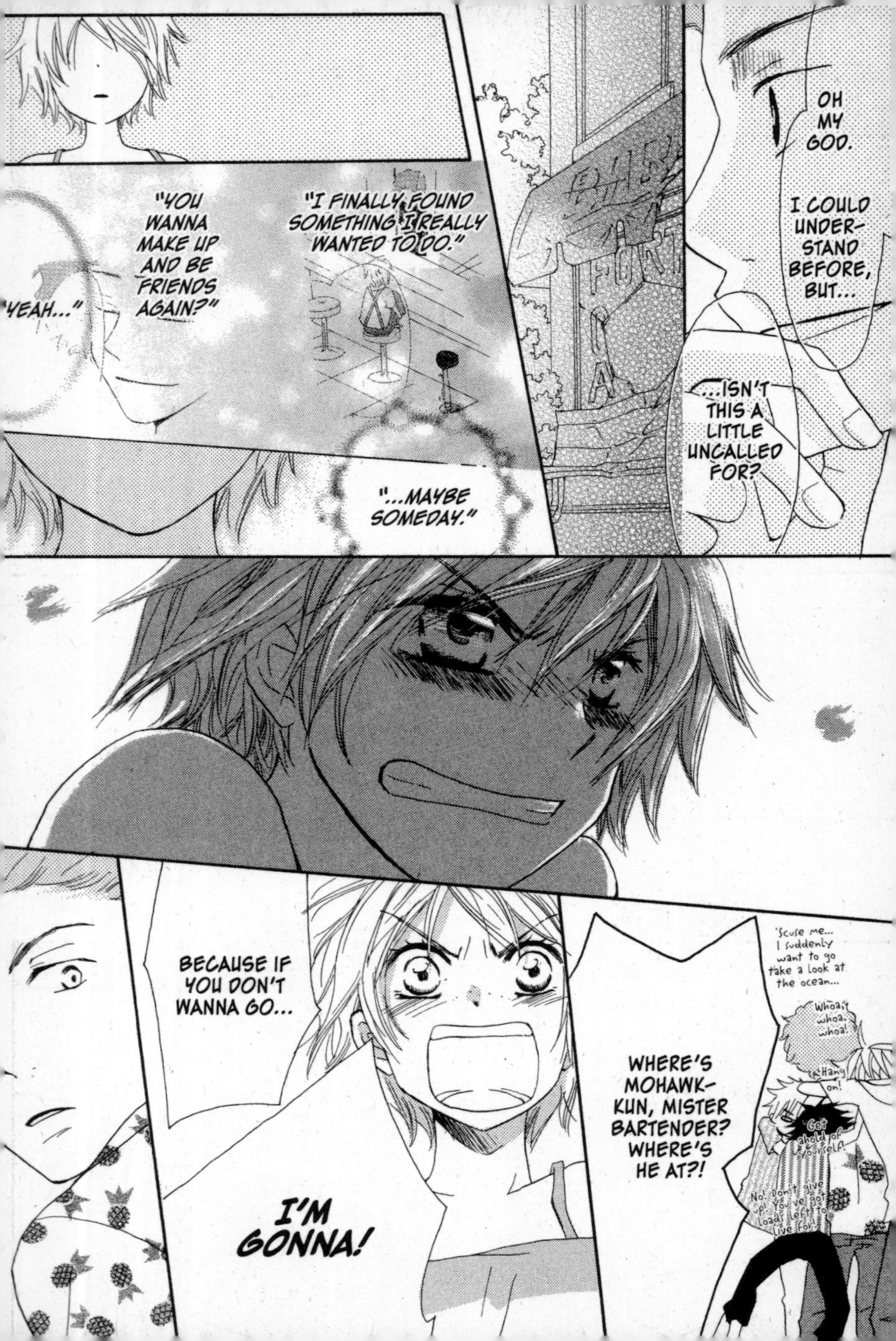
OH MY GOD.
I COULD UNDERSTAND BEFORE, BUT...
...ISN'T THIS A LITTLE UNCALLED FOR?
"I FINALLY FOUND SOMETHING I REALLY WANTED TO DO."
"YOU WANNA MAKE UP AND BE FRIENDS AGAIN?"
"YEAH..."
"...MAYBE SOMEDAY."
'Scuse me... I suddenly want to go take a look at the ocean...
Whoa! whoa! whoa!
Hang on!
Get ahold of yourself!
No! Don't give up! You've got loads left to live for!
WHERE'S MOHAWK-KUN, MISTER BARTENDER? WHERE'S HE AT?!
BECAUSE IF YOU DON'T WANNA GO...
I'M GONNA!

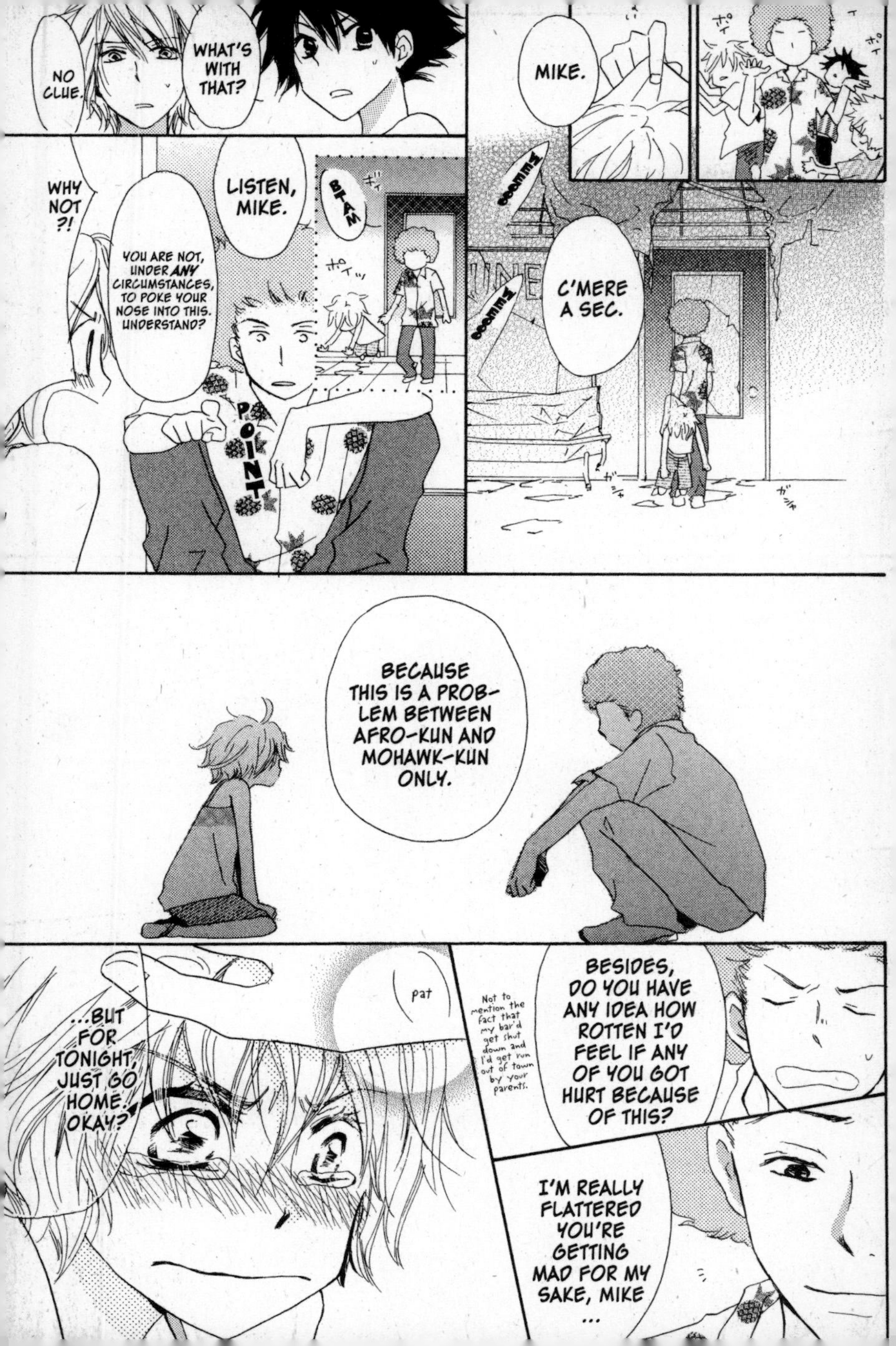
MIKE.
woomm
woomm
C'MERE A SEC.
WHAT'S WITH THAT?
NO CLUE.
LISTEN, MIKE.
BTAM
YOU ARE NOT, UNDER ANY CIRCUMSTANCES, TO POKE YOUR NOSE INTO THIS. UNDERSTAND?
POINT
WHY NOT ?!
BECAUSE THIS IS A PROB-LEM BETWEEN AFRO-KUN AND MOHAWK-KUN ONLY.
BESIDES, DO YOU HAVE ANY IDEA HOW ROTTEN I'D FEEL IF ANY OF YOU GOT HURT BECAUSE OF THIS?
Not to mention the fact that my bar'd get shut down and I'd get run out of town by your parents.
I'M REALLY FLATTERED YOU'RE GETTING MAD FOR MY SAKE, MIKE ...
pat
...BUT FOR TONIGHT, JUST GO HOME. OKAY?

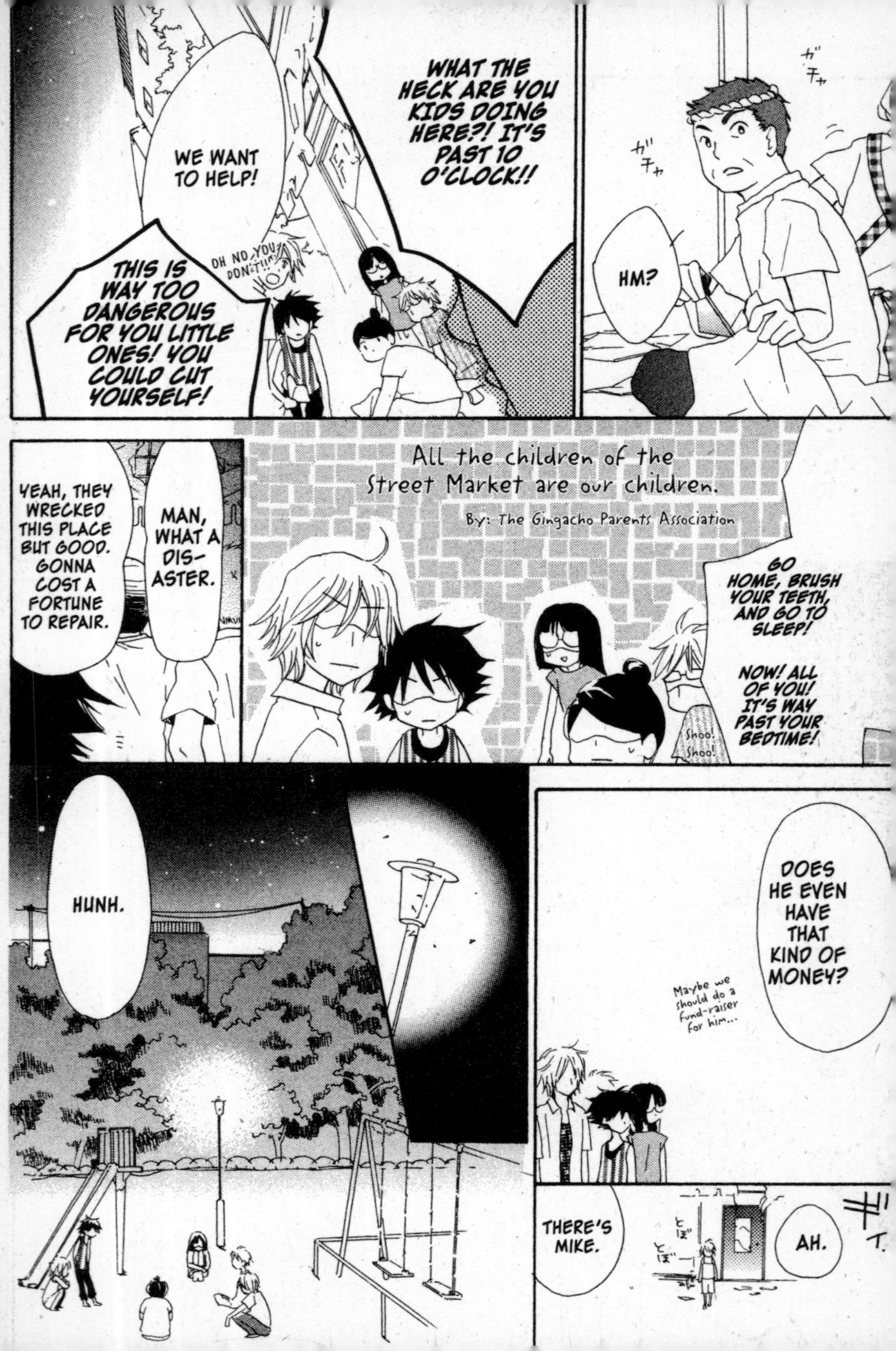

ガチャ
ガチャ
HM?
WHAT THE HECK ARE YOU KIDS DOING HERE?! IT'S PAST 10 O'CLOCK!!
WE WANT TO HELP!
OH NO YOU DON'T!!
THIS IS WAY TOO DANGEROUS FOR YOU LITTLE ONES! YOU COULD CUT YOURSELF!
GO HOME, BRUSH YOUR TEETH, AND GO TO SLEEP!
NOW! ALL OF YOU! IT'S WAY PAST YOUR BEDTIME!
Shoo! Shoo!
All the children of the Street Market are our children.
By: The Gingacho Parents Association
MAN, WHAT A DIS-ASTER.
YEAH, THEY WRECKED THIS PLACE BUT GOOD. GONNA COST A FORTUNE TO REPAIR.
DOES HE EVEN HAVE THAT KIND OF MONEY?
Maybe we should do a fund-raiser for him...
ギィ
AH.
とぼ
とぼ
THERE'S MIKE.
HUNH.

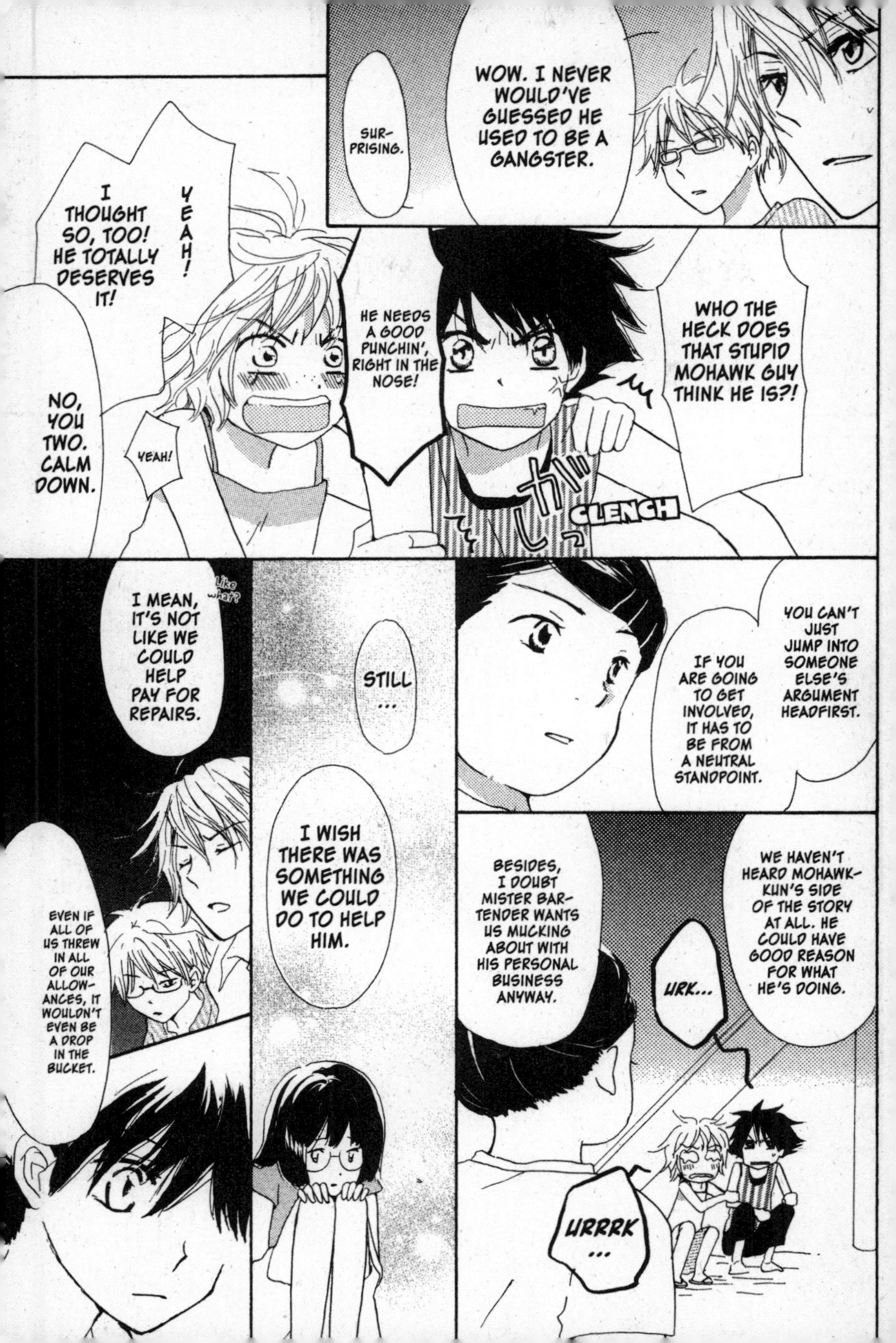

WOW. I NEVER WOULD'VE GUESSED HE USED TO BE A GANGSTER.
SUR-PRISING.
WHO THE HECK DOES THAT STUPID MOHAWK GUY THINK HE IS?!
CLENCH
HE NEEDS A GOOD PUNCHIN', RIGHT IN THE NOSE!
YEAH!
I THOUGHT SO, TOO! HE TOTALLY DESERVES IT!
YEAH!
NO, YOU TWO. CALM DOWN.
YOU CAN'T JUST JUMP INTO SOMEONE ELSE'S ARGUMENT HEADFIRST.
IF YOU ARE GOING TO GET INVOLVED, IT HAS TO BE FROM A NEUTRAL STANDPOINT.
WE HAVEN'T HEARD MOHAWK-KUN'S SIDE OF THE STORY AT ALL. HE COULD HAVE GOOD REASON FOR WHAT HE'S DOING.
BESIDES, I DOUBT MISTER BAR-TENDER WANTS US MUCKING ABOUT WITH HIS PERSONAL BUSINESS ANYWAY.
URK...
URRRK ...
STILL ...
I WISH THERE WAS SOMETHING WE COULD DO TO HELP HIM.
Like what?
I MEAN, IT'S NOT LIKE WE COULD HELP PAY FOR REPAIRS.
EVEN IF ALL OF US THREW IN ALL OF OUR ALLOW-ANCES, IT WOULDN'T EVEN BE A DROP IN THE BUCKET.

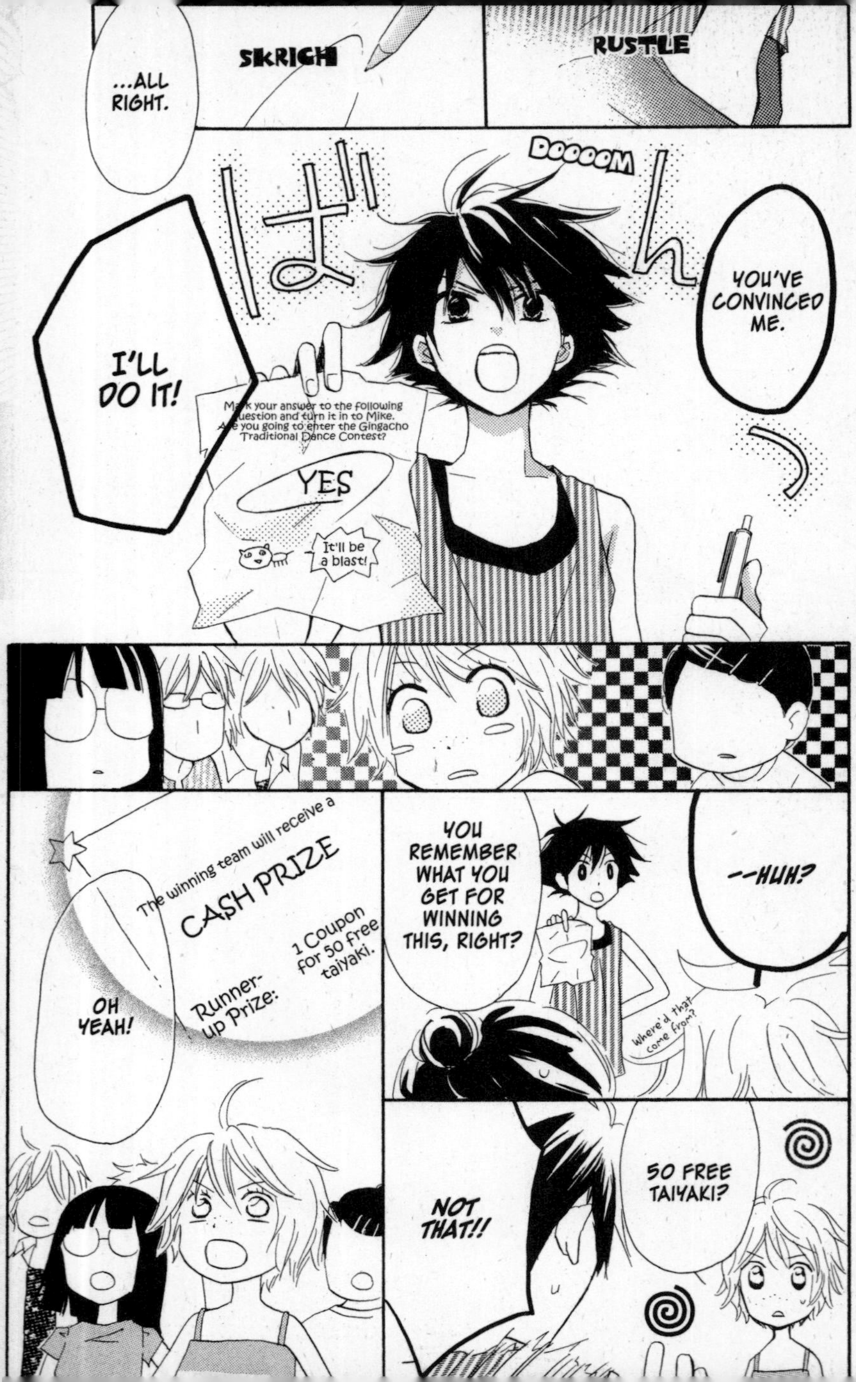
RUSTLE
SKRICH
...ALL RIGHT.
DOOOOM
ばん
YOU'VE CONVINCED ME.
I'LL DO IT!
Mark your answer to the following question and turn it in to Mike.
Are you going to enter the Gingacho Traditional Dance Contest?
YES
It'll be a blast!
--HUH?
YOU REMEMBER WHAT YOU GET FOR WINNING THIS, RIGHT?
Where'd that come from?
50 FREE TAIYAKI?
NOT THAT!!
The winning team will receive a
CASH PRIZE
Runner-up Prize:
1 Coupon for 50 free taiyaki.
OH YEAH!

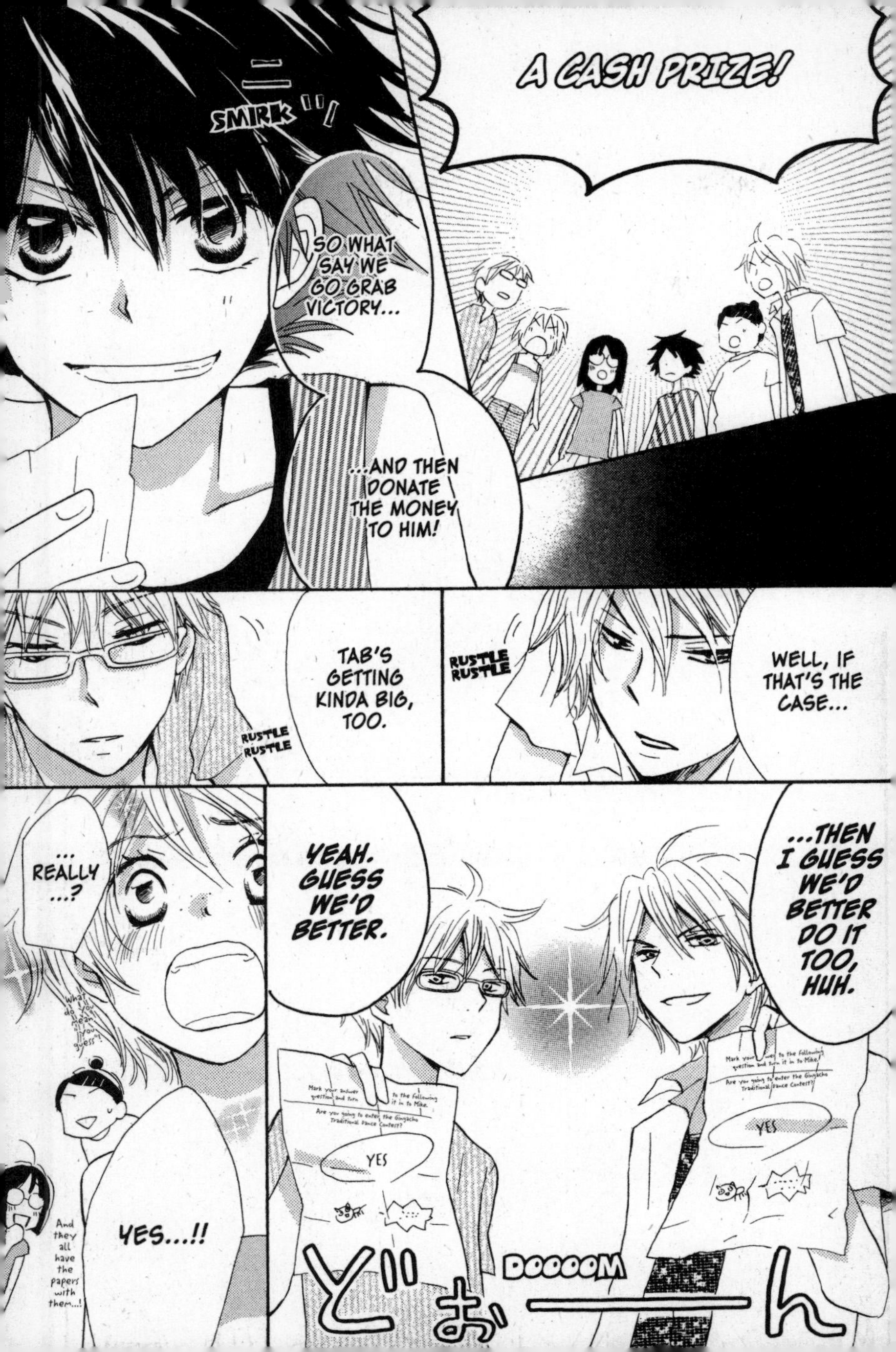
A CASH PRIZE!
SMIRK
SO WHAT SAY WE GO GRAB VICTORY...
...AND THEN DONATE THE MONEY TO HIM!
RUSTLE RUSTLE
WELL, IF THAT'S THE CASE...
TAB'S GETTING KINDA BIG, TOO.
RUSTLE RUSTLE
...THEN I GUESS WE'D BETTER DO IT TOO, HUH.
Mark your answer to the following question and turn it in to Mike.
Are you going to enter the Gingacho Traditional Dance Contest?
YES
YEAH. GUESS WE'D BETTER.
Mark your answer to the following question and turn it in to Mike.
Are you going to enter the Gingacho Traditional Dance Contest?
YES
DOOOOM
どぉーーん
...REALLY...?
What do you mean "you guess"?!
YES...!!
And they all have the papers with them...!

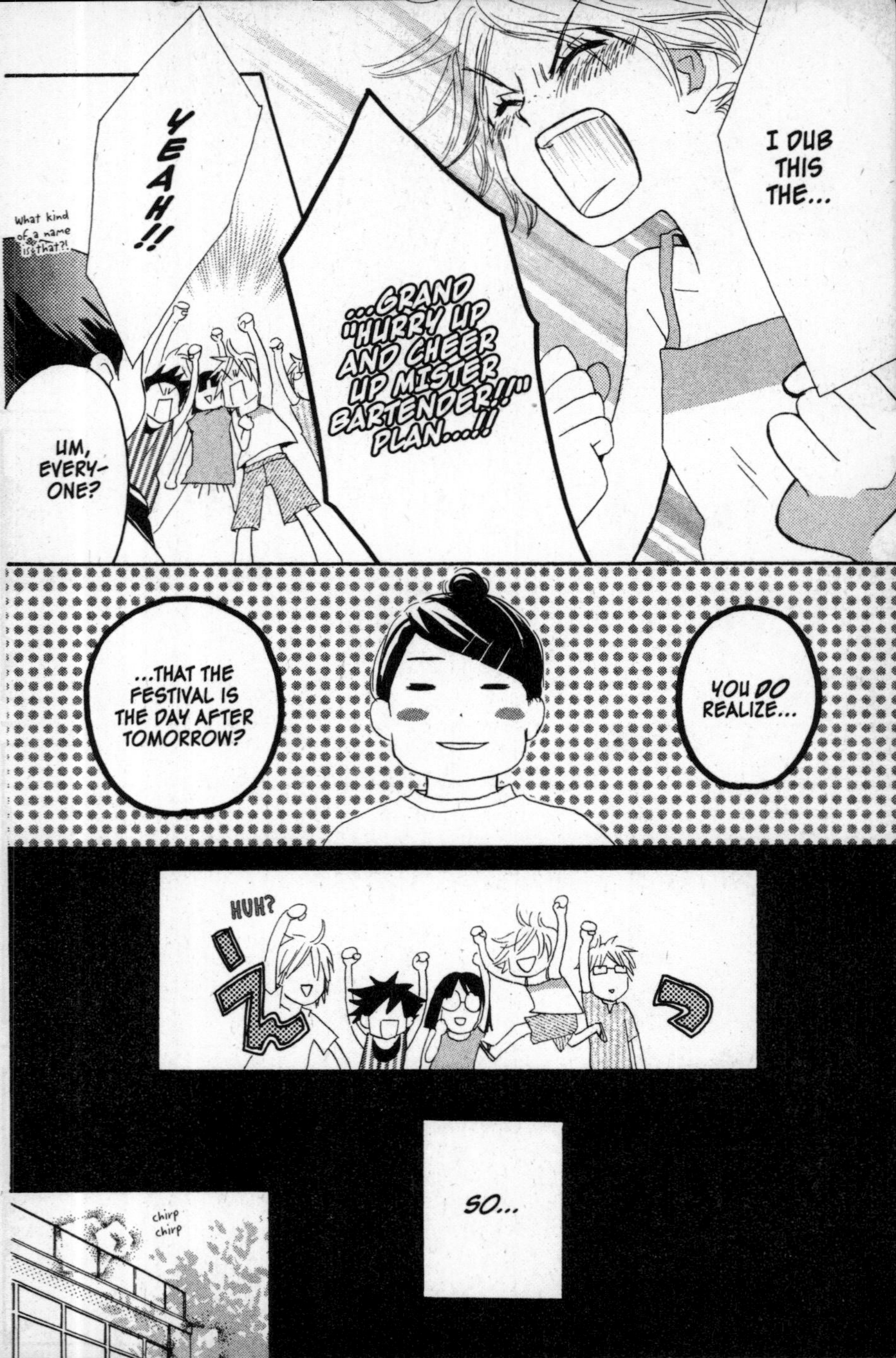
I DUB THIS THE...
...GRAND "HURRY UP AND CHEER UP MISTER BARTENDER!!" PLAN...!!
YEAH!!
What kind of a name is that?!
UM, EVERY-ONE?
YOU DO REALIZE...
...THAT THE FESTIVAL IS THE DAY AFTER TOMORROW?
HUH?
SO...
chirp chirp

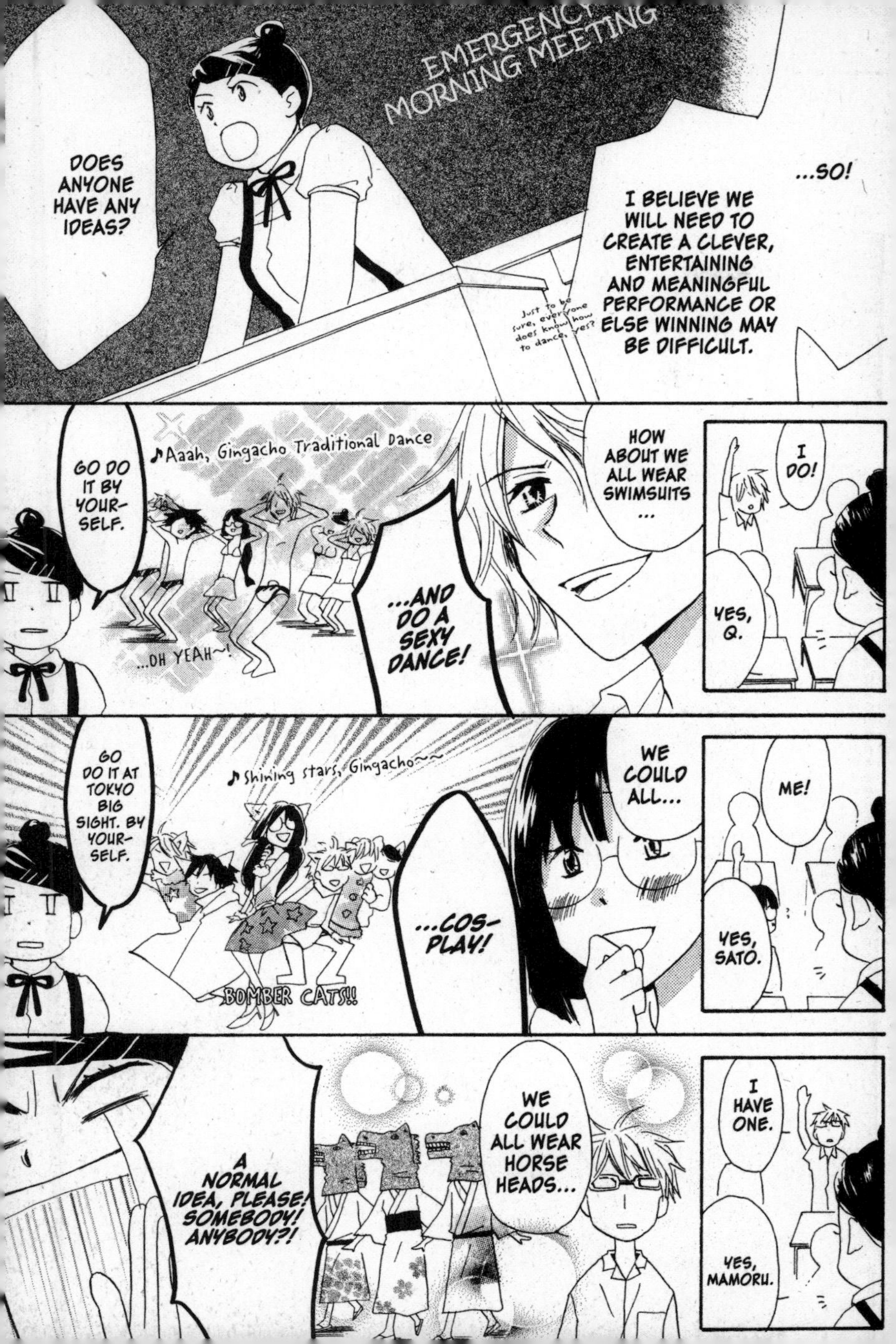

...SO!
I BELIEVE WE WILL NEED TO CREATE A CLEVER, ENTERTAINING AND MEANINGFUL PERFORMANCE OR ELSE WINNING MAY BE DIFFICULT.
Just to be sure, everyone does know how to dance, yes?
EMERGENCY MORNING MEETING
DOES ANYONE HAVE ANY IDEAS?
I DO!
YES, Q.
HOW ABOUT WE ALL WEAR SWIMSUITS...
...AND DO A SEXY DANCE!
♪Aaah, Gingacho Traditional Dance
...OH YEAH~!
GO DO IT BY YOURSELF.
ME!
YES, SATO.
WE COULD ALL...
...COSPLAY!
♪Shining stars, Gingacho~~
BOMBER CATS!!
GO DO IT AT TOKYO BIG SIGHT. BY YOURSELF.
I HAVE ONE.
YES, MAMORU.
WE COULD ALL WEAR HORSE HEADS...
A NORMAL IDEA, PLEASE! SOMEBODY! ANYBODY?!

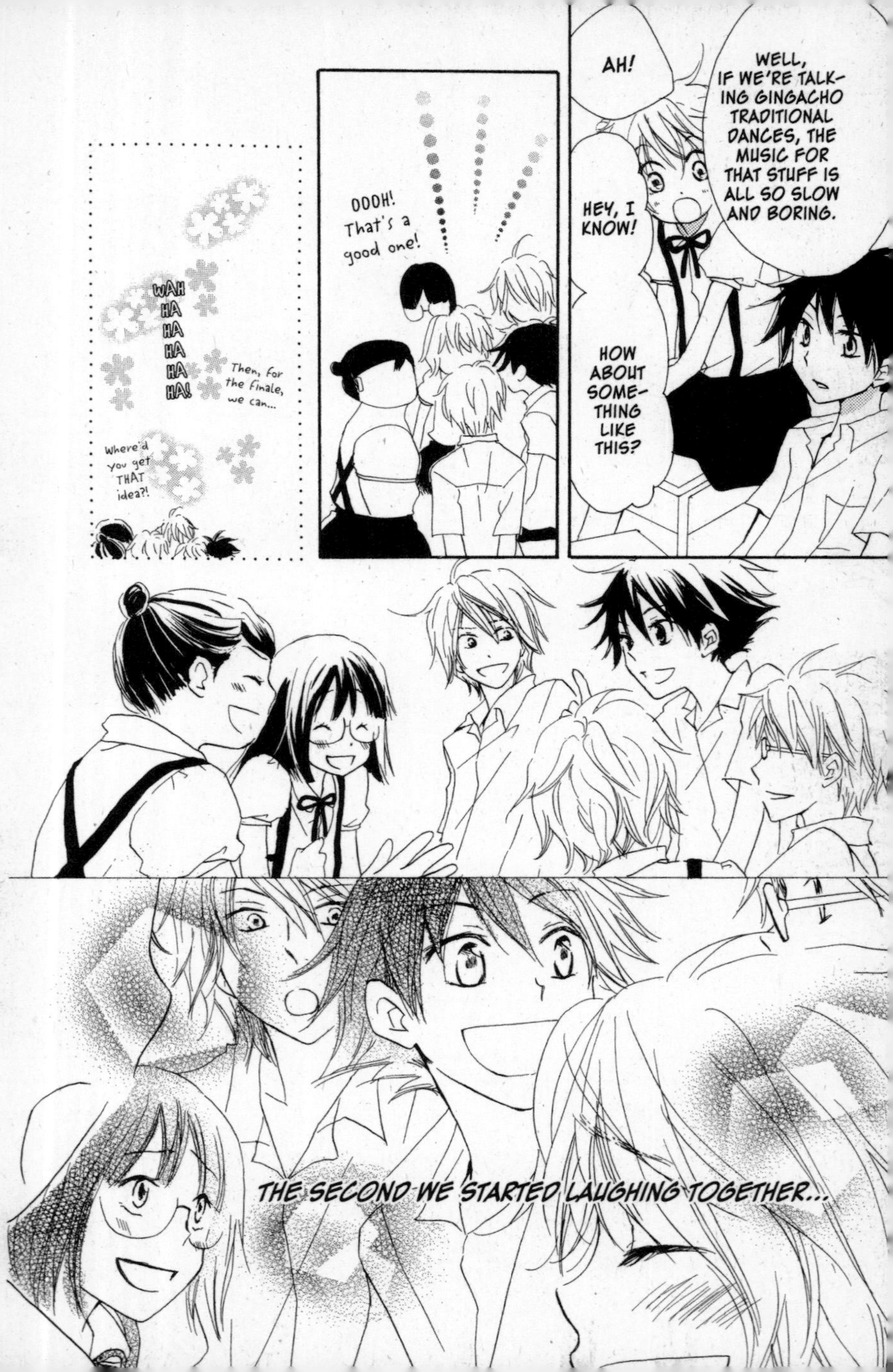
WELL, IF WE'RE TALKING GINGACHO TRADITIONAL DANCES, THE MUSIC FOR THAT STUFF IS ALL SO SLOW AND BORING.
AH!
HEY, I KNOW!
HOW ABOUT SOMETHING LIKE THIS?
OOOH! That's a good one!
WAH HA HA HA HA HA!
Then, for the finale, we can...
Where'd you get THAT idea?!
THE SECOND WE STARTED LAUGHING TOGETHER...

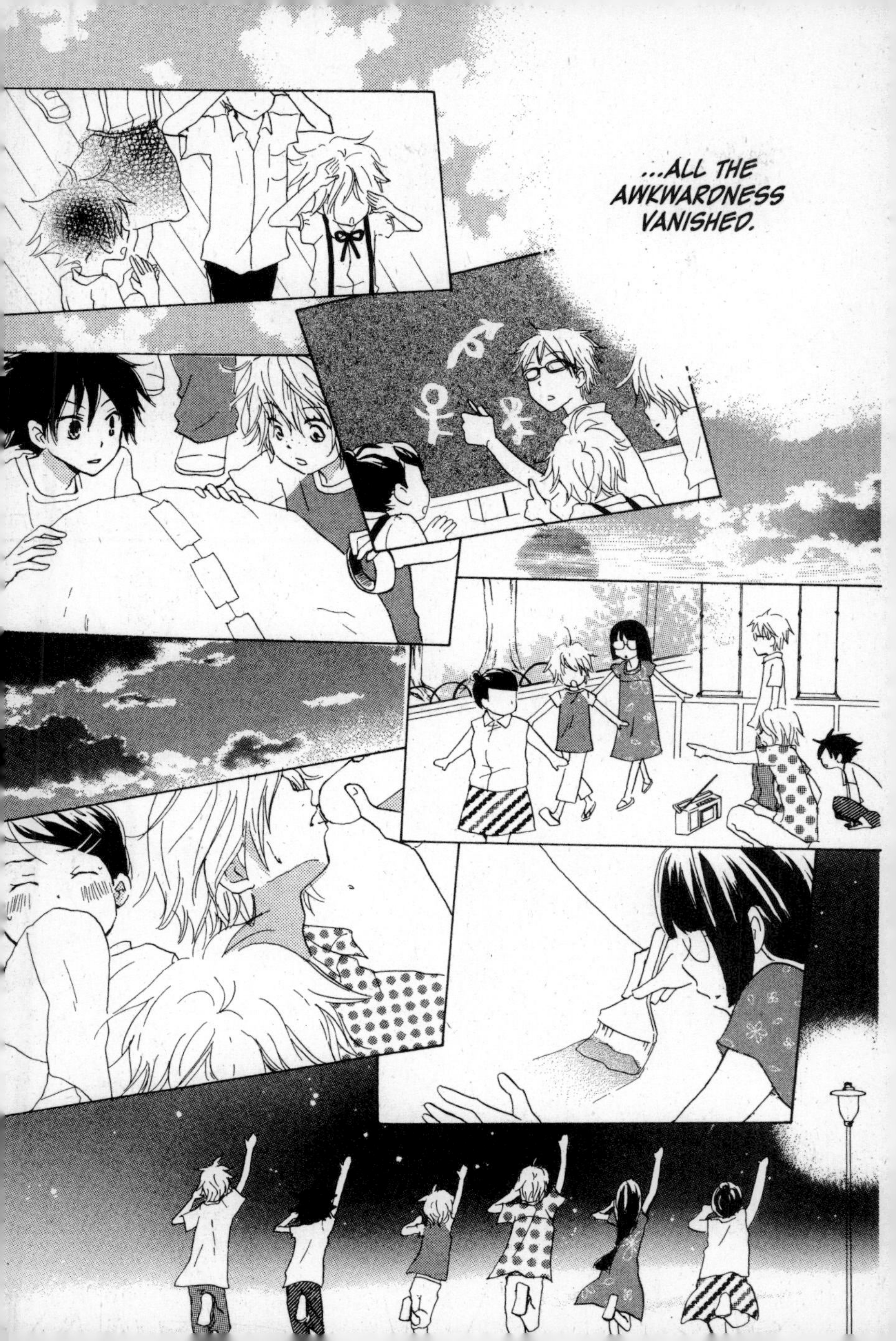
...ALL THE AWKWARDNESS VANISHED.

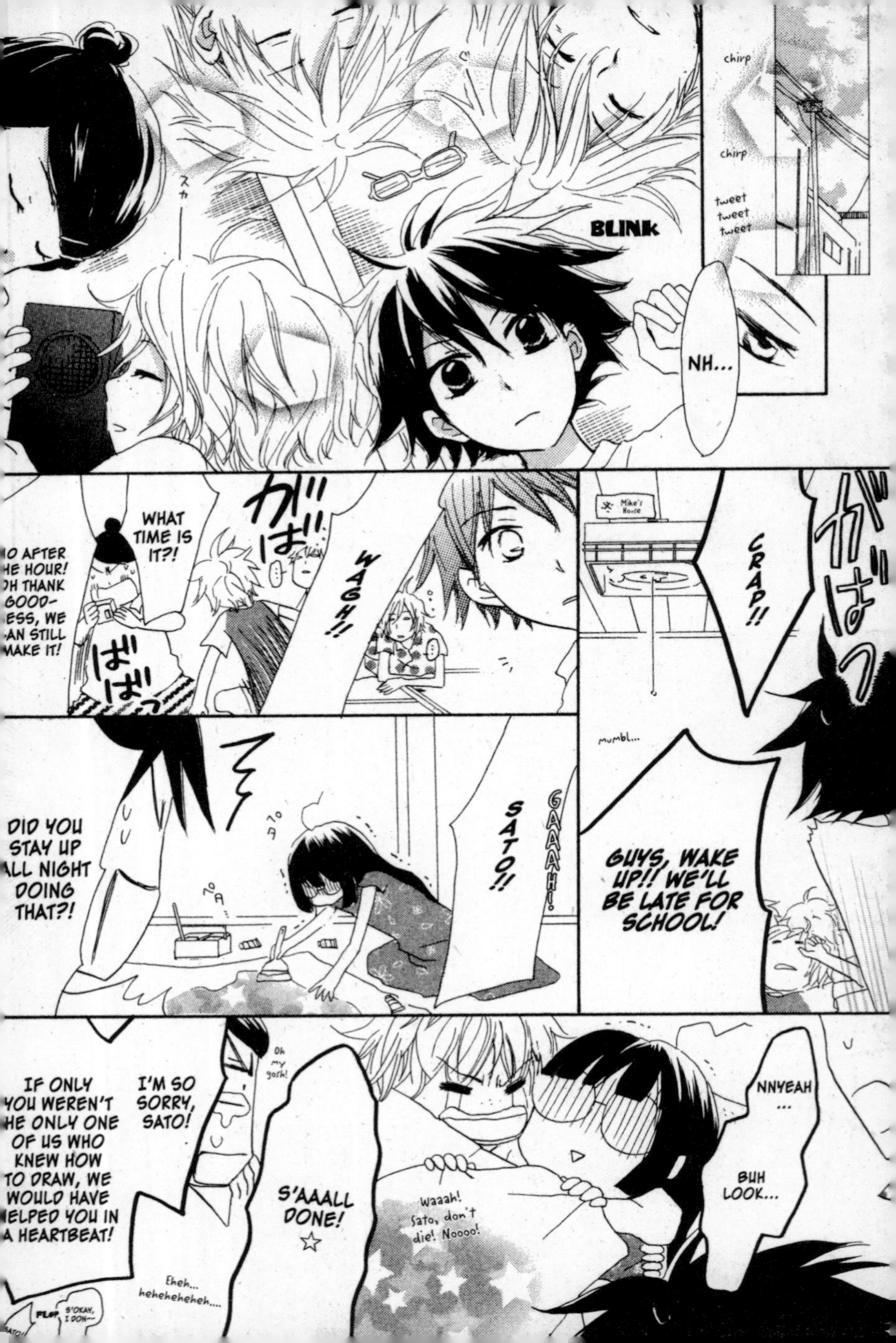
chirp
chirp
tweet
tweet
tweet
NH...
BLINK
スカー
がばっ
CRAP!!
WAGH!!
...
WHAT TIME IS IT?!
...
O AFTER HE HOUR! OH THANK GOOD-ESS, WE AN STILL MAKE IT!
ばばっ
mumbl...
GUYS, WAKE UP!! WE'LL BE LATE FOR SCHOOL!
SATO!!
GAAAAH!
DID YOU STAY UP LL NIGHT DOING THAT?!
NNYEAH...
BUH LOOK...
S'AAALL DONE! ☆
Waaah! Sato, don't die! Noooo!
Oh my gosh!
I'M SO SORRY, SATO!
IF ONLY YOU WEREN'T HE ONLY ONE OF US WHO KNEW HOW TO DRAW, WE WOULD HAVE HELPED YOU IN A HEARTBEAT!
Eheh... heheheheheh....
FLOP
S'OKAY, I DON--
SATO!!

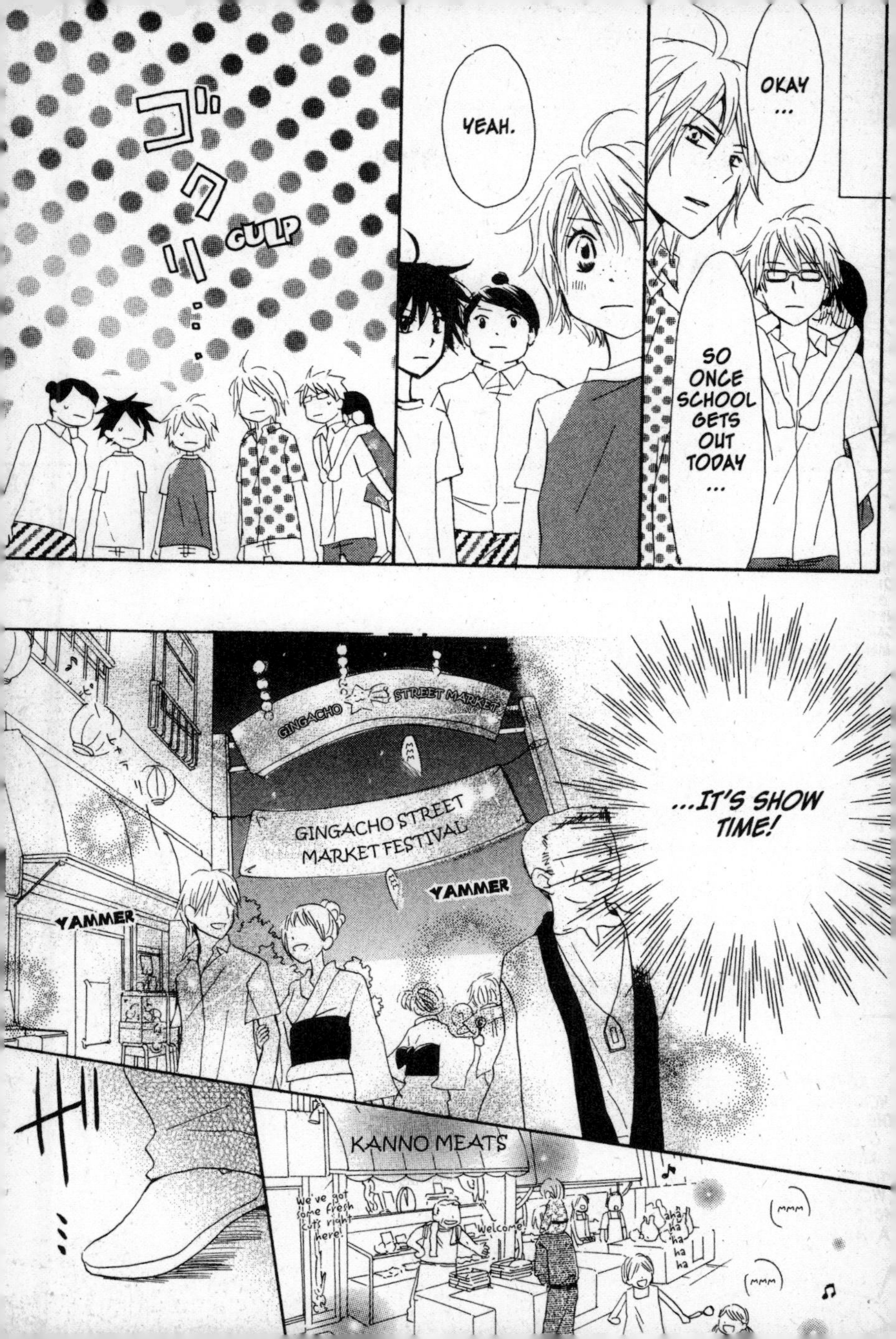
OKAY ...
SO ONCE SCHOOL GETS OUT TODAY ...
YEAH.
GULP
...IT'S SHOW TIME!
GINGACHO STREET MARKET
GINGACHO STREET MARKET FESTIVAL
YAMMER
YAMMER
KANNO MEATS
(MMM)
aha ha ha ha ha
Welcome!
We've got some fresh cuts right here!
(MMM)

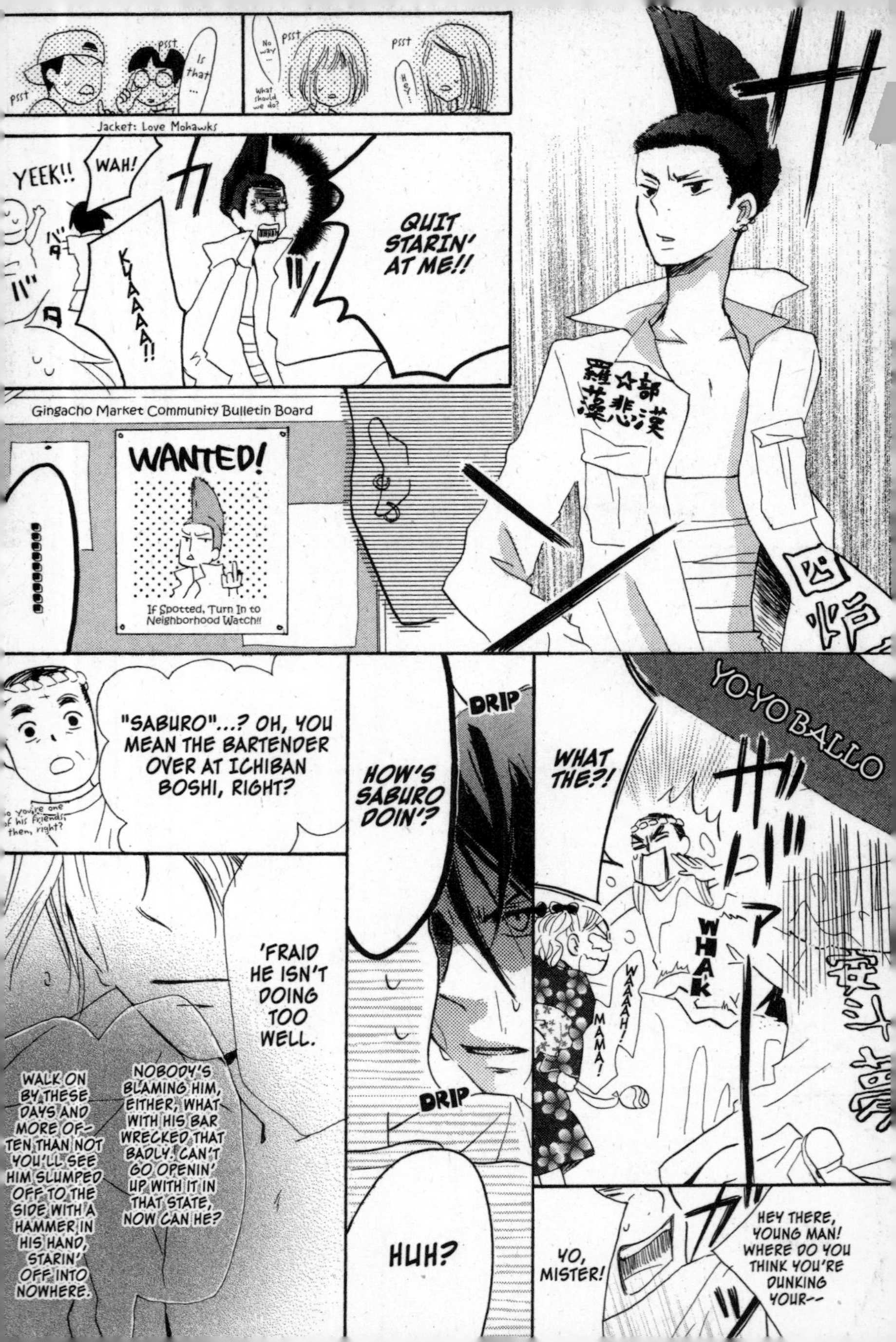

No way...
What should we do?
psst
Hey...
psst
psst
Is that...
psst
Jacket: Love Mohawks
QUIT STARIN' AT ME!!
KYAAAAA!!
WAH!
YEEK!!
Gingacho Market Community Bulletin Board
WANTED!
If Spotted, Turn In to Neighborhood Watch!!
YO-YO BALLO
WHAT THE?!
WHAK
WAAAAH!
MAMA! MAMA!
HEY THERE, YOUNG MAN! WHERE DO YOU THINK YOU'RE DUNKING YOUR--
YO, MISTER!
DRIP
HOW'S SABURO DOIN'?
DRIP
HUH?
"SABURO"...? OH, YOU MEAN THE BARTENDER OVER AT ICHIBAN BOSHI, RIGHT?
So you're one of his friends, then, right?
'FRAID HE ISN'T DOING TOO WELL.
NOBODY'S BLAMING HIM, EITHER, WHAT WITH HIS BAR WRECKED THAT BADLY. CAN'T GO OPENIN' UP WITH IT IN THAT STATE, NOW CAN HE?
WALK ON BY THESE DAYS AND MORE OFTEN THAN NOT YOU'LL SEE HIM SLUMPED OFF TO THE SIDE WITH A HAMMER IN HIS HAND, STARIN' OFF INTO NOWHERE.

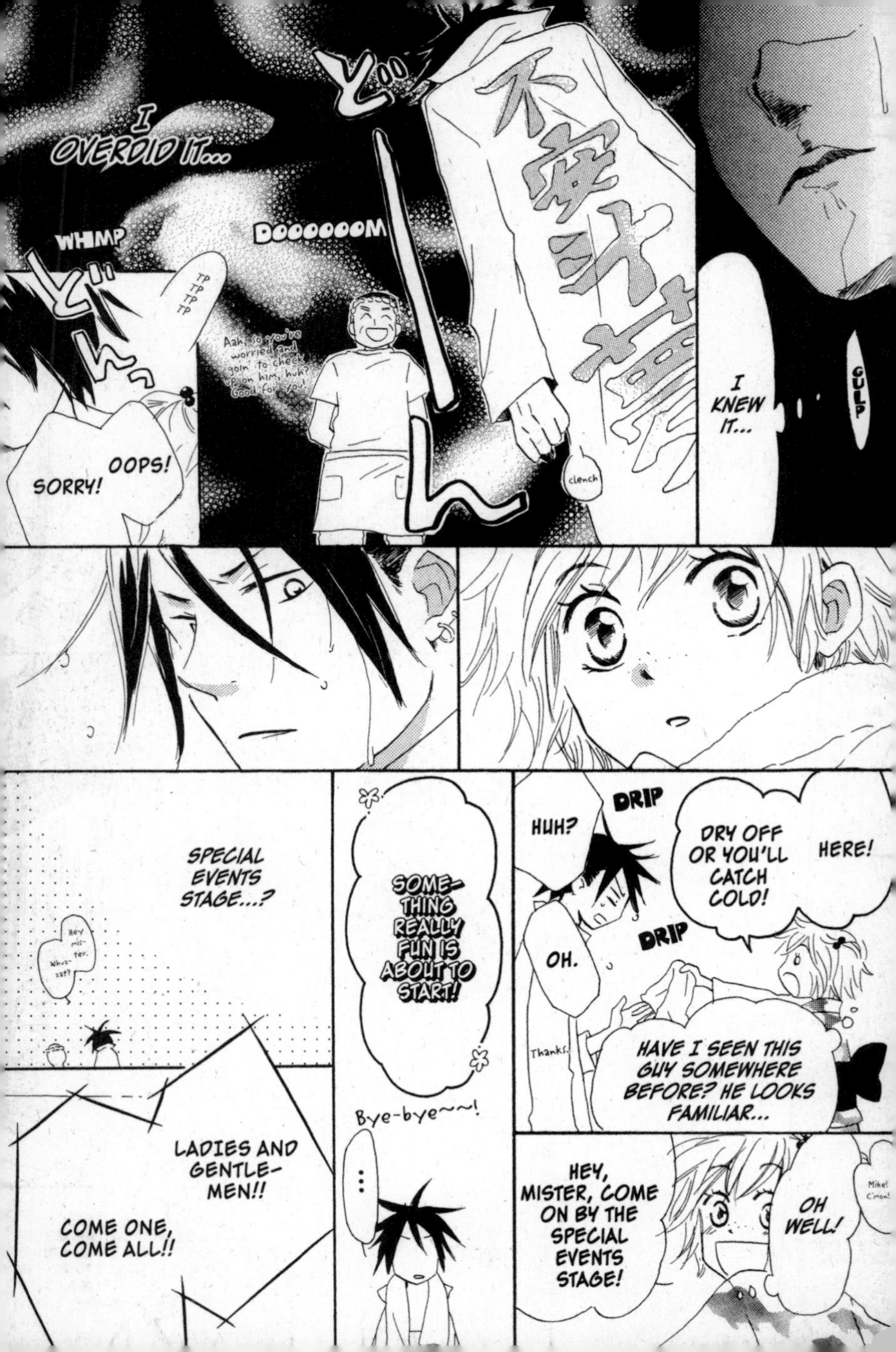
GULP
I KNEW IT...
I OVERDID IT...
DOOOOOOM
clench
Aah, so you're worried and goin' to check up on him, huh? Good for you!
TP TP TP TP
WHIMP
OOPS!
SORRY!
HERE!
DRY OFF OR YOU'LL CATCH COLD!
DRIP
HUH?
DRIP
OH.
Thanks.
HAVE I SEEN THIS GUY SOMEWHERE BEFORE? HE LOOKS FAMILIAR...
Mike! C'mon!
OH WELL!
HEY, MISTER, COME ON BY THE SPECIAL EVENTS STAGE!
SOME-THING REALLY FUN IS ABOUT TO START!
Bye-bye~~!
...
SPECIAL EVENTS STAGE...?
Hey mis-ter. Whuz-zat?
LADIES AND GENTLE-MEN!!
COME ONE, COME ALL!!

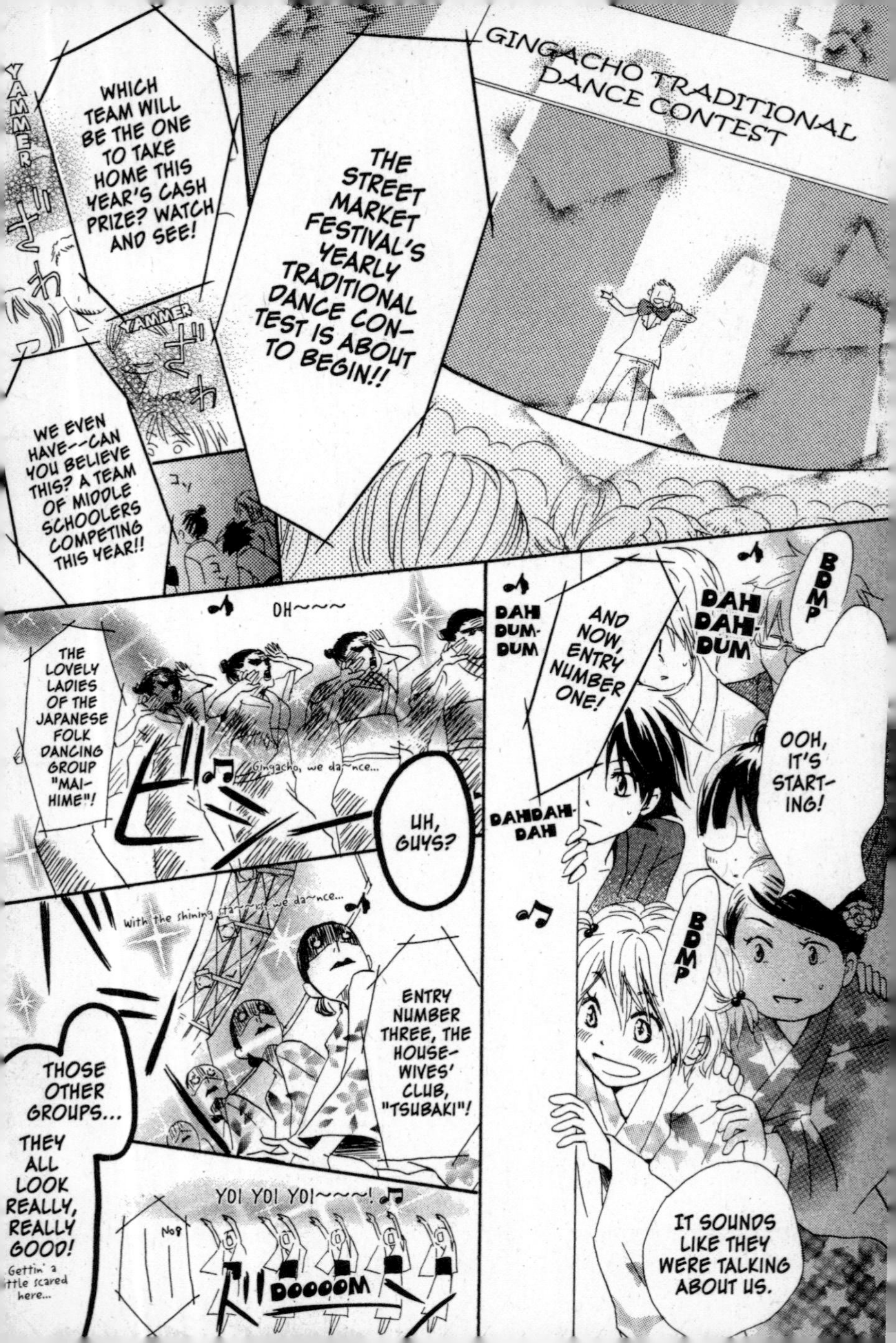
GINGACHO TRADITIONAL DANCE CONTEST
THE STREET MARKET FESTIVAL'S YEARLY TRADITIONAL DANCE CONTEST IS ABOUT TO BEGIN!!
WHICH TEAM WILL BE THE ONE TO TAKE HOME THIS YEAR'S CASH PRIZE? WATCH AND SEE!
YAMMER
YAMMER
WE EVEN HAVE--CAN YOU BELIEVE THIS? A TEAM OF MIDDLE SCHOOLERS COMPETING THIS YEAR!!
BDMP
DAH DAH-DUM
AND NOW, ENTRY NUMBER ONE!
DAH DUM-DUM
OOH, IT'S STARTING!
DAHDAH-DAH
BDMP
IT SOUNDS LIKE THEY WERE TALKING ABOUT US.
OH~~~
THE LOVELY LADIES OF THE JAPANESE FOLK DANCING GROUP "MAI-HIME"!
Gingacho, we da~nce...
UH, GUYS?
With the shining sta~~rs we da~nce...
ENTRY NUMBER THREE, THE HOUSE-WIVES' CLUB, "TSUBAKI"!
THOSE OTHER GROUPS...
THEY ALL LOOK REALLY, REALLY GOOD!
Gettin' a little scared here...
YOI YOI YOI~~~!
No8
DOOOOM

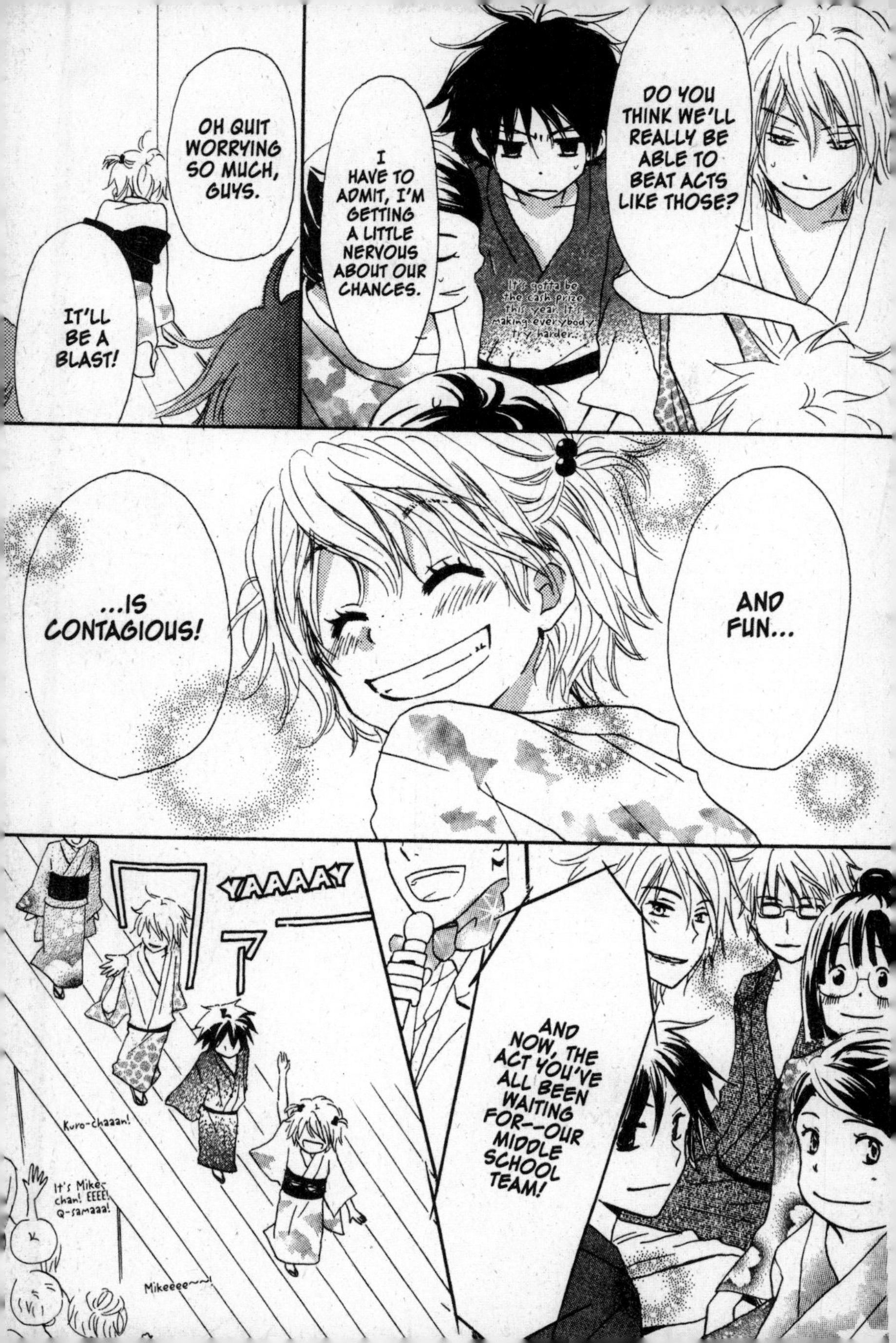
DO YOU THINK WE'LL REALLY BE ABLE TO BEAT ACTS LIKE THOSE?
I HAVE TO ADMIT, I'M GETTING A LITTLE NERVOUS ABOUT OUR CHANCES.
It's gotta be the cash prize this year. It's making everybody try harder...
OH QUIT WORRYING SO MUCH, GUYS.
IT'LL BE A BLAST!
AND FUN...
...IS CONTAGIOUS!
AND NOW, THE ACT YOU'VE ALL BEEN WAITING FOR--OUR MIDDLE SCHOOL TEAM!
YAAAAY
Kuro-chaaan!
It's Mike-chan! EEEE! Q-samaaa!
Mikeeee~~!

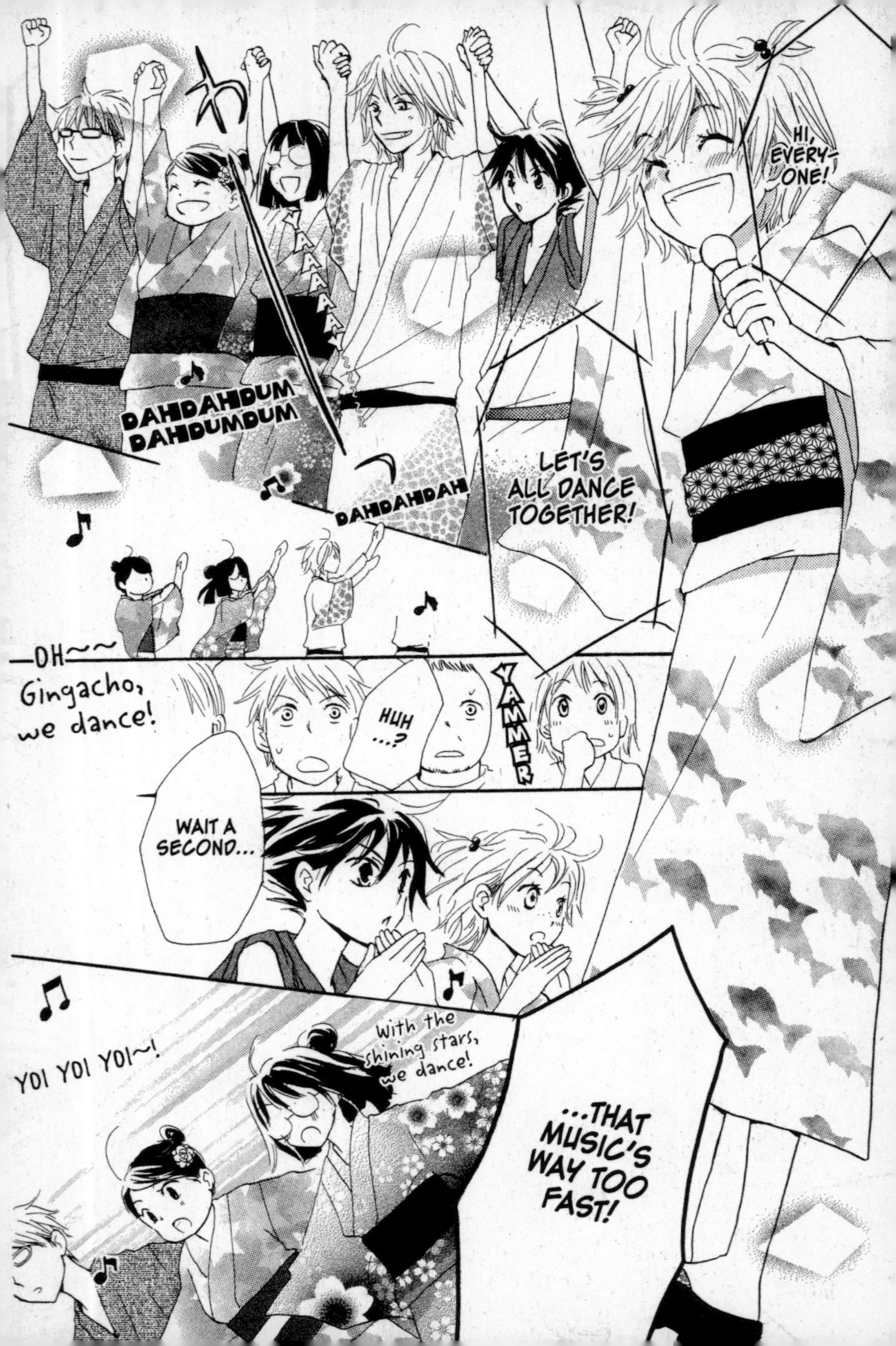

HI, EVERY-ONE!
LET'S ALL DANCE TOGETHER!
YAAAAAAA
DAHDAHDUM DAHDUMDUM
DAHDAHDAH
—OH~~
Gingacho, we dance!
YAMMER
HUH ...?
WAIT A SECOND...
...THAT MUSIC'S WAY TOO FAST!
With the shining stars, we dance!
YOI YOI YOI~!

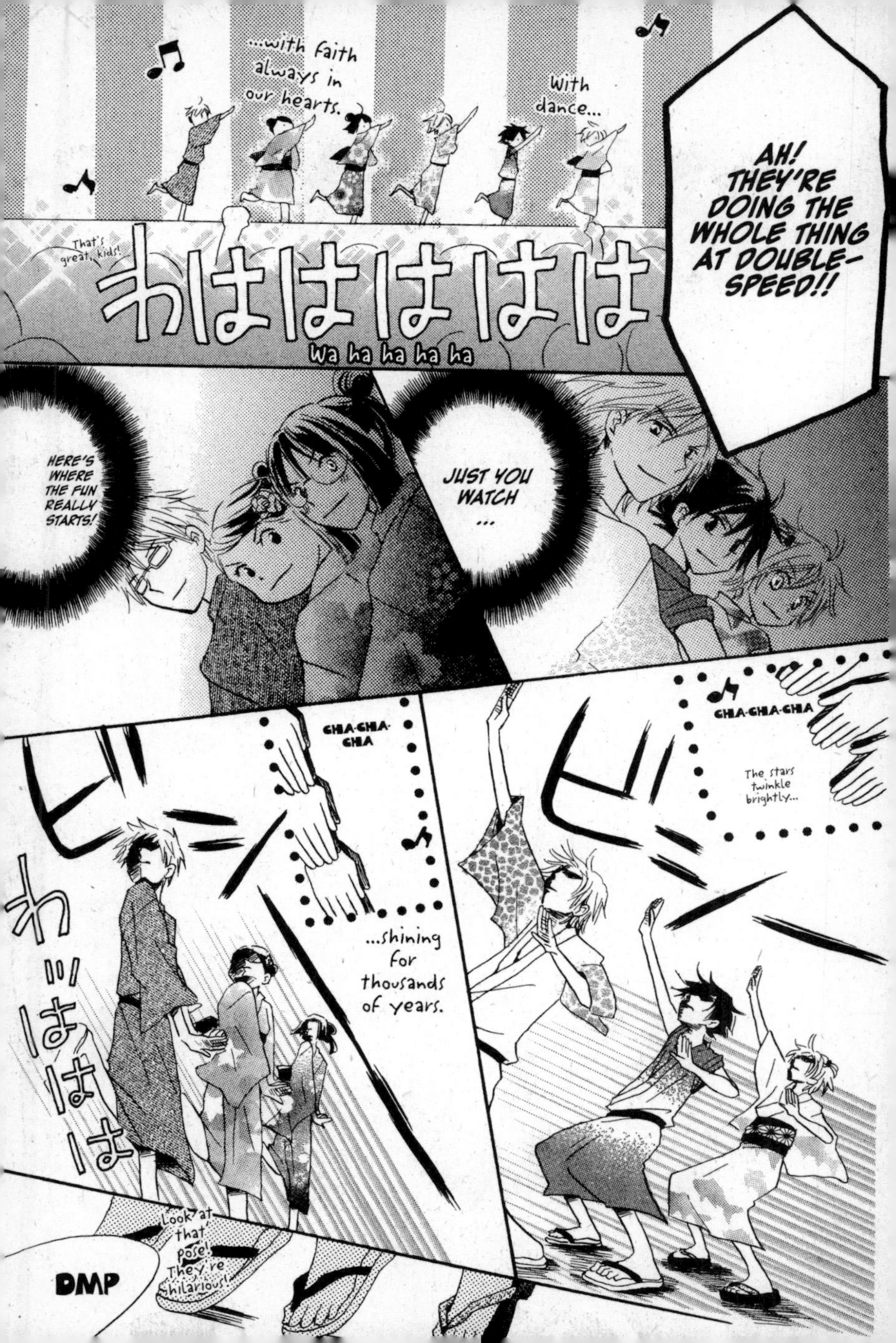
AH! THEY'RE DOING THE WHOLE THING AT DOUBLE-SPEED!!
With dance...
...with faith always in our hearts.
That's great, kids!
わははははは
Wa ha ha ha ha
JUST YOU WATCH ...
HERE'S WHERE THE FUN REALLY STARTS!
CHA-CHA-CHA
The stars twinkle brightly...
CHA-CHA-CHA
...shining for thousands of years.
わはは
Look at that pose! They're hilarious!

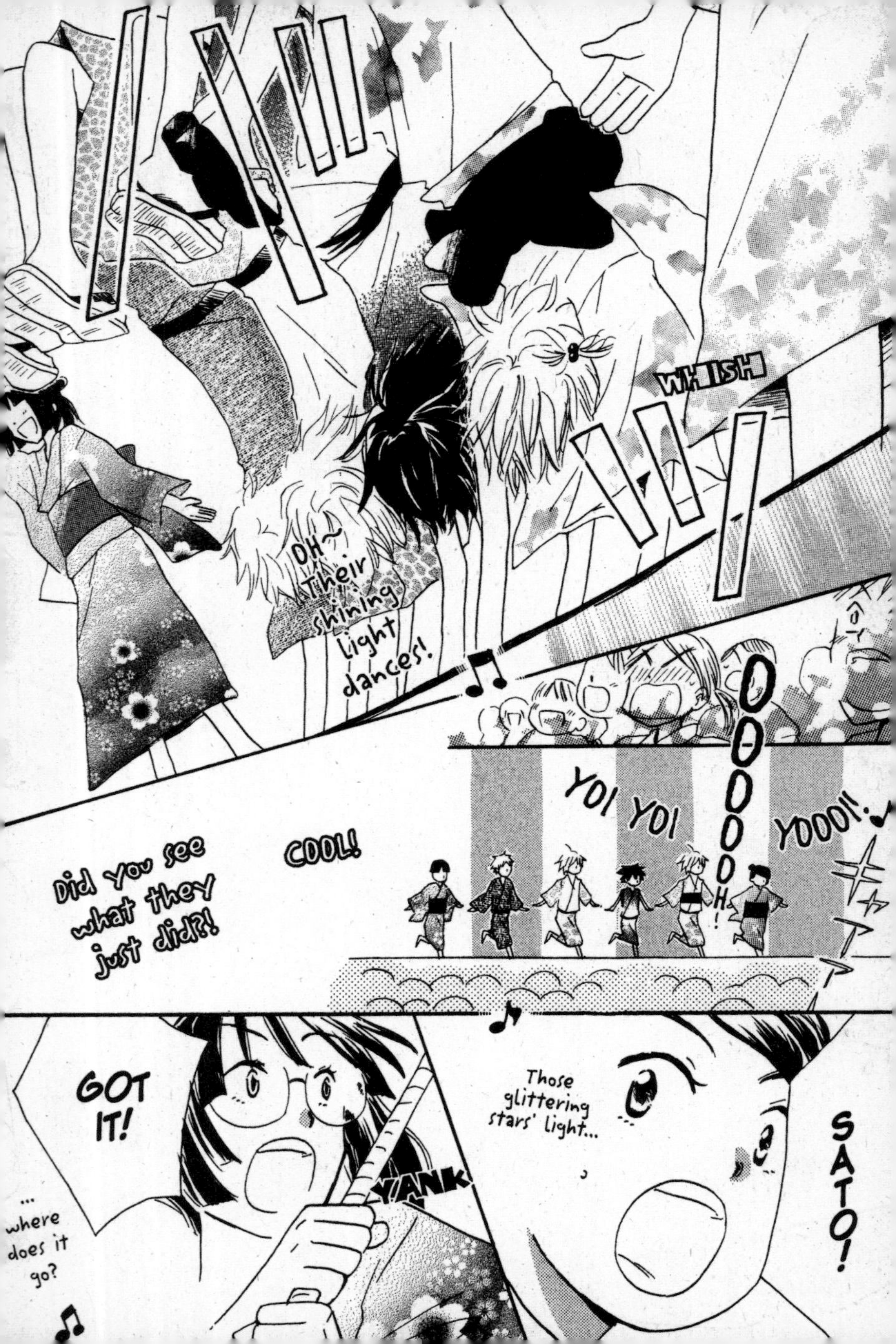

WHISH
OH~ Their shining light dances!
YOI YOI YOOO!!
OOOOOOOOH!
COOL!
Did you see what they just did?!
SATO!
Those glittering stars' light...
GOT IT!
YANK
...where does it go?

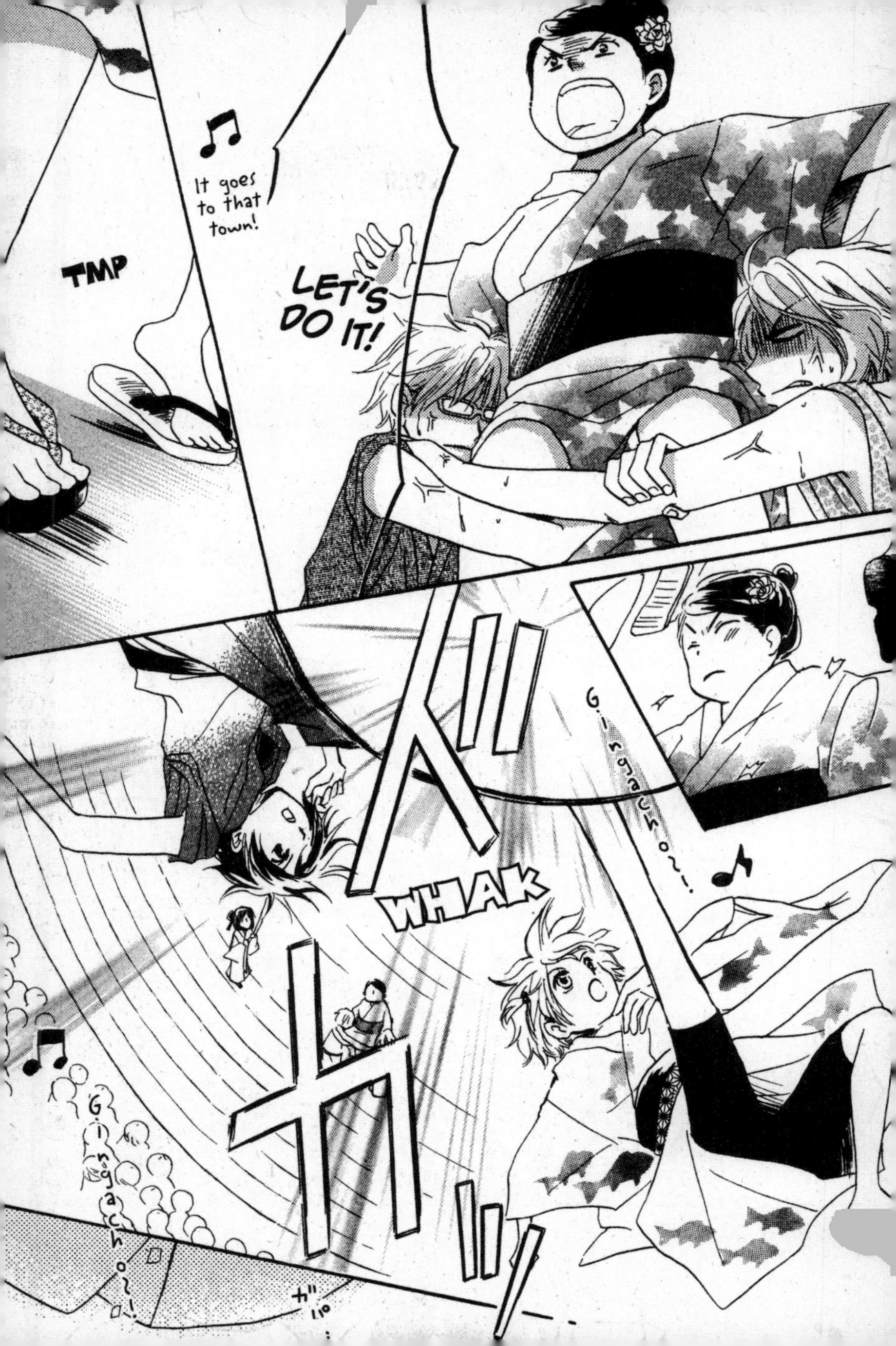
LET'S DO IT!
It goes to that town!
TMP
Gingacho~!
WHAK
Gingacho~!

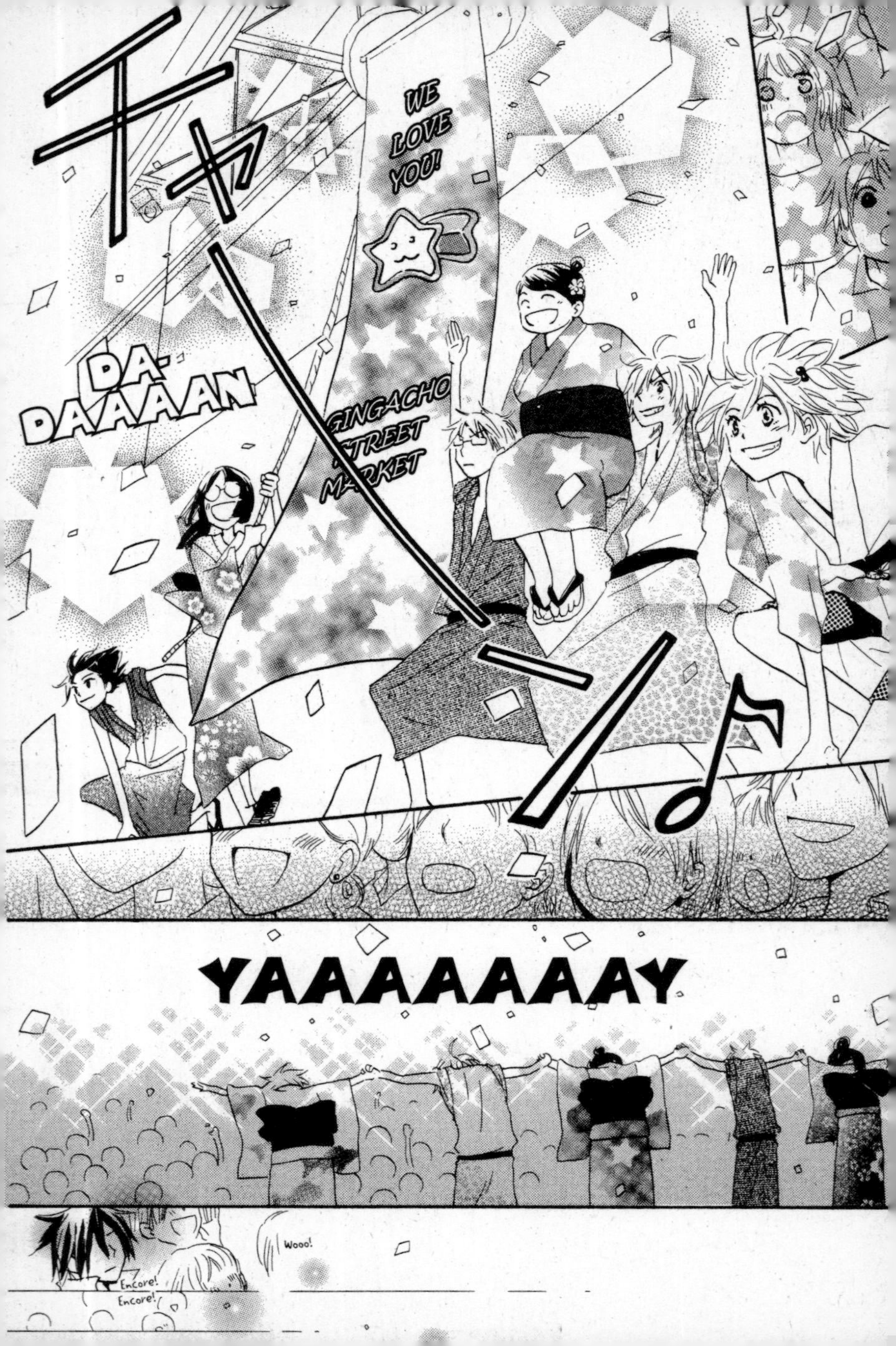
WE LOVE YOU!
GINGACHO STREET MARKET
チャ
DA-DAAAAAN
YAAAAAAAY
Wooo!
Encore!
Encore!

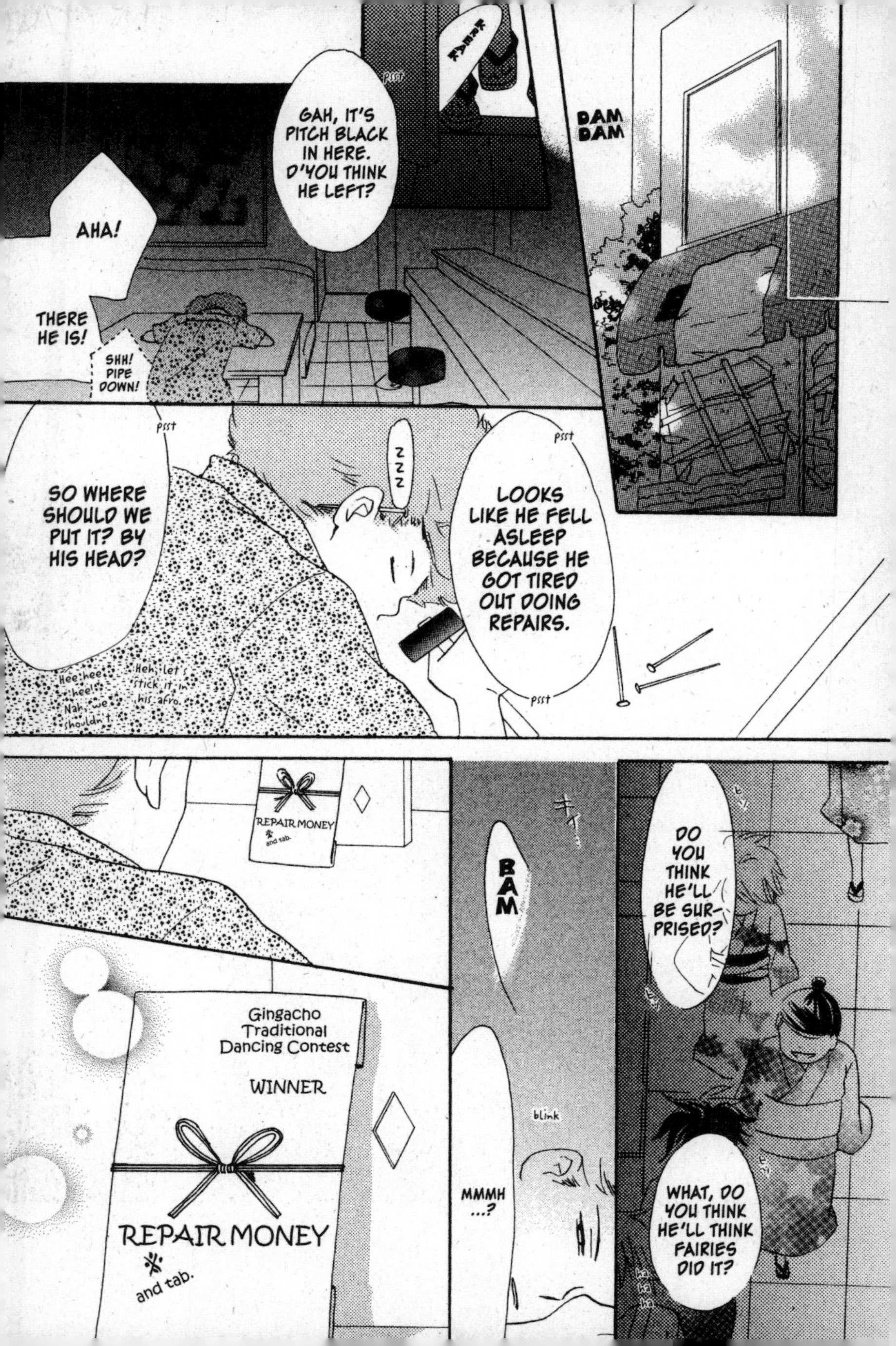
DAM
DAM
psst
GAH, IT'S PITCH BLACK IN HERE. D'YOU THINK HE LEFT?
AHA!
THERE HE IS!
SHH! PIPE DOWN!
psst
LOOKS LIKE HE FELL ASLEEP BECAUSE HE GOT TIRED OUT DOING REPAIRS.
psst
Z Z Z
psst
SO WHERE SHOULD WE PUT IT? BY HIS HEAD?
Heh, let's stick it in his afro.
Hee hee hee! Nah, we shouldn't.
DO YOU THINK HE'LL BE SUR-PRISED?
WHAT, DO YOU THINK HE'LL THINK FAIRIES DID IT?
BAM
blink
MMMH ...?
REPAIR MONEY
and tab.
Gingacho Traditional Dancing Contest
WINNER
REPAIR MONEY
and tab.

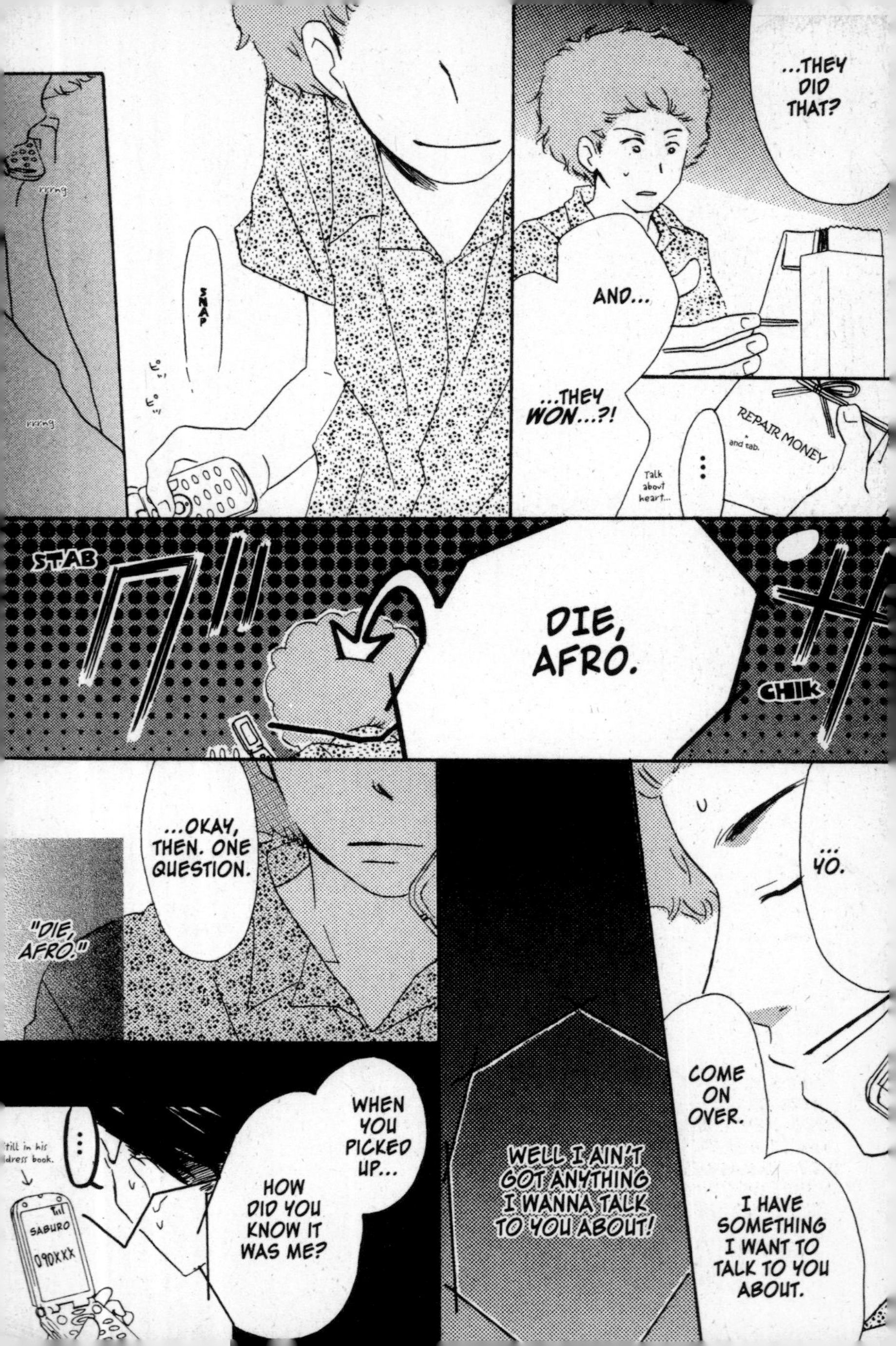
...THEY DID THAT?
AND...
...THEY WON...?!
REPAIR MONEY
and tab.
...
Talk about heart...
SNAP
rrrng
rrrng
DIE, AFRO.
STAB
CHIK
...YO.
COME ON OVER.
I HAVE SOMETHING I WANT TO TALK TO YOU ABOUT.
WELL I AIN'T GOT ANYTHING I WANNA TALK TO YOU ABOUT!
...OKAY, THEN. ONE QUESTION.
"DIE, AFRO."
WHEN YOU PICKED UP...
HOW DID YOU KNOW IT WAS ME?
...
till in his ddress book.
SABURO
090XXX

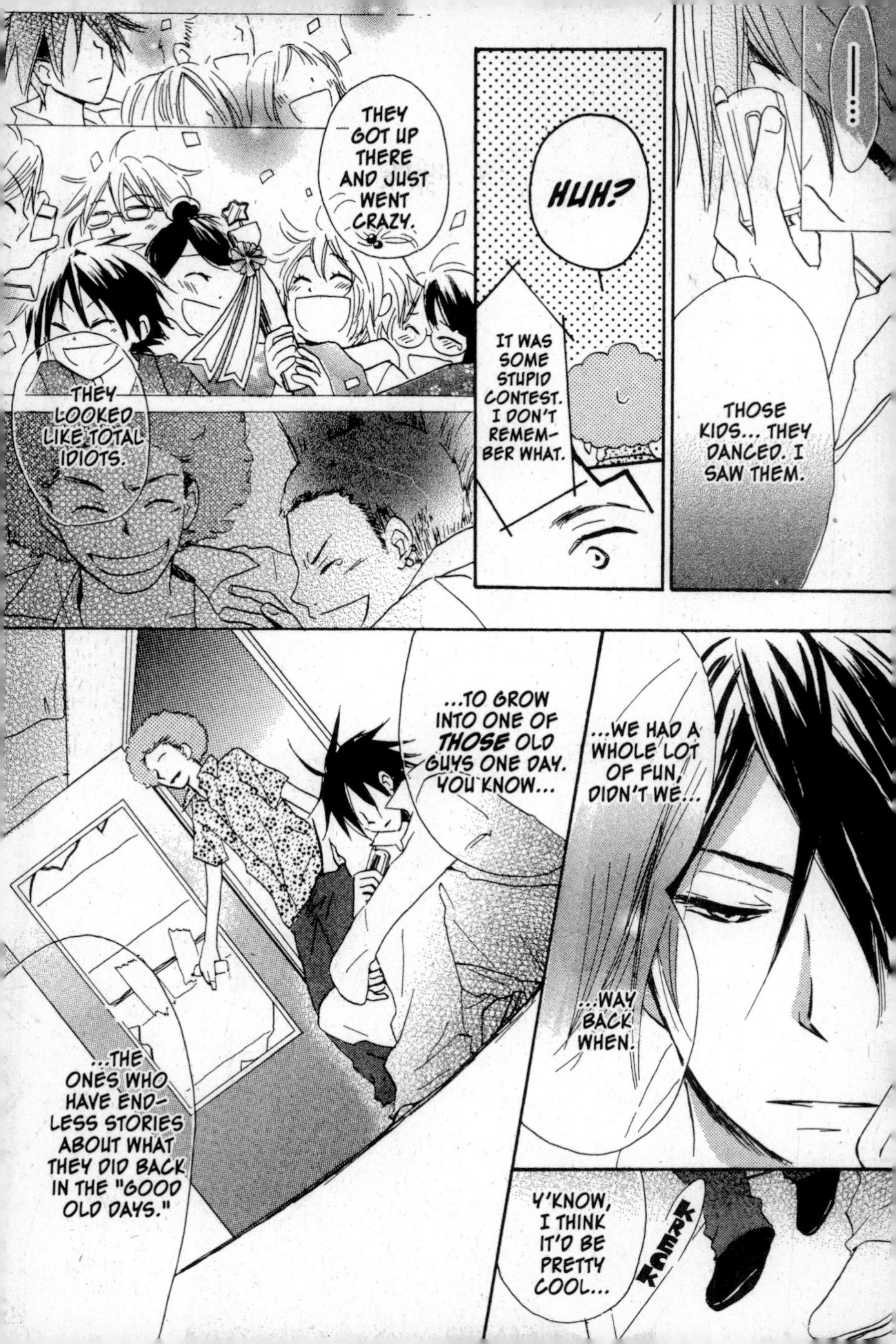
—...
THOSE KIDS... THEY DANCED. I SAW THEM.
HUH?
IT WAS SOME STUPID CONTEST. I DON'T REMEMBER WHAT.
THEY GOT UP THERE AND JUST WENT CRAZY.
THEY LOOKED LIKE TOTAL IDIOTS.
...WE HAD A WHOLE LOT OF FUN, DIDN'T WE...
...WAY BACK WHEN.
Y'KNOW, I THINK IT'D BE PRETTY COOL...
KRECK
...TO GROW INTO ONE OF *THOSE* OLD GUYS ONE DAY. YOU KNOW...
...THE ONES WHO HAVE ENDLESS STORIES ABOUT WHAT THEY DID BACK IN THE "GOOD OLD DAYS."

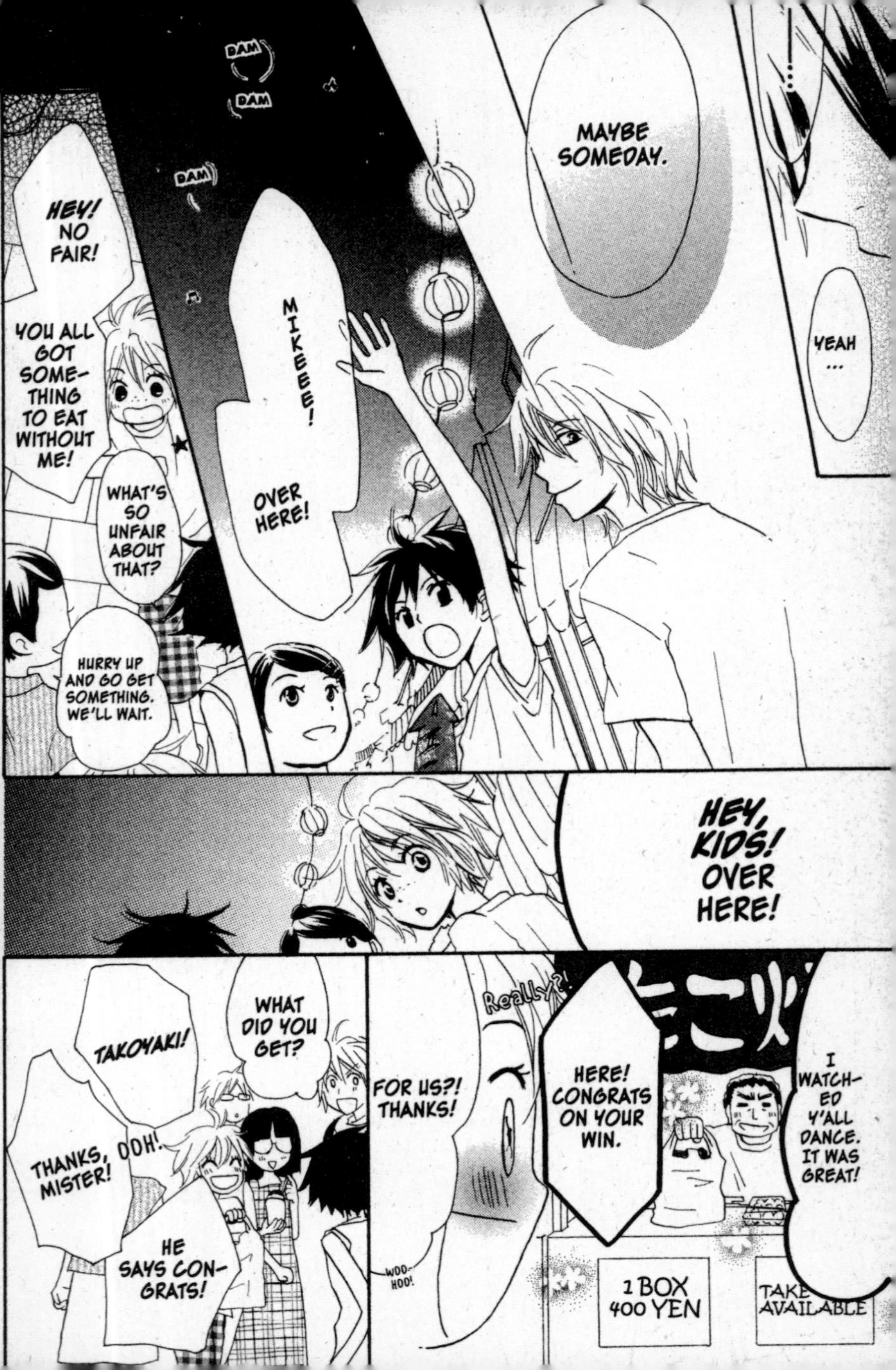
...
YEAH ...
MAYBE SOMEDAY.
DAM
DAM
DAM
MIKEEEE!
OVER HERE!
HEY! NO FAIR!
YOU ALL GOT SOMETHING TO EAT WITHOUT ME!
WHAT'S SO UNFAIR ABOUT THAT?
HURRY UP AND GO GET SOMETHING. WE'LL WAIT.
HEY, KIDS! OVER HERE!
I WATCHED Y'ALL DANCE. IT WAS GREAT!
HERE! CONGRATS ON YOUR WIN.
Really?!
FOR US?! THANKS!
WOO-HOO!
1 BOX 400 YEN
TAKE AVAILABLE
WHAT DID YOU GET?
TAKOYAKI!
OOH!
THANKS, MISTER!
HE SAYS CON-GRATS!

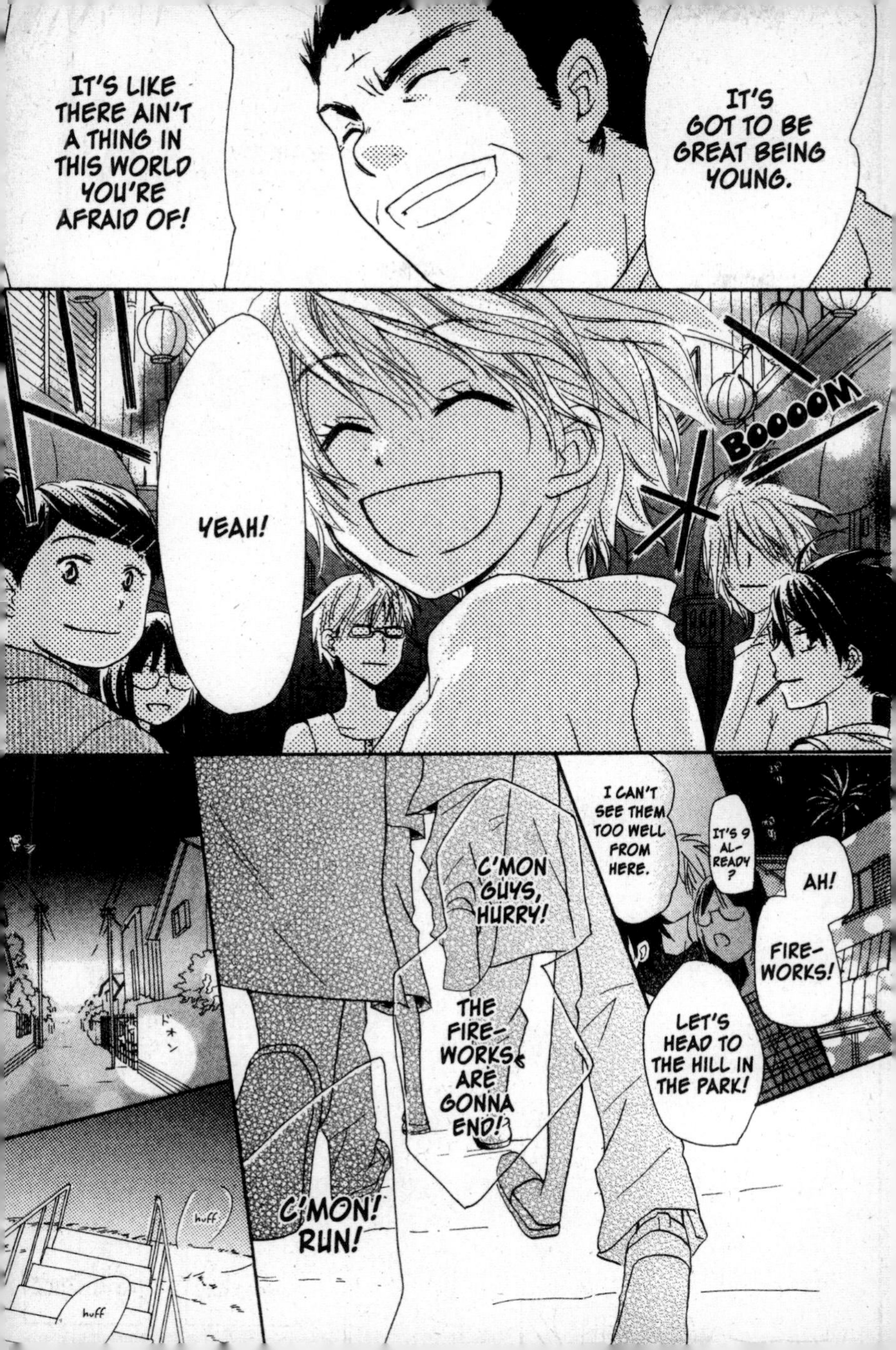
IT'S GOT TO BE GREAT BEING YOUNG.
IT'S LIKE THERE AIN'T A THING IN THIS WORLD YOU'RE AFRAID OF!
BOOOOM
YEAH!
I CAN'T SEE THEM TOO WELL FROM HERE.
IT'S 9 ALREADY?
AH!
FIRE-WORKS!
LET'S HEAD TO THE HILL IN THE PARK!
C'MON GUYS, HURRY!
THE FIRE-WORKS ARE GONNA END!
C'MON! RUN!
ドオン
huff
huff

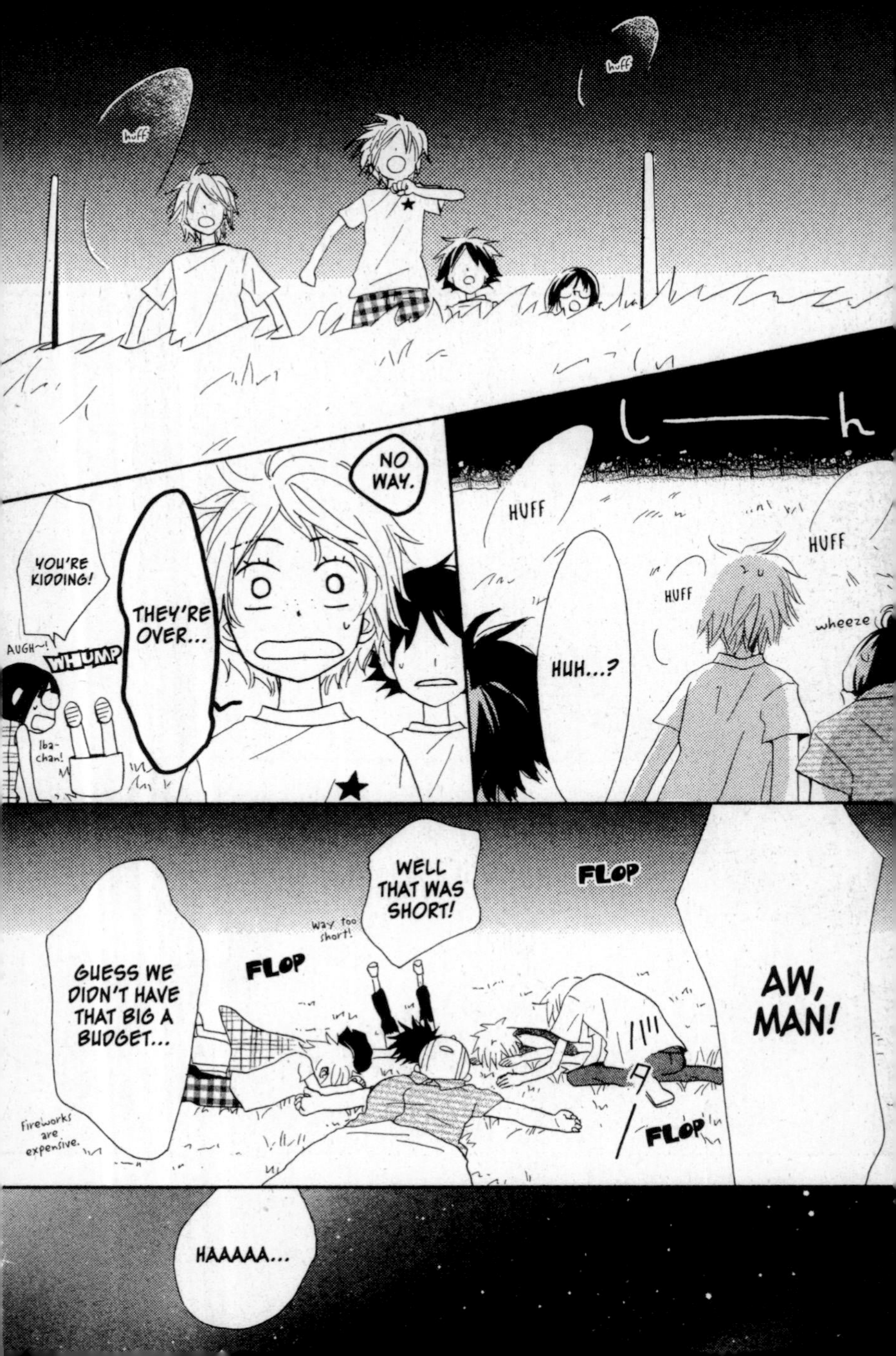
huff
huff
HUFF
HUFF
HUFF
wheeze
HUH...?
NO WAY.
THEY'RE OVER...
YOU'RE KIDDING!
AUGH~!
WHUMP
Iba-chan!
AW, MAN!
FLOP
WELL THAT WAS SHORT!
Way too short!
FLOP
GUESS WE DIDN'T HAVE THAT BIG A BUDGET...
Fireworks are expensive.
FLOP
HAAAAA...

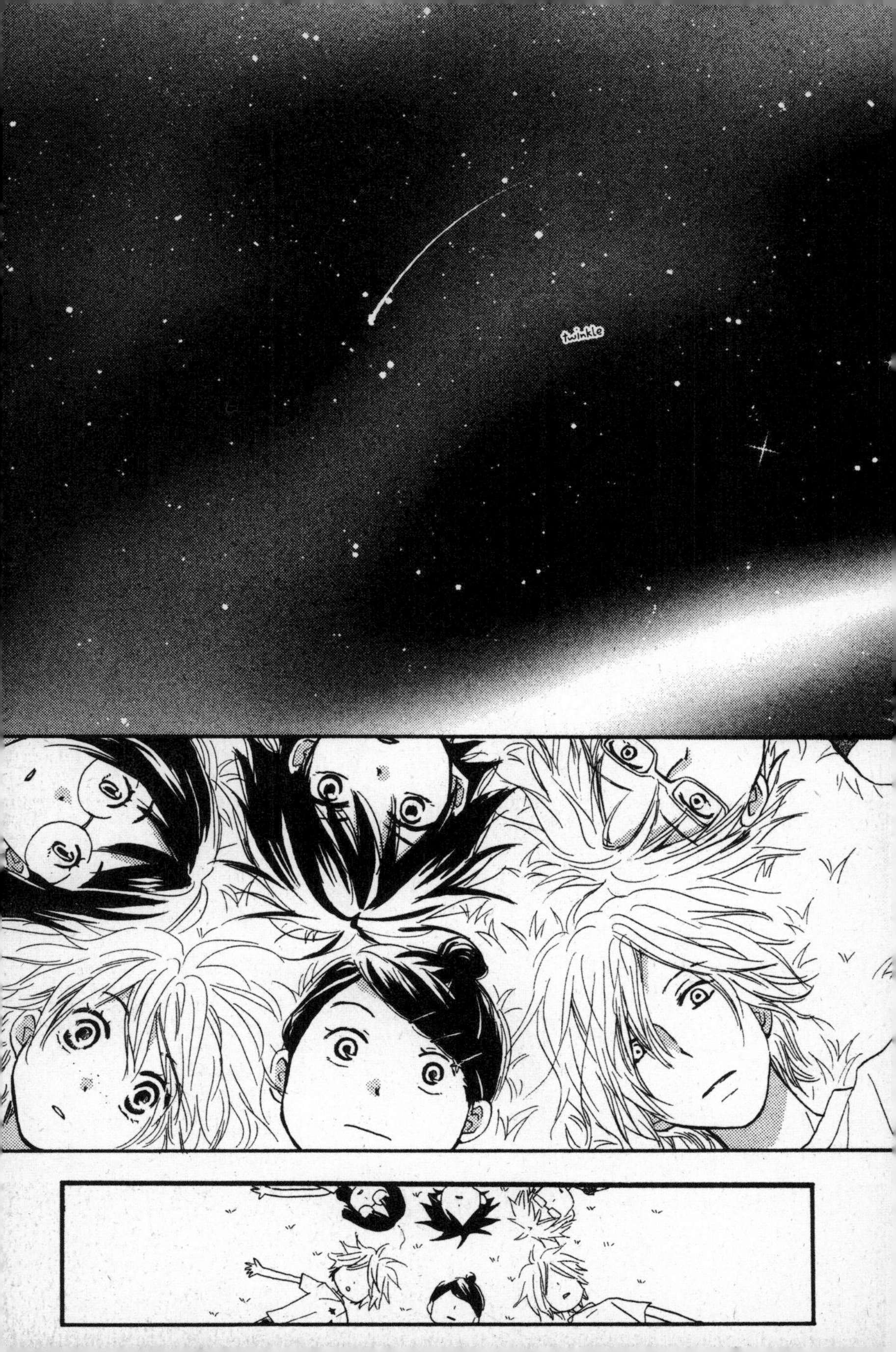
twinkle

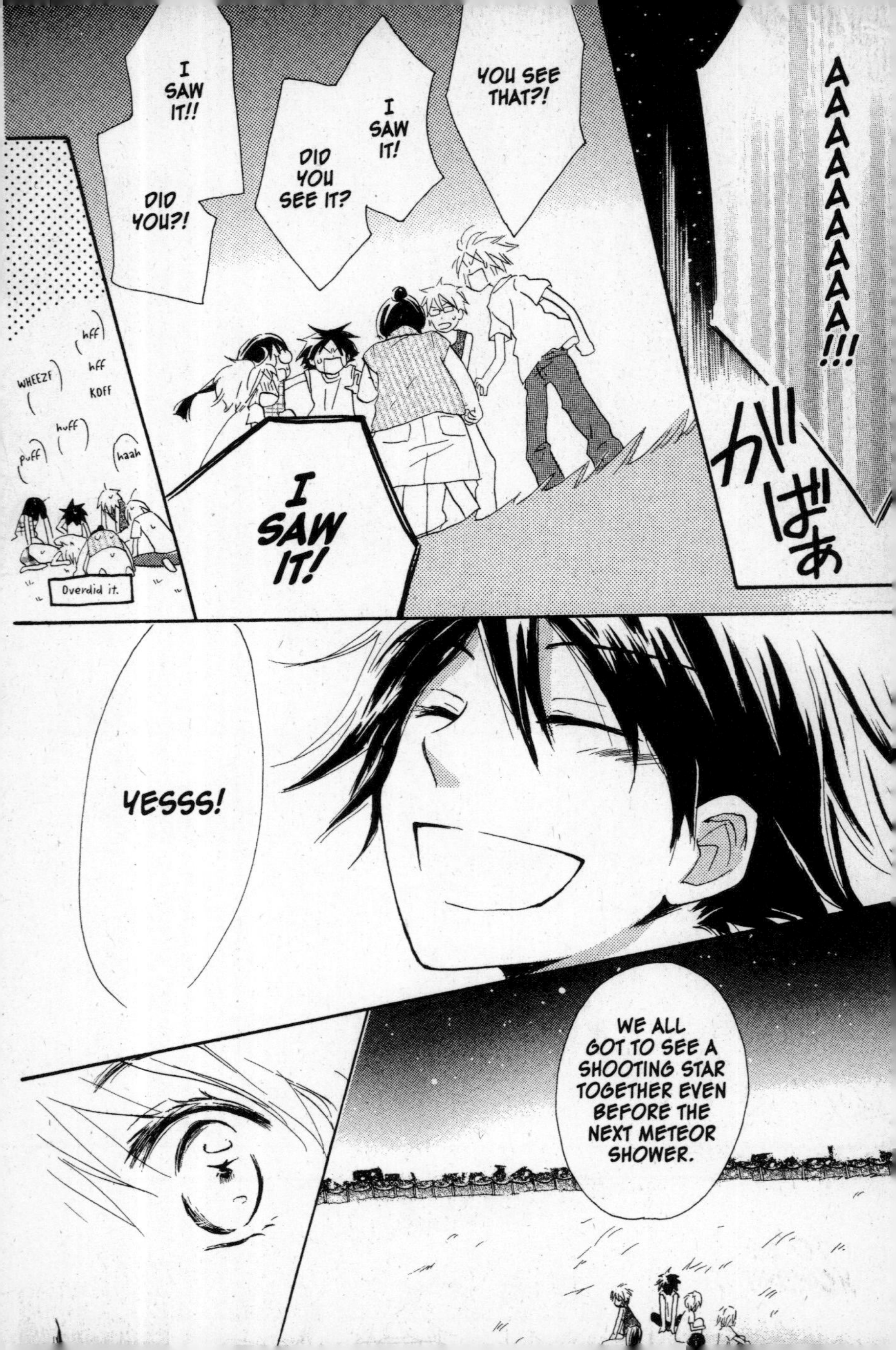
AAAAAAAAA!!!
がばぁ
YOU SEE THAT?!
I SAW IT!
DID YOU SEE IT?
I SAW IT!!
DID YOU?!
I SAW IT!
hff
hff
KOFF
WHEEZF
huff
puff
haah
Overdid it.
YESSS!
WE ALL GOT TO SEE A SHOOTING STAR TOGETHER EVEN BEFORE THE NEXT METEOR SHOWER.

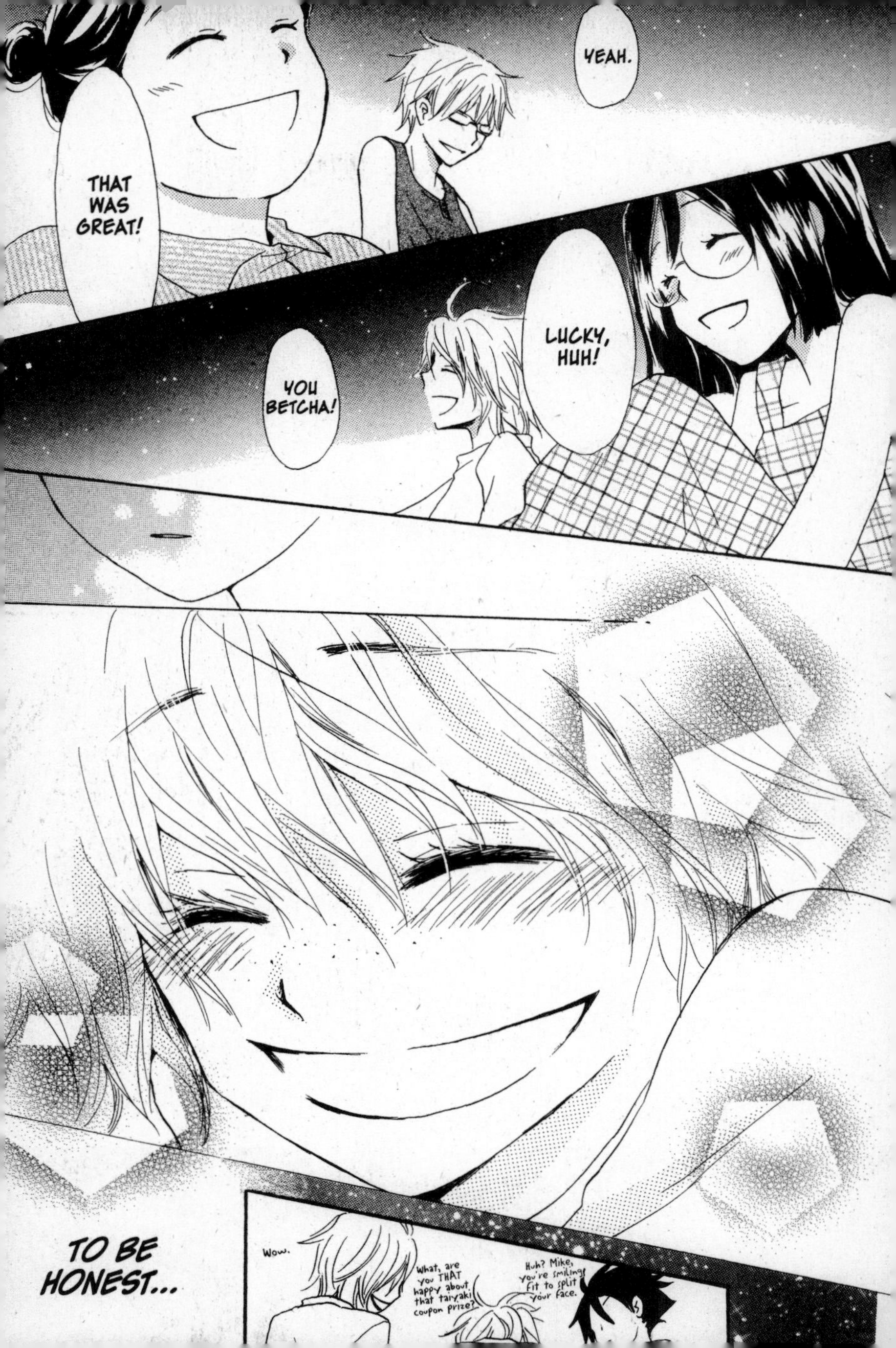
YEAH.
THAT WAS GREAT!
LUCKY, HUH!
YOU BETCHA!
Huh? Mike, you're smiling fit to split your face.
What, are you THAT happy about that taiyaki coupon prize?
Wow.
TO BE HONEST...

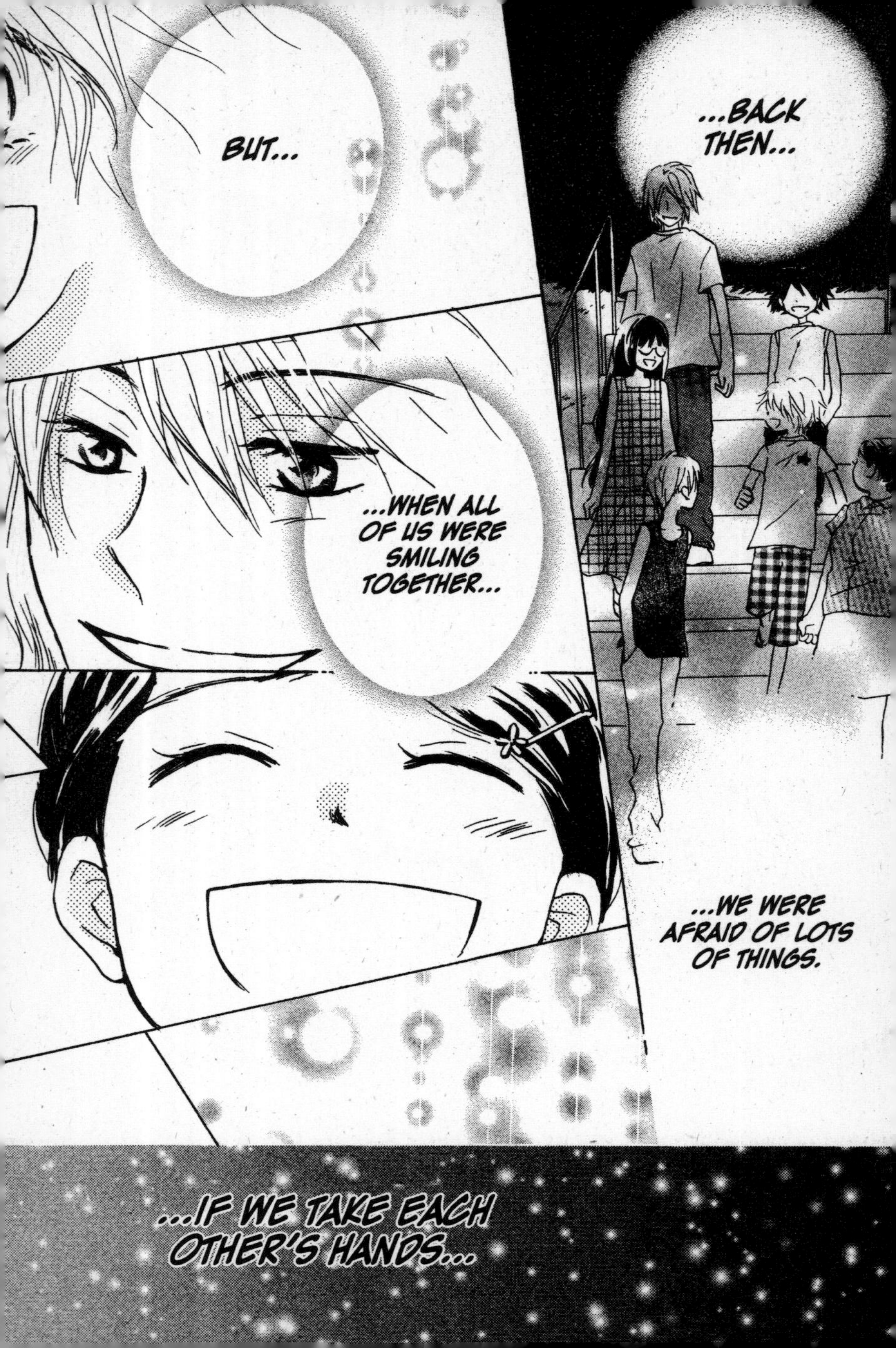
...BACK THEN...
...WE WERE AFRAID OF LOTS OF THINGS.
BUT...
...WHEN ALL OF US WERE SMILING TOGETHER...
...IF WE TAKE EACH OTHER'S HANDS...

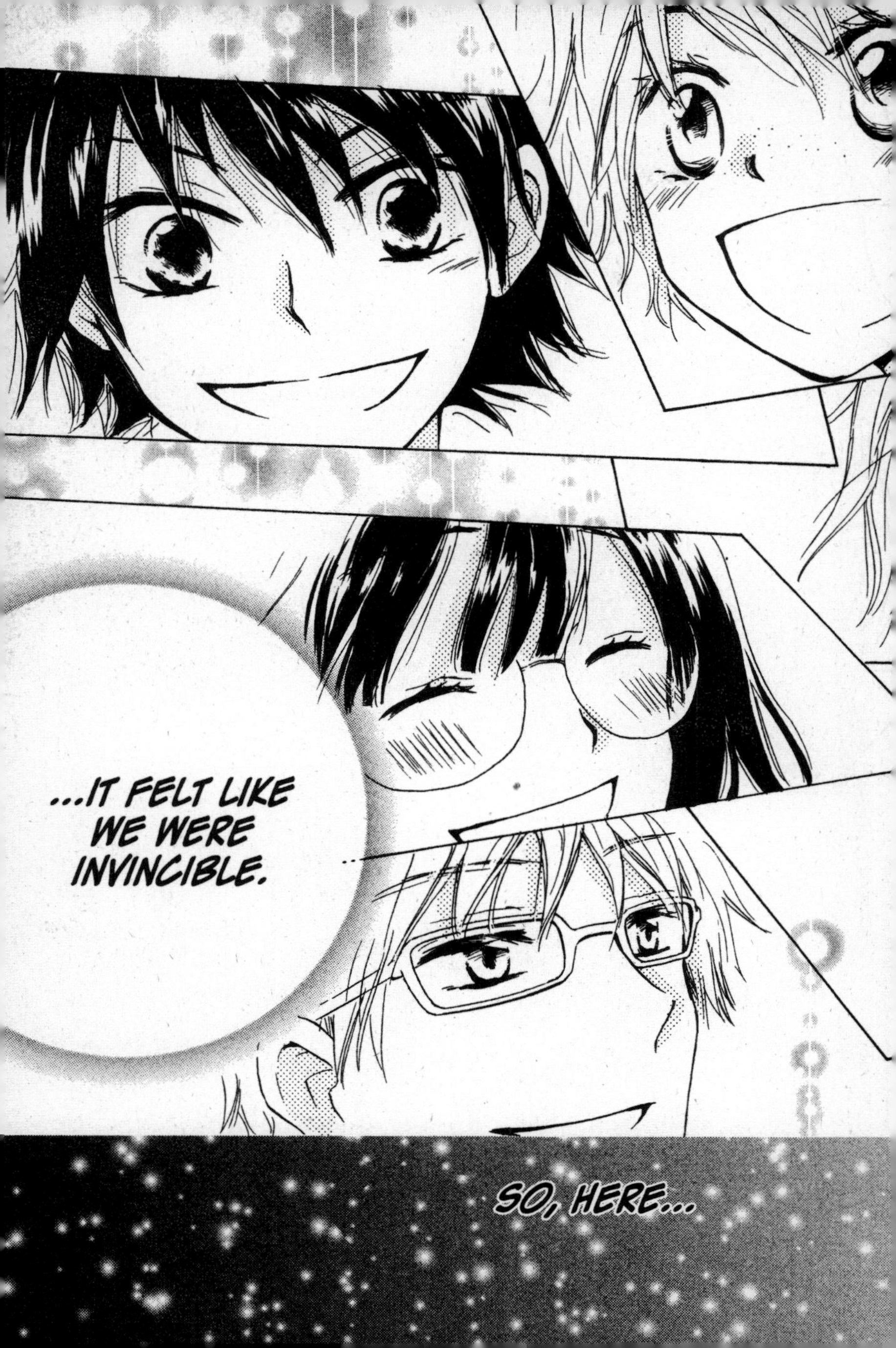
...IT FELT LIKE WE WERE INVINCIBLE.
SO, HERE...

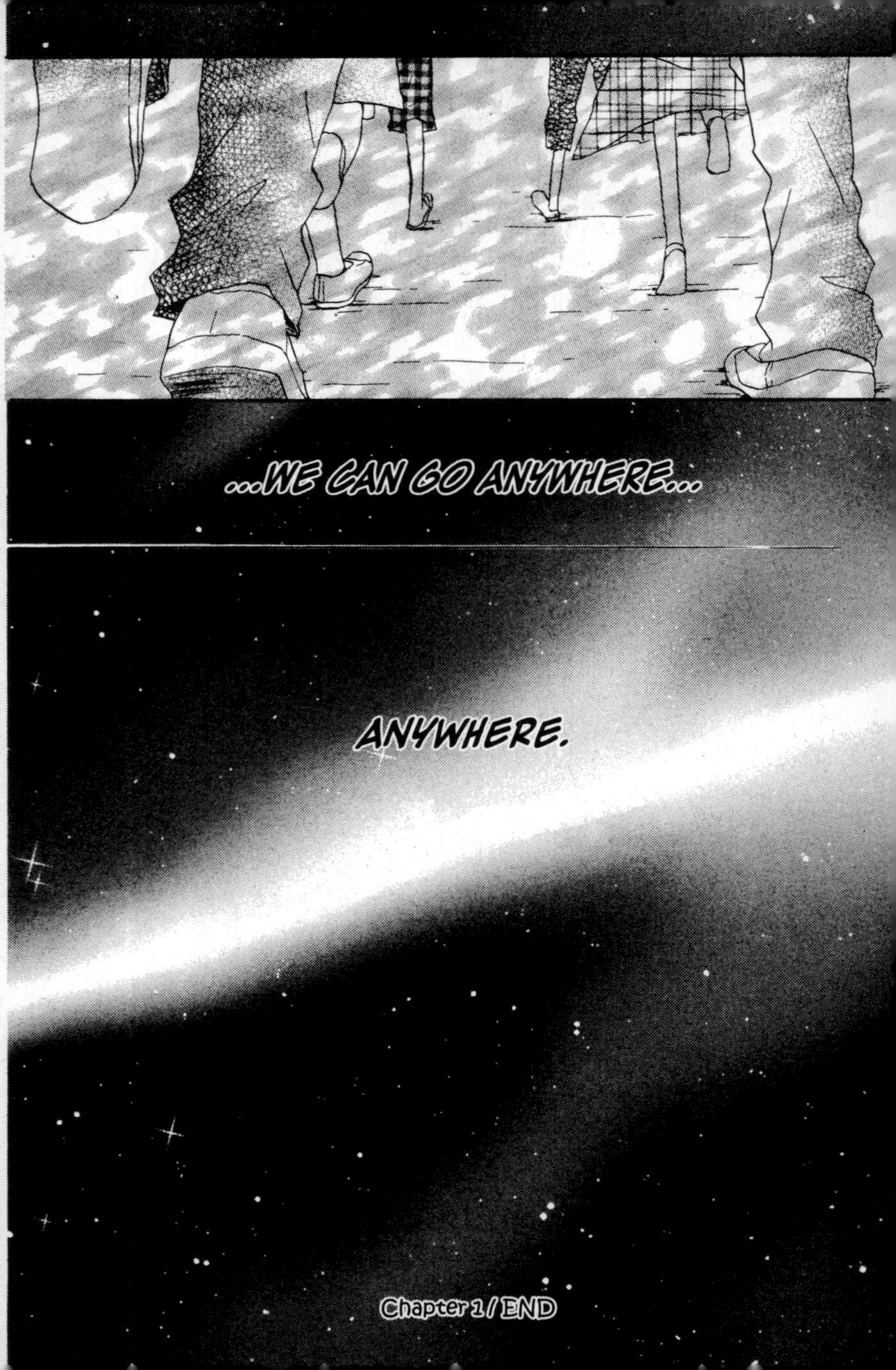
...WE CAN GO ANYWHERE...
ANYWHERE.
Chapter 1 / END

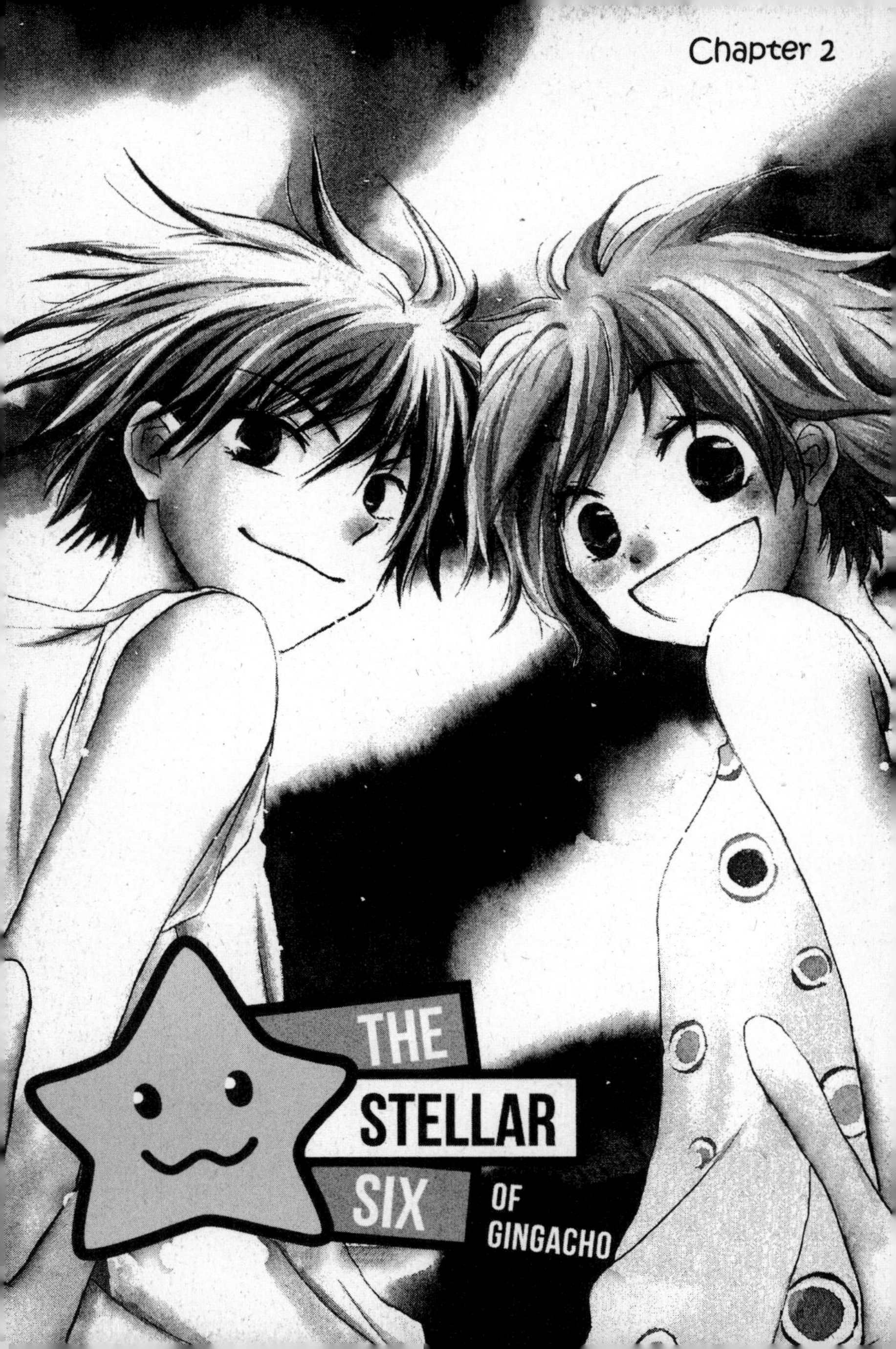
Chapter 2
THE
STELLAR
SIX
OF
GINGACHO

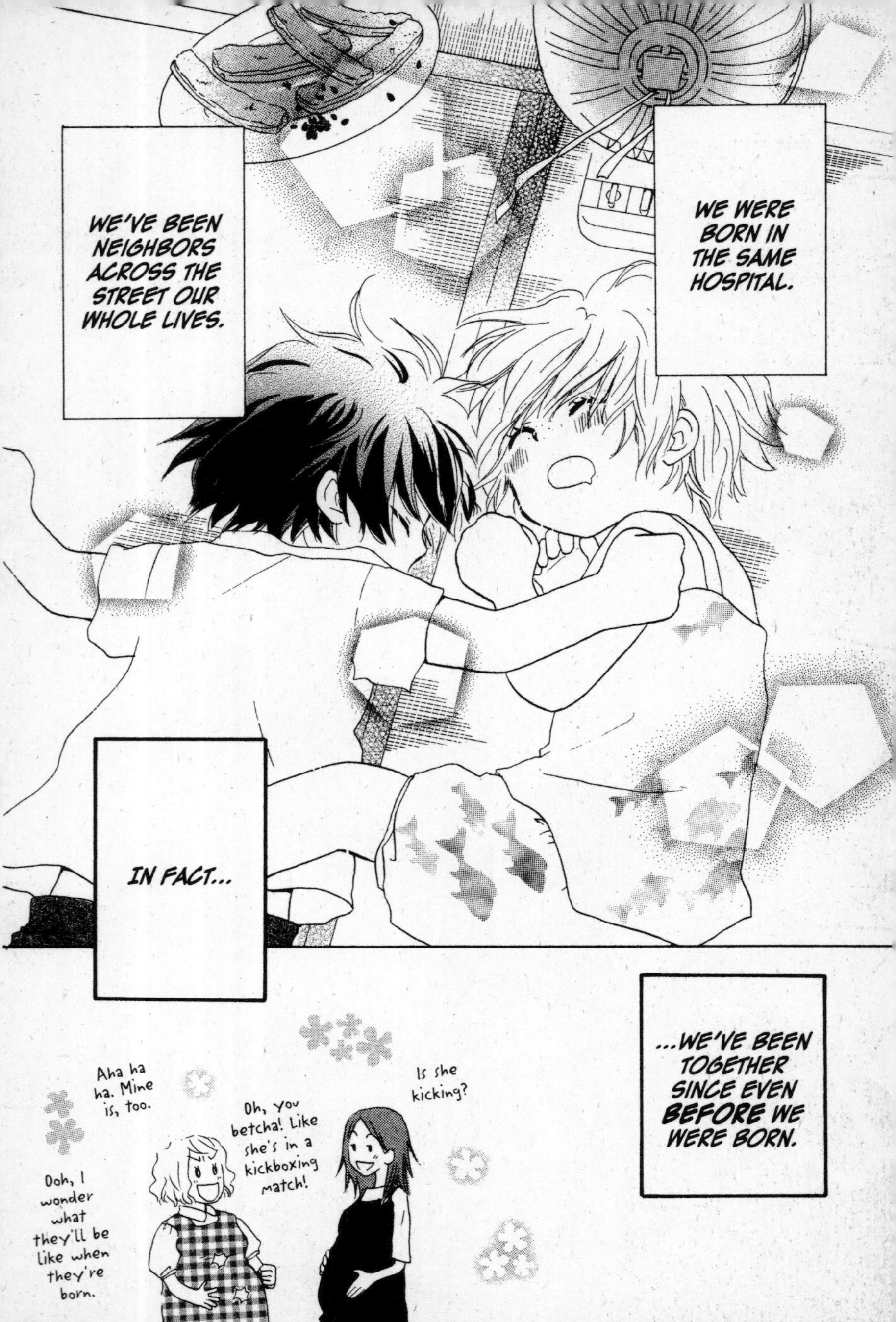
WE WERE BORN IN THE SAME HOSPITAL.
WE'VE BEEN NEIGHBORS ACROSS THE STREET OUR WHOLE LIVES.
IN FACT...
...WE'VE BEEN TOGETHER SINCE EVEN BEFORE WE WERE BORN.
Is she kicking?
Oh, you betcha! Like she's in a kickboxing match!
Aha ha ha. Mine is, too.
Ooh, I wonder what they'll be like when they're born.

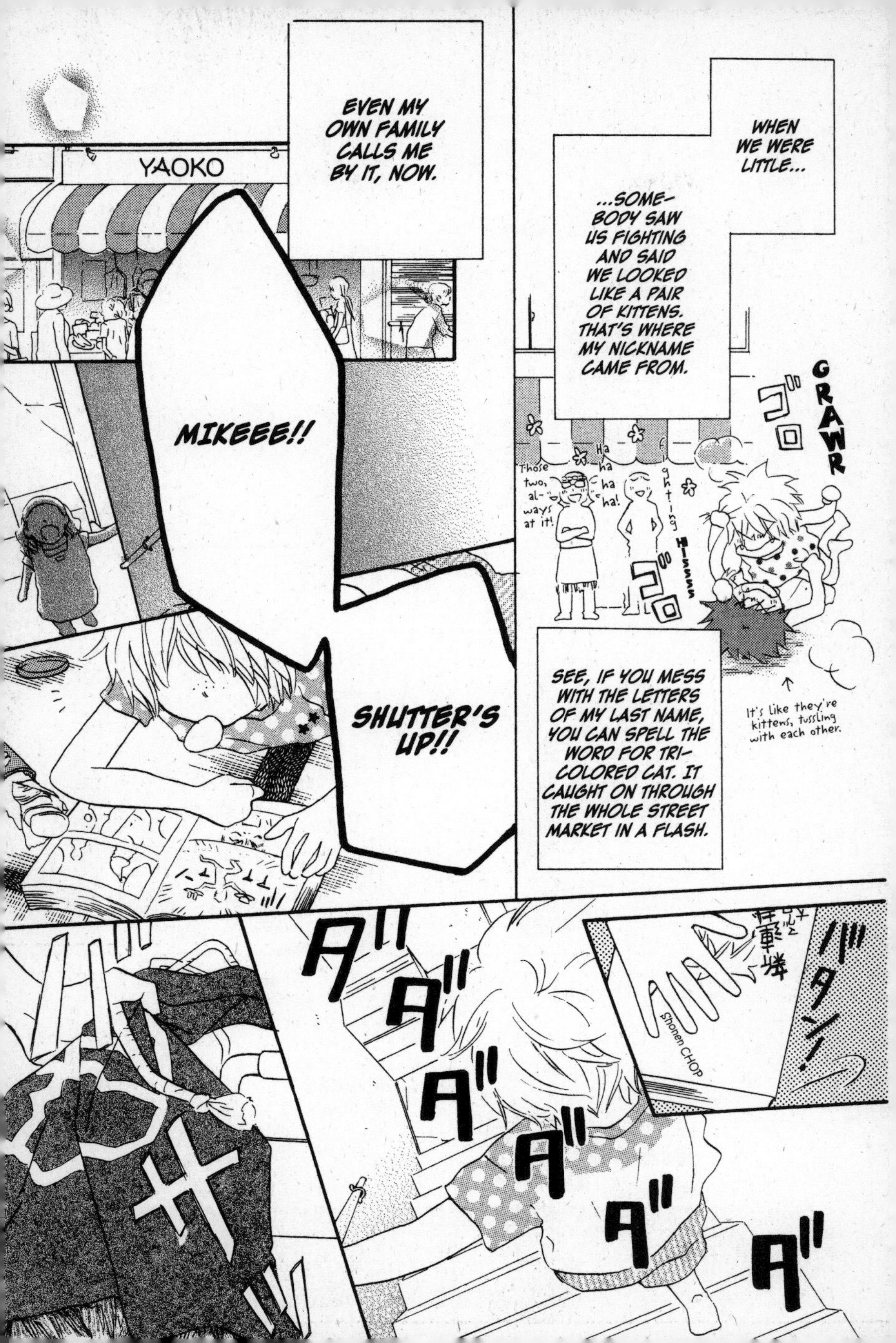
WHEN WE WERE LITTLE...
...SOME-BODY SAW US FIGHTING AND SAID WE LOOKED LIKE A PAIR OF KITTENS. THAT'S WHERE MY NICKNAME CAME FROM.
GRAWR
ゴロ
Ha ha ha ha!
Those two, al-ways at it!
fighting
HISSSS
ゴロ
SEE, IF YOU MESS WITH THE LETTERS OF MY LAST NAME, YOU CAN SPELL THE WORD FOR TRI-COLORED CAT. IT CAUGHT ON THROUGH THE WHOLE STREET MARKET IN A FLASH.
It's like they're kittens, tussling with each other.
YAOKO
EVEN MY OWN FAMILY CALLS ME BY IT, NOW.
MIKEEE!!
SHUTTER'S UP!!
バタン!
Shonen CHOP

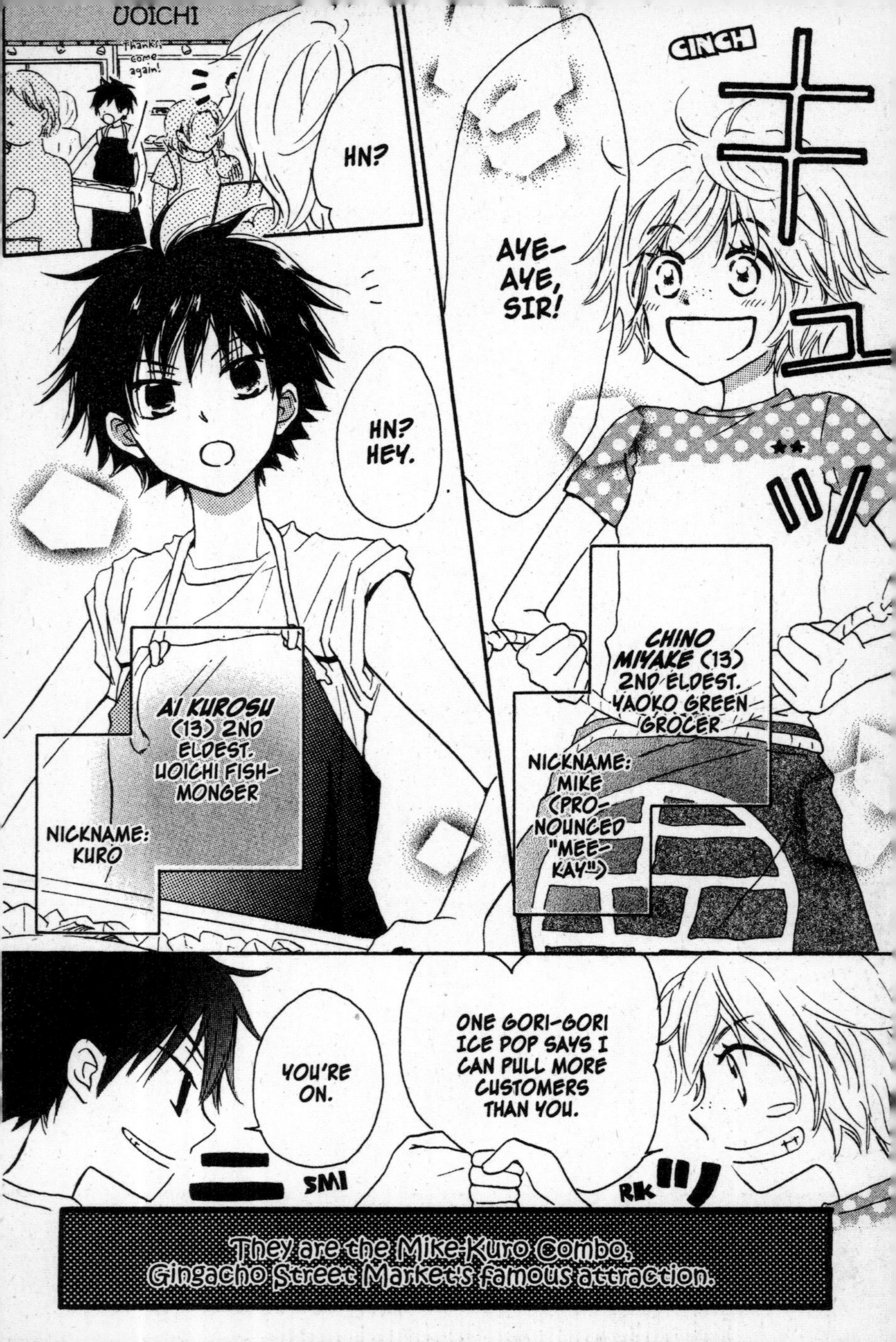
CINCH
AYE-AYE, SIR!
CHINO MIYAKE (13) 2ND ELDEST. YAOKO GREEN GROCER
NICKNAME: MIKE (PRONOUNCED "MEE-KAY")
UOICHI
Thanks, come again!
HN?
HN? HEY.
AI KUROSU (13) 2ND ELDEST. UOICHI FISHMONGER
NICKNAME: KURO
ONE GORI-GORI ICE POP SAYS I CAN PULL MORE CUSTOMERS THAN YOU.
YOU'RE ON.
SMI
RK
They are the Mike-Kuro Combo, Gingacho Street Market's famous attraction.

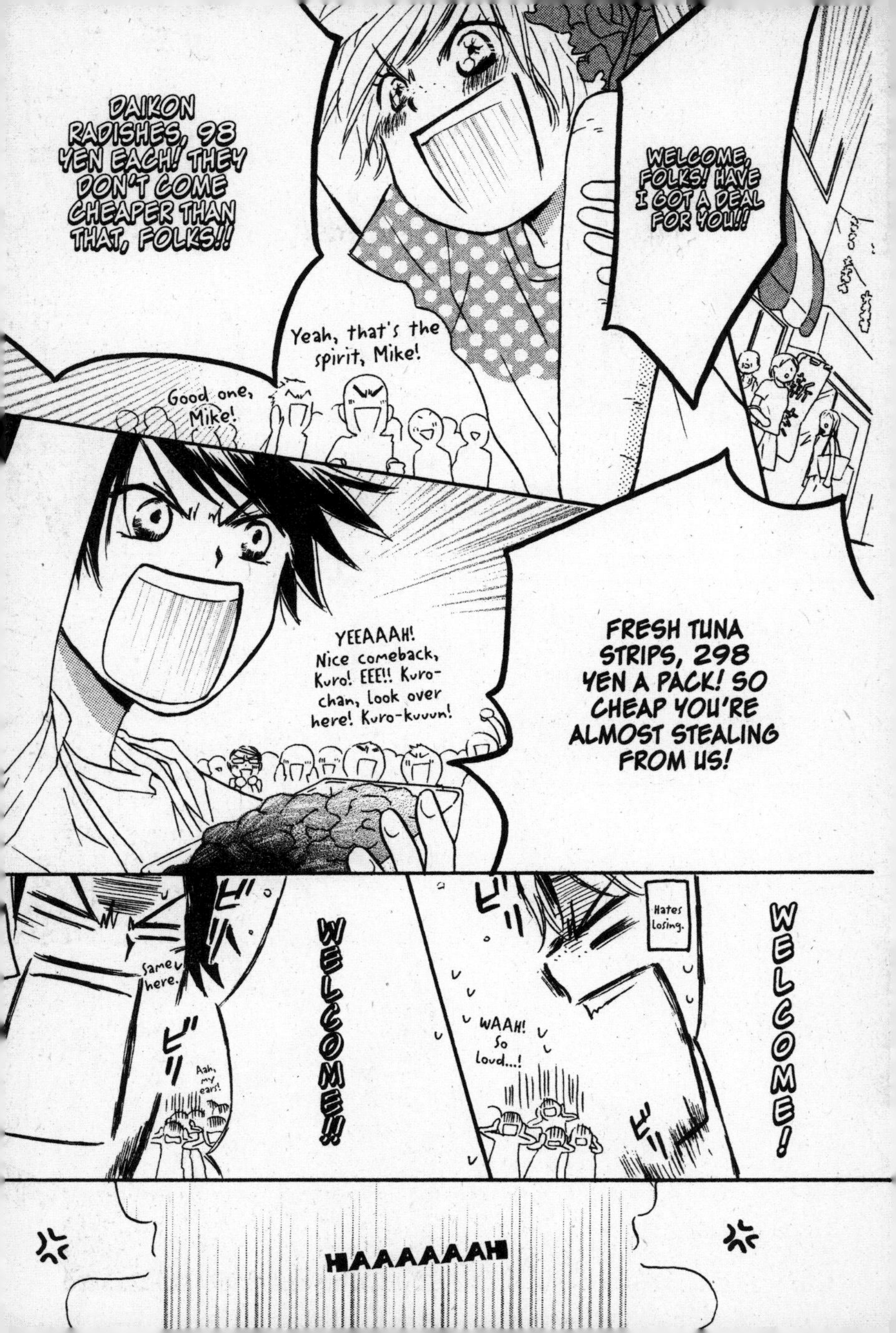

WELCOME, FOLKS! HAVE I GOT A DEAL FOR YOU!!
DAIKON RADISHES, 98 YEN EACH! THEY DON'T COME CHEAPER THAN THAT, FOLKS!!
Yeah, that's the spirit, Mike!
Good one, Mike!
FRESH TUNA STRIPS, 298 YEN A PACK! SO CHEAP YOU'RE ALMOST STEALING FROM US!
YEEAAAH! Nice comeback, Kuro! EEE!! Kuro-chan, look over here! Kuro-kuuun!
WELCOME!
Hates losing.
WAAH! So loud...!
WELCOME!!
Same here.
Aah, my ears!
HAAAAAAH

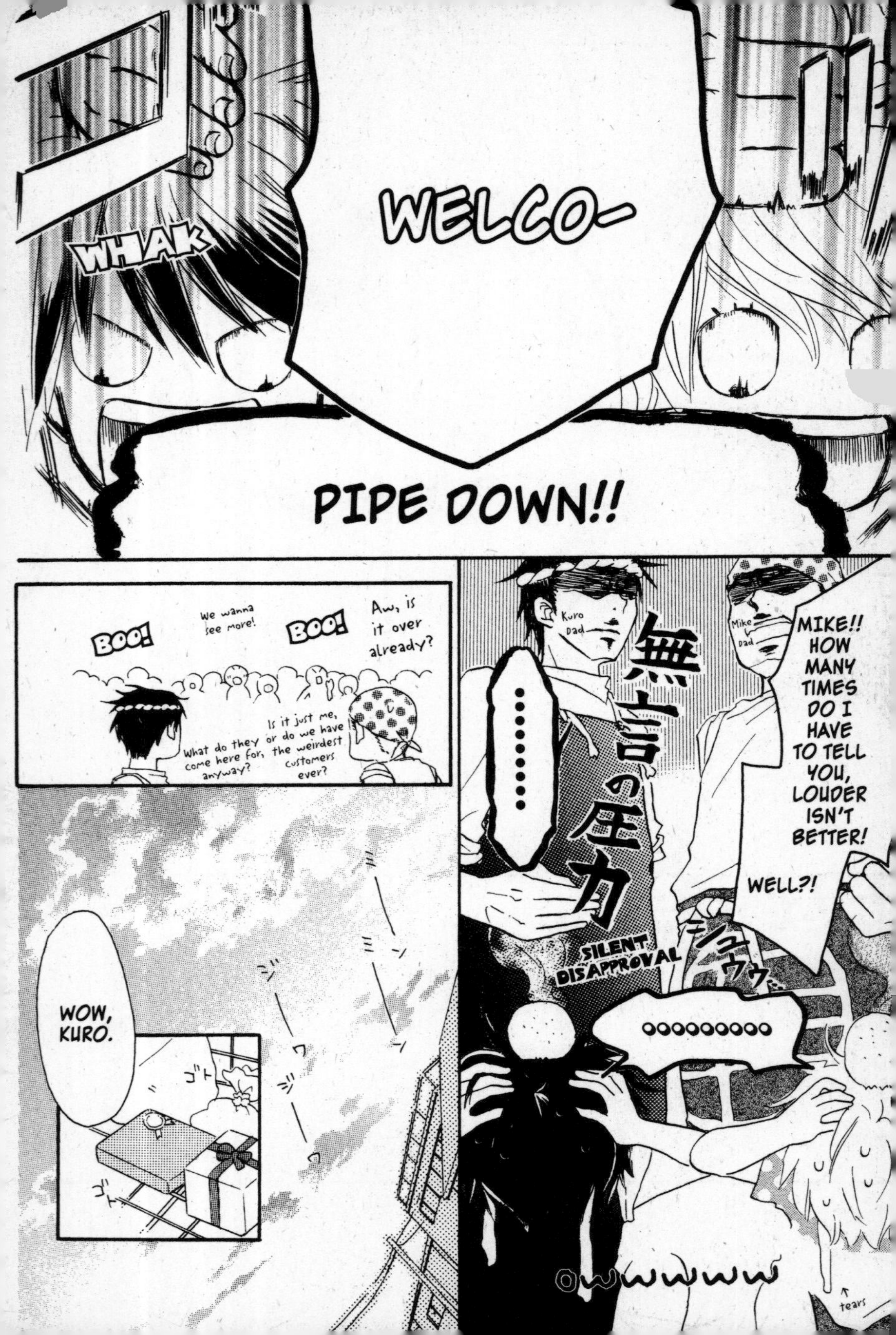
WELCO-
WHAK
PIPE DOWN!!
Kuro Dad
Mike Dad
MIKE!! HOW MANY TIMES DO I HAVE TO TELL YOU, LOUDER ISN'T BETTER!
WELL?!
無言の圧力
SILENT DISAPPROVAL
シュウウ…
OWWWWWW
tears
Aw, is it over already?
BOO!
We wanna see more!
BOO!
Is it just me, or do we have the weirdest customers ever?
What do they come here for, anyway?
WOW, KURO.
ゴト
ゴト

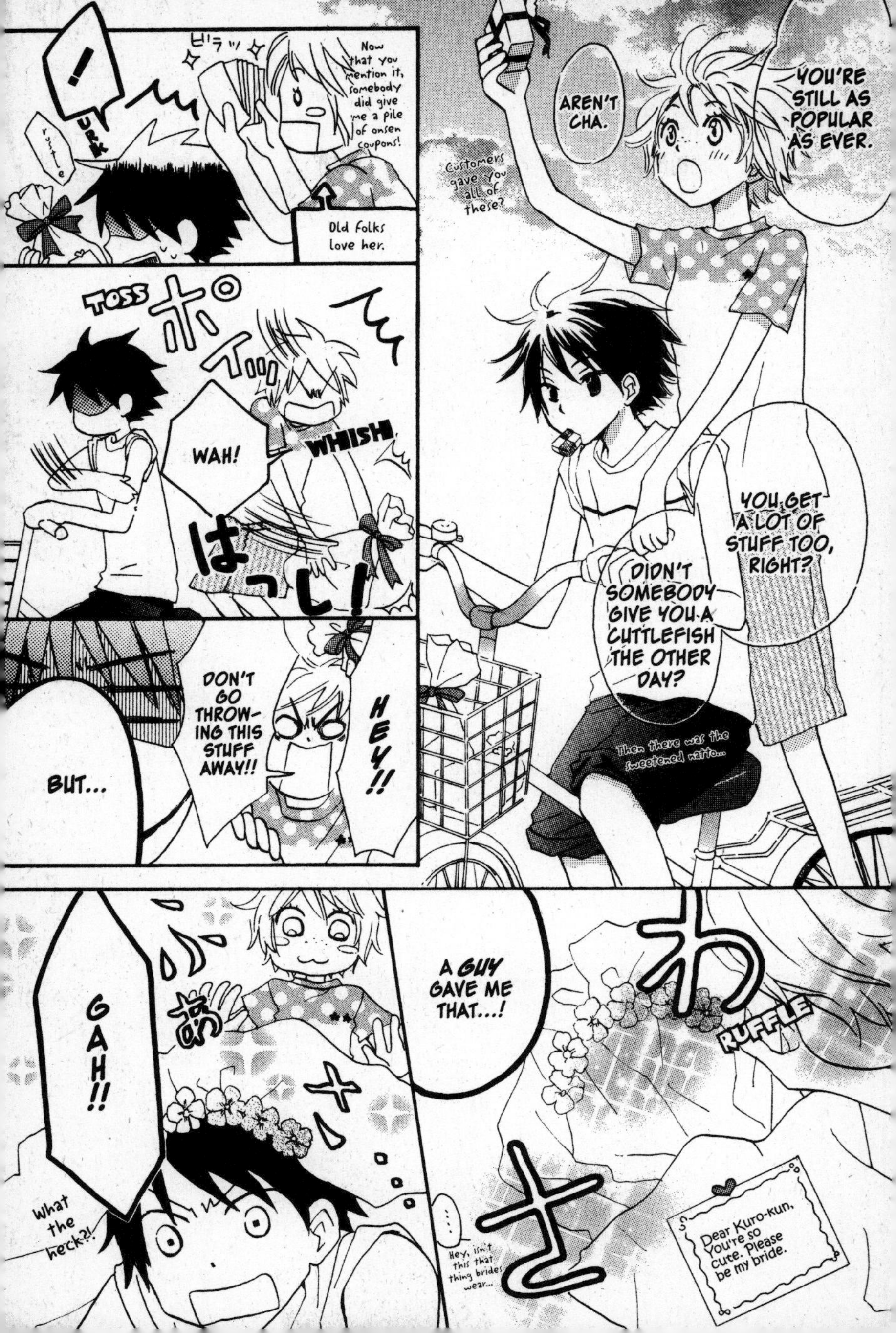
YOU'RE STILL AS POPULAR AS EVER.
AREN'T CHA.
Customers gave you all of these?
YOU GET A LOT OF STUFF TOO, RIGHT?
DIDN'T SOMEBODY GIVE YOU A CUTTLEFISH THE OTHER DAY?
Then there was the sweetened natto...
Now that you mention it, somebody did give me a pile of onsen coupons!
Old folks love her.
!
URK
rustle
TOSS
WAH!
WHISH
HEY!!
DON'T GO THROWING THIS STUFF AWAY!!
BUT...
RUFFLE
Dear Kuro-kun, You're so cute. Please be my bride.
Hey, isn't this thing brides wear...
....
A GUY GAVE ME THAT...!
GAH!!
What the heck?!

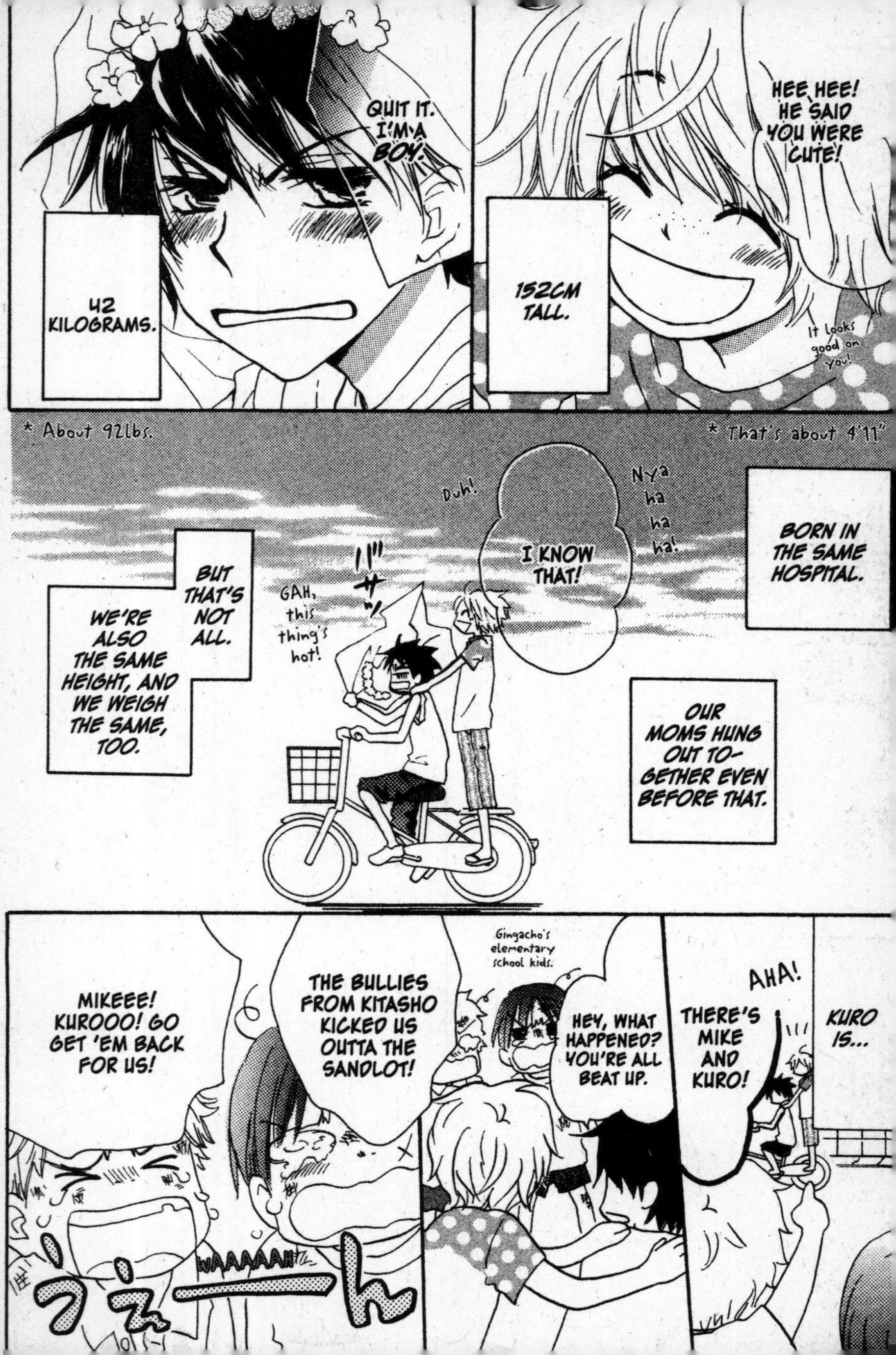
HEE HEE! HE SAID YOU WERE CUTE!
152CM TALL.
It looks good on you!
* That's about 4'11"
QUIT IT. I'M A BOY.
42 KILOGRAMS.
* About 92lbs.
BORN IN THE SAME HOSPITAL.
OUR MOMS HUNG OUT TO-GETHER EVEN BEFORE THAT.
Nya ha ha ha!
I KNOW THAT!
Duh!
GAH, this thing's hot!
BUT THAT'S NOT ALL.
WE'RE ALSO THE SAME HEIGHT, AND WE WEIGH THE SAME, TOO.
KURO IS...
AHA!
THERE'S MIKE AND KURO!
HEY, WHAT HAPPENED? YOU'RE ALL BEAT UP.
Gingacho's elementary school kids.
THE BULLIES FROM KITASHO KICKED US OUTTA THE SANDLOT!
MIKEEE! KUROOO! GO GET 'EM BACK FOR US!
WAAAAAAH

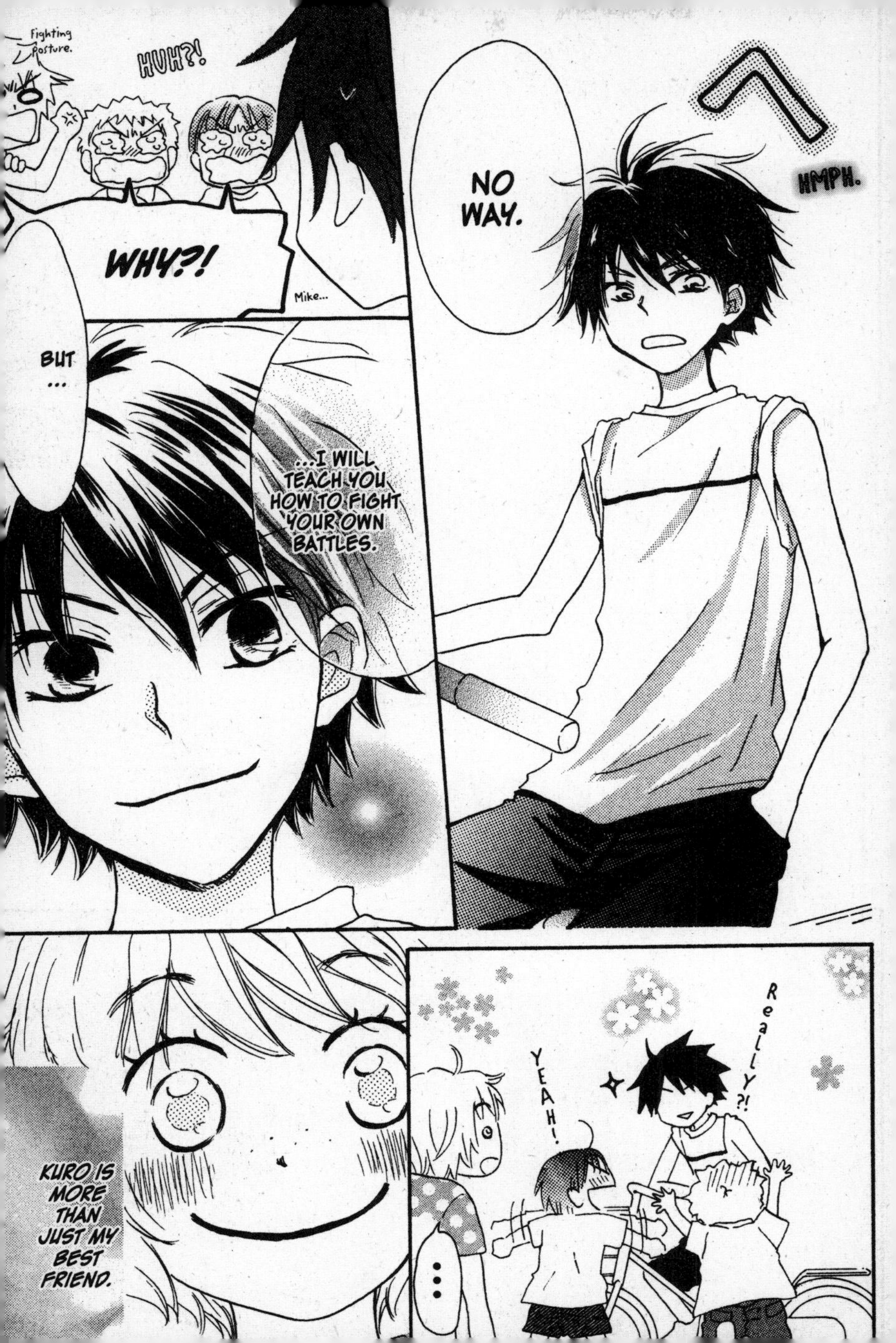
NO WAY.
HMPH.
HUH?!
Fighting posture.
WHY?!
Mike...
BUT ...
...I WILL TEACH YOU HOW TO FIGHT YOUR OWN BATTLES.
Really?!
YEAH!
...
KURO IS MORE THAN JUST MY BEST FRIEND.

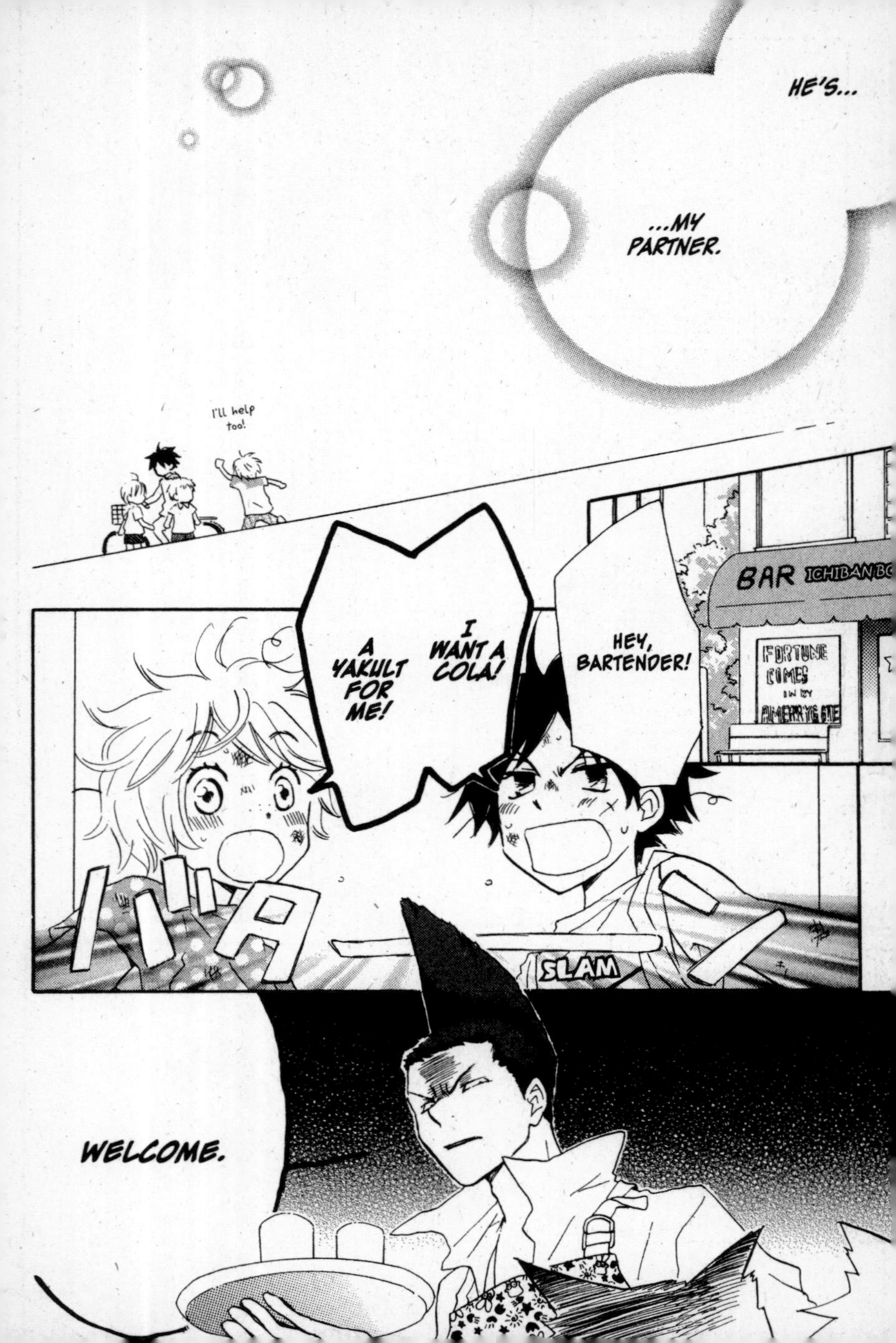
HE'S...
...MY PARTNER.
I'll help too!
BAR
FORTUNE COMES
HEY, BARTENDER!
I WANT A COLA!
A YAKULT FOR ME!
SLAM
WELCOME.

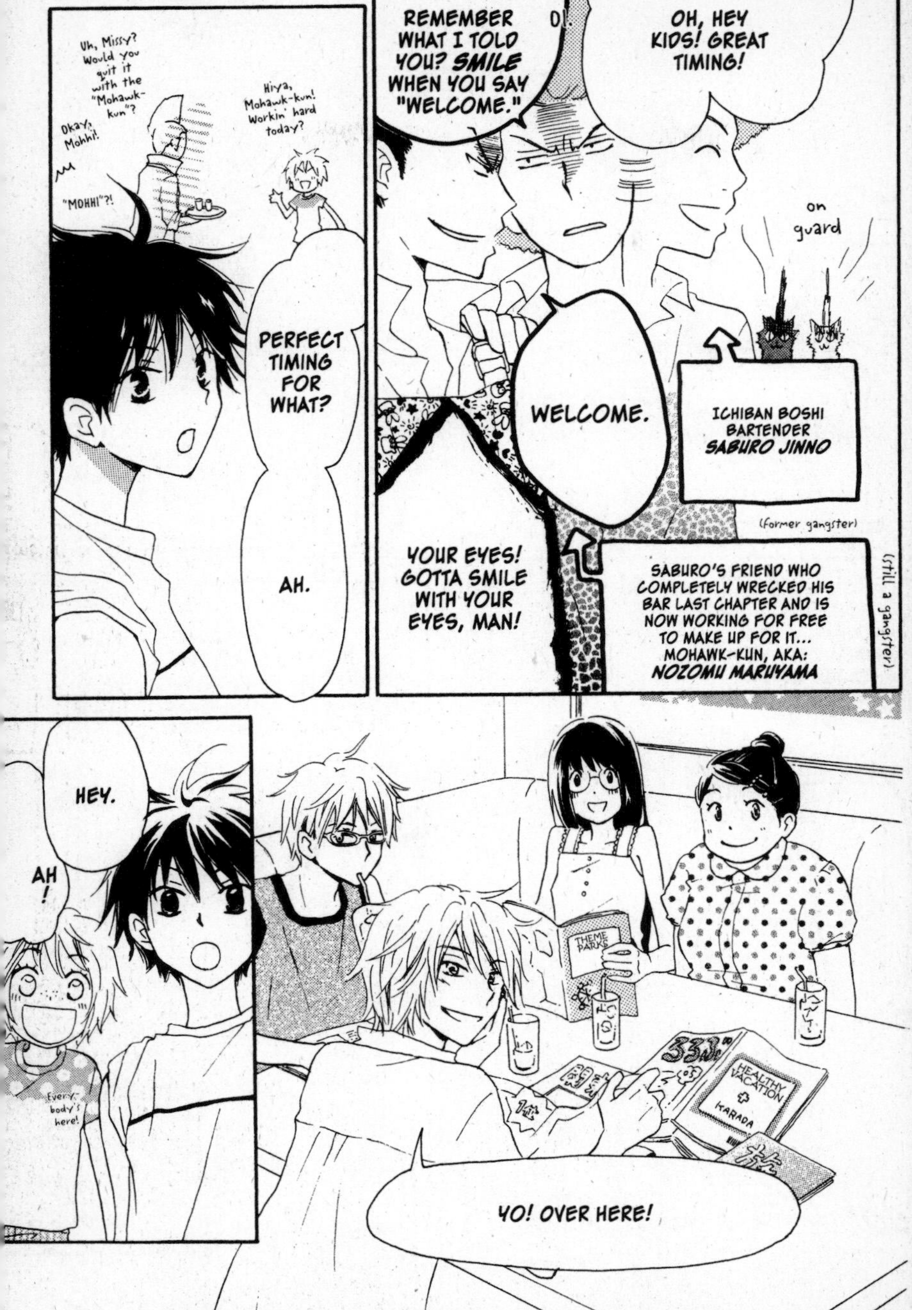
OH, HEY KIDS! GREAT TIMING!
OI.
REMEMBER WHAT I TOLD YOU? SMILE WHEN YOU SAY "WELCOME."
on guard
WELCOME.
ICHIBAN BOSHI BARTENDER SABURO JINNO
(former gangster)
SABURO'S FRIEND WHO COMPLETELY WRECKED HIS BAR LAST CHAPTER AND IS NOW WORKING FOR FREE TO MAKE UP FOR IT... MOHAWK-KUN, AKA: NOZOMU MARUYAMA
(still a gangster)
YOUR EYES! GOTTA SMILE WITH YOUR EYES, MAN!
Hiya, Mohawk-kun! Workin' hard today?
Uh, Missy? Would you quit it with the "Mohawk-kun"?
Okay, Mohhi!
"MOHHI"?!
PERFECT TIMING FOR WHAT?
AH.
YO! OVER HERE!
THEME PARKS
HEALTHY VACATION
KARADA
HEY.
AH!
Every-body's here!

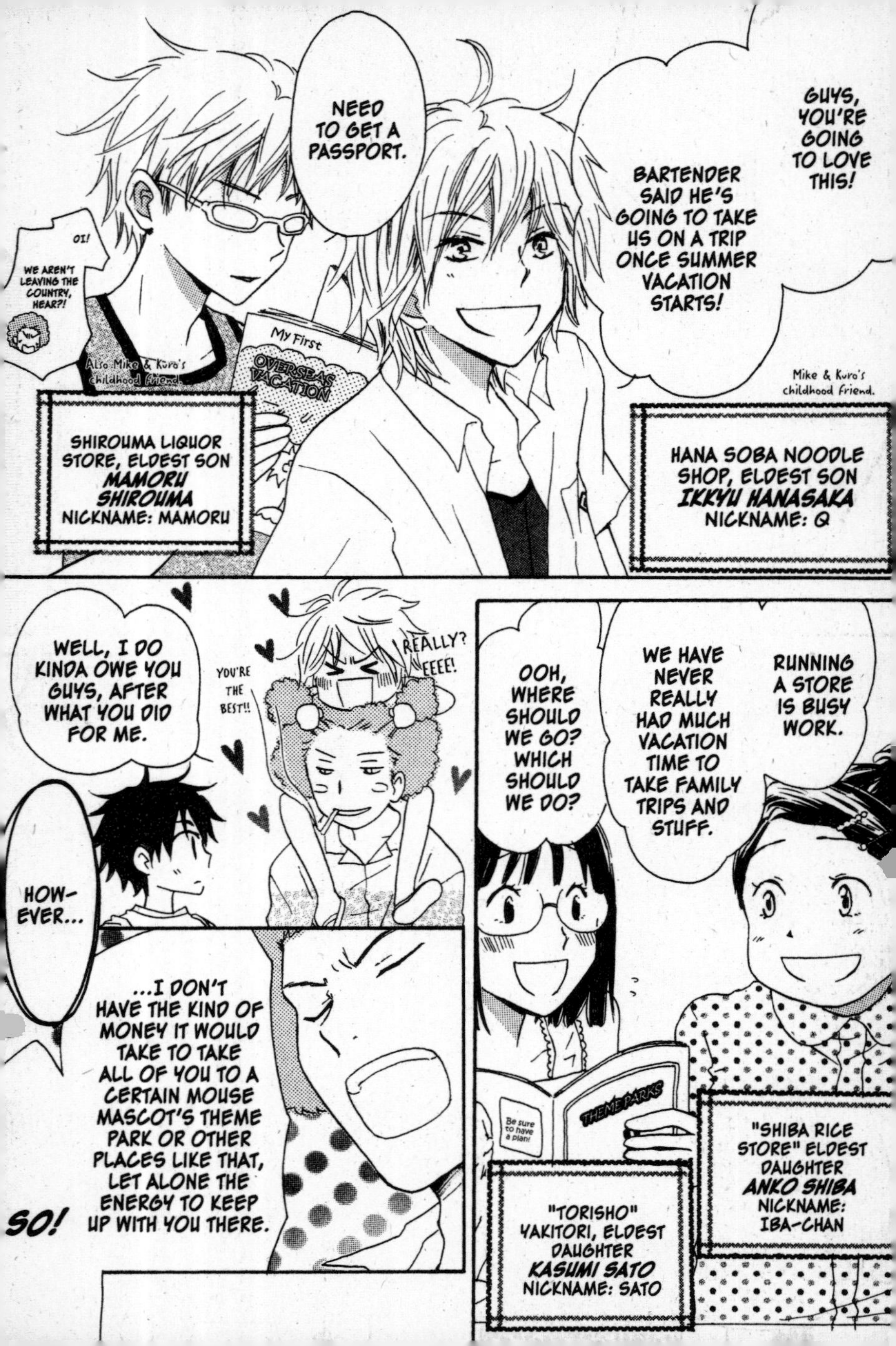
GUYS, YOU'RE GOING TO LOVE THIS!
BARTENDER SAID HE'S GOING TO TAKE US ON A TRIP ONCE SUMMER VACATION STARTS!
Mike & Kuro's childhood friend.
HANA SOBA NOODLE SHOP, ELDEST SON **IKKYU HANASAKA** NICKNAME: Q
NEED TO GET A PASSPORT.
My First OVERSEAS VACATION
SHIROUMA LIQUOR STORE, ELDEST SON **MAMORU SHIROUMA** NICKNAME: MAMORU
Also Mike & Kuro's childhood friend.
OI!
WE AREN'T LEAVING THE COUNTRY, HEAR?!
RUNNING A STORE IS BUSY WORK.
WE HAVE NEVER REALLY HAD MUCH VACATION TIME TO TAKE FAMILY TRIPS AND STUFF.
OOH, WHERE SHOULD WE GO? WHICH SHOULD WE DO?
THEME PARKS
Be sure to have a plan!
"SHIBA RICE STORE" ELDEST DAUGHTER **ANKO SHIBA** NICKNAME: IBA-CHAN
"TORISHO" YAKITORI, ELDEST DAUGHTER **KASUMI SATO** NICKNAME: SATO
REALLY? EEEE!
YOU'RE THE BEST!!
WELL, I DO KINDA OWE YOU GUYS, AFTER WHAT YOU DID FOR ME.
HOW-EVER...
...I DON'T HAVE THE KIND OF MONEY IT WOULD TAKE TO TAKE ALL OF YOU TO A CERTAIN MOUSE MASCOT'S THEME PARK OR OTHER PLACES LIKE THAT, LET ALONE THE ENERGY TO KEEP UP WITH YOU THERE.
SO!

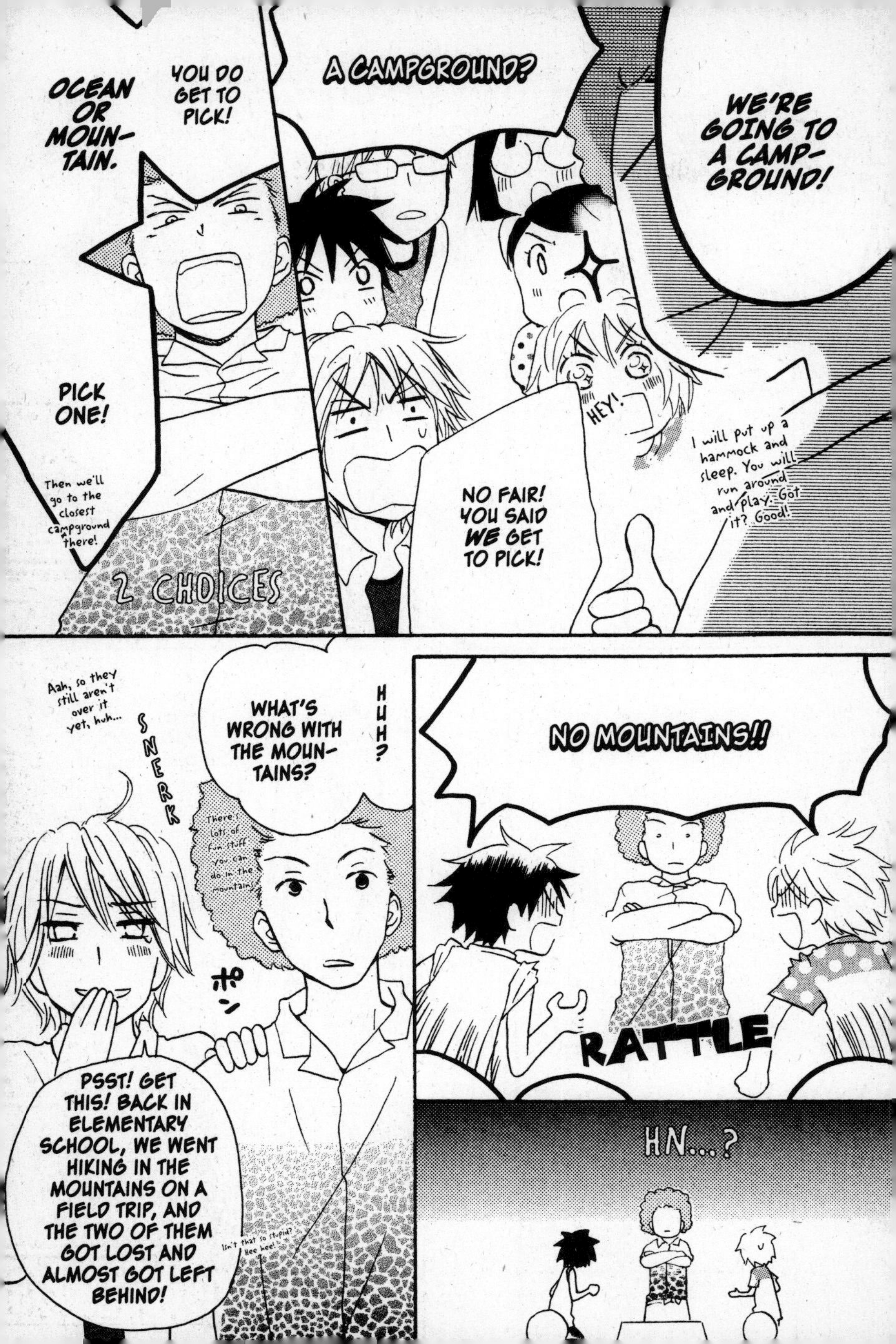
WE'RE GOING TO A CAMP-GROUND!
A CAMPGROUND?
HEY!
I will put up a hammock and sleep. You will run around and play. Got it? Good!
NO FAIR! YOU SAID WE GET TO PICK!
YOU DO GET TO PICK!
OCEAN OR MOUN-TAIN.
PICK ONE!
Then we'll go to the closest campground there!
2 CHOICES
NO MOUNTAINS!!
RATTLE
HN...?
HUH?
WHAT'S WRONG WITH THE MOUN-TAINS?
There's lots of fun stuff you can do in the mountains
Aah, so they still aren't over it yet, huh...
SNERK
ポン
PSST! GET THIS! BACK IN ELEMENTARY SCHOOL, WE WENT HIKING IN THE MOUNTAINS ON A FIELD TRIP, AND THE TWO OF THEM GOT LOST AND ALMOST GOT LEFT BEHIND!
Isn't that so stupid? Hee hee!

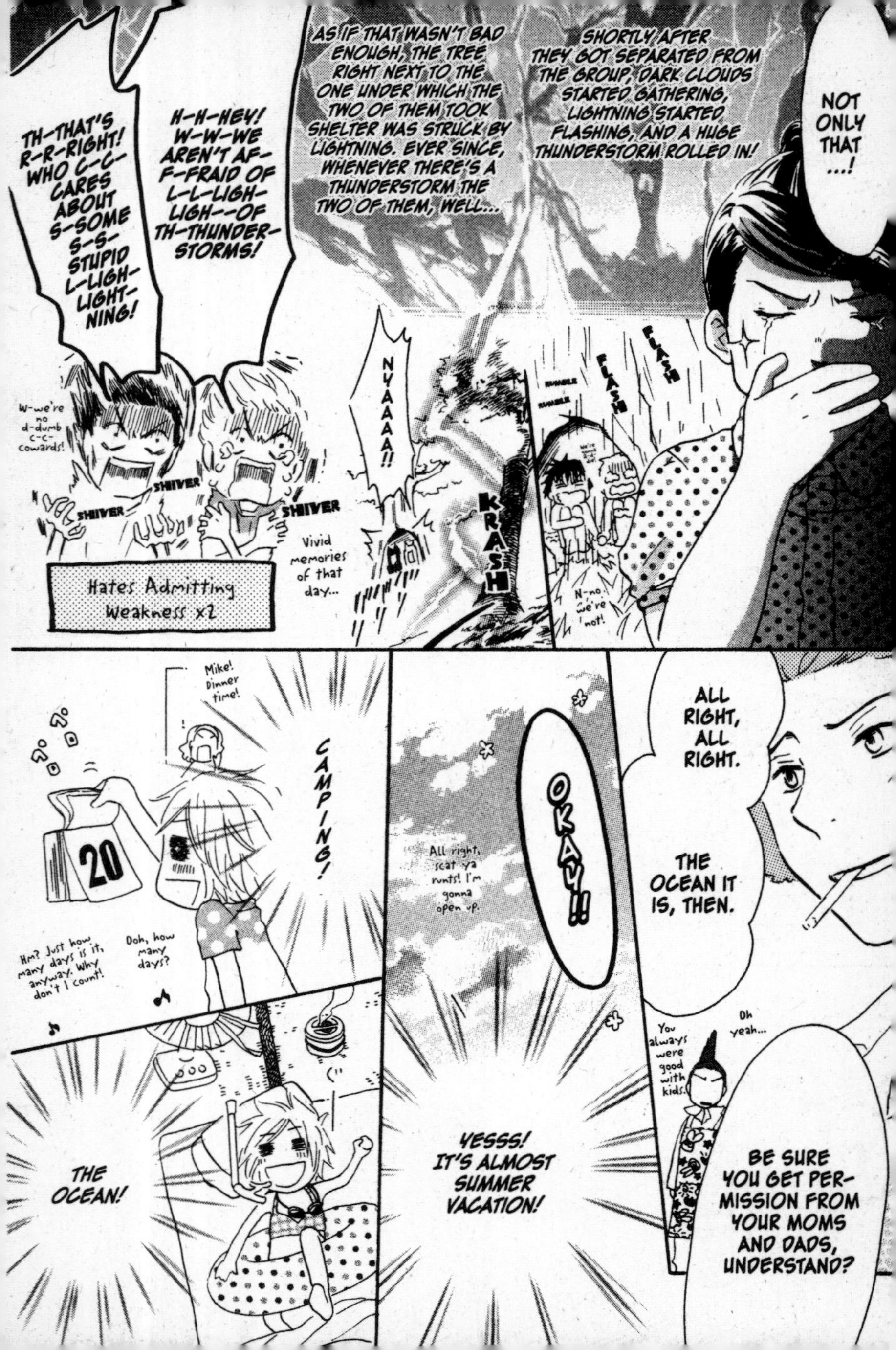
NOT ONLY THAT ...!
SHORTLY AFTER THEY GOT SEPARATED FROM THE GROUP, DARK CLOUDS STARTED GATHERING, LIGHTNING STARTED FLASHING, AND A HUGE THUNDERSTORM ROLLED IN!
AS IF THAT WASN'T BAD ENOUGH, THE TREE RIGHT NEXT TO THE ONE UNDER WHICH THE TWO OF THEM TOOK SHELTER WAS STRUCK BY LIGHTNING. EVER SINCE, WHENEVER THERE'S A THUNDERSTORM THE TWO OF THEM, WELL...
FLASH
FLASH
RUMBLE
RUMBLE
N-no we're not!
KRASH
NYAAAAA!!
Vivid memories of that day...
H-H-HEY! W-W-WE AREN'T AF-F-FRAID OF L-L-LIGH-LIGH-LIGH--OF TH-THUNDER-STORMS!
TH-THAT'S R-R-RIGHT! WHO C-C-CARES ABOUT S-SOME S-S-STUPID L-LIGH-LIGHT-NING!
W-we're no d-dumb c-c-cowards!
SHIVER
SHIVER
SHIVER
Hates Admitting Weakness x2
ALL RIGHT, ALL RIGHT.
THE OCEAN IT IS, THEN.
Oh yeah...
You always were good with kids.
BE SURE YOU GET PER-MISSION FROM YOUR MOMS AND DADS, UNDERSTAND?
OKAY!!
All right, scat ya runts! I'm gonna open up.
YESSS! IT'S ALMOST SUMMER VACATION!
Mike! Dinner time!
CAMPING!
Ooh, how many days?
Hm? Just how many days is it, anyway. Why don't I count!
20
THE OCEAN!

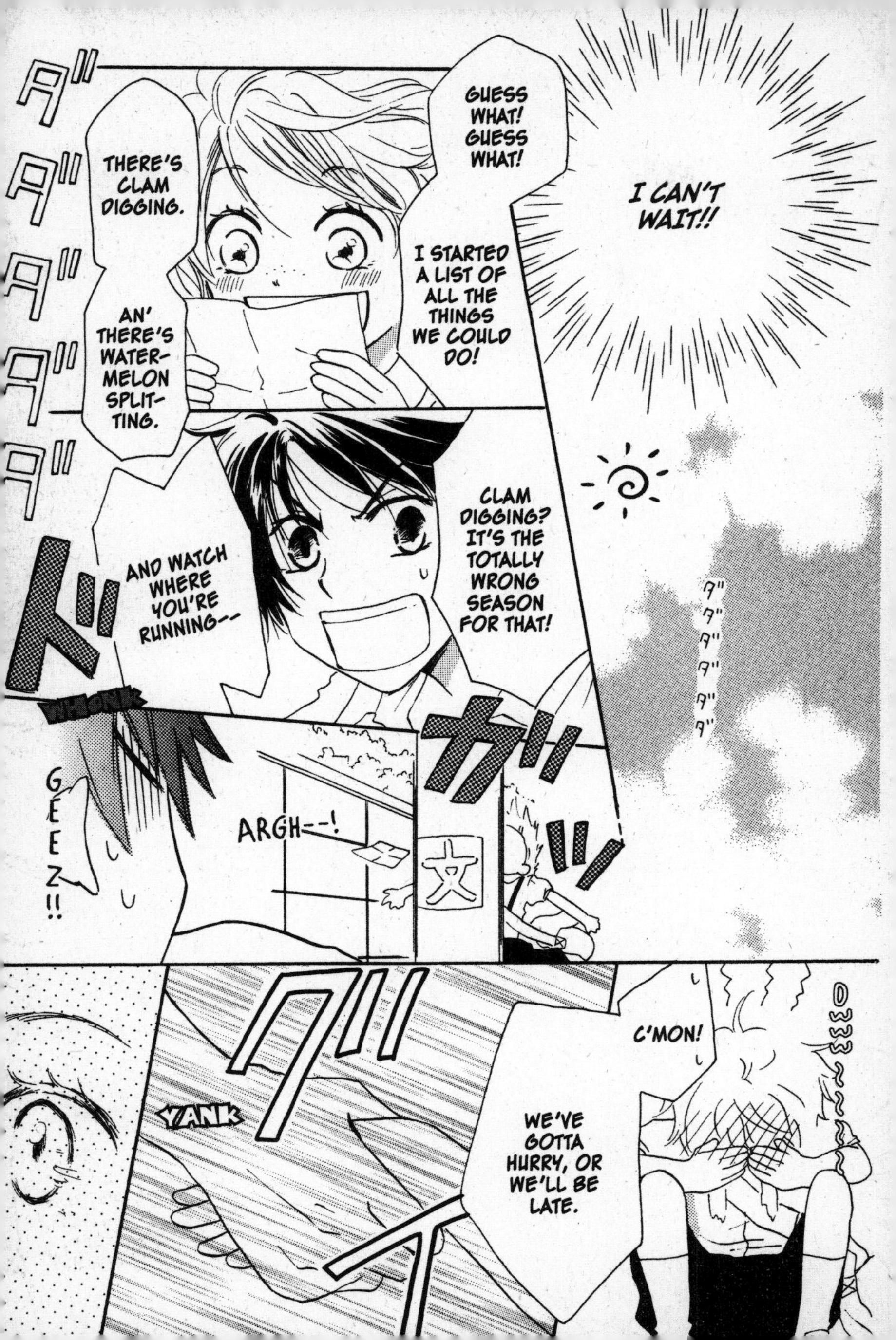
I CAN'T WAIT!!
ダ" ダ" ダ" ダ" ダ" ダ"
GUESS WHAT! GUESS WHAT!
I STARTED A LIST OF ALL THE THINGS WE COULD DO!
THERE'S CLAM DIGGING.
AN' THERE'S WATER-MELON SPLIT-TING.
ダダダダダ
CLAM DIGGING? IT'S THE TOTALLY WRONG SEASON FOR THAT!
AND WATCH WHERE YOU'RE RUNNING--
ド
ガッ
ARGH--!
WHONK
GEEZ!!
OWWW~~~
C'MON!
WE'VE GOTTA HURRY, OR WE'LL BE LATE.
グイ
YANK

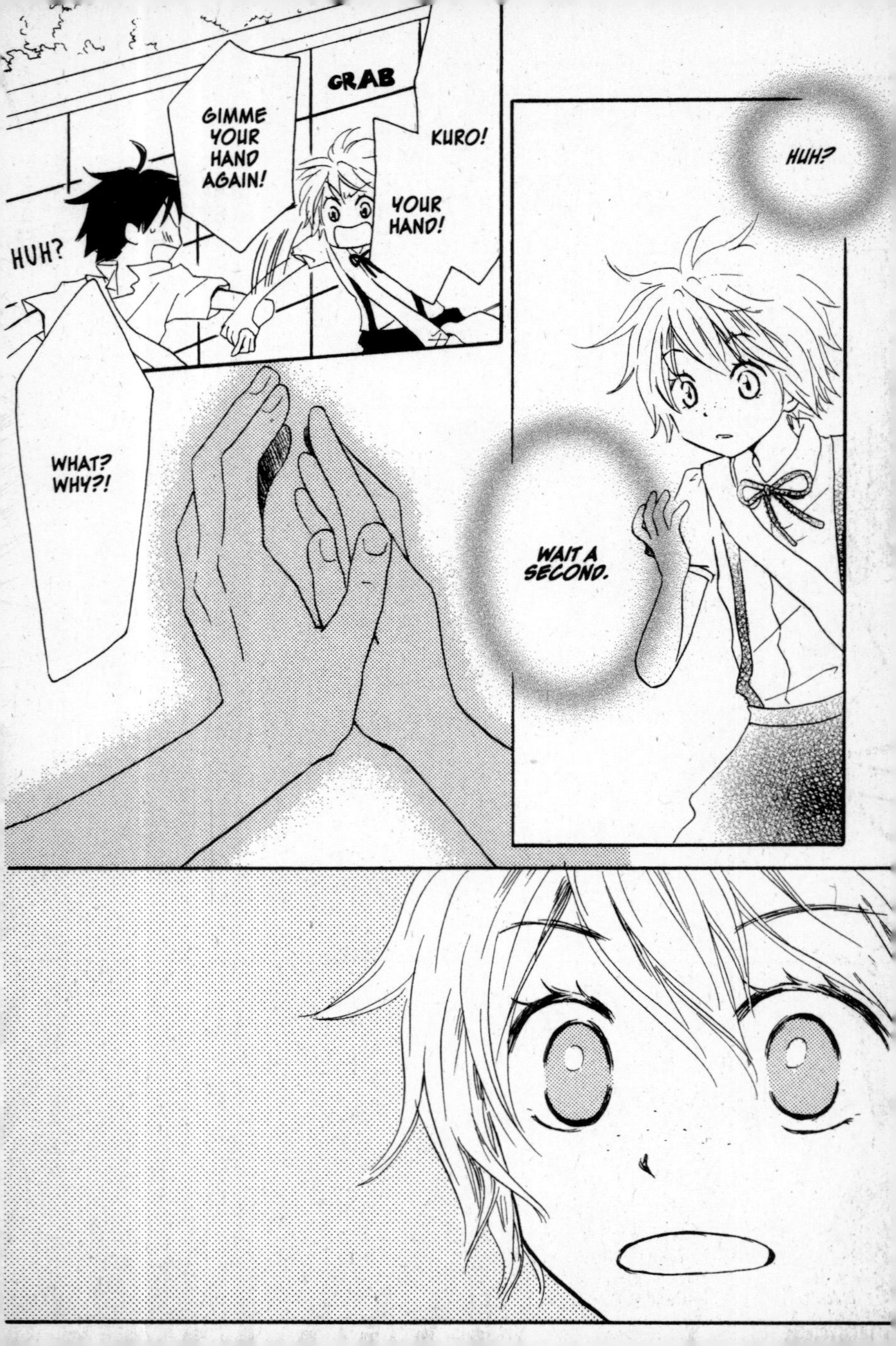
HUH?
WAIT A SECOND.
KURO!
GRAB
GIMME YOUR HAND AGAIN!
YOUR HAND!
HUH?
WHAT? WHY?!

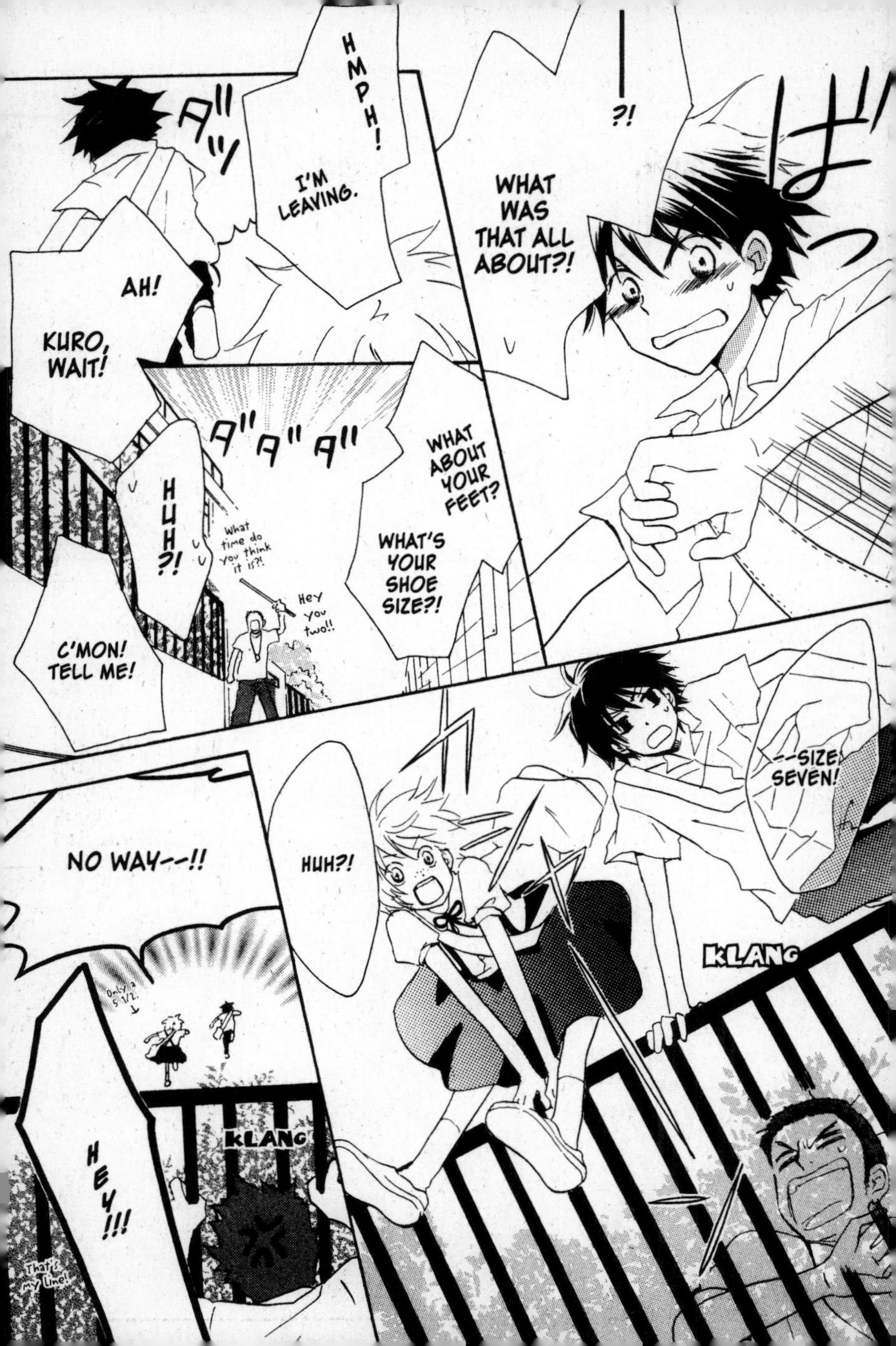
ぱっ
—?!
WHAT WAS THAT ALL ABOUT?!
HMPH!
I'M LEAVING.
ダッ
AH!
KURO, WAIT!
WHAT ABOUT YOUR FEET?
WHAT'S YOUR SHOE SIZE?!
ダダダ
Hey you two!!
What time do you think it is?!
HUH?!
C'MON! TELL ME!
--SIZE SEVEN!
KLANG
HUH?!
NO WAY--!!
Only a 5 1/2.
KLANG
HEY!!!
That's my line!

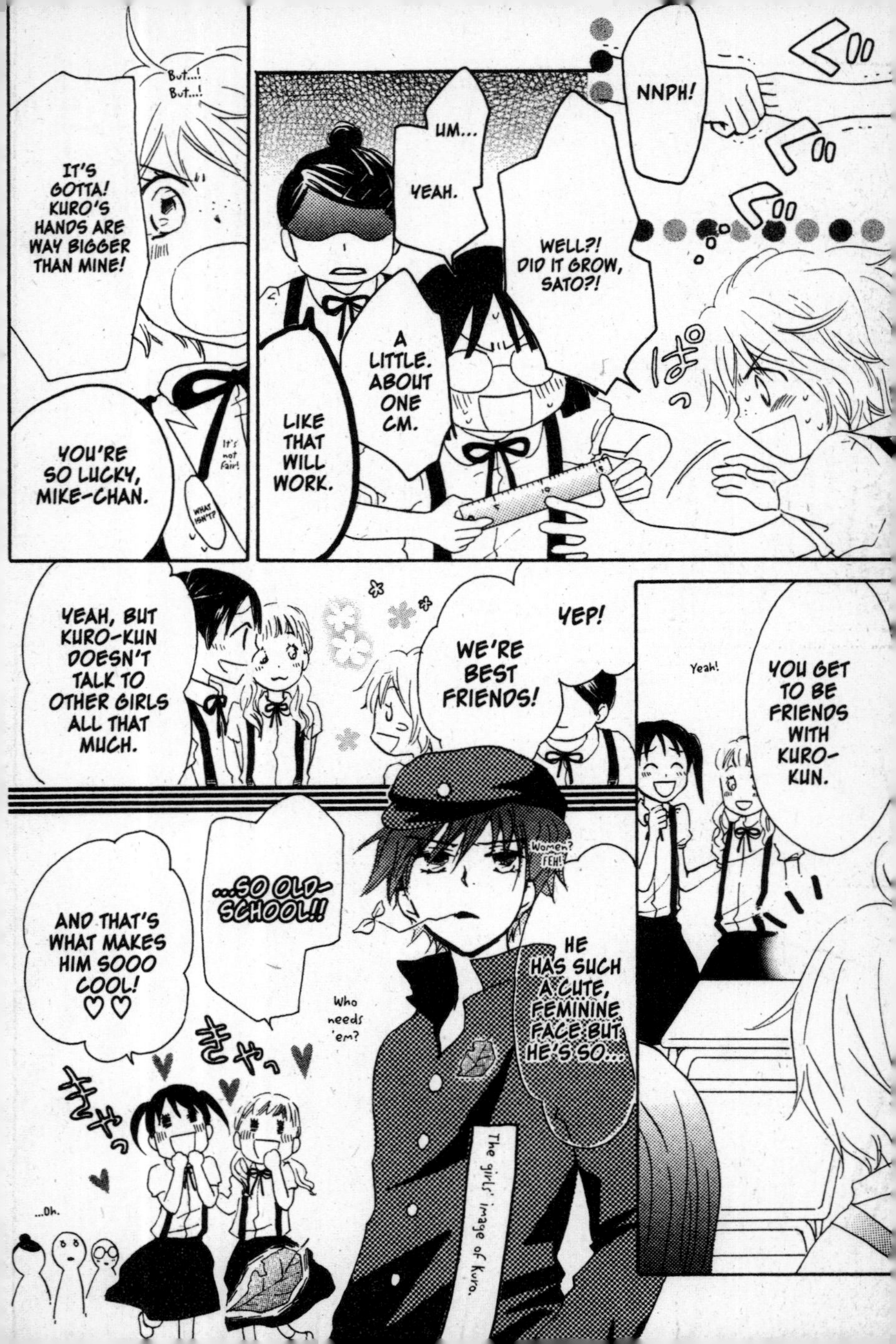

NNPH!
くっ
くっ
くっ
WELL?! DID IT GROW, SATO?!
ぱっ
UM...
YEAH.
A LITTLE. ABOUT ONE CM.
LIKE THAT WILL WORK.
But...! But...!
IT'S GOTTA! KURO'S HANDS ARE WAY BIGGER THAN MINE!
YOU'RE SO LUCKY, MIKE-CHAN.
It's not fair!
WHAT ISN'T?
YOU GET TO BE FRIENDS WITH KURO-KUN.
Yeah!
YEP!
WE'RE BEST FRIENDS!
YEAH, BUT KURO-KUN DOESN'T TALK TO OTHER GIRLS ALL THAT MUCH.
HE HAS SUCH A CUTE, FEMININE FACE BUT HE'S SO...
...SO OLD-SCHOOL!!
Women? FEH!
Who needs 'em?
The girls' image of Kuro.
AND THAT'S WHAT MAKES HIM SOOO COOL! ♡♡
きゃっ
きゃっ
...Oh.

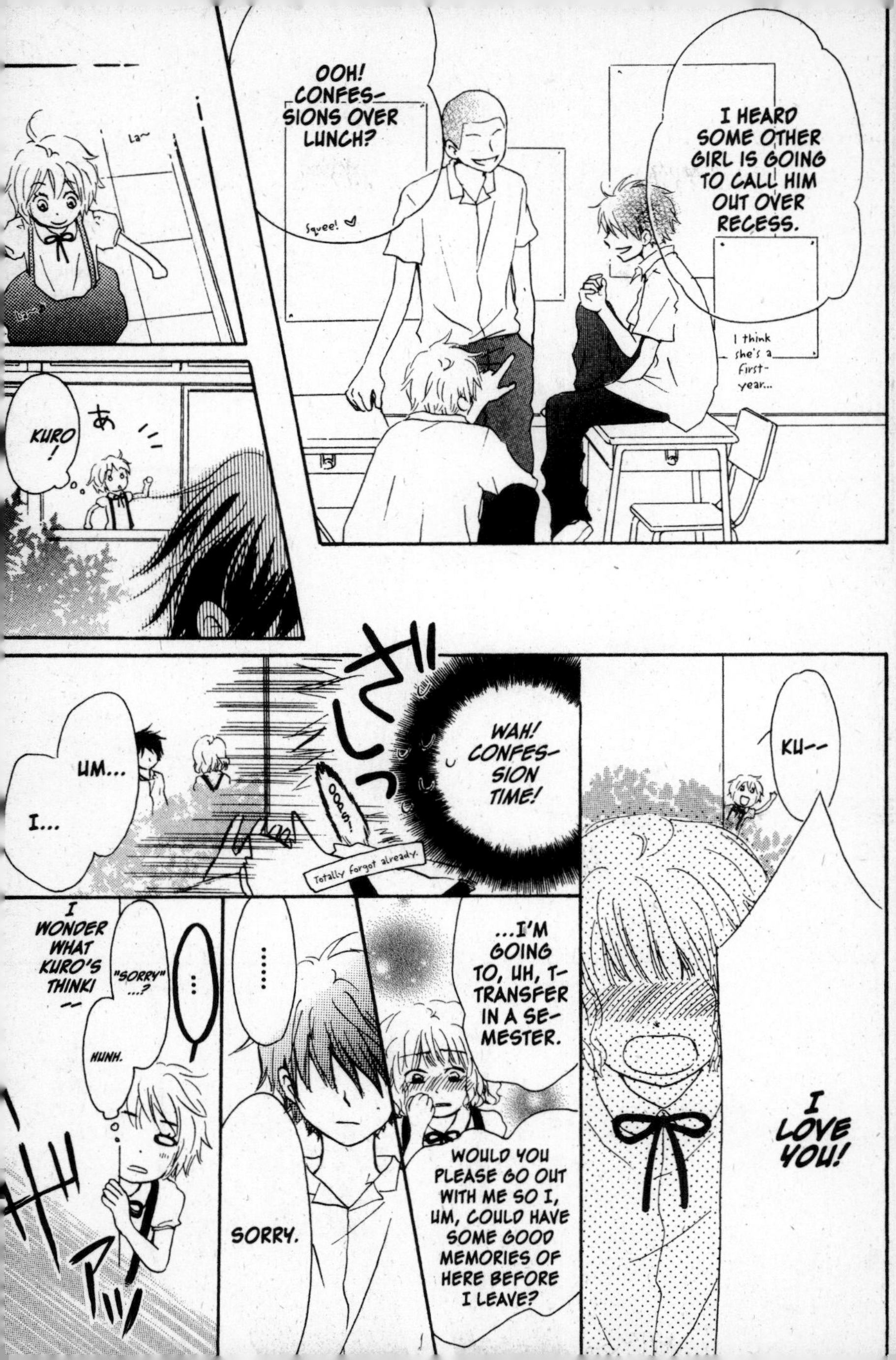

I HEARD SOME OTHER GIRL IS GOING TO CALL HIM OUT OVER RECESS.
I think she's a first-year...
OOH! CONFESSIONS OVER LUNCH?
Squee!
La~
La~
KURO!
あ
KU--
I LOVE YOU!
WAH! CONFESSION TIME!
OOPS!
Totally forgot already.
UM...
I...
...I'M GOING TO, UH, T-TRANSFER IN A SEMESTER.
WOULD YOU PLEASE GO OUT WITH ME SO I, UM, COULD HAVE SOME GOOD MEMORIES OF HERE BEFORE I LEAVE?
......
SORRY.
...
I WONDER WHAT KURO'S THINKI--
"SORRY" ...?
HUNH.

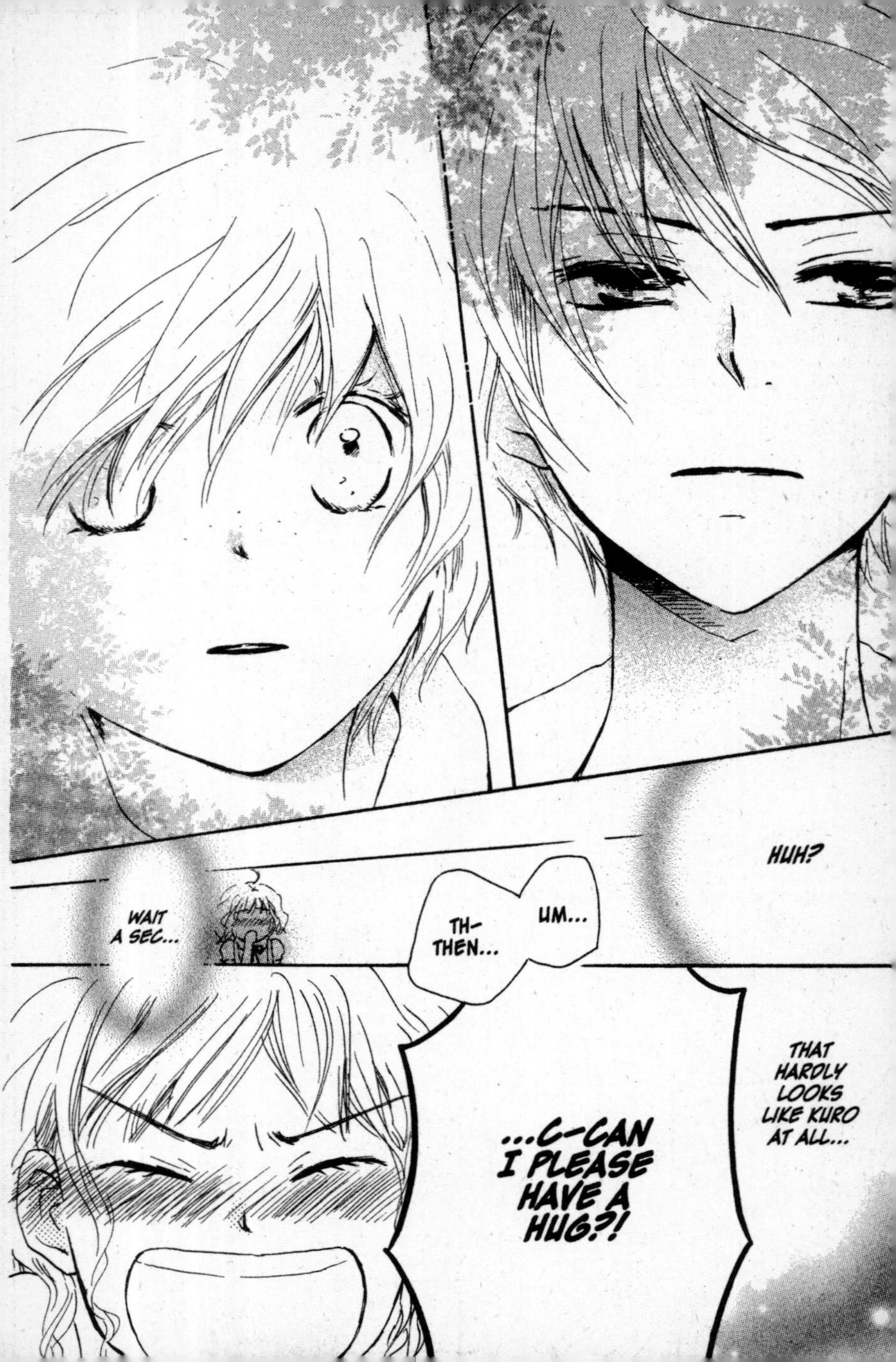
HUH?
UM...
TH- THEN...
WAIT A SEC...
THAT HARDLY LOOKS LIKE KURO AT ALL...
...C-CAN I PLEASE HAVE A HUG?!

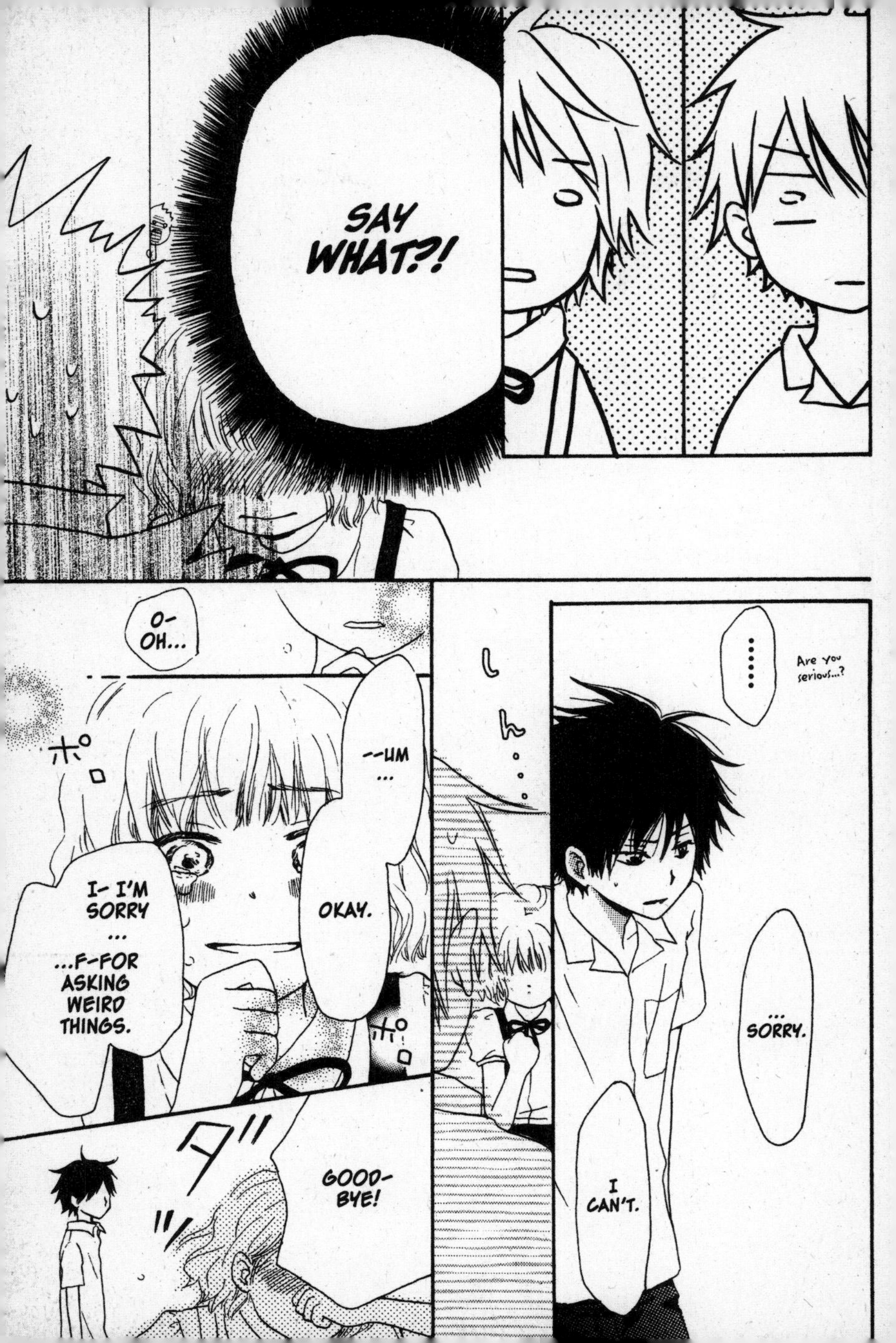
SAY WHAT?!
......
Are you serious...?
...SORRY.
I CAN'T.
しん...
O-OH...
--UM ...
OKAY.
ポロ
I- I'M SORRY ... ...F-FOR ASKING WEIRD THINGS.
ポロ
ダッ
GOOD-BYE!

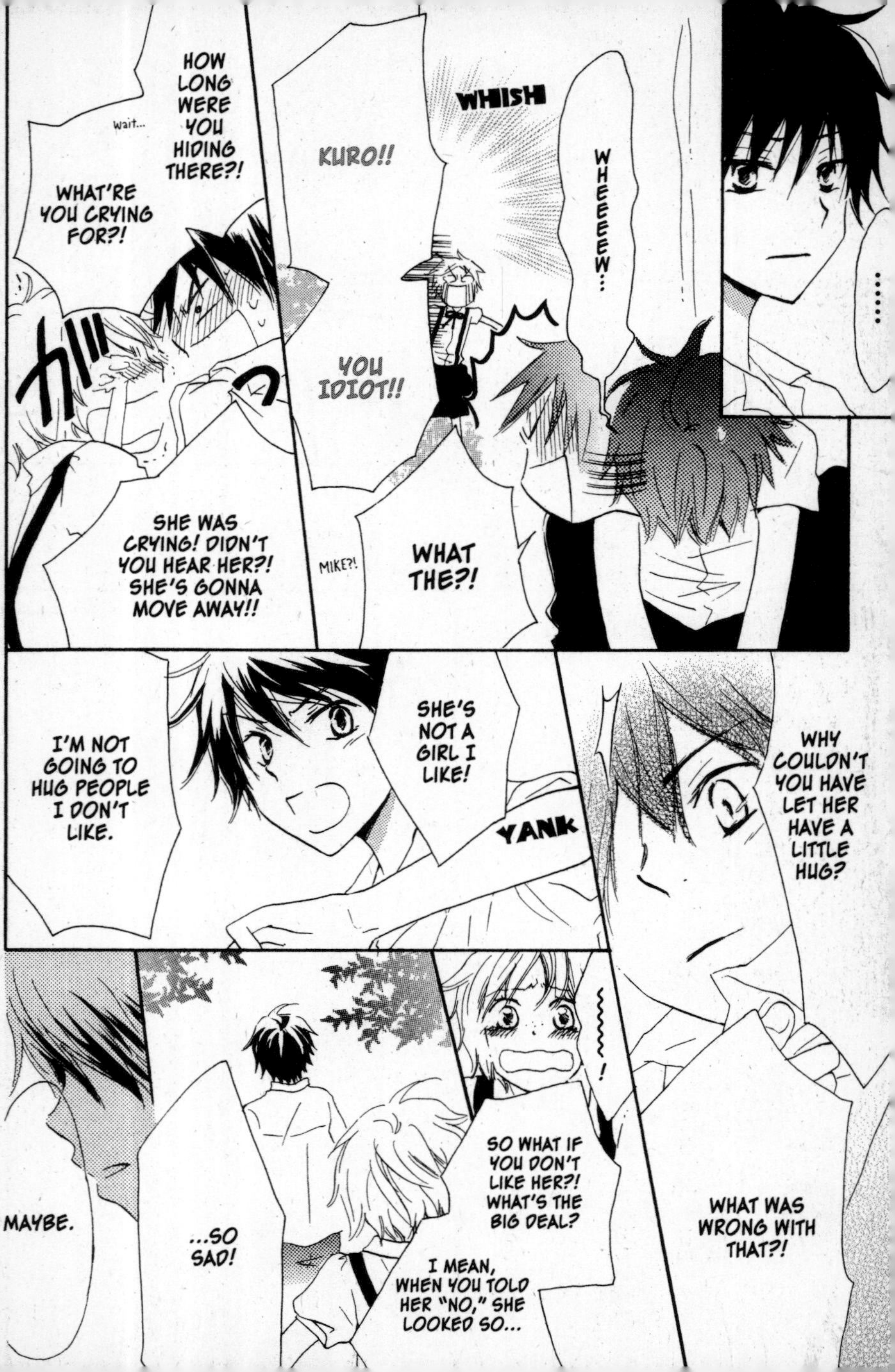
......
WHEEEEW...
WHISH
KURO!!
YOU IDIOT!!
WHAT THE?!
MIKE?!
HOW LONG WERE YOU HIDING THERE?!
wait...
WHAT'RE YOU CRYING FOR?!
SHE WAS CRYING! DIDN'T YOU HEAR HER?! SHE'S GONNA MOVE AWAY!!
WHY COULDN'T YOU HAVE LET HER HAVE A LITTLE HUG?
YANK
SHE'S NOT A GIRL I LIKE!
I'M NOT GOING TO HUG PEOPLE I DON'T LIKE.
WHAT WAS WRONG WITH THAT?!
~~~!
SO WHAT IF YOU DON'T LIKE HER?! WHAT'S THE BIG DEAL?
I MEAN, WHEN YOU TOLD HER "NO," SHE LOOKED SO...
...SO SAD!
MAYBE.
~~~

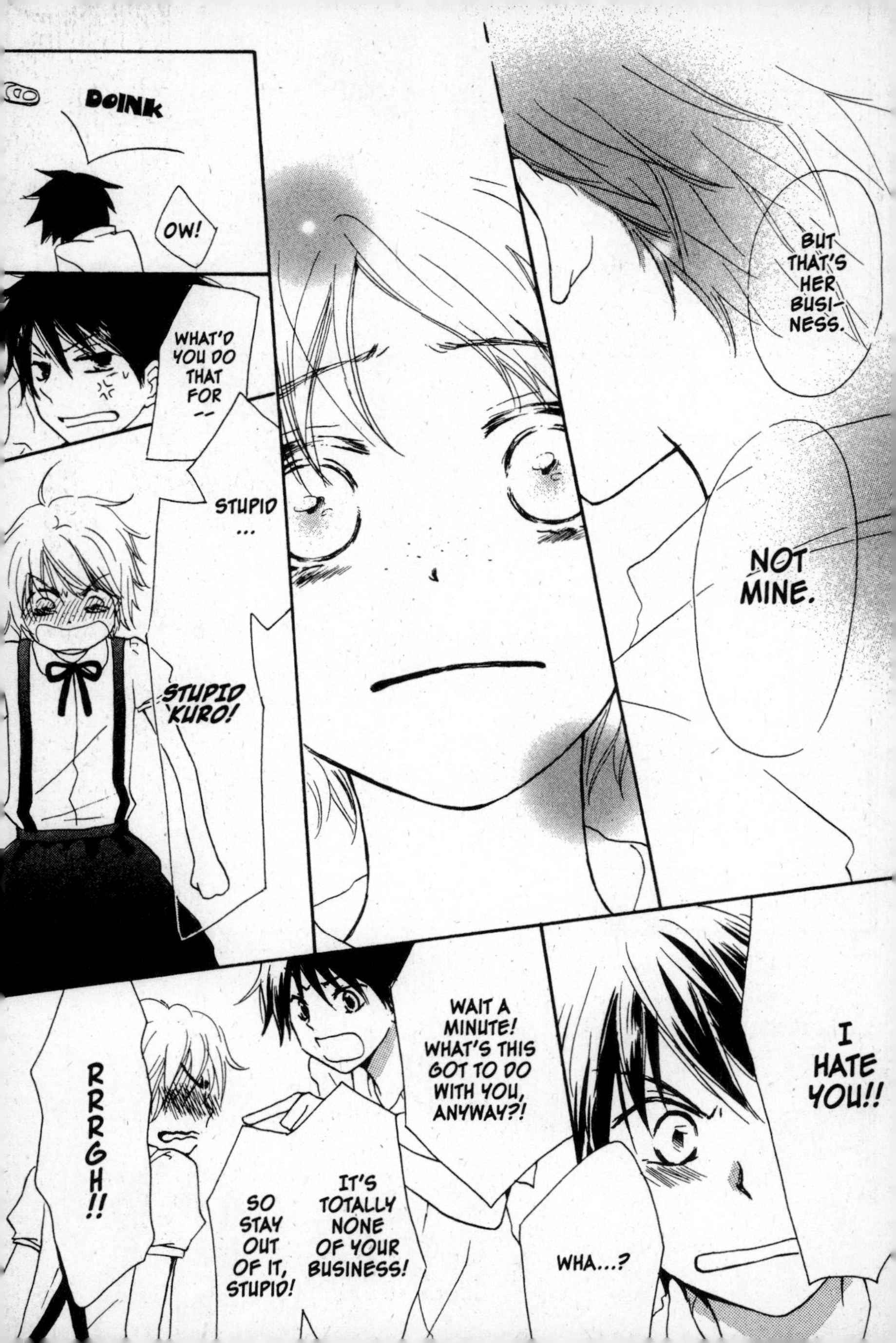

BUT THAT'S HER BUSI-NESS.
NOT MINE.
DOINK
OW!
WHAT'D YOU DO THAT FOR --
STUPID ...
STUPID KURO!
I HATE YOU!!
WHA...?
WAIT A MINUTE! WHAT'S THIS GOT TO DO WITH YOU, ANYWAY?!
IT'S TOTALLY NONE OF YOUR BUSINESS!
SO STAY OUT OF IT, STUPID!
RRRGH!!

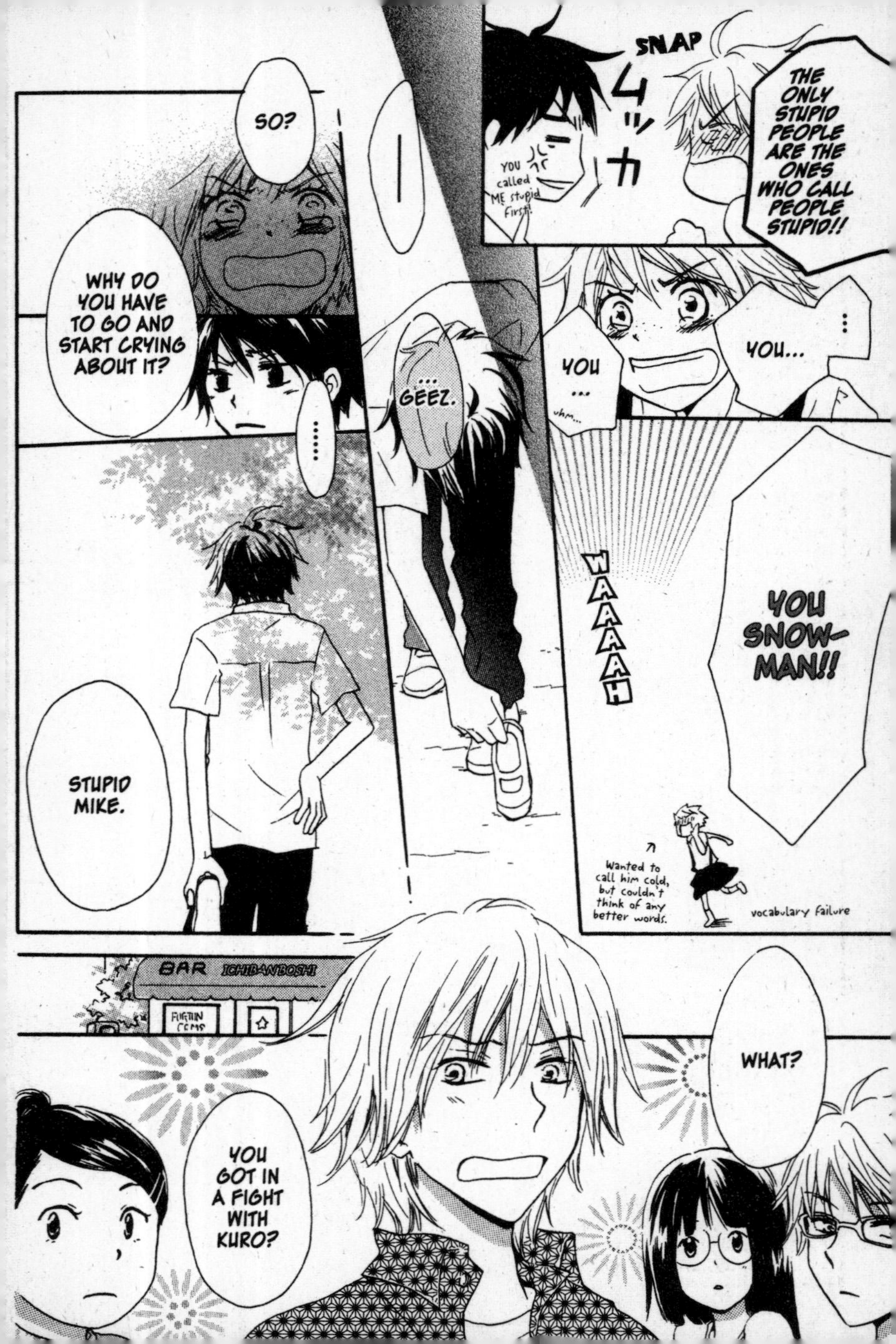

SNAP
ムッカ
THE ONLY STUPID PEOPLE ARE THE ONES WHO CALL PEOPLE STUPID!!
YOU called ME stupid first!
...
YOU...
YOU ...
uhm...
YOU SNOW-MAN!!
WAAAAAH
Wanted to call him cold, but couldn't think of any better words.
vocabulary failure
... GEEZ.
......
SO?
WHY DO YOU HAVE TO GO AND START CRYING ABOUT IT?
STUPID MIKE.
BAR ICHIBANBOSHI
WHAT?
YOU GOT IN A FIGHT WITH KURO?

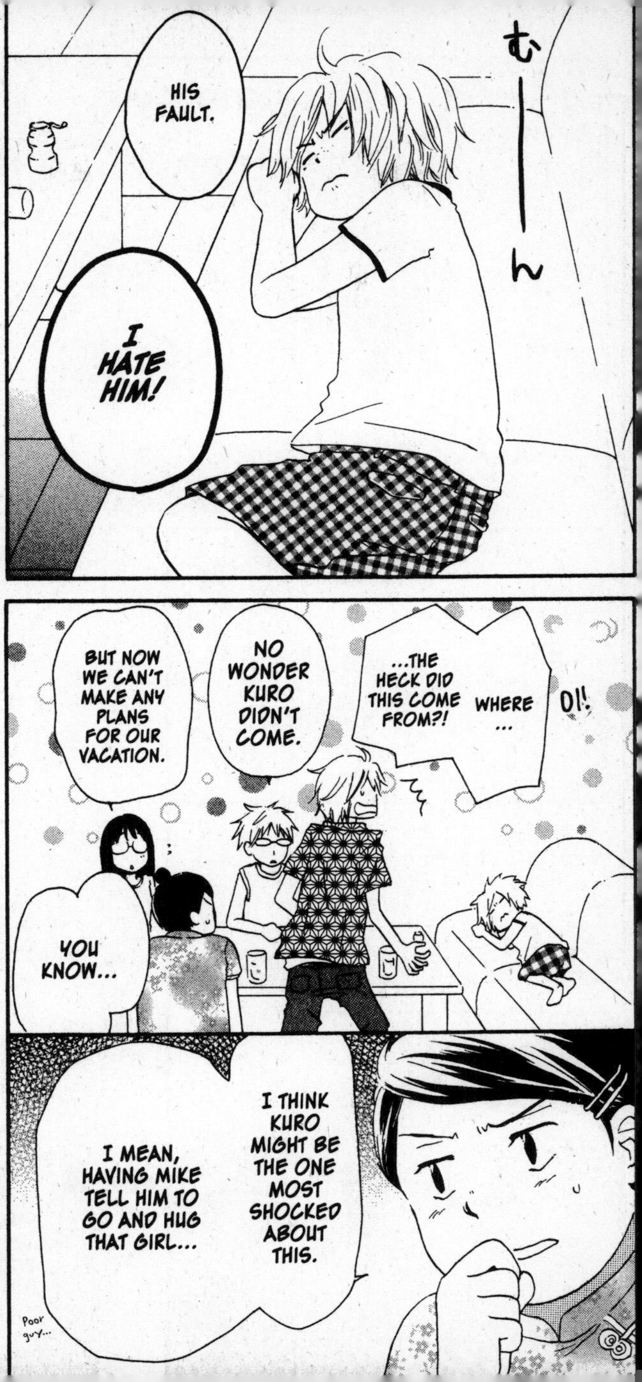
むーん
HIS FAULT.
I HATE HIM!
OI!
WHERE ...
...THE HECK DID THIS COME FROM?!
NO WONDER KURO DIDN'T COME.
BUT NOW WE CAN'T MAKE ANY PLANS FOR OUR VACATION.
YOU KNOW...
I THINK KURO MIGHT BE THE ONE MOST SHOCKED ABOUT THIS.
I MEAN, HAVING MIKE TELL HIM TO GO AND HUG THAT GIRL...
Poor guy...

3

I'm drawing a lot of inspiration for the Gingacho Street Market from my own childhood. When I was little, I lived near a street market a lot like it. Many of the kids in my elementary school lived there. They all had their homes on that one narrow street, and everybody always said "Oh, there's the rice shop's girl" or "He's the grocery store's kid." I don't know why, but I was strangely jealous of that. Of course, I didn't actually realize this until I had already come up with the base concepts for this story.

The summer Obon festival of the Dead was always huge where I grew up, too. Maybe because they handed out ice cream to all the kids at 9pm. Friends and I went after that ice cream all the way up through high school. We got it, too.

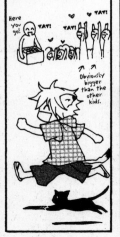

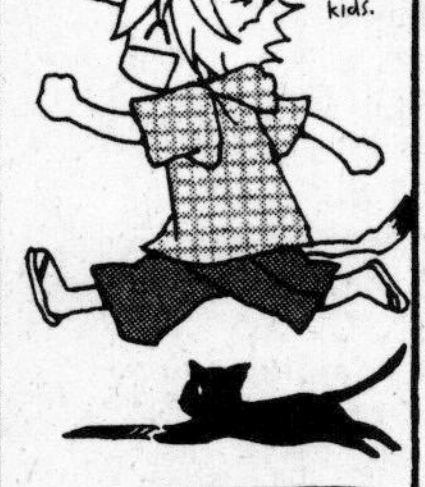
Here you go!
YAY!
YAY!
YAY!
Obviously bigger than the other kids.

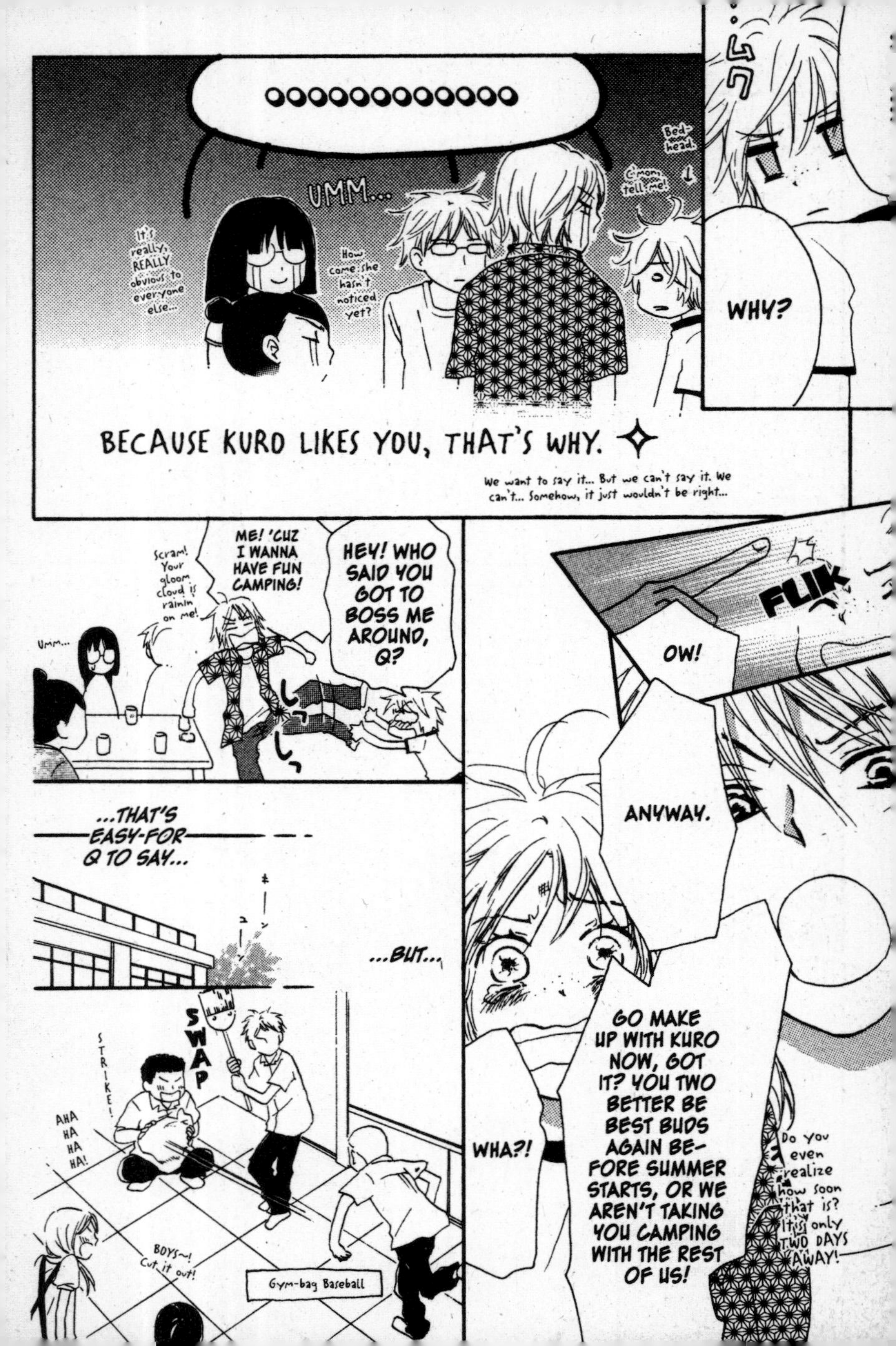

WHY?
OOOOOOOOOOOOO
Bed-head.
C'mon, tell me!
UMM...
How come she hasn't noticed yet?
It's really, REALLY obvious to everyone else...
BECAUSE KURO LIKES YOU, THAT'S WHY.
We want to say it... But we can't say it. We can't... Somehow, it just wouldn't be right...
FLIK
OW!
ANYWAY.
GO MAKE UP WITH KURO NOW, GOT IT? YOU TWO BETTER BE BEST BUDS AGAIN BE-FORE SUMMER STARTS, OR WE AREN'T TAKING YOU CAMPING WITH THE REST OF US!
Do you even realize how soon that is? It's only TWO DAYS AWAY!
WHA?!
HEY! WHO SAID YOU GOT TO BOSS ME AROUND, Q?
ME! 'CUZ I WANNA HAVE FUN CAMPING!
Scram! Your gloom cloud is rainin on me!
Umm...
...THAT'S EASY FOR Q TO SAY...
...BUT...
SWAP
STRIKE!
AHA HA HA HA!
BOYS~! Cut it out!
Gym-bag Baseball

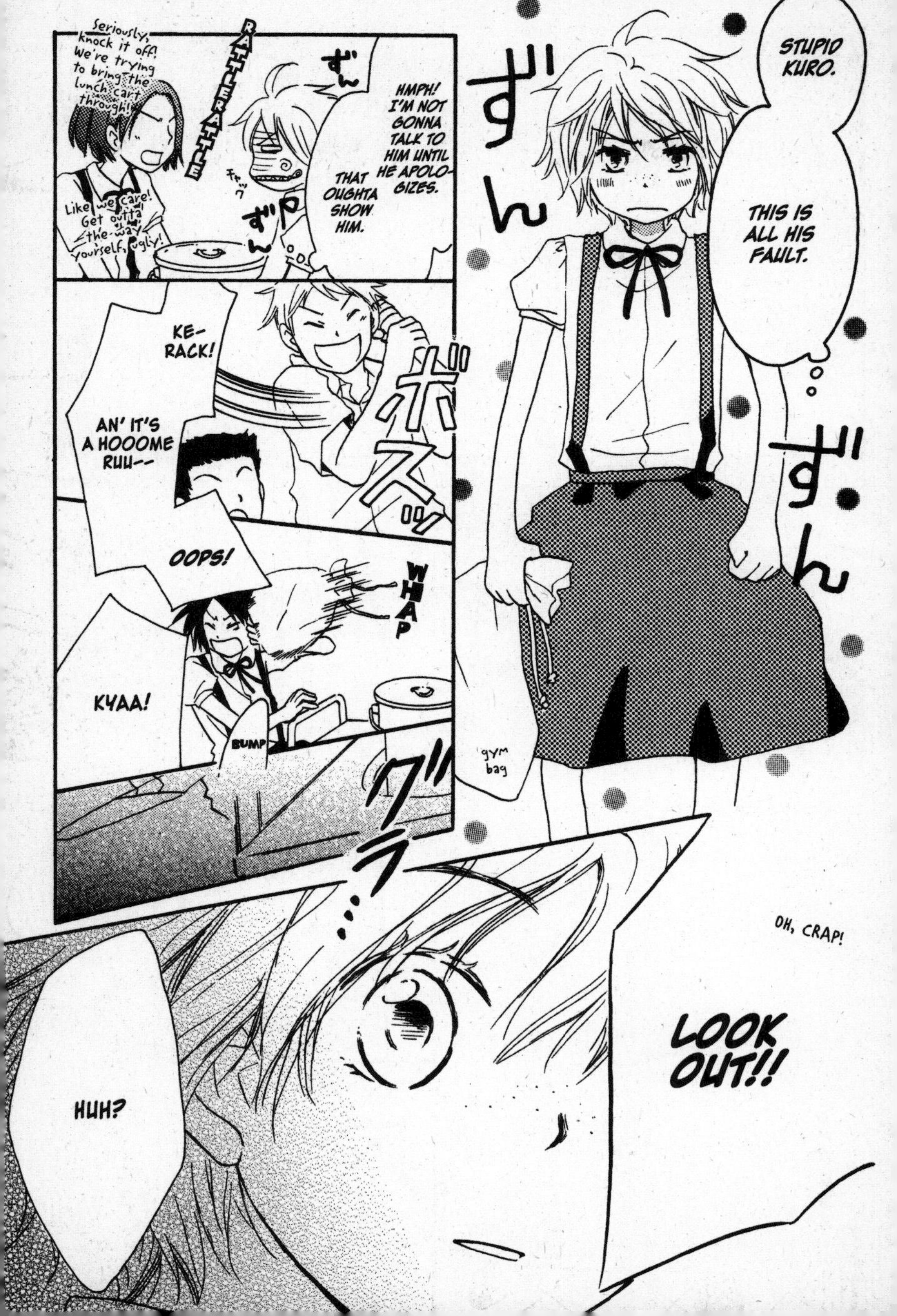
STUPID KURO.
THIS IS ALL HIS FAULT.
ずん
ずん
gym bag
HMPH! I'M NOT GONNA TALK TO HIM UNTIL HE APOLOGIZES.
THAT OUGHTA SHOW HIM.
ずん
RATTLERATTLE
Seriously, knock it off! We're trying to bring the lunch cart through!!
Like we care! Get outta the way yourself, ugly!
ずん
KE-RACK!
AN' IT'S A HOOOME RUU--
ボス
OOPS!
WHAP
KYAA!
BUMP
グラ…
OH, CRAP!
LOOK OUT!!
HUH?

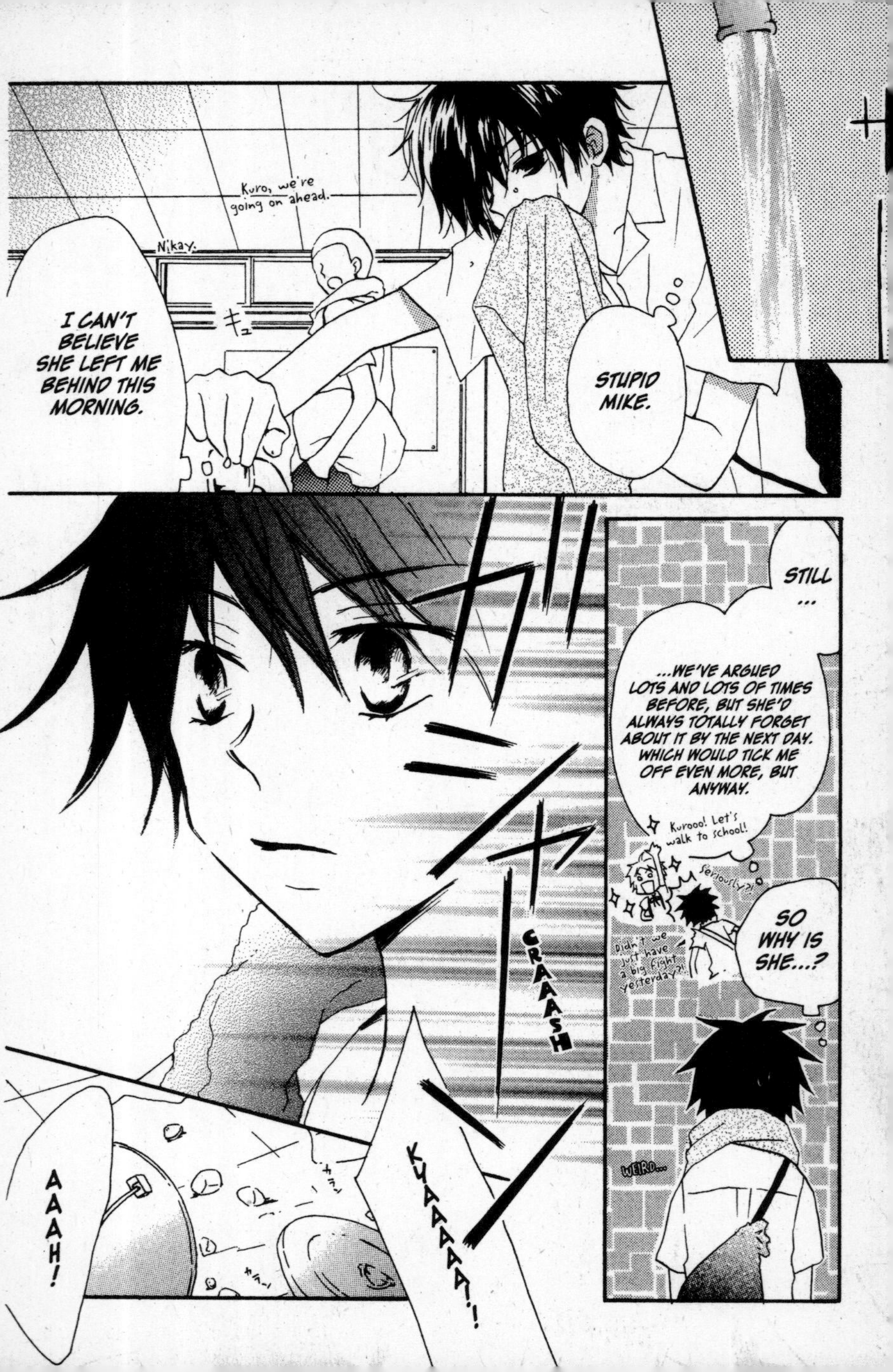
Kuro, we're going on ahead.
Nikay.
キュ
STUPID MIKE.
I CAN'T BELIEVE SHE LEFT ME BEHIND THIS MORNING.
STILL...
...WE'VE ARGUED LOTS AND LOTS OF TIMES BEFORE, BUT SHE'D ALWAYS TOTALLY FORGET ABOUT IT BY THE NEXT DAY. WHICH WOULD TICK ME OFF EVEN MORE, BUT ANYWAY.
Kurooo! Let's walk to school!
Seriously?!
Didn't we just have a big fight yesterday?!
SO WHY IS SHE...?
WEIRD...
CRAAASH
KYAAAAA!!
AAAAH!

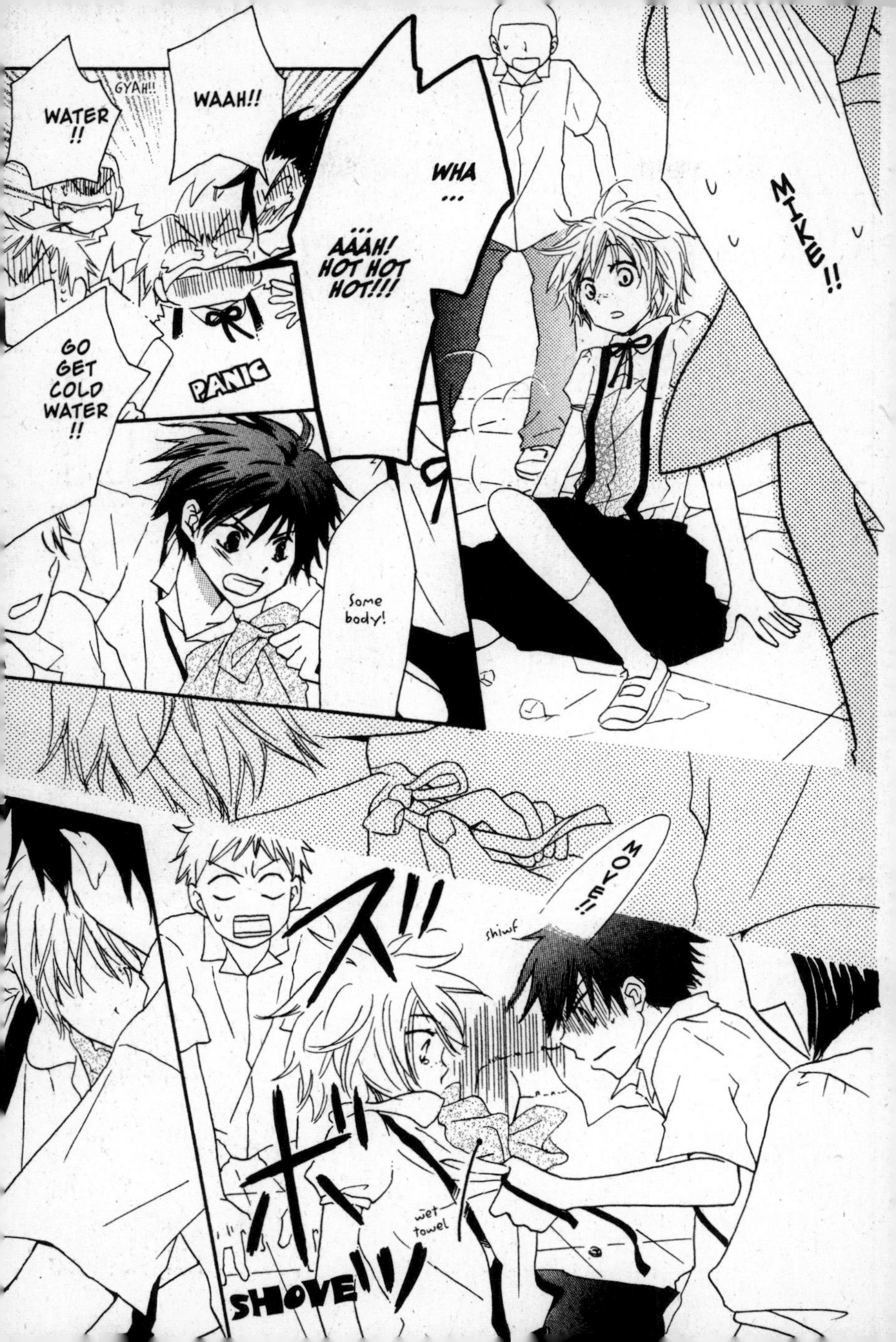
MIKE!!
WHA...
...AAAH! HOT HOT HOT!!!
WAAH!!
GYAH!!
WATER!!
PANIC
GO GET COLD WATER!!
Some body!
MOVE!!
wet towel
SHOVE

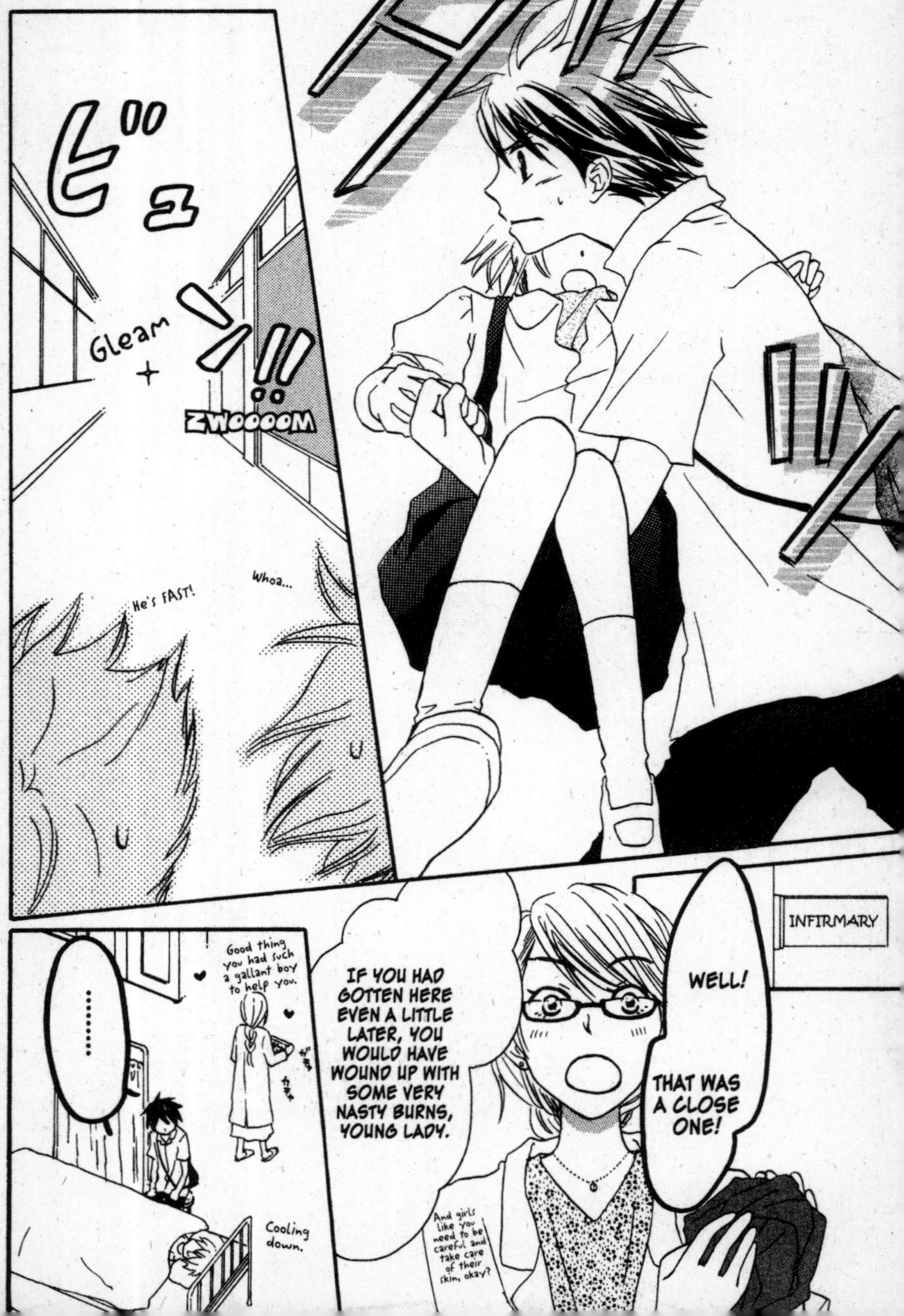

Gleam
ZWOOOOM
Whoa...
He's FAST!
INFIRMARY
WELL!
THAT WAS A CLOSE ONE!
IF YOU HAD GOTTEN HERE EVEN A LITTLE LATER, YOU WOULD HAVE WOUND UP WITH SOME VERY NASTY BURNS, YOUNG LADY.
And girls like you need to be careful and take care of their skin, okay?
....
Good thing you had such a gallant boy to help you.
Cooling down.

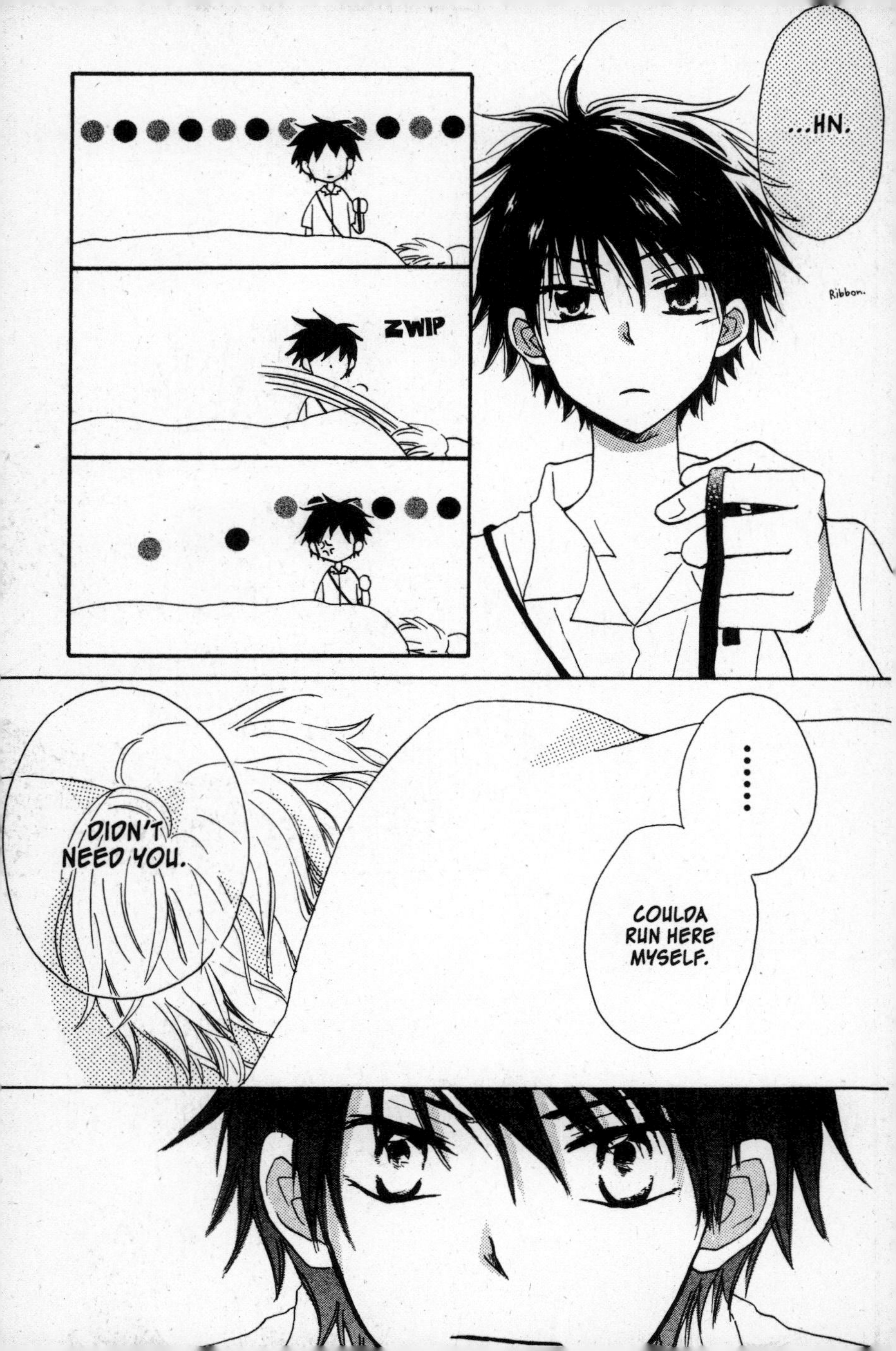
...HN.
Ribbon.
ZWIP
......
COULDA RUN HERE MYSELF.
DIDN'T NEED YOU.

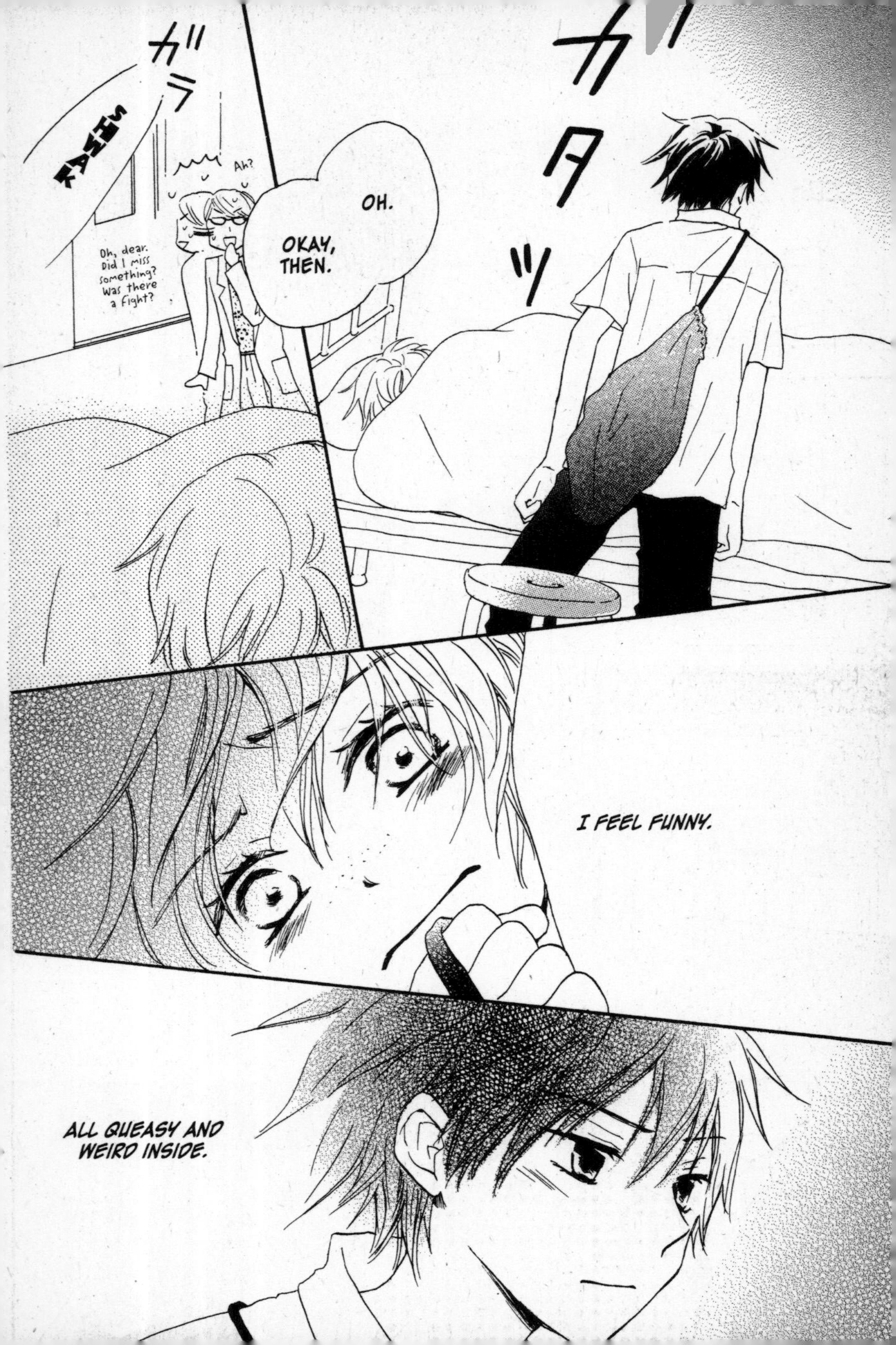
ガタッ
OH.
OKAY, THEN.
ガラ
KASHS
Ah?
Oh, dear. Did I miss something? Was there a fight?
I FEEL FUNNY.
ALL QUEASY AND WEIRD INSIDE.

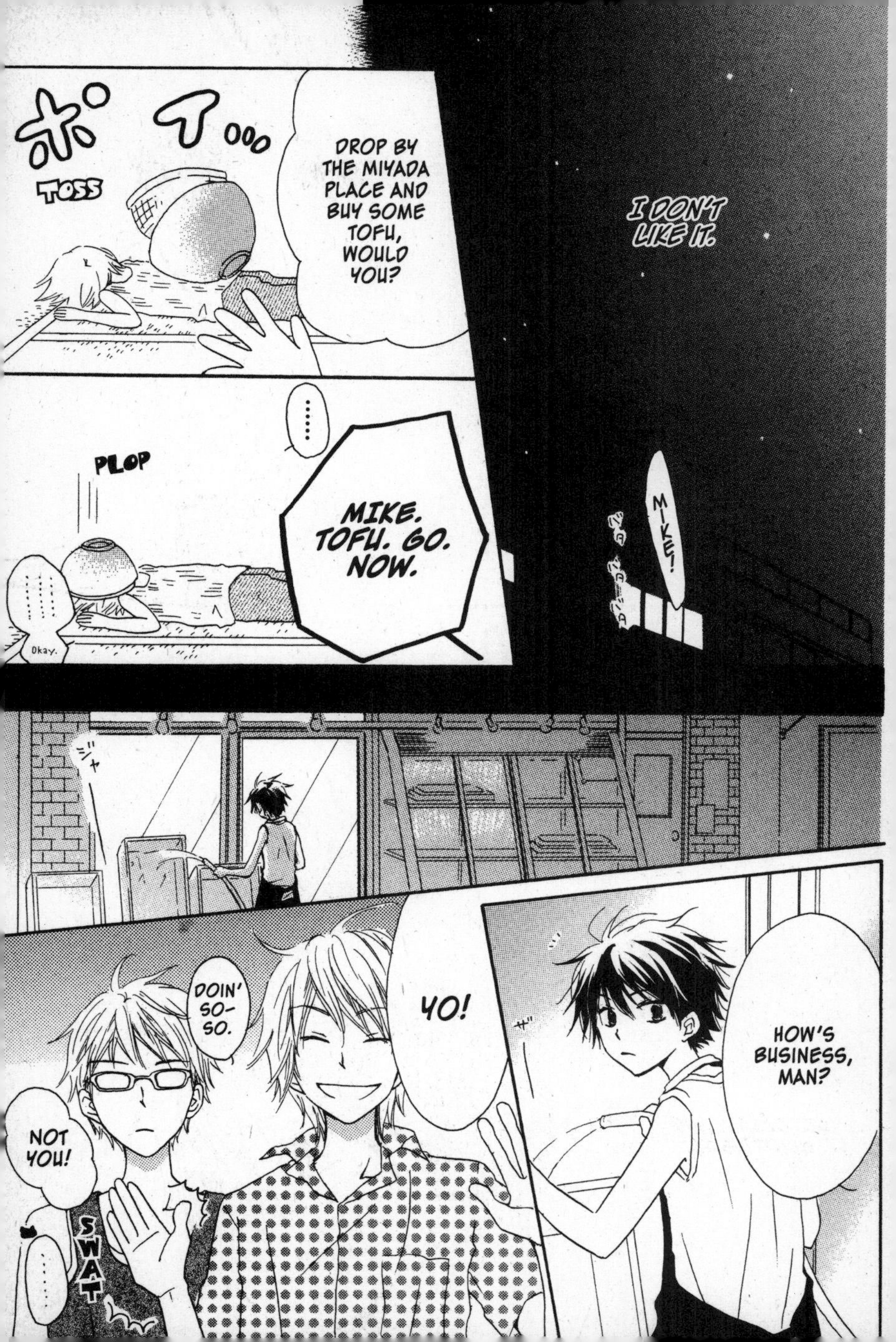
I DON'T LIKE IT.
MIKE!
ポイ
TOSS
DROP BY THE MIYADA PLACE AND BUY SOME TOFU, WOULD YOU?
......
PLOP
MIKE. TOFU. GO. NOW.
......
Okay.
HOW'S BUSINESS, MAN?
YO!
DOIN' SO-SO.
NOT YOU!
SWAT
......

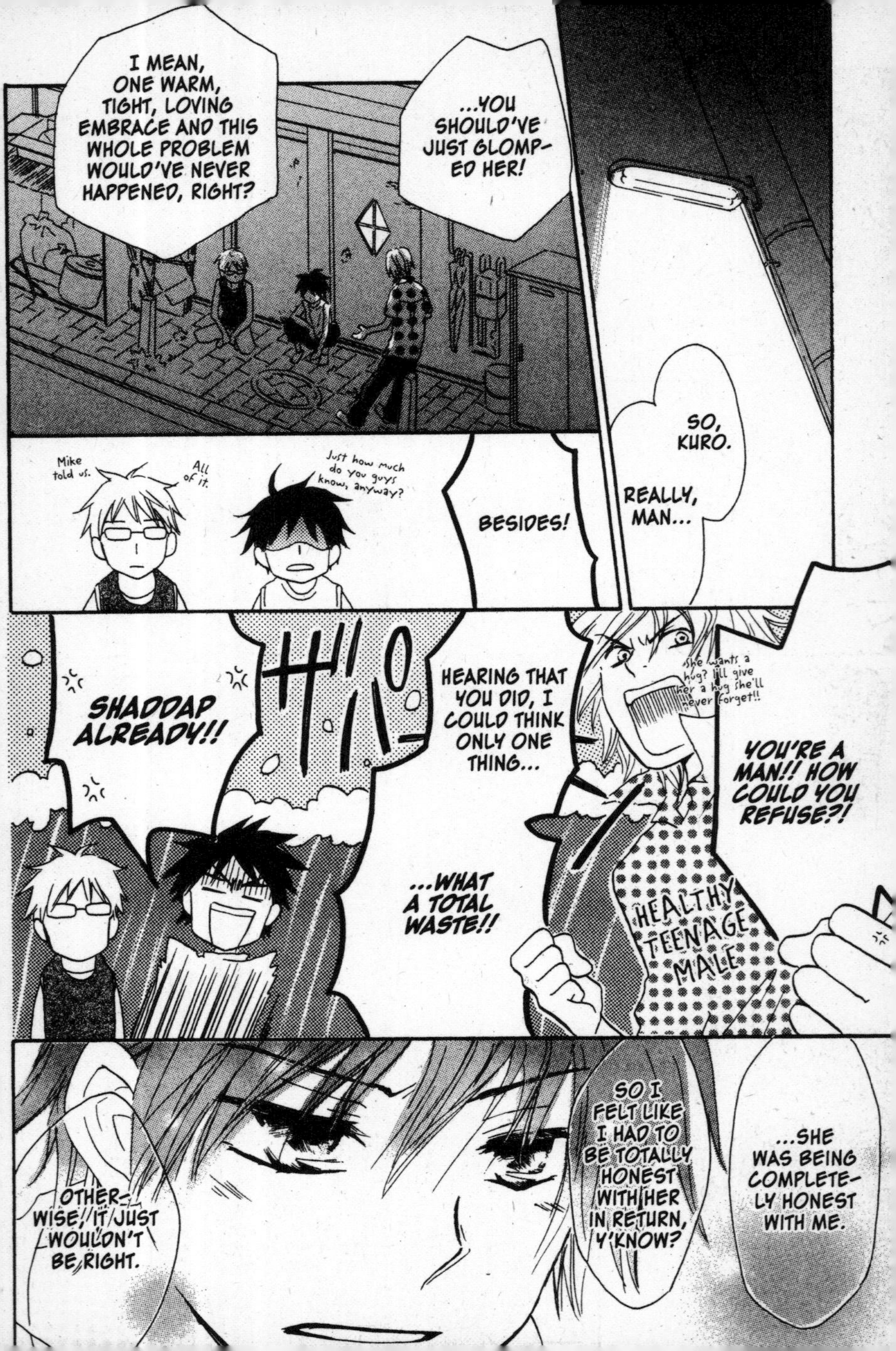
SO, KURO.
REALLY, MAN...
...YOU SHOULD'VE JUST GLOMP-ED HER!
I MEAN, ONE WARM, TIGHT, LOVING EMBRACE AND THIS WHOLE PROBLEM WOULD'VE NEVER HAPPENED, RIGHT?
BESIDES!
Just how much do you guys know, anyway?
All of it.
Mike told us.
YOU'RE A MAN!! HOW COULD YOU REFUSE?!
She wants a hug? I'll give her a hug she'll never forget!!
HEARING THAT YOU DID, I COULD THINK ONLY ONE THING...
HEALTHY TEENAGE MALE
...WHAT A TOTAL WASTE!!
SHADDAP ALREADY!!
...SHE WAS BEING COMPLETE-LY HONEST WITH ME.
SO I FELT LIKE I HAD TO BE TOTALLY HONEST WITH HER IN RETURN, Y'KNOW?
OTHER-WISE, IT JUST WOULDN'T BE RIGHT.

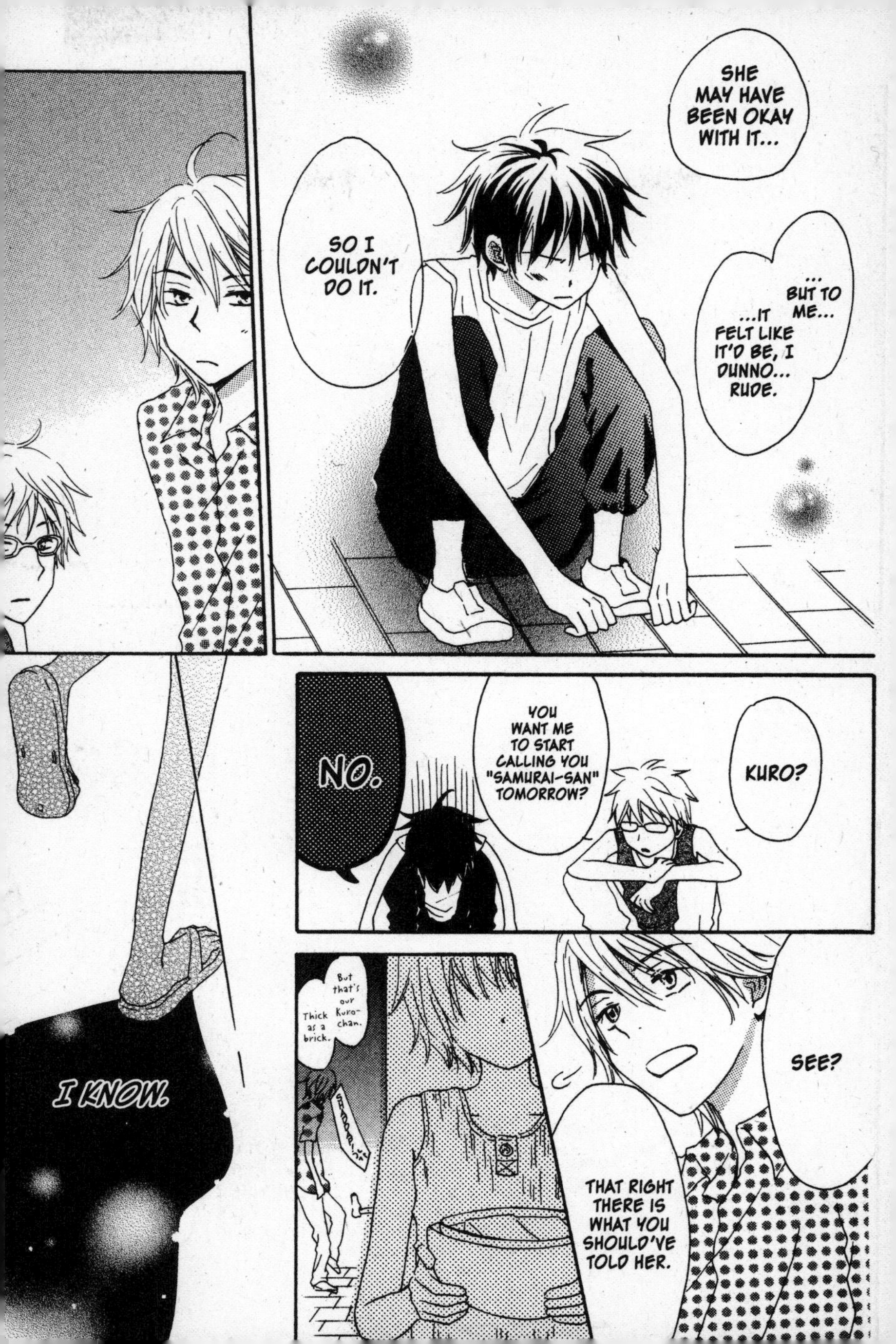
SHE MAY HAVE BEEN OKAY WITH IT...
...BUT TO ME...
...IT FELT LIKE IT'D BE, I DUNNO... RUDE.
SO I COULDN'T DO IT.
KURO?
YOU WANT ME TO START CALLING YOU "SAMURAI-SAN" TOMORROW?
NO.
SEE?
THAT RIGHT THERE IS WHAT YOU SHOULD'VE TOLD HER.
But that's our Kuro-chan.
Thick as a brick.
I KNOW.

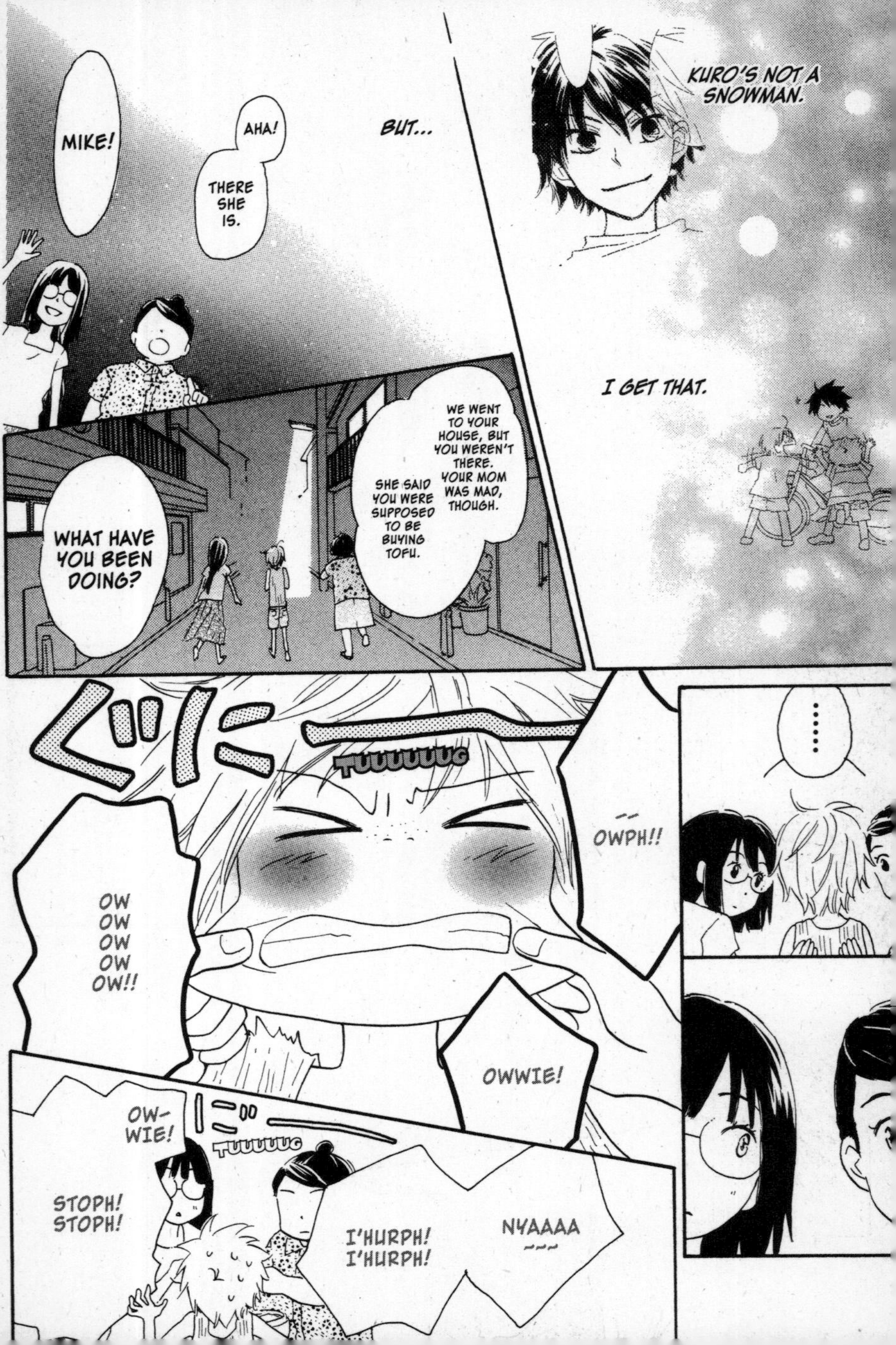
KURO'S NOT A SNOWMAN.
I GET THAT.
BUT...
AHA!
THERE SHE IS.
MIKE!
WE WENT TO YOUR HOUSE, BUT YOU WEREN'T THERE. YOUR MOM WAS MAD, THOUGH.
SHE SAID YOU WERE SUPPOSED TO BE BUYING TOFU.
WHAT HAVE YOU BEEN DOING?
......
--OWPH!!
TUUUUUUG
OW OW OW OW OW!!
OWWIE!
NYAAAA
I'HURPH! I'HURPH!
STOPH! STOPH!
OW-WIE!
TUUUUUG

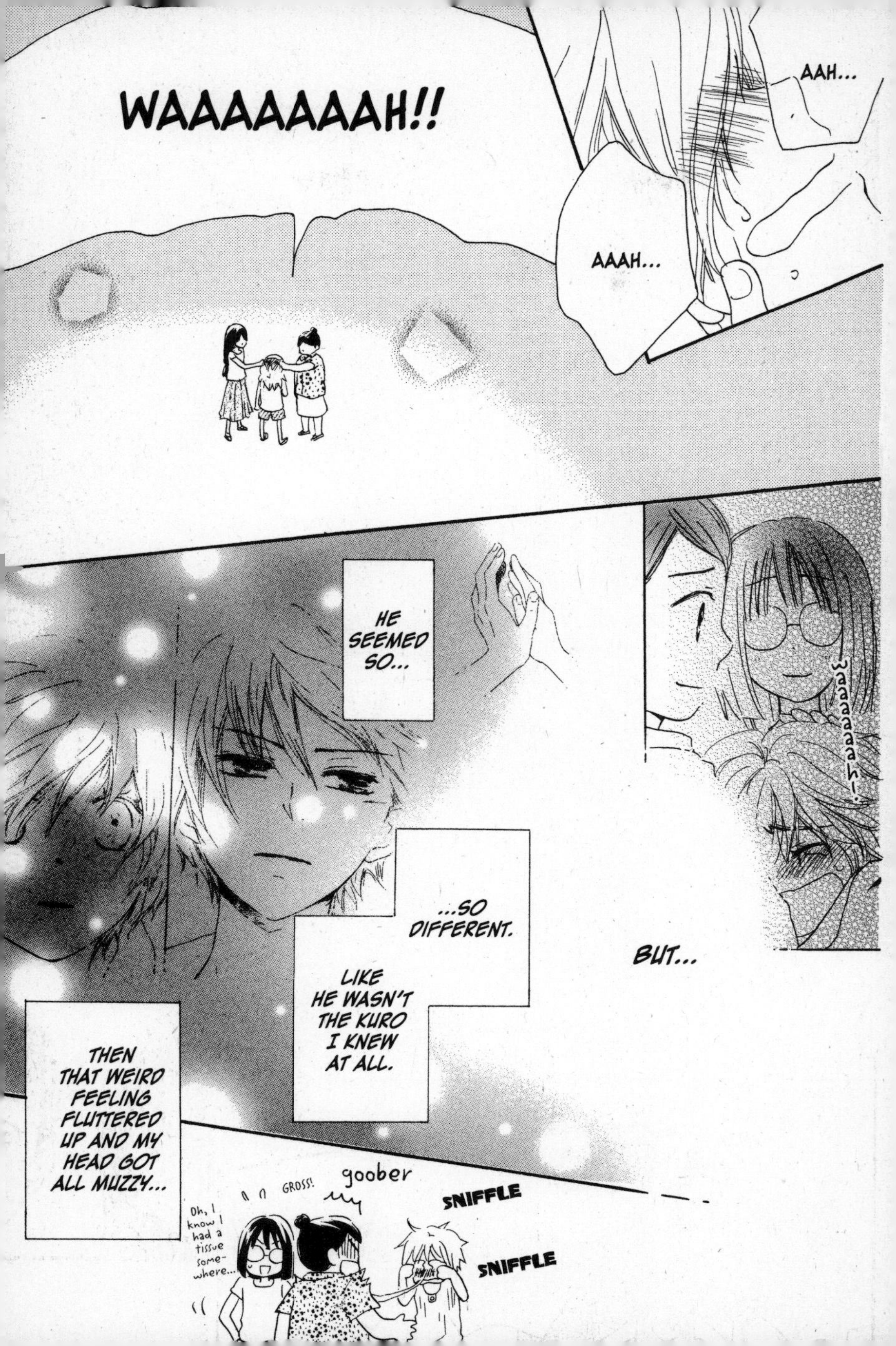
AAH...
AAAH...
WAAAAAAAAH!!
Waaaaaaah!..
BUT...
HE SEEMED SO...
...SO DIFFERENT.
LIKE HE WASN'T THE KURO I KNEW AT ALL.
THEN THAT WEIRD FEELING FLUTTERED UP AND MY HEAD GOT ALL MUZZY...
SNIFFLE
SNIFFLE
goober
GROSS!
Oh, I know I had a tissue somewhere...

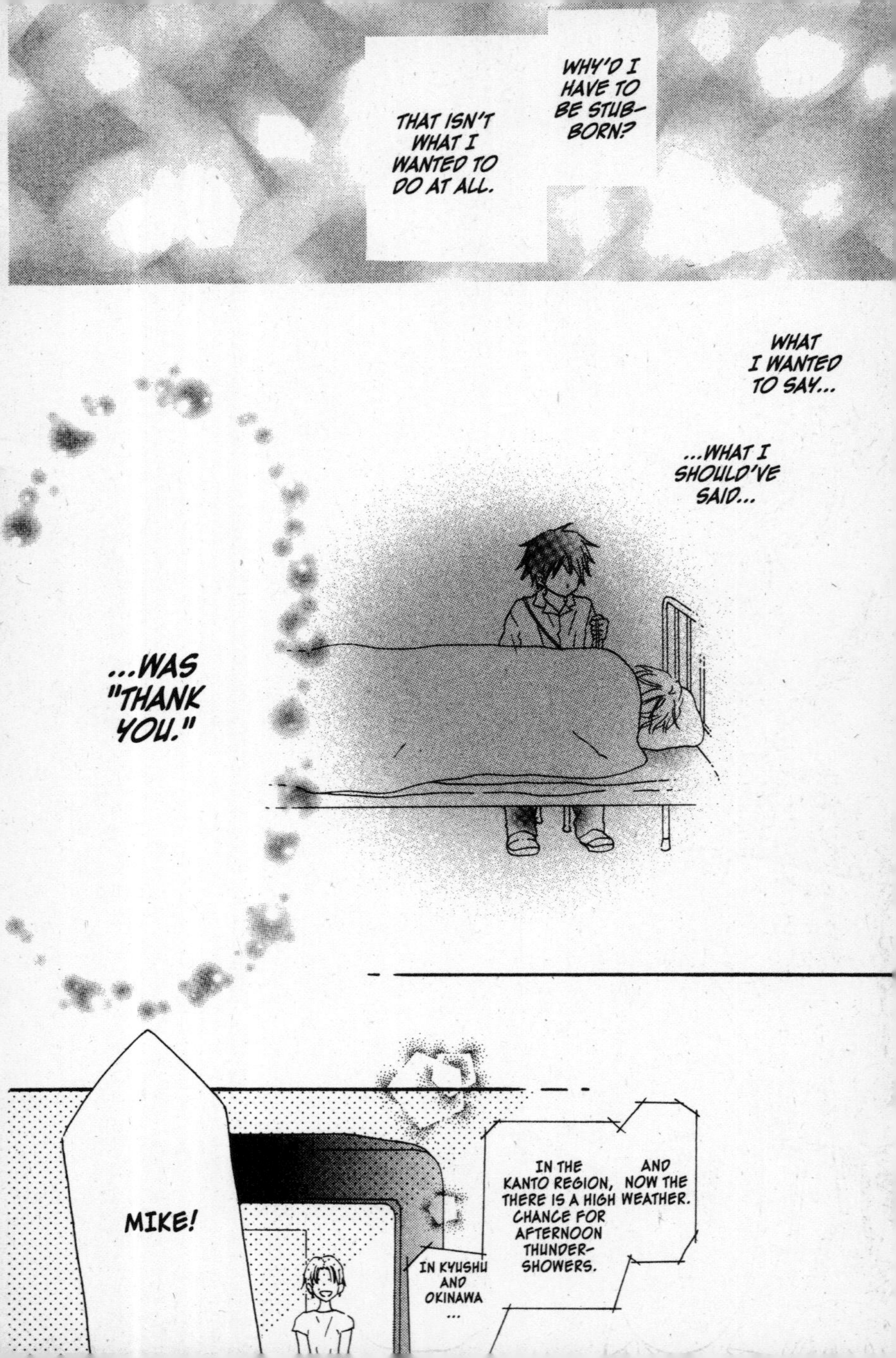
WHY'D I HAVE TO BE STUB-BORN?
THAT ISN'T WHAT I WANTED TO DO AT ALL.
WHAT I WANTED TO SAY...
...WHAT I SHOULD'VE SAID...
...WAS "THANK YOU."
AND NOW THE WEATHER.
IN THE KANTO REGION, THERE IS A HIGH CHANCE FOR AFTERNOON THUNDER-SHOWERS.
IN KYUSHU AND OKINAWA ...
MIKE!

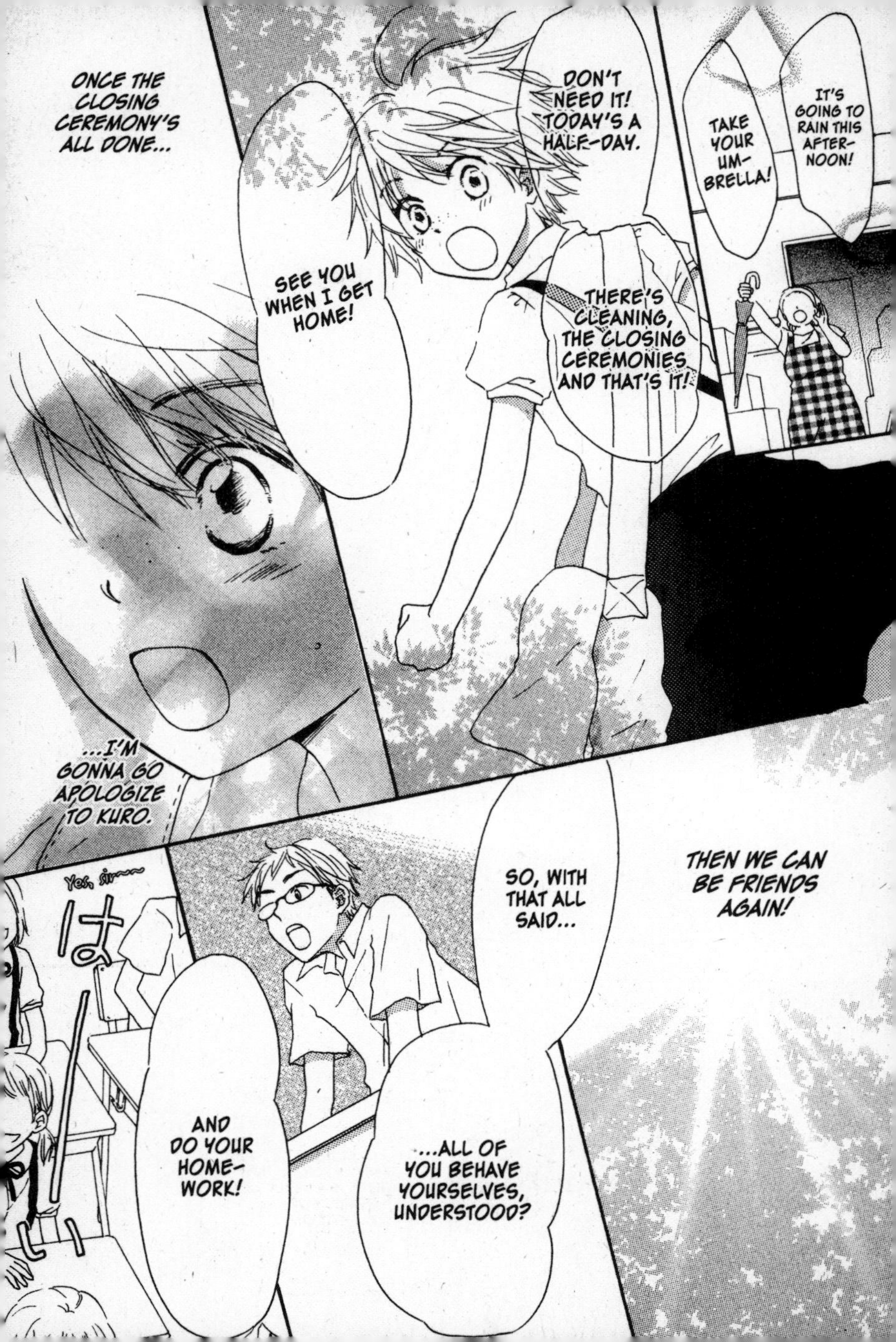
IT'S GOING TO RAIN THIS AFTER-NOON!
TAKE YOUR UM-BRELLA!
DON'T NEED IT! TODAY'S A HALF-DAY.
THERE'S CLEANING, THE CLOSING CEREMONIES AND THAT'S IT!
SEE YOU WHEN I GET HOME!
ONCE THE CLOSING CEREMONY'S ALL DONE...
...I'M GONNA GO APOLOGIZE TO KURO.
THEN WE CAN BE FRIENDS AGAIN!
SO, WITH THAT ALL SAID...
...ALL OF YOU BEHAVE YOURSELVES, UNDERSTOOD?
AND DO YOUR HOME-WORK!
はーい
Yes, sir~~

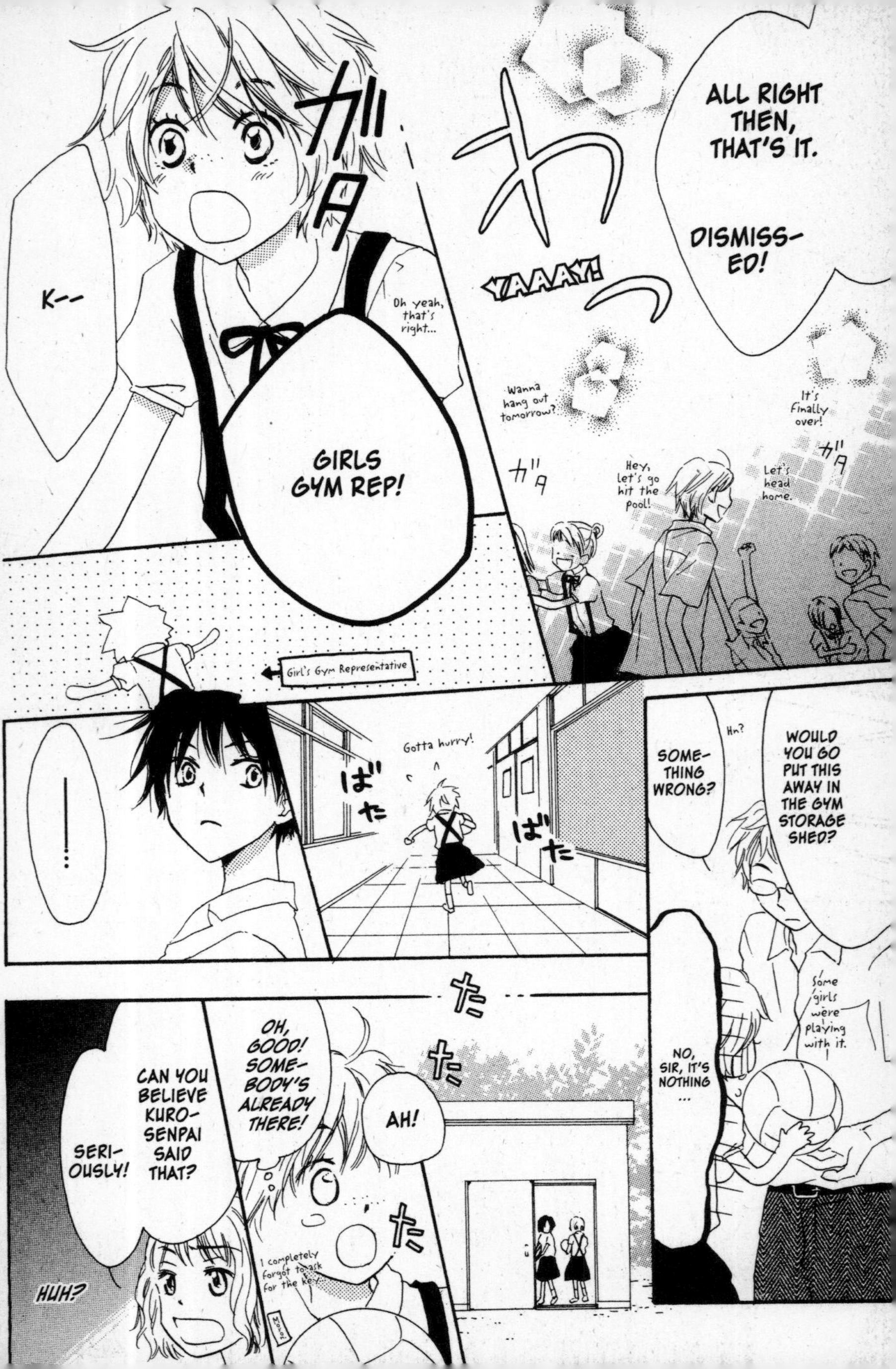
ALL RIGHT THEN, THAT'S IT.
DISMISS-ED!
わっ
YAAAY!
It's finally over!
ガタ
Let's head home.
Hey, let's go hit the pool!
ガタ
Wanna hang out tomorrow?
ガタ
K--
Oh yeah, that's right...
GIRLS GYM REP!
Girl's Gym Representative
WOULD YOU GO PUT THIS AWAY IN THE GYM STORAGE SHED?
Hn?
SOME-THING WRONG?
NO, SIR, IT'S NOTHING...
Some girls were playing with it.
Gotta hurry!
ばた
ばた
!...
たっ
たっ
たっ
AH!
OH, GOOD! SOME-BODY'S ALREADY THERE!
I completely forgot to ask for the key.
CAN YOU BELIEVE KURO-SENPAI SAID THAT?
SERI-OUSLY!
HUH?

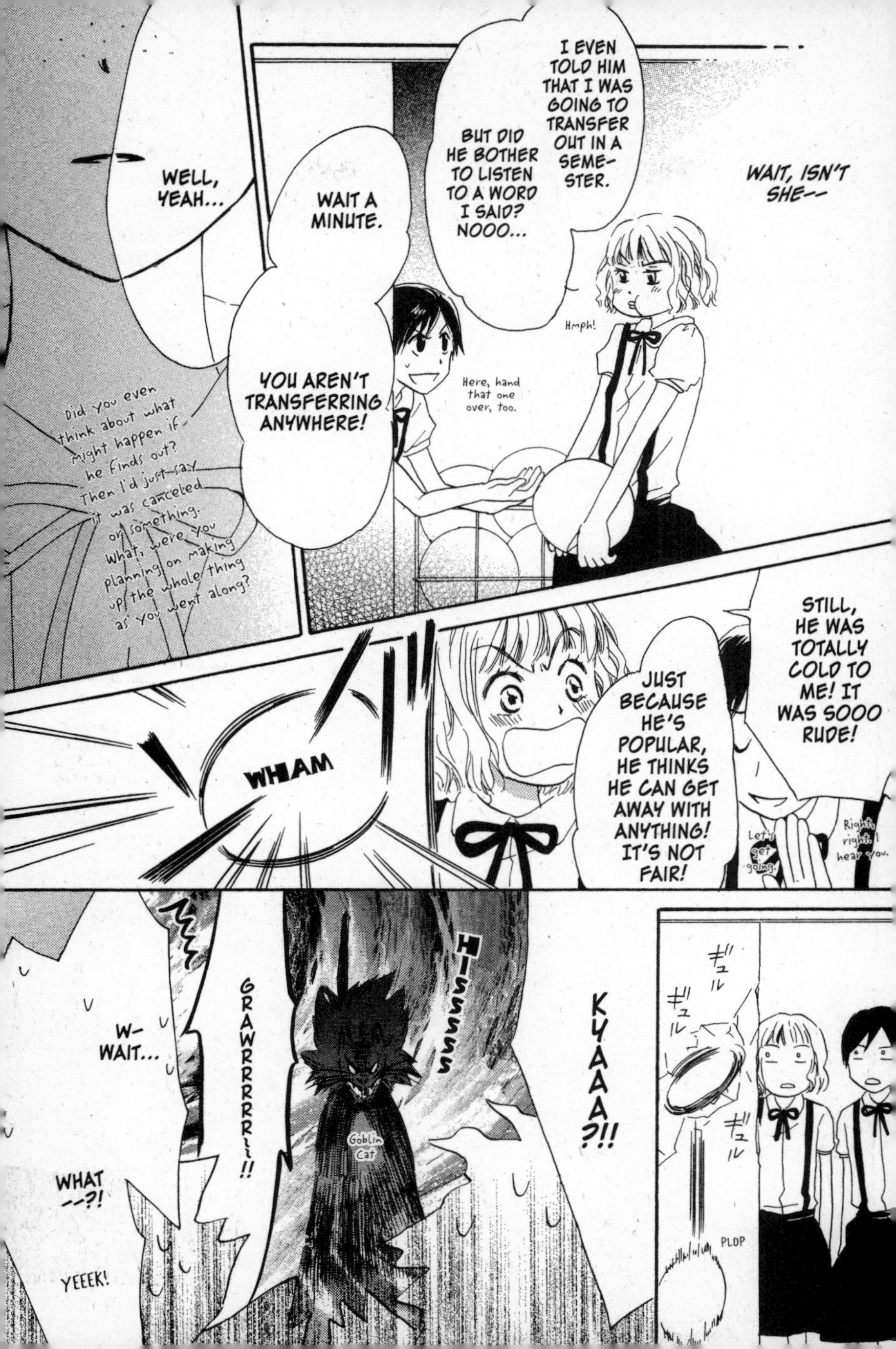
WAIT, ISN'T SHE--
I EVEN TOLD HIM THAT I WAS GOING TO TRANSFER OUT IN A SEMESTER.
BUT DID HE BOTHER TO LISTEN TO A WORD I SAID? NOOO...
Hmph!
WAIT A MINUTE.
Here, hand that one over, too.
YOU AREN'T TRANSFERRING ANYWHERE!
WELL, YEAH...
Did you even think about what might happen if he finds out?
Then I'd just say it was canceled or something.
What, were you planning on making up the whole thing as you went along?
STILL, HE WAS TOTALLY COLD TO ME! IT WAS SOOO RUDE!
Right, right. I hear you.
Let's get going.
JUST BECAUSE HE'S POPULAR, HE THINKS HE CAN GET AWAY WITH ANYTHING! IT'S NOT FAIR!
WHAM
ギュル
ギュル
ギュル
PLOP
KYAAAA?!!
HISSSSSS
GRAWRRRRRR!!
Goblin Cat
W-WAIT...
WHAT--?!
YEEEK!

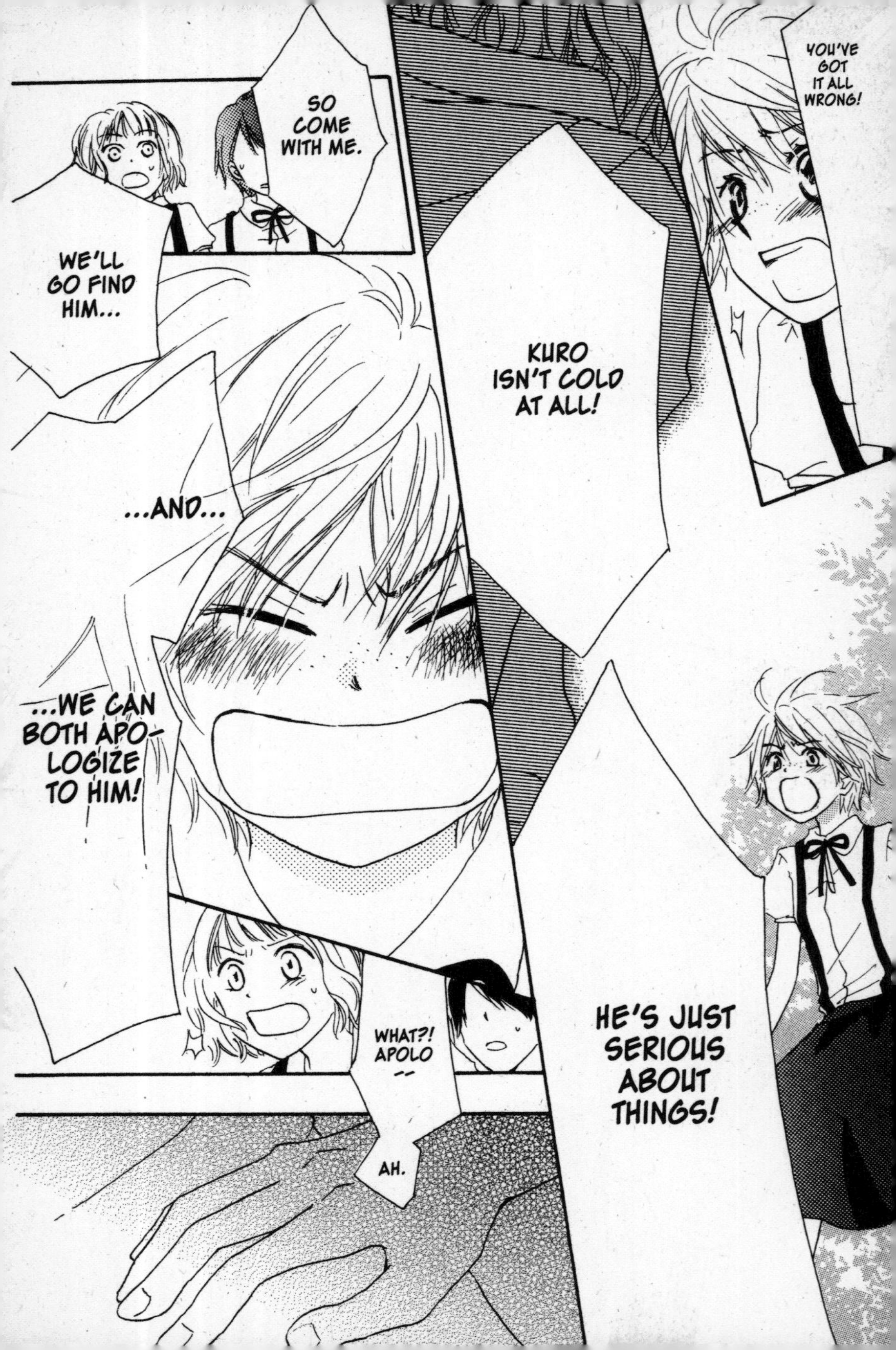
YOU'VE GOT IT ALL WRONG!
KURO ISN'T COLD AT ALL!
HE'S JUST SERIOUS ABOUT THINGS!
SO COME WITH ME.
WE'LL GO FIND HIM...
...AND...
...WE CAN BOTH APO-LOGIZE TO HIM!
WHAT?! APOLO --
AH.

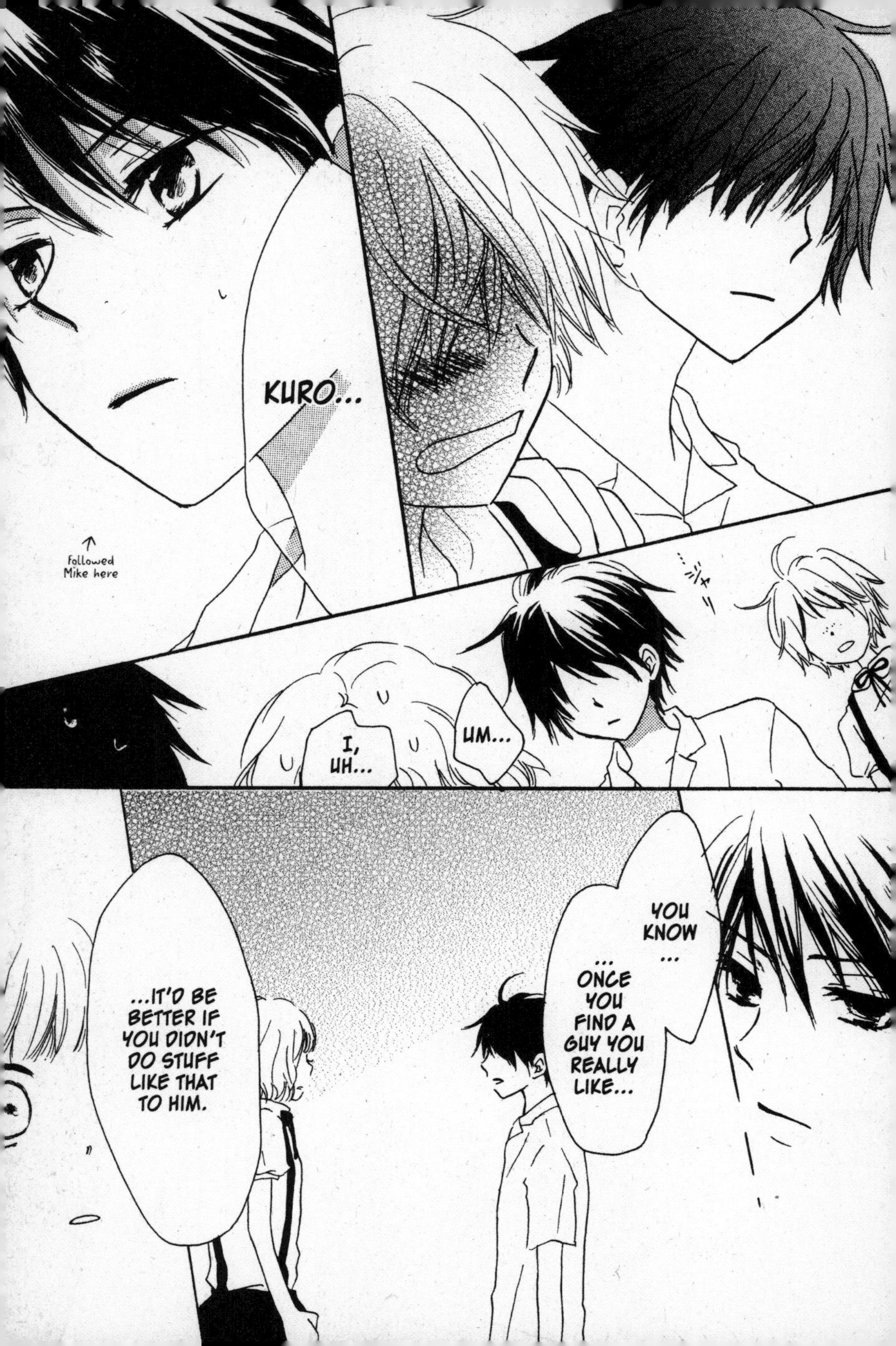
KURO...
Followed Mike here
UM...
I, UH...
YOU KNOW ... ONCE YOU FIND A GUY YOU REALLY LIKE...
...IT'D BE BETTER IF YOU DIDN'T DO STUFF LIKE THAT TO HIM.

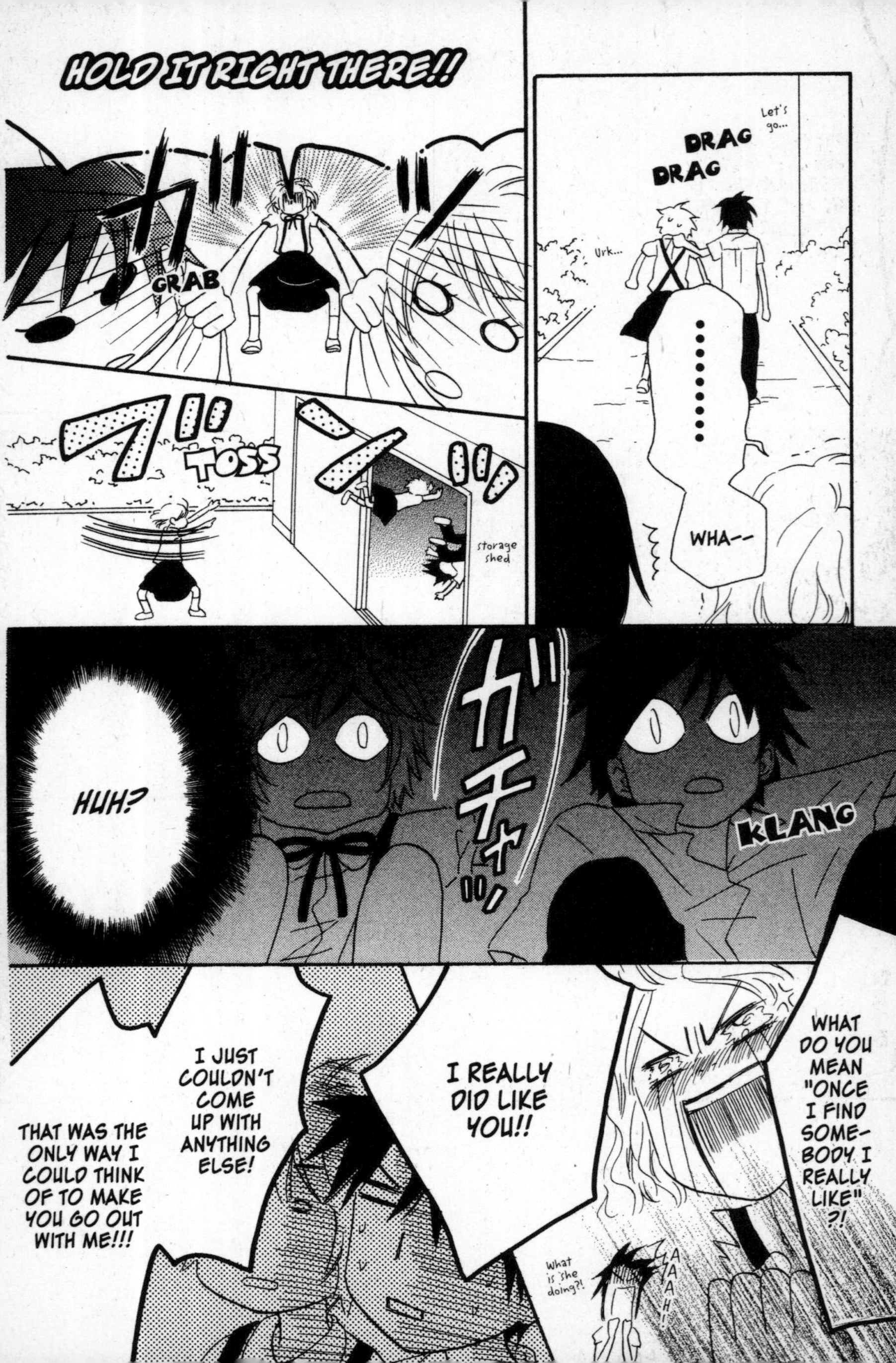

Let's go...
DRAG
DRAG
Urk...
....
WHA--
HOLD IT RIGHT THERE!!
GRAB
TOSS
storage shed
KLANG
HUH?
WHAT DO YOU MEAN "ONCE I FIND SOMEBODY I REALLY LIKE"?!
What is she doing?!
I REALLY DID LIKE YOU!!
I JUST COULDN'T COME UP WITH ANYTHING ELSE!
THAT WAS THE ONLY WAY I COULD THINK OF TO MAKE YOU GO OUT WITH ME!!!

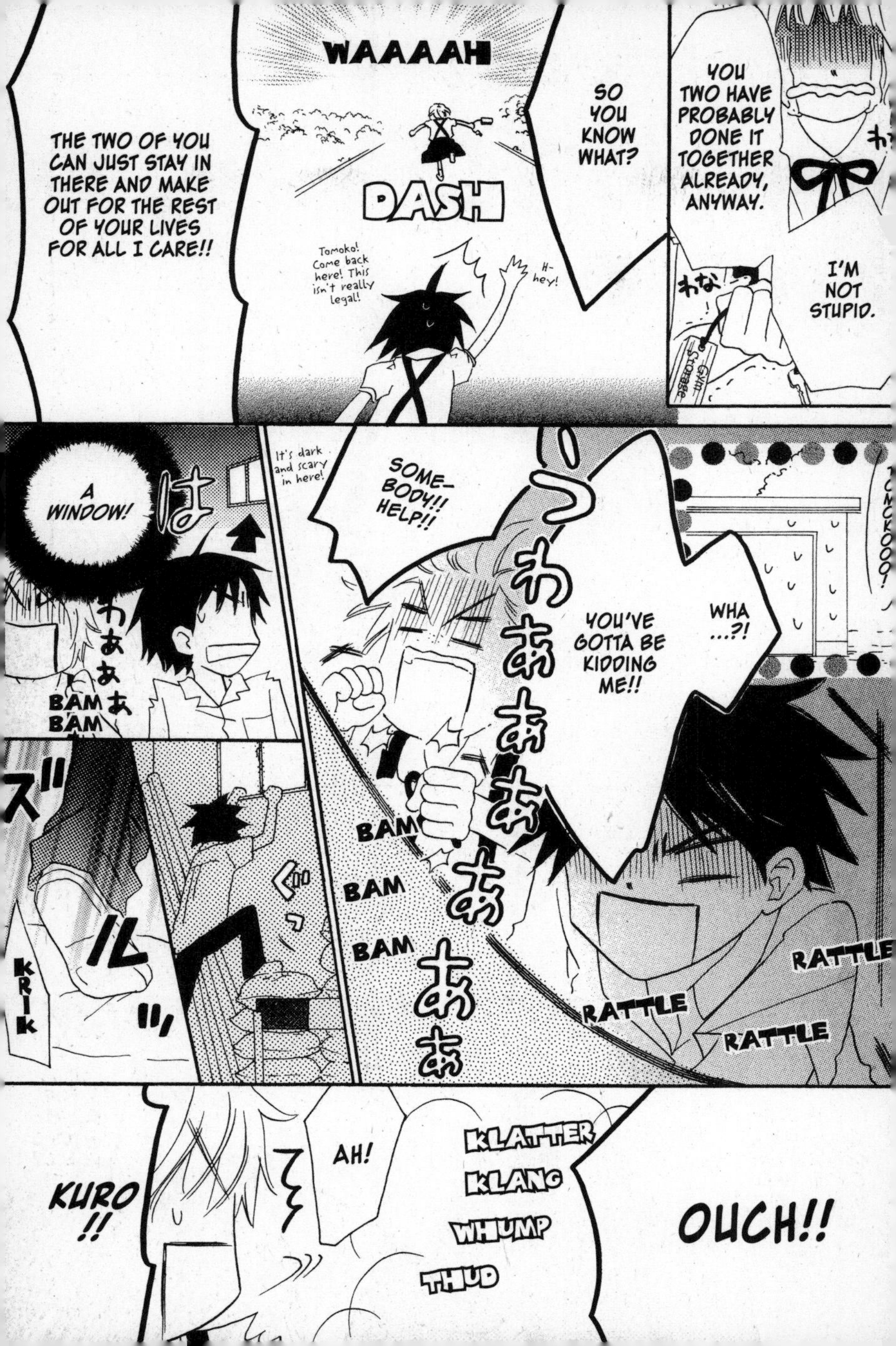

YOU TWO HAVE PROBABLY DONE IT TOGETHER ALREADY, ANYWAY.
I'M NOT STUPID.
Gym Storage
SO YOU KNOW WHAT?
THE TWO OF YOU CAN JUST STAY IN THERE AND MAKE OUT FOR THE REST OF YOUR LIVES FOR ALL I CARE!!
WAAAAH
DASH
H-hey!
Tomoko! Come back here! This isn't really legal!
TOMOKOOO!
WHA ...?!
YOU'VE GOTTA BE KIDDING ME!!
SOME-BODY!! HELP!!
It's dark and scary in here!
うわあああああああ
BAM
BAM
BAM
RATTLE
RATTLE
RATTLE
A WINDOW!
は
わあああ
BAM BAM
ズル
KRIK
OUCH!!
KLATTER
KLANG
WHUMP
THUD
AH!
KURO!!

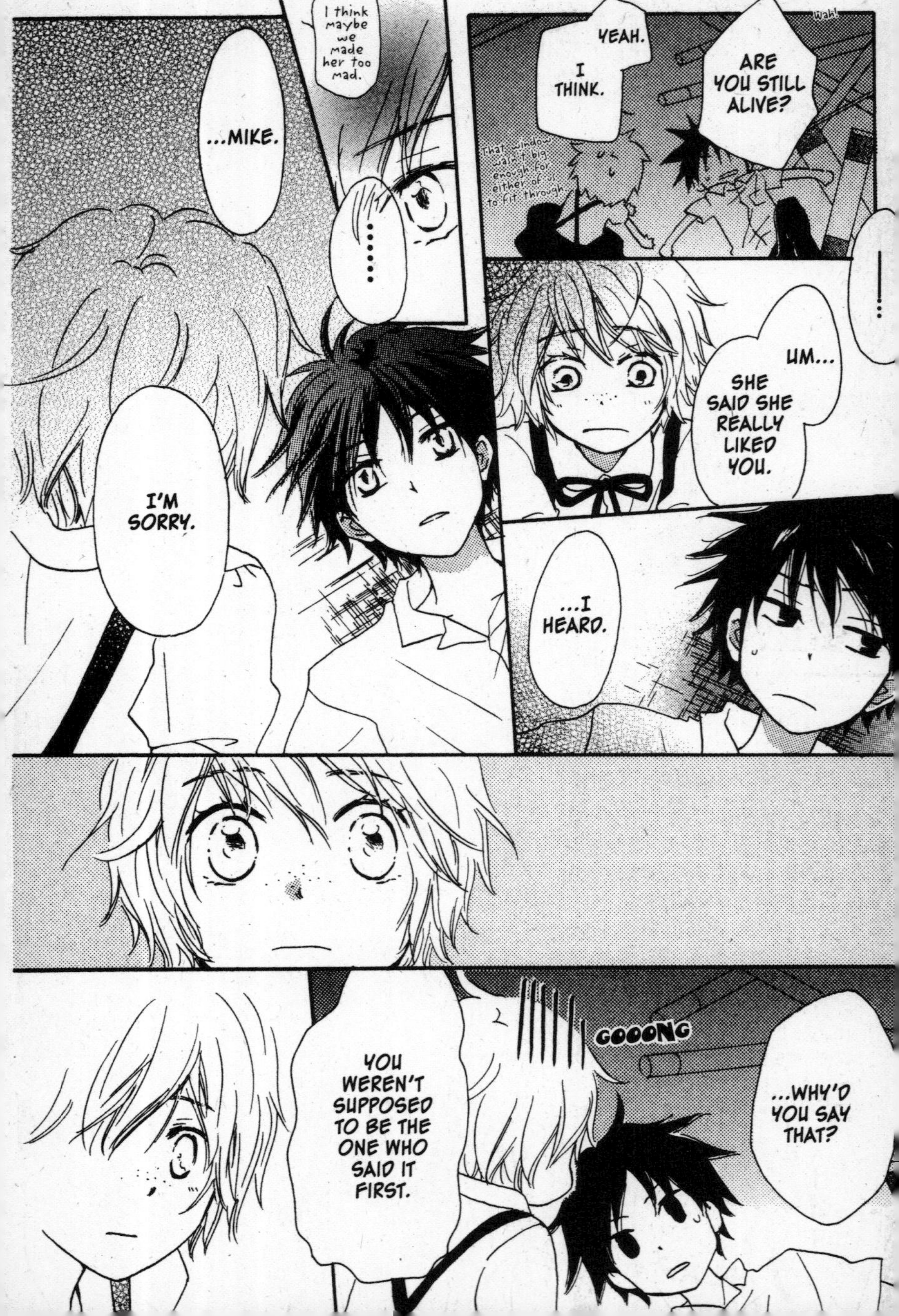
Wah!
ARE YOU STILL ALIVE?
YEAH. I THINK.
That window wasn't big enough for either of us to fit through.
!...
UM... SHE SAID SHE REALLY LIKED YOU.
...I HEARD.
I think maybe we made her too mad.
......
...MIKE.
I'M SORRY.
...WHY'D YOU SAY THAT?
GOOONG
YOU WEREN'T SUPPOSED TO BE THE ONE WHO SAID IT FIRST.

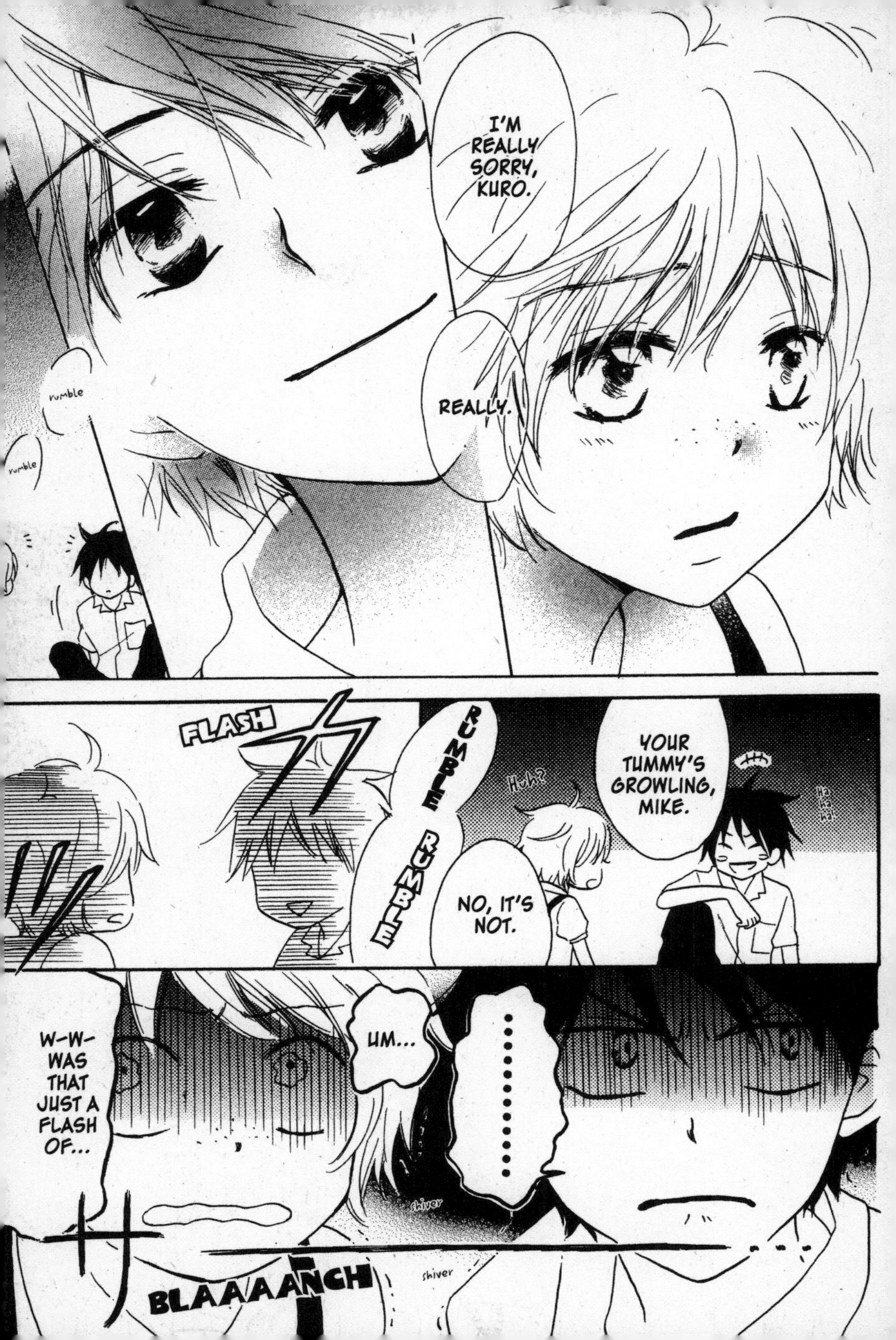
I'M REALLY SORRY, KURO.
REALLY.
rumble
rumble
YOUR TUMMY'S GROWLING, MIKE.
Ha ha ha
Huh?
NO, IT'S NOT.
RUMBLE RUMBLE
FLASH
......
UM...
W-W-WAS THAT JUST A FLASH OF...
shiver
shiver
BLAAAAANCH

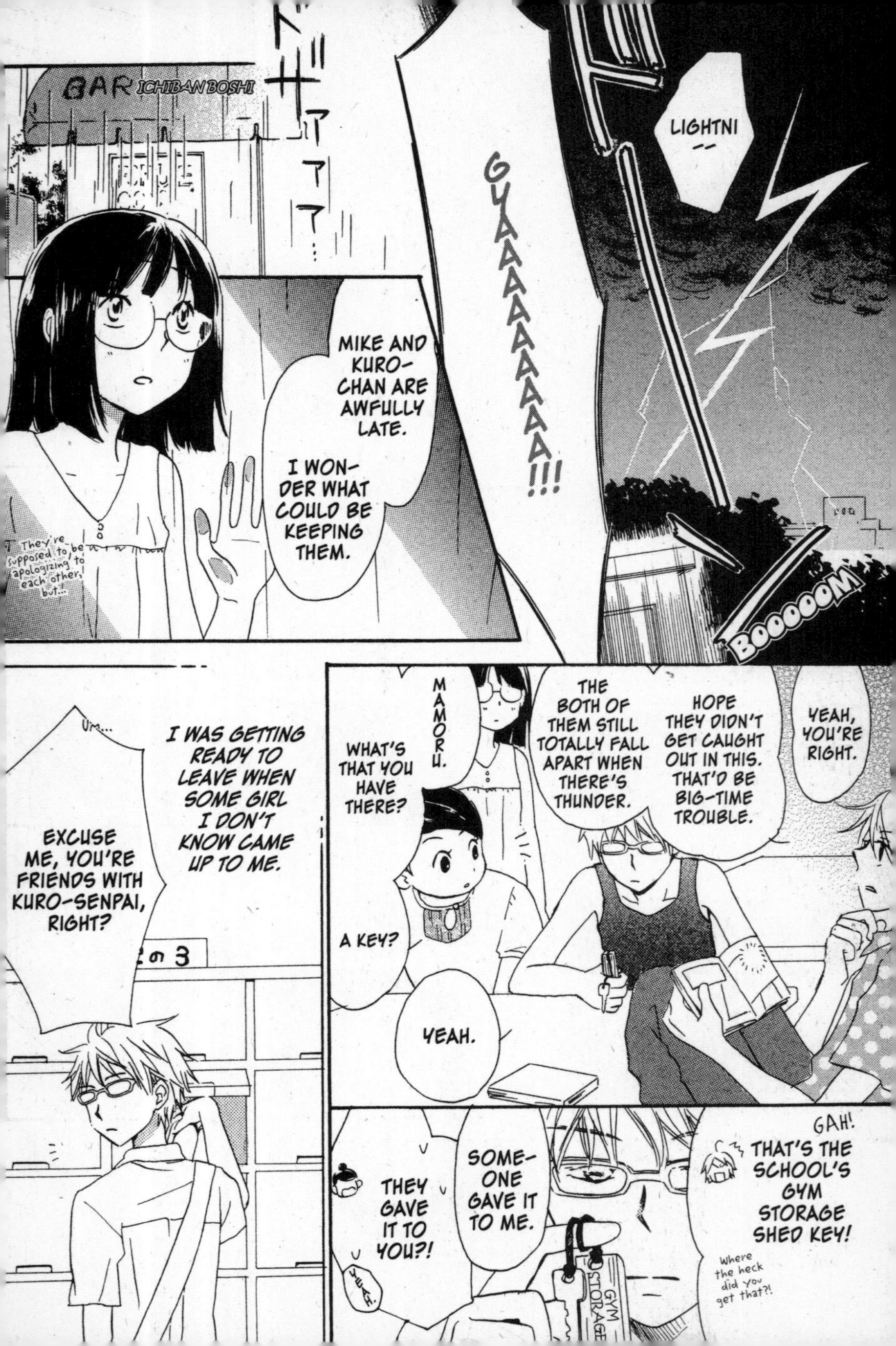
LIGHTNI --
GYAAAAAAAAAA!!!
BOOOOOM
BAR ICHIBAN BOSHI
ドザァァァ…
MIKE AND KURO-CHAN ARE AWFULLY LATE.
I WONDER WHAT COULD BE KEEPING THEM.
They're supposed to be apologizing to each other, but...
YEAH, YOU'RE RIGHT.
HOPE THEY DIDN'T GET CAUGHT OUT IN THIS. THAT'D BE BIG-TIME TROUBLE.
THE BOTH OF THEM STILL TOTALLY FALL APART WHEN THERE'S THUNDER.
MAMORU.
WHAT'S THAT YOU HAVE THERE?
A KEY?
YEAH.
GAH! THAT'S THE SCHOOL'S GYM STORAGE SHED KEY!
Where the heck did you get that?!
SOME-ONE GAVE IT TO ME.
THEY GAVE IT TO YOU?!
YEAH.
GYM STORAGE
I WAS GETTING READY TO LEAVE WHEN SOME GIRL I DON'T KNOW CAME UP TO ME.
Um...
EXCUSE ME, YOU'RE FRIENDS WITH KURO-SENPAI, RIGHT?

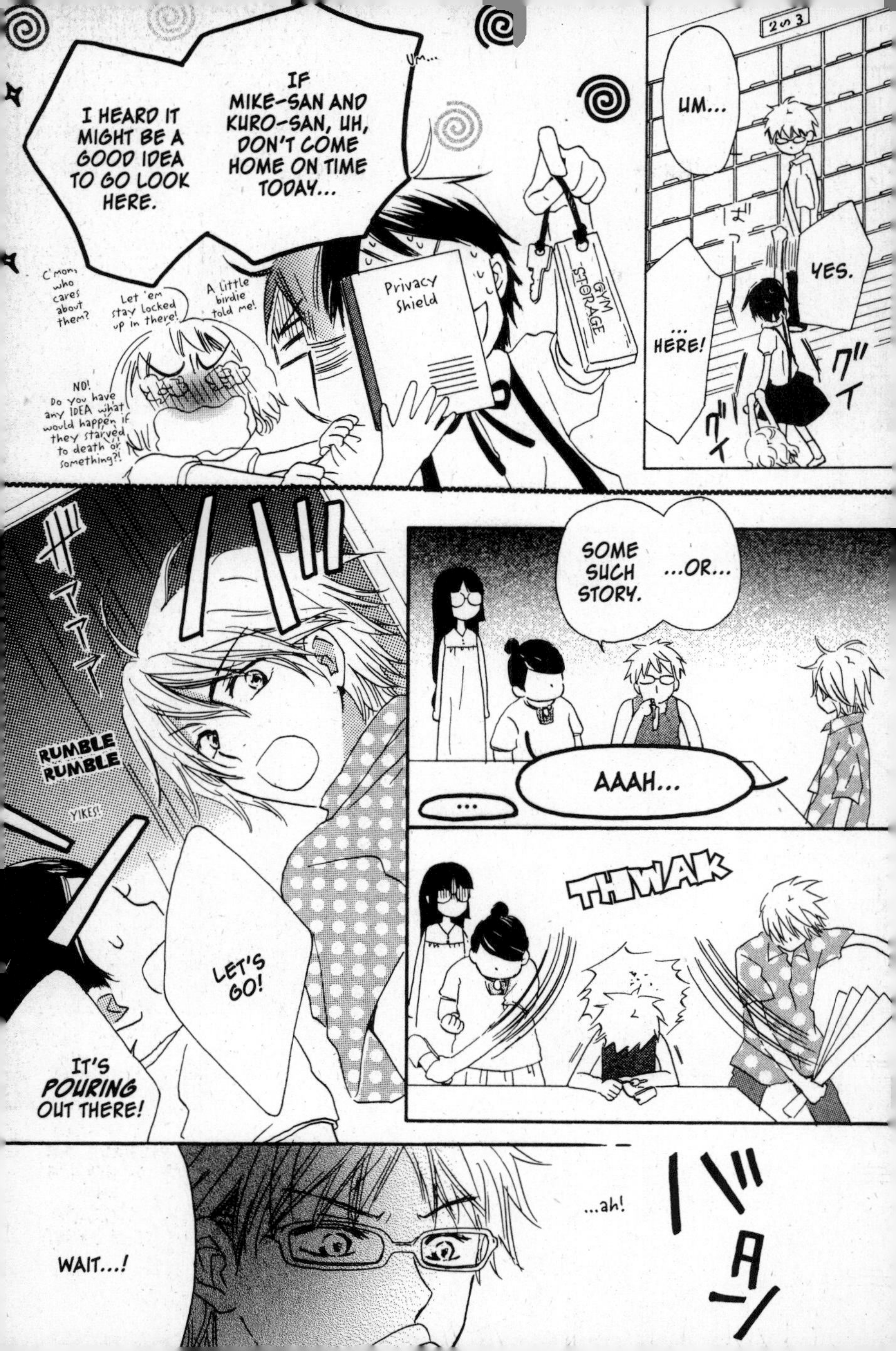
UM...
YES.
...HERE!
UM...
IF MIKE-SAN AND KURO-SAN, UH, DON'T COME HOME ON TIME TODAY...
I HEARD IT MIGHT BE A GOOD IDEA TO GO LOOK HERE.
Privacy Shield
GYM STORAGE
A little birdie told me!
Let 'em stay locked up in there!
C'mon, who cares about them?
NO! Do you have any IDEA what would happen if they starved to death or something?!
SOME SUCH STORY.
...OR...
AAAH...
...
THWAK
RUMBLE RUMBLE
YIKES!
LET'S GO!
IT'S POURING OUT THERE!
...ah!
WAIT...!
バタン

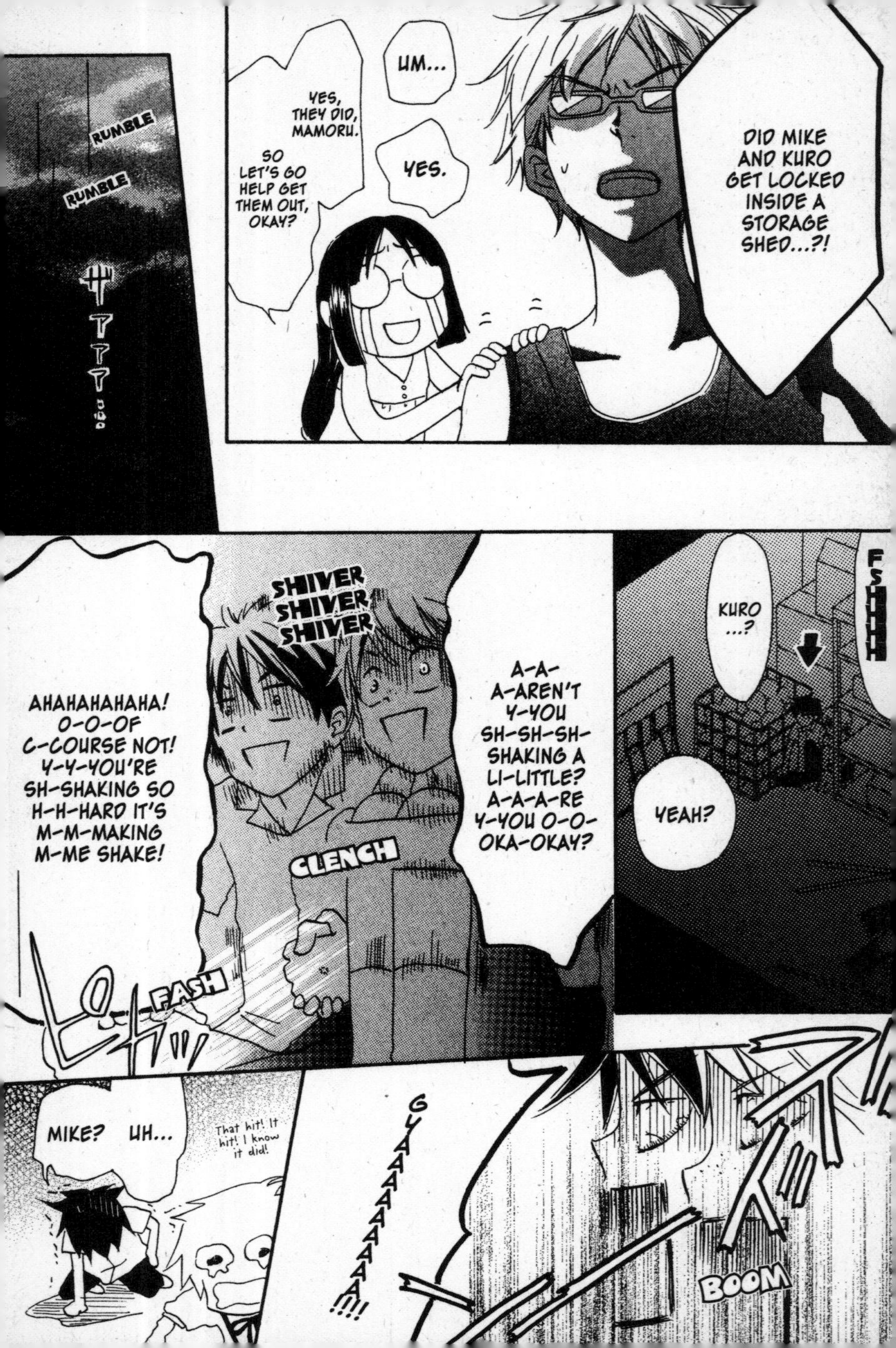
DID MIKE AND KURO GET LOCKED INSIDE A STORAGE SHED...?!
UM...
YES, THEY DID, MAMORU.
YES.
SO LET'S GO HELP GET THEM OUT, OKAY?
RUMBLE
RUMBLE
FSHHHH
KURO ...?
YEAH?
SHIVER SHIVER SHIVER
A-A-A-AREN'T Y-YOU SH-SH-SH-SHAKING A LI-LITTLE? A-A-A-RE Y-YOU O-O-OKA-OKAY?
AHAHAHAHAHA! O-O-OF C-COURSE NOT! Y-Y-YOU'RE SH-SHAKING SO H-H-HARD IT'S M-M-MAKING M-ME SHAKE!
CLENCH
FASH
BOOM
GUAAAAAAAAAA!!!!
MIKE? UH...
That hit! It hit! I know it did!

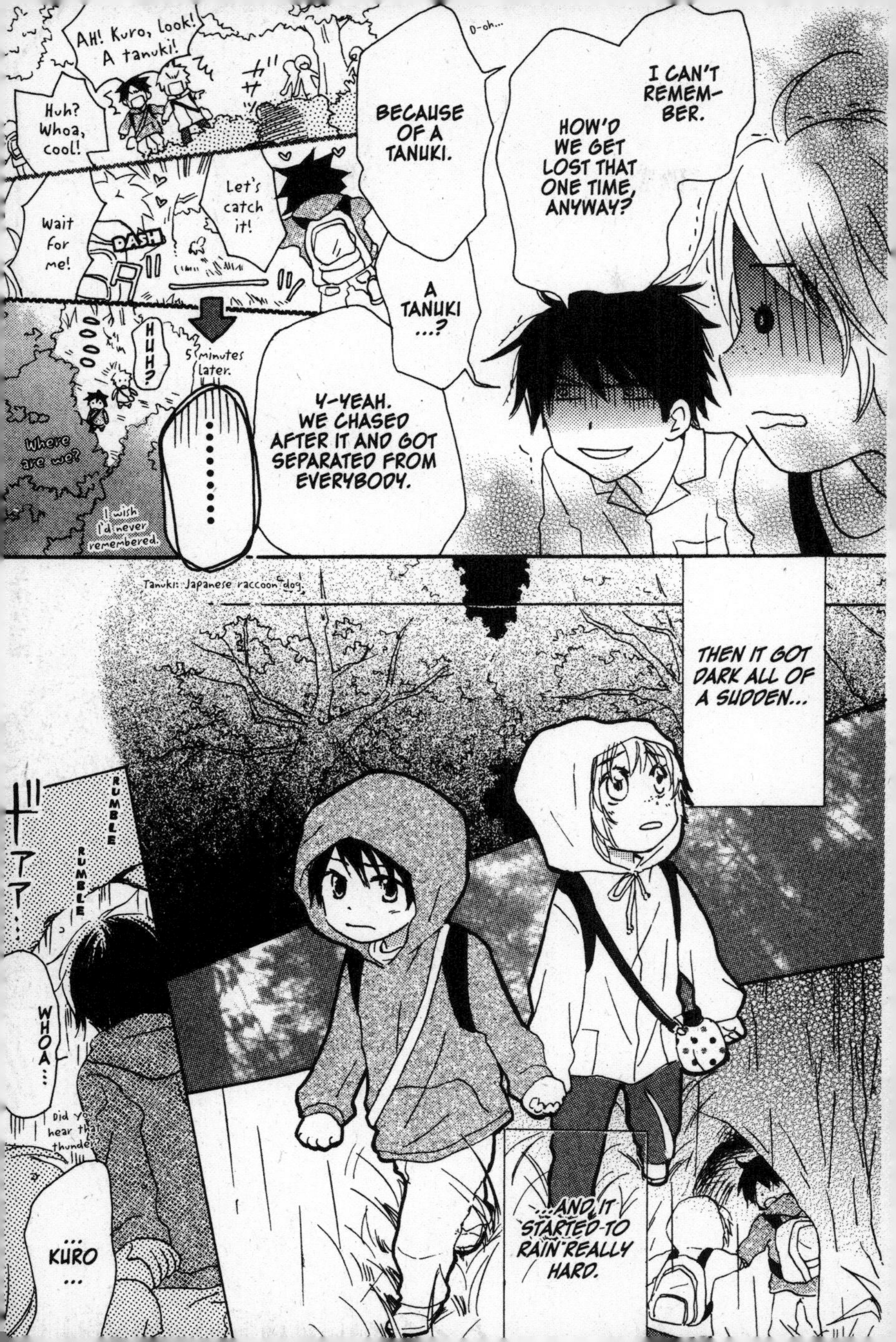
I CAN'T REMEMBER.
HOW'D WE GET LOST THAT ONE TIME, ANYWAY?
O-oh...
BECAUSE OF A TANUKI.
A TANUKI ...?
Y-YEAH. WE CHASED AFTER IT AND GOT SEPARATED FROM EVERYBODY.
AH! Kuro, look! A tanuki!
Huh? Whoa, cool!
Let's catch it!
Wait for me!
DASH
5 minutes later.
......
HUH?
Where are we?
I wish I'd never remembered.
THEN IT GOT DARK ALL OF A SUDDEN...
RUMBLE
RUMBLE
WHOA...
Did yo hear tha thunde
... KURO ...
...AND IT STARTED TO RAIN REALLY HARD.
Tanuki: Japanese raccoon dog.

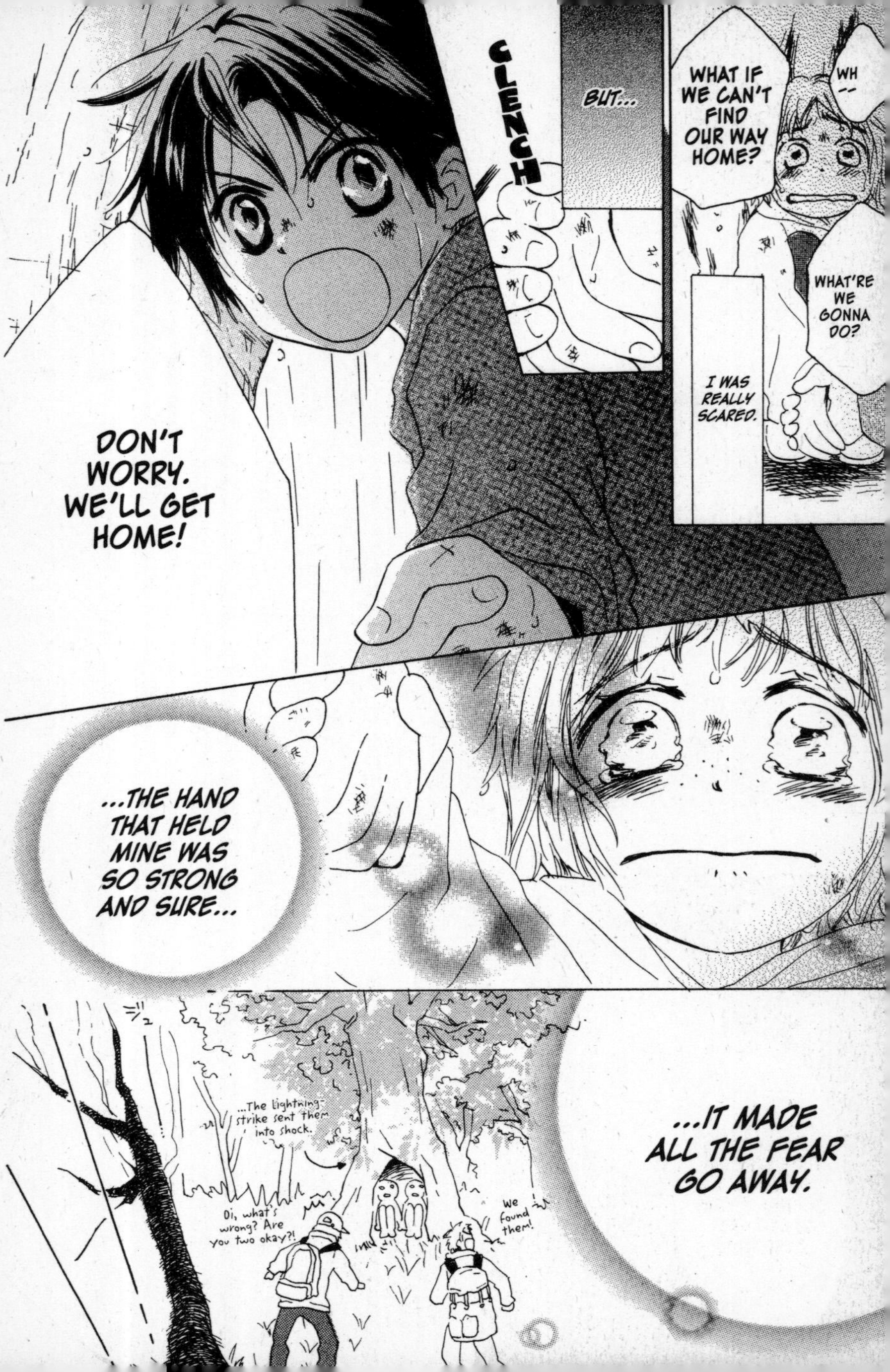
WH--
WHAT IF WE CAN'T FIND OUR WAY HOME?
WHAT'RE WE GONNA DO?
I WAS REALLY SCARED.
BUT...
CLENCH
DON'T WORRY. WE'LL GET HOME!
...THE HAND THAT HELD MINE WAS SO STRONG AND SURE...
...IT MADE ALL THE FEAR GO AWAY.
We found them!
...The lightning-strike sent them into shock.
Oi, what's wrong? Are you two okay?!

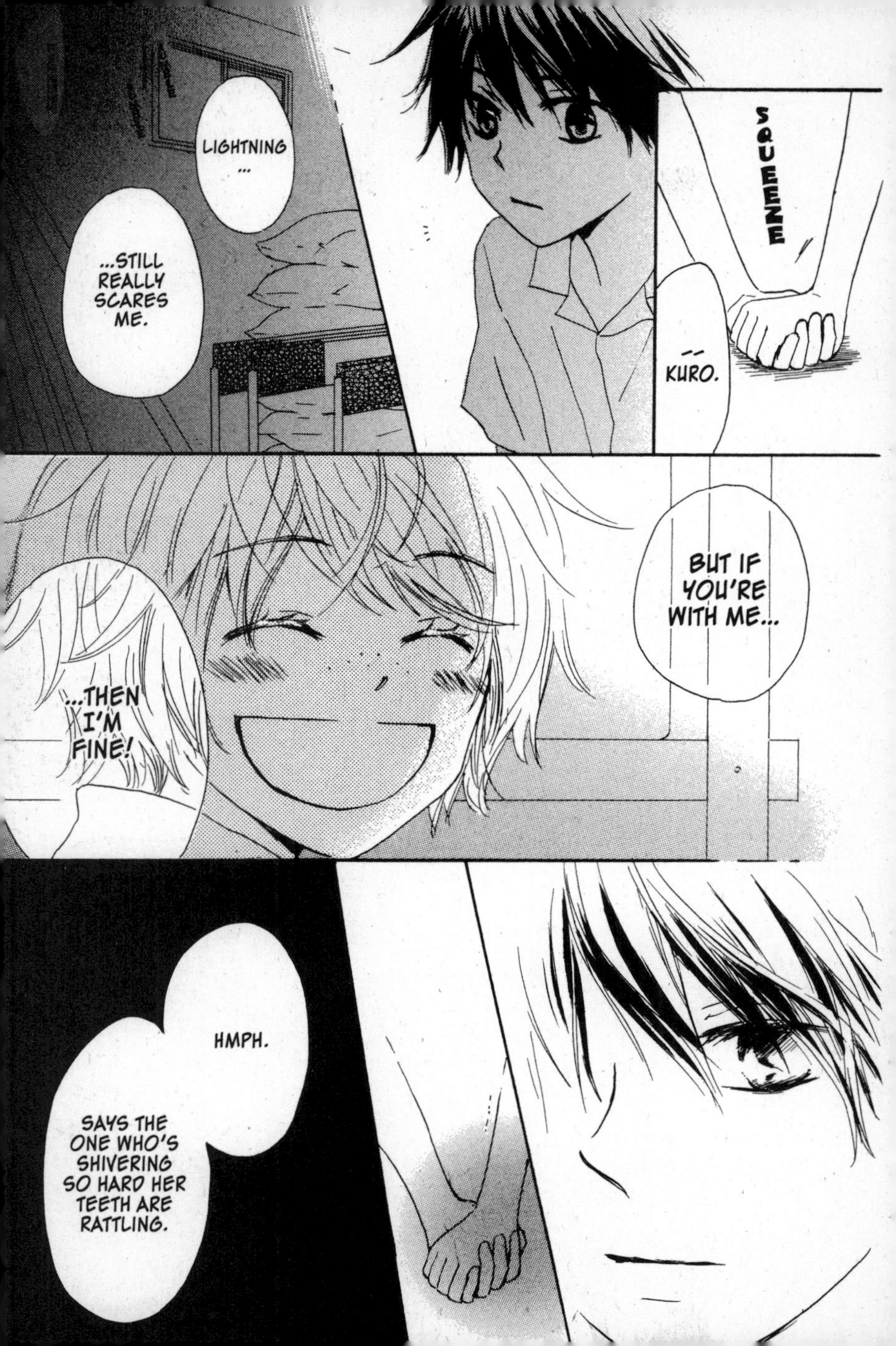
SQUEEZE
--KURO.
LIGHTNING...
...STILL REALLY SCARES ME.
BUT IF YOU'RE WITH ME...
...THEN I'M FINE!
HMPH.
SAYS THE ONE WHO'S SHIVERING SO HARD HER TEETH ARE RATTLING.

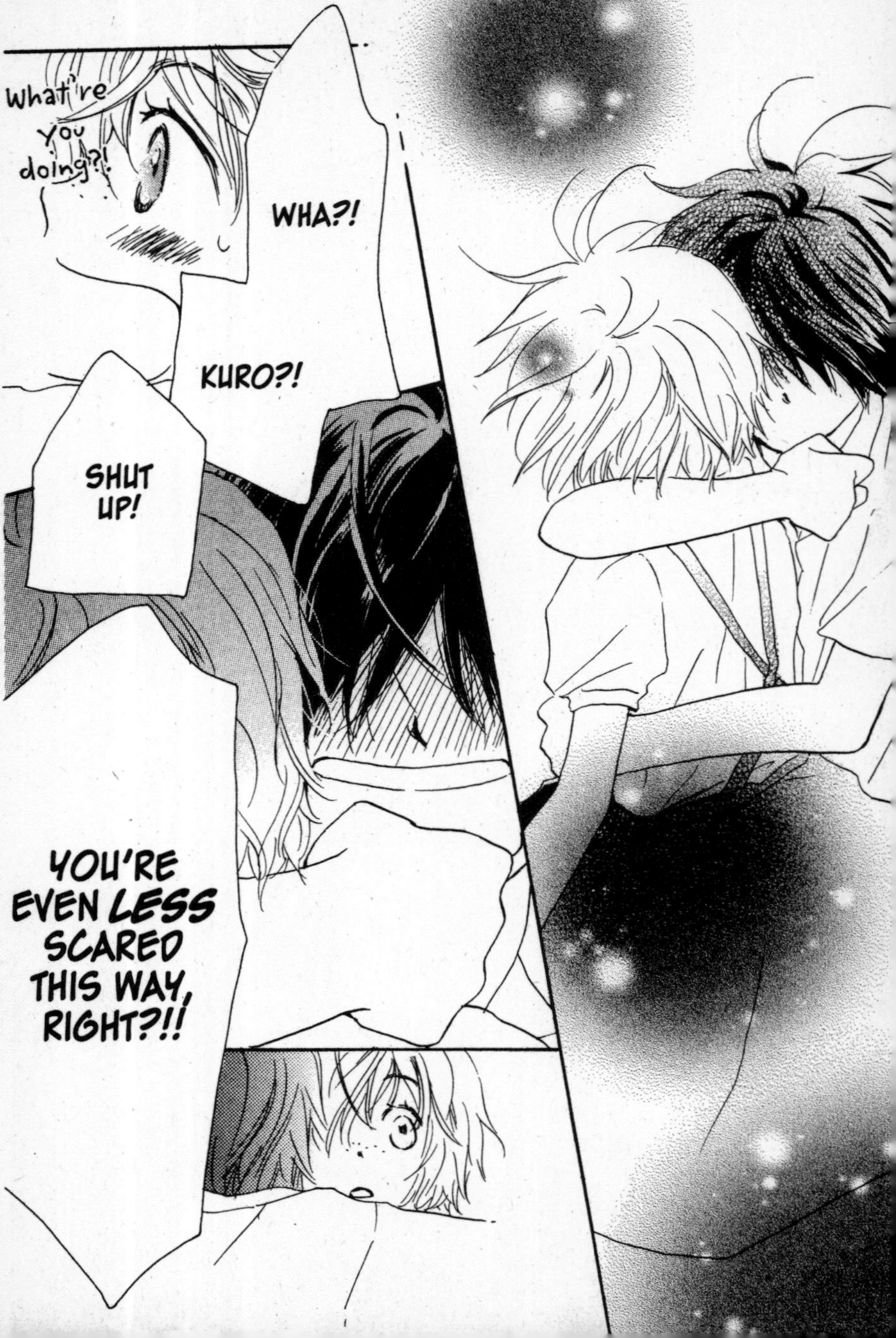

YOU'RE EVEN LESS SCARED THIS WAY, RIGHT?!!
What're you doing?!
WHA?!
KURO?!
SHUT UP!

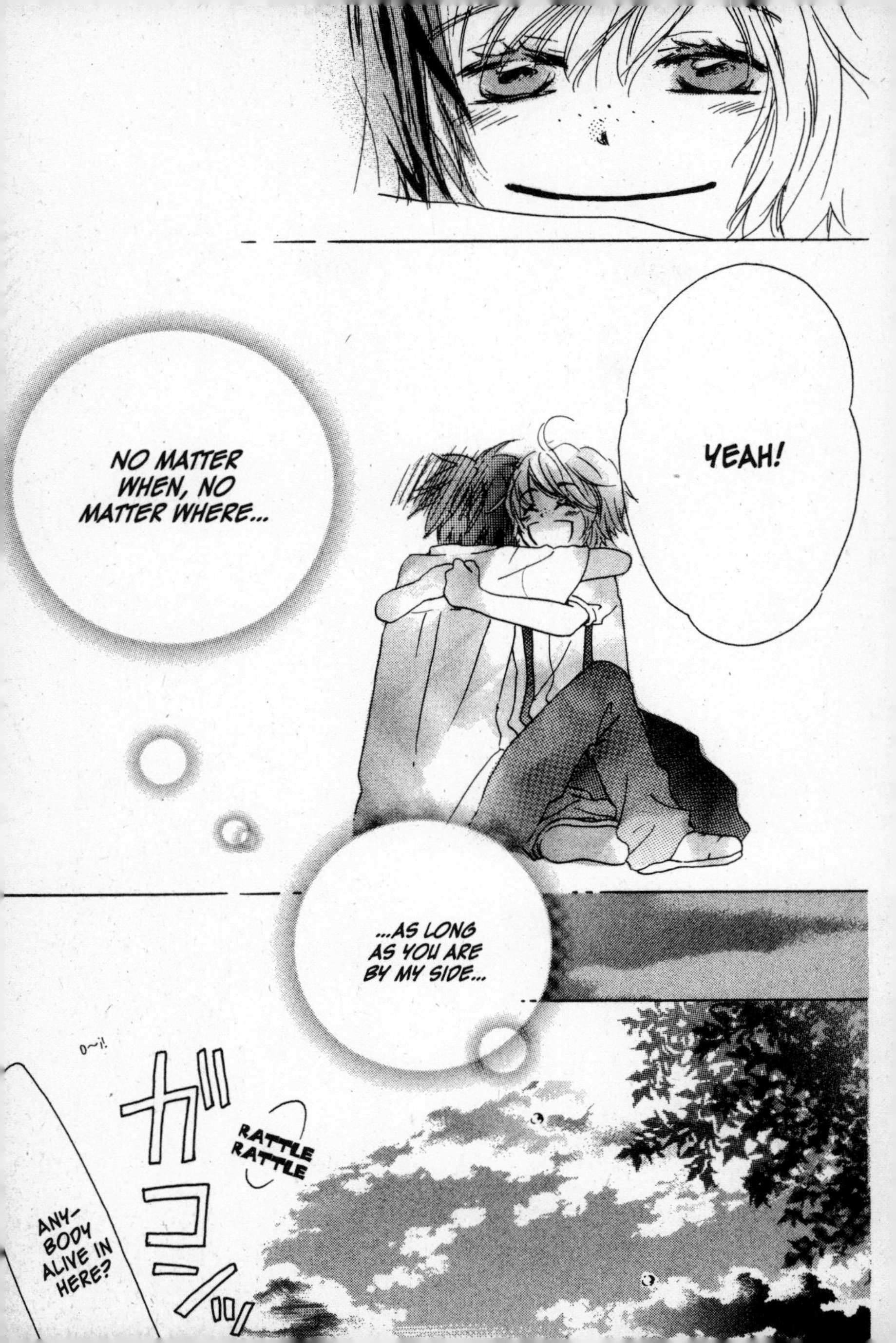
YEAH!
NO MATTER WHEN, NO MATTER WHERE...
...AS LONG AS YOU ARE BY MY SIDE...
RATTLE RATTLE
ガコン
O~i!
ANY-BODY ALIVE IN HERE?

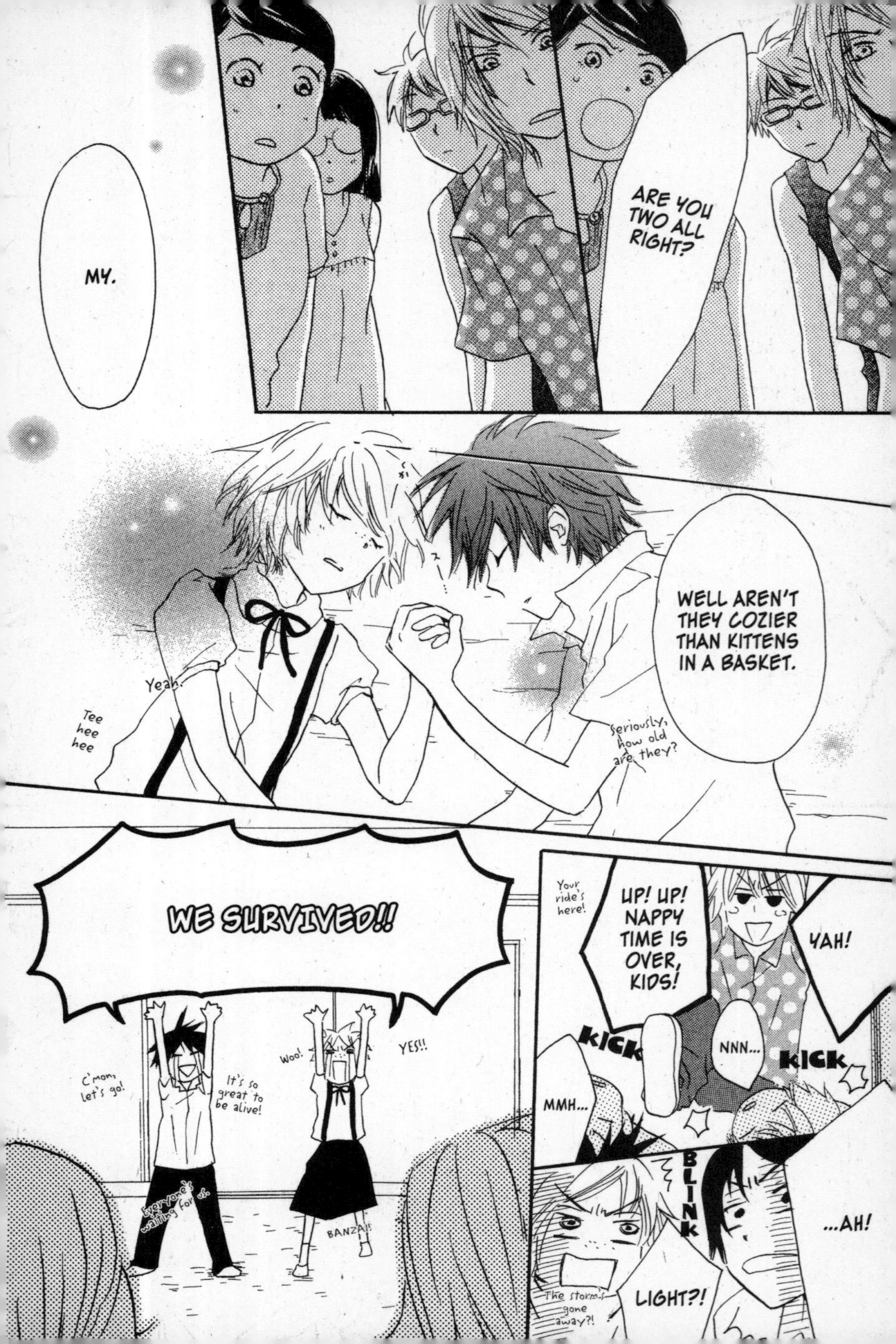
ARE YOU TWO ALL RIGHT?
MY.
WELL AREN'T THEY COZIER THAN KITTENS IN A BASKET.
Seriously, how old are they?
Yeah.
Tee hee hee
YAH!
UP! UP! NAPPY TIME IS OVER, KIDS!
Your ride's here!
KICK
NNN...
KICK
MMH...
...AH!
BLINK
LIGHT?!
The storm's gone away?!
WE SURVIVED!!
YES!!
Woo!
It's so great to be alive!
C'mon, let's go!
BANZAI!
Everyone's waiting for us.

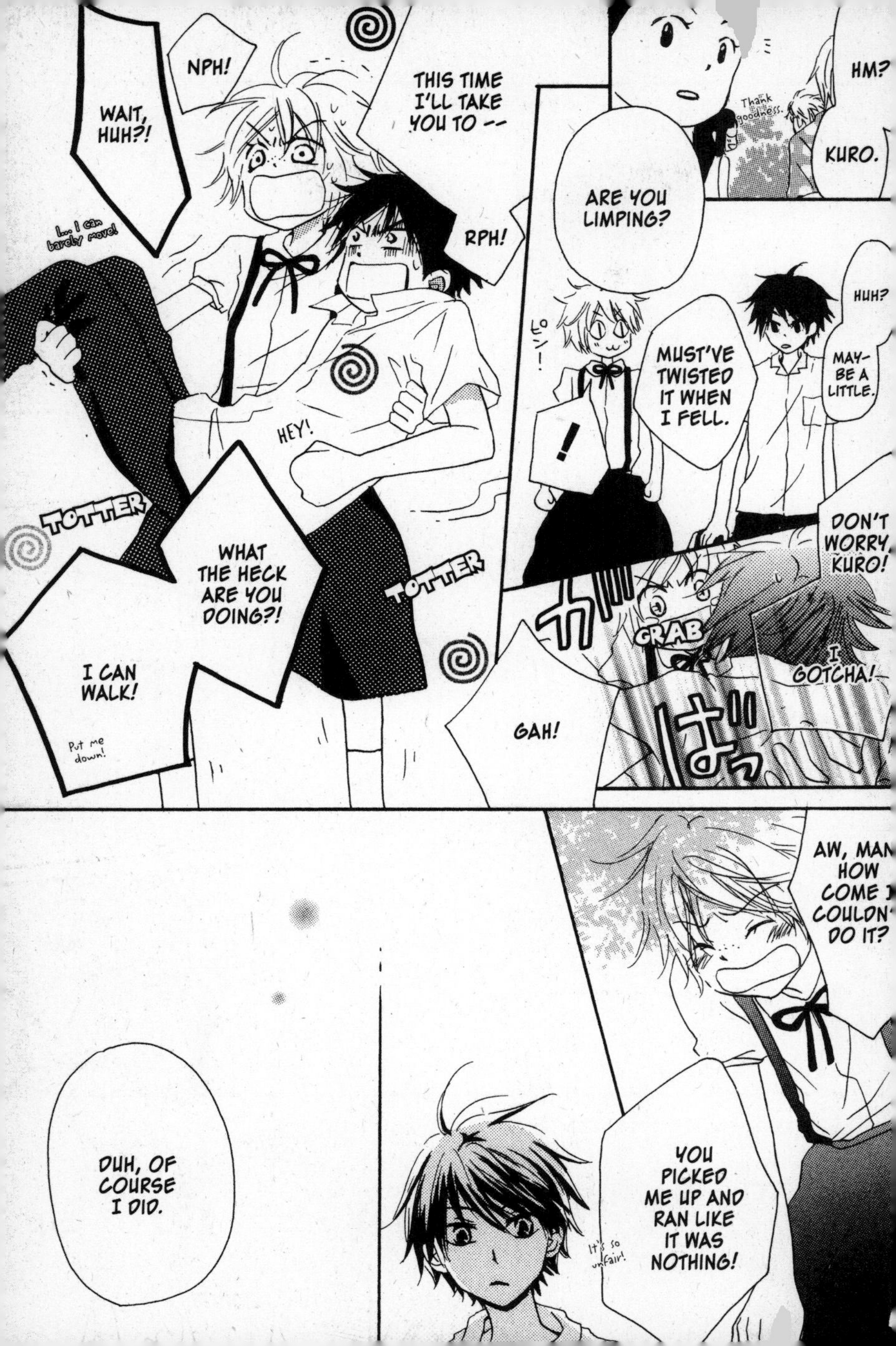
HM?
KURO.
Thank goodness.
ARE YOU LIMPING?
HUH?
MAY-BE A LITTLE.
!
MUST'VE TWISTED IT WHEN I FELL.
DON'T WORRY, KURO!
I GOTCHA!
GRAB
GAH!
THIS TIME I'LL TAKE YOU TO --
NPH!
RPH!
WAIT, HUH?!
I... I can barely move!
HEY!
TOTTER
TOTTER
WHAT THE HECK ARE YOU DOING?!
I CAN WALK!
Put me down!
AW, MAN HOW COME I COULDN'T DO IT?
YOU PICKED ME UP AND RAN LIKE IT WAS NOTHING!
It's so unfair!
DUH, OF COURSE I DID.

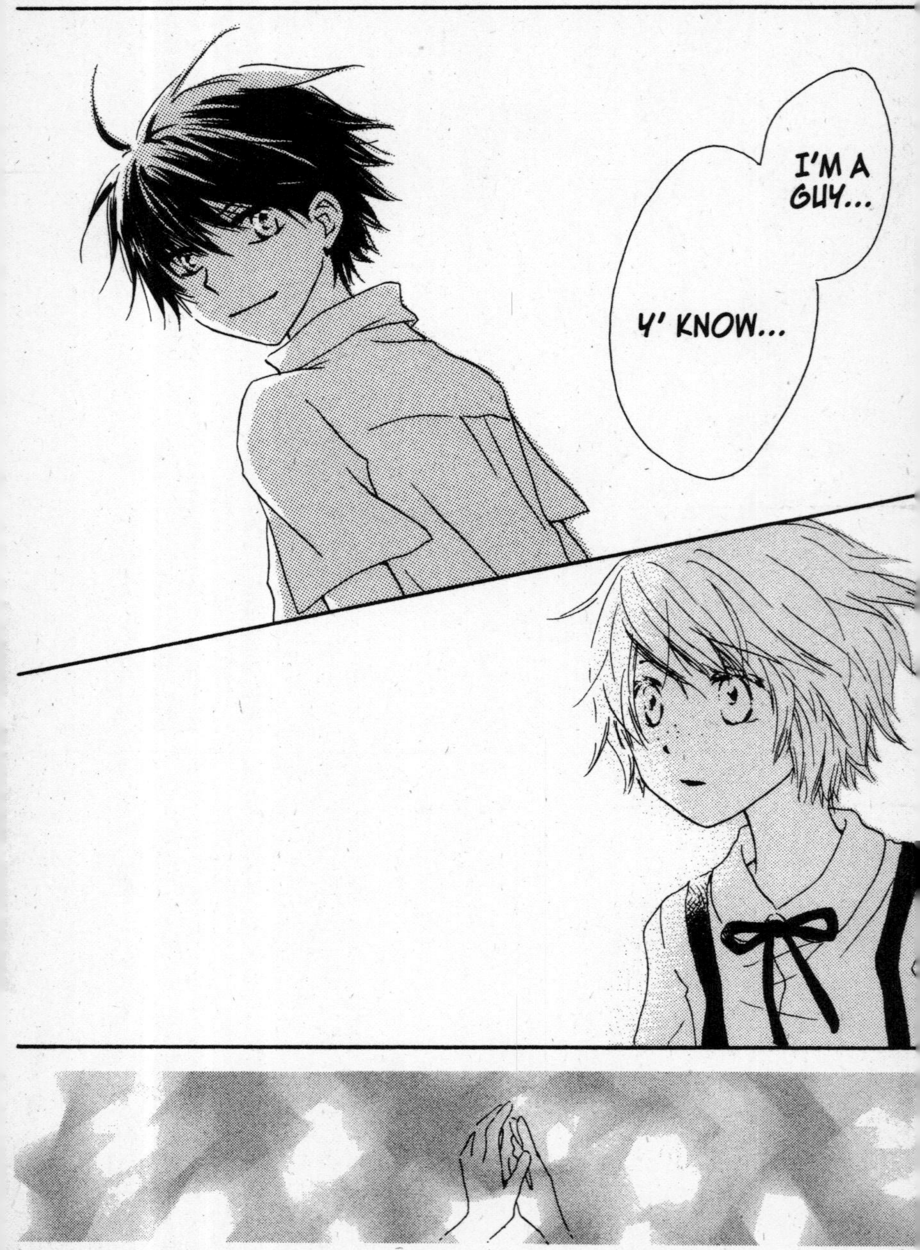
I'M A GUY...
Y' KNOW...

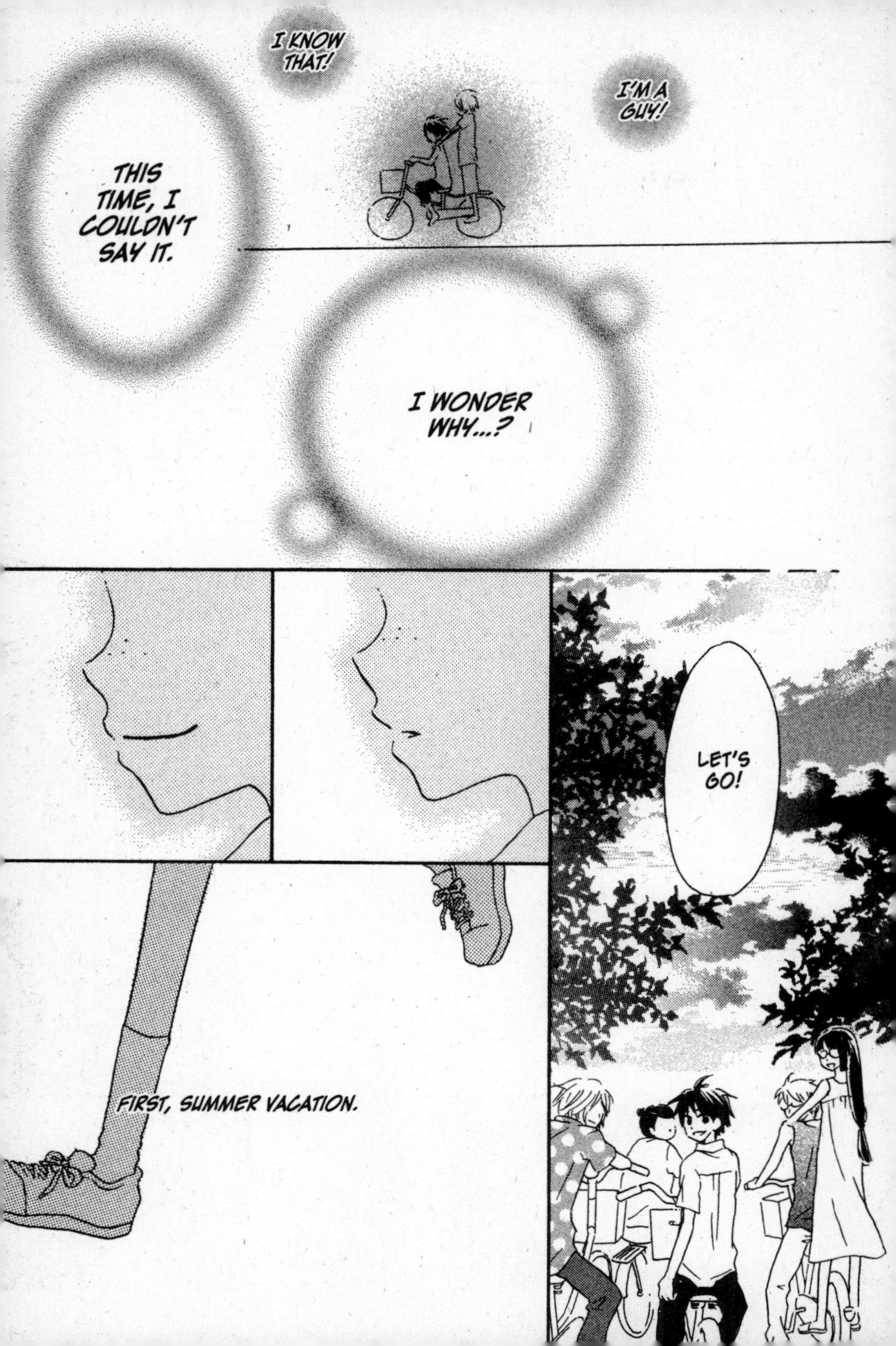
I'M A GUY!
I KNOW THAT!
THIS TIME, I COULDN'T SAY IT.
I WONDER WHY...?
LET'S GO!
FIRST, SUMMER VACATION.

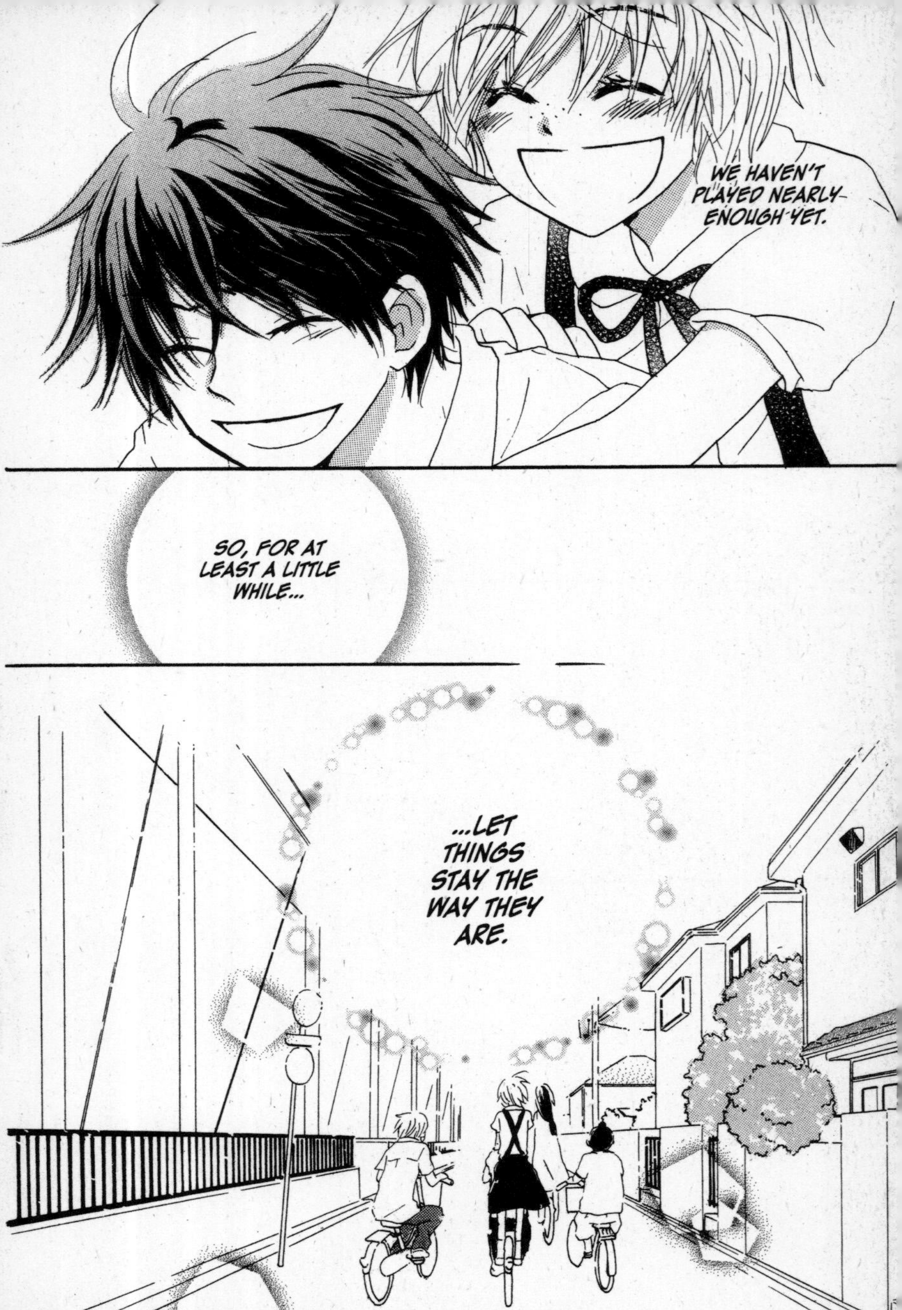
WE HAVEN'T PLAYED NEARLY ENOUGH YET.
SO, FOR AT LEAST A LITTLE WHILE...
...LET THINGS STAY THE WAY THEY ARE.
Chapter 2 / END

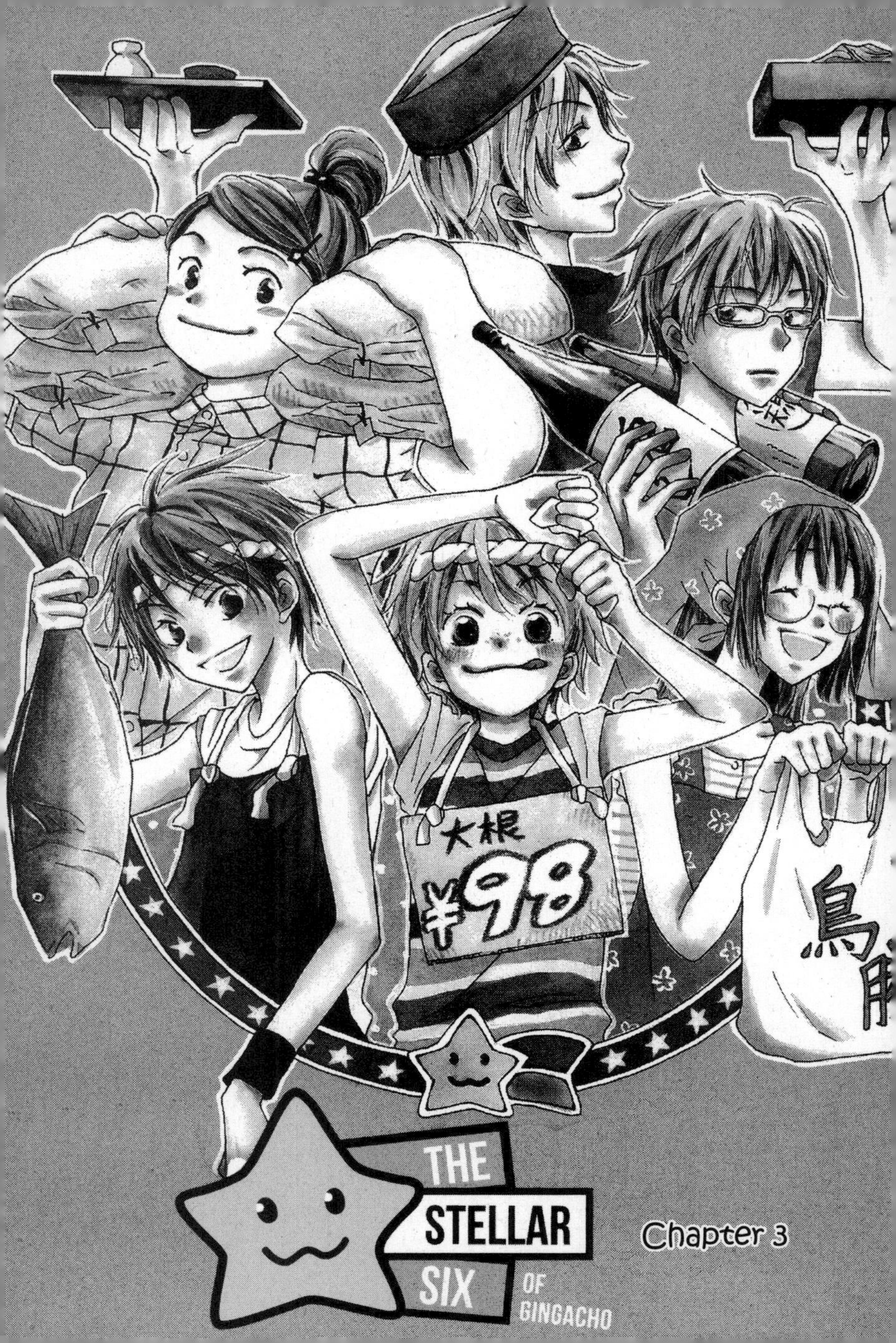
大根
¥98
鳥
THE STELLAR SIX OF GINGACHO
Chapter 3

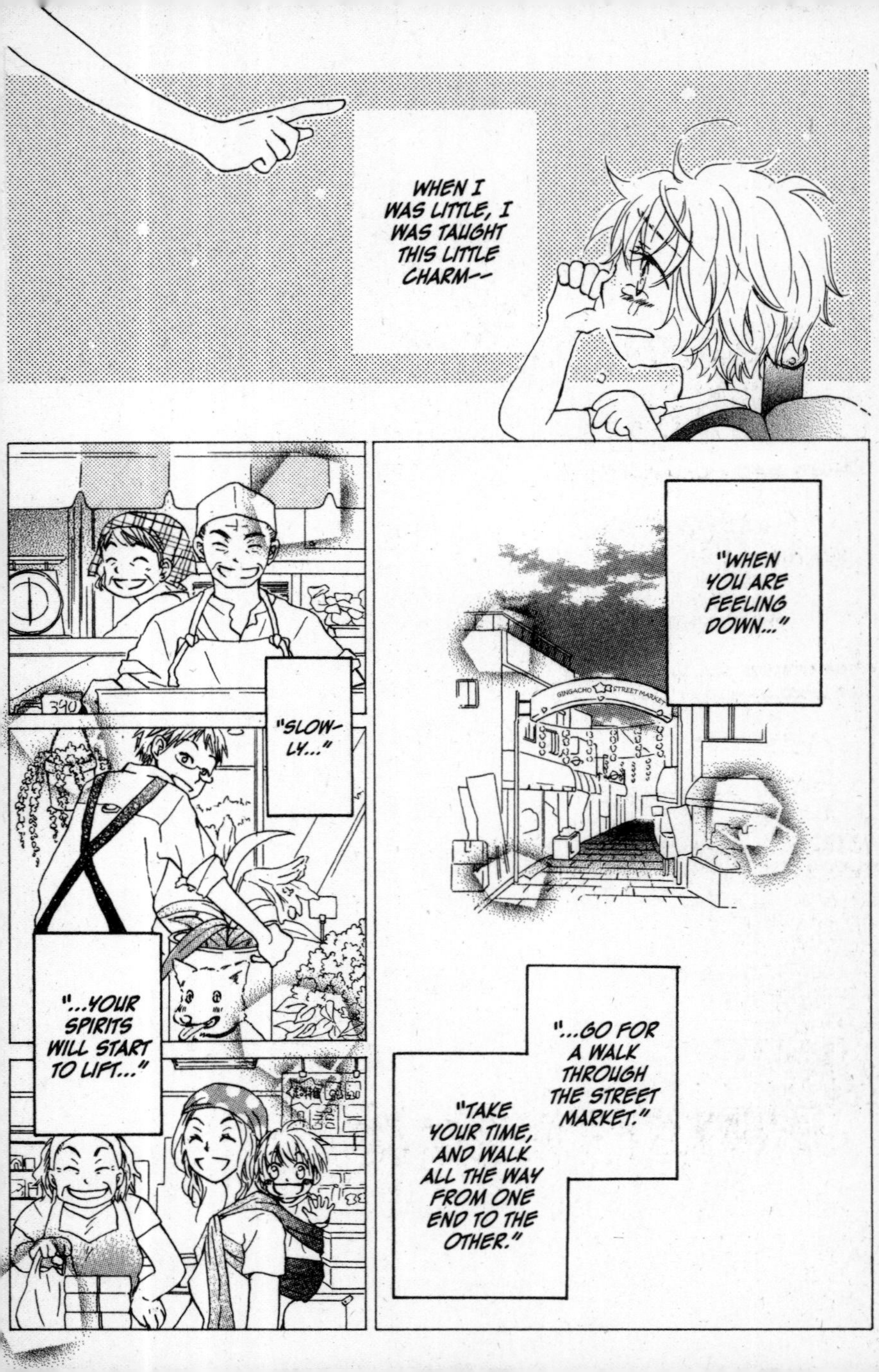
WHEN I WAS LITTLE, I WAS TAUGHT THIS LITTLE CHARM--
"WHEN YOU ARE FEELING DOWN..."
GINGACHO STREET MARKET
"...GO FOR A WALK THROUGH THE STREET MARKET."
"TAKE YOUR TIME, AND WALK ALL THE WAY FROM ONE END TO THE OTHER."
390
"SLOW-LY..."
"...YOUR SPIRITS WILL START TO LIFT..."

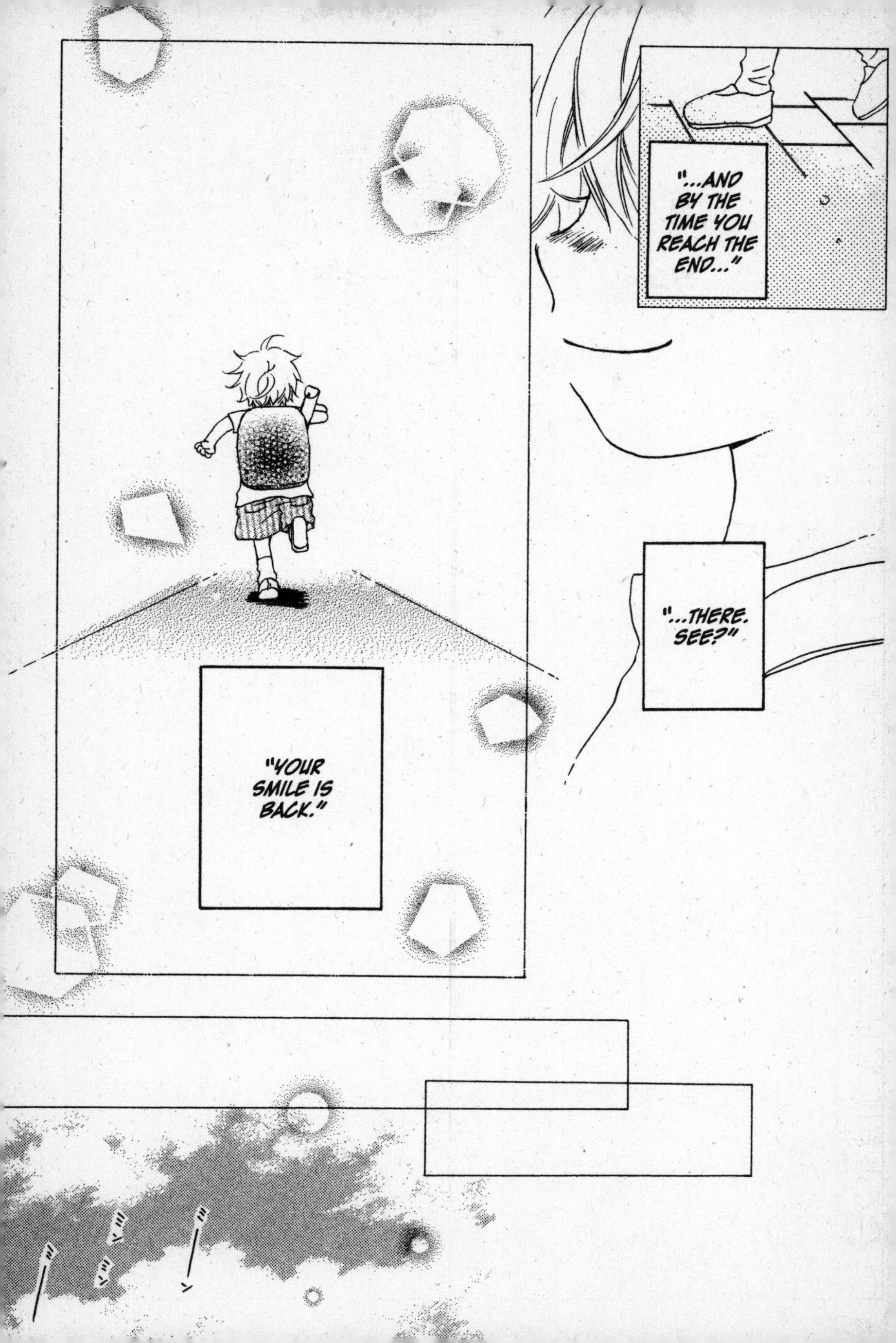
"...AND BY THE TIME YOU REACH THE END..."
"...THERE. SEE?"
"YOUR SMILE IS BACK."

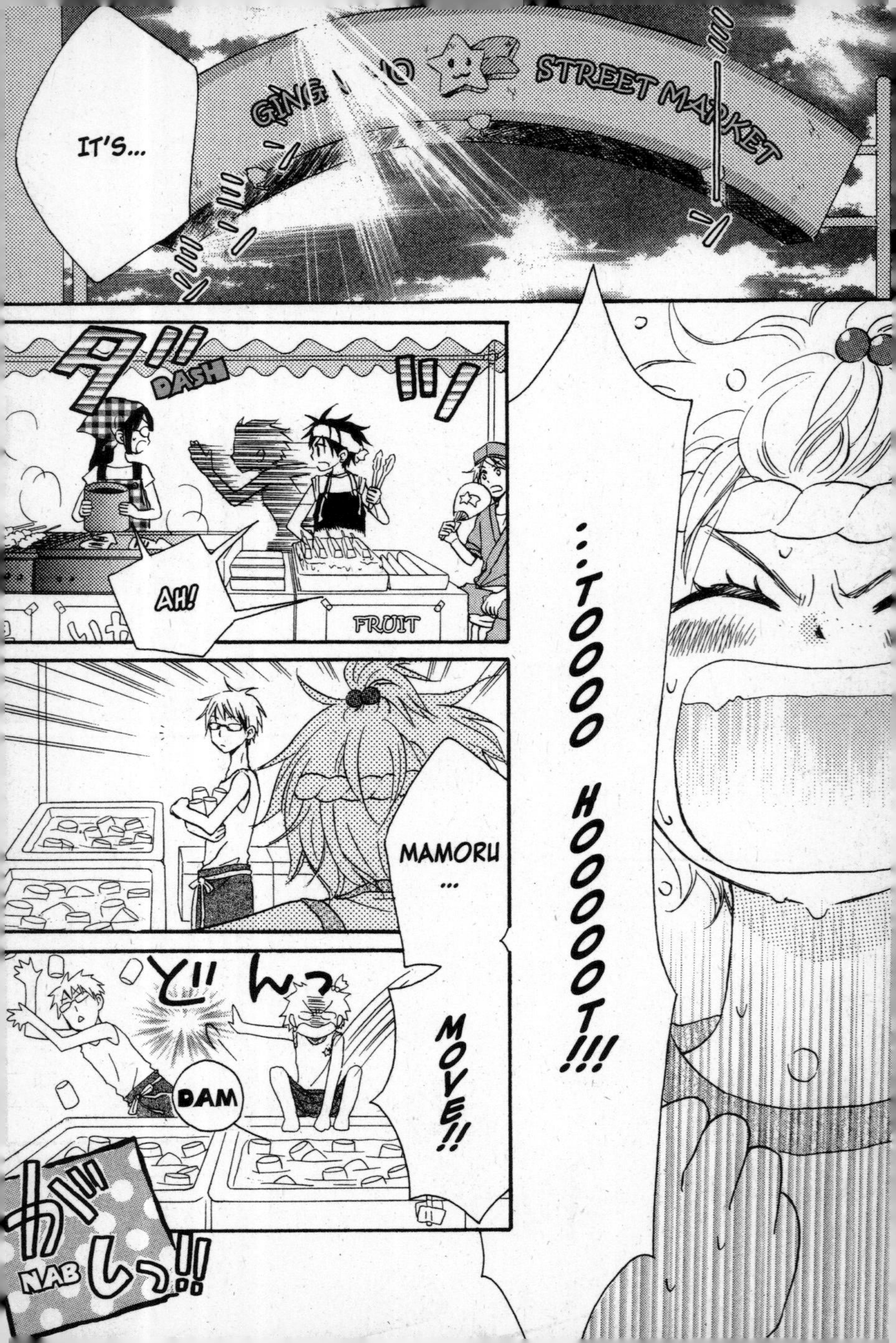
IT'S...
GING O
STREET MARKET
...TOOOOO HOOOOOOOT!!!
タッ
DASH
AH!
FRUIT
MAMORU
...
どんっ
DAM
MOVE!!
がしっ!!
NAB

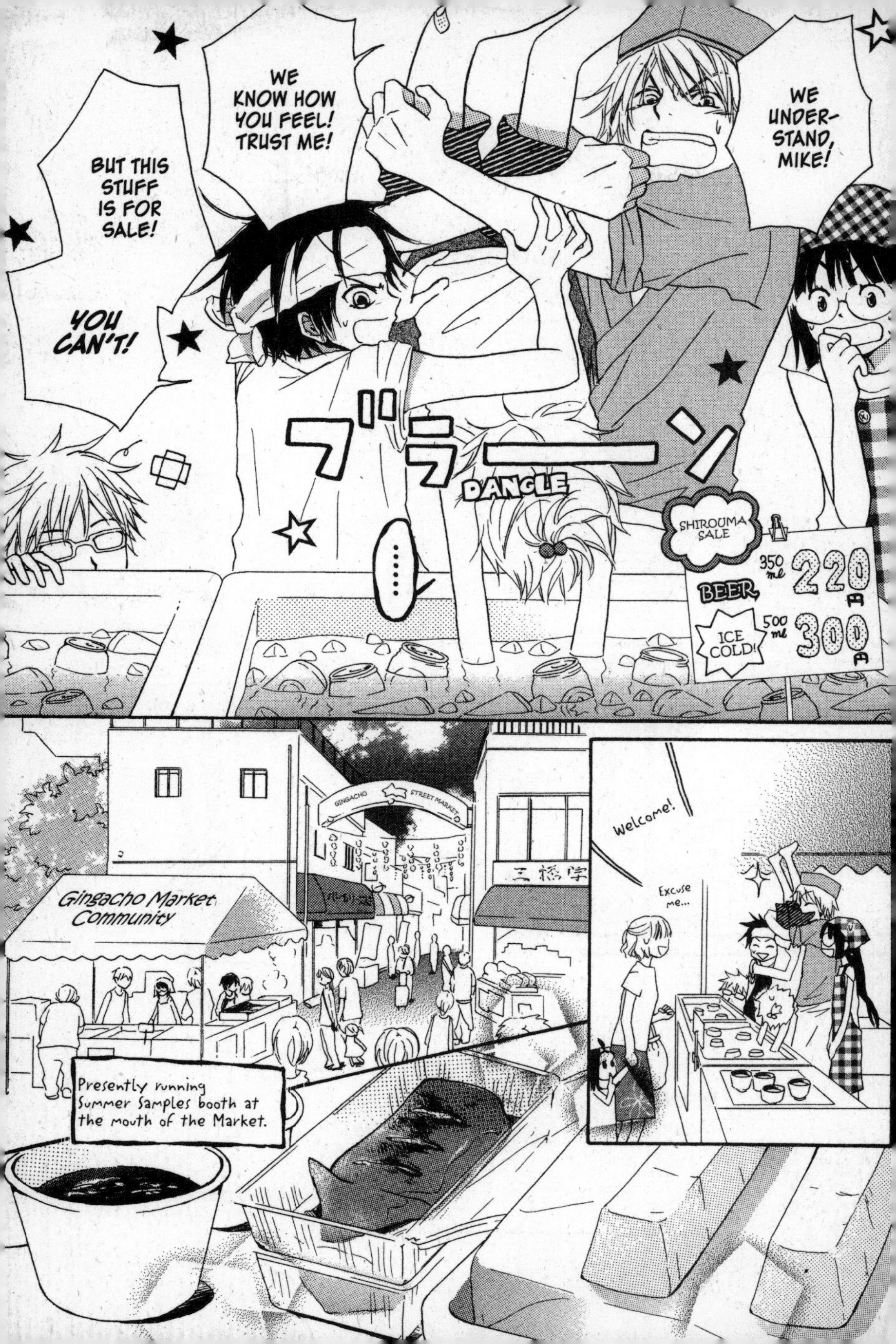
WE UNDER-STAND, MIKE!
WE KNOW HOW YOU FEEL! TRUST ME!
BUT THIS STUFF IS FOR SALE!
YOU CAN'T!
ブラーーン
DANGLE
......
SHIROUMA SALE
BEER
350 ml 220円
500 ml 300円
ICE COLD!
Welcome!
Excuse me...
GINGACHO STREET MARKET
Gingacho Market Community
Presently running Summer Samples booth at the mouth of the Market.

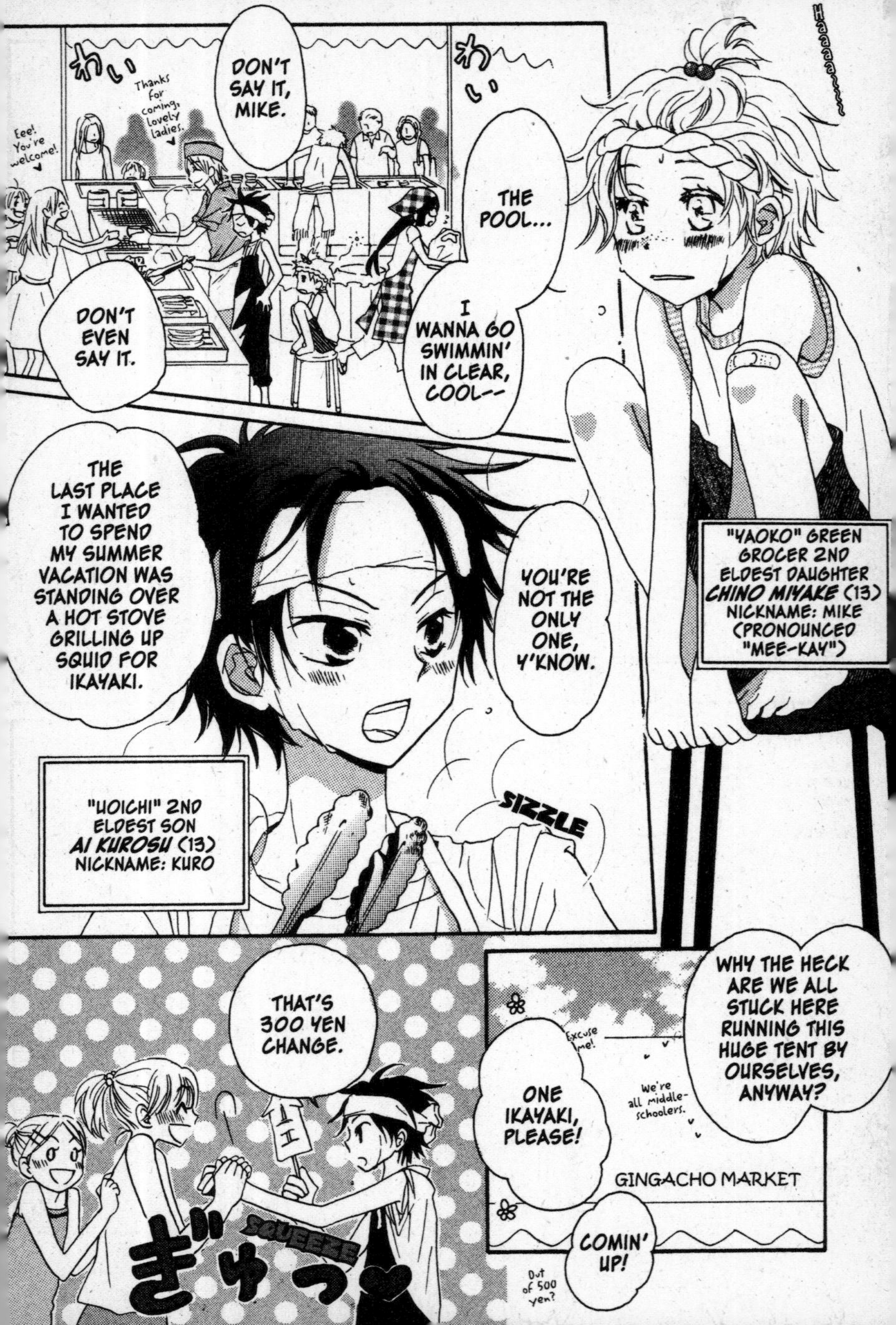
Haaaa~~~
THE POOL...
I WANNA GO SWIMMIN' IN CLEAR, COOL--
"YAOKO" GREEN GROCER 2ND ELDEST DAUGHTER
CHINO MIYAKE (13)
NICKNAME: MIKE (PRONOUNCED "MEE-KAY")
DON'T SAY IT, MIKE.
わい
Thanks for coming, lovely ladies.
Eee! You're welcome!
わい
DON'T EVEN SAY IT.
YOU'RE NOT THE ONLY ONE, Y'KNOW.
THE LAST PLACE I WANTED TO SPEND MY SUMMER VACATION WAS STANDING OVER A HOT STOVE GRILLING UP SQUID FOR IKAYAKI.
SIZZLE
"UOICHI" 2ND ELDEST SON
AI KUROSU (13)
NICKNAME: KURO
WHY THE HECK ARE WE ALL STUCK HERE RUNNING THIS HUGE TENT BY OURSELVES, ANYWAY?
Excuse me!
We're all middle-schoolers.
ONE IKAYAKI, PLEASE!
GINGACHO MARKET
COMIN' UP!
Out of 500 yen?
THAT'S 300 YEN CHANGE.
SQUEEEZE
ぎゅっ

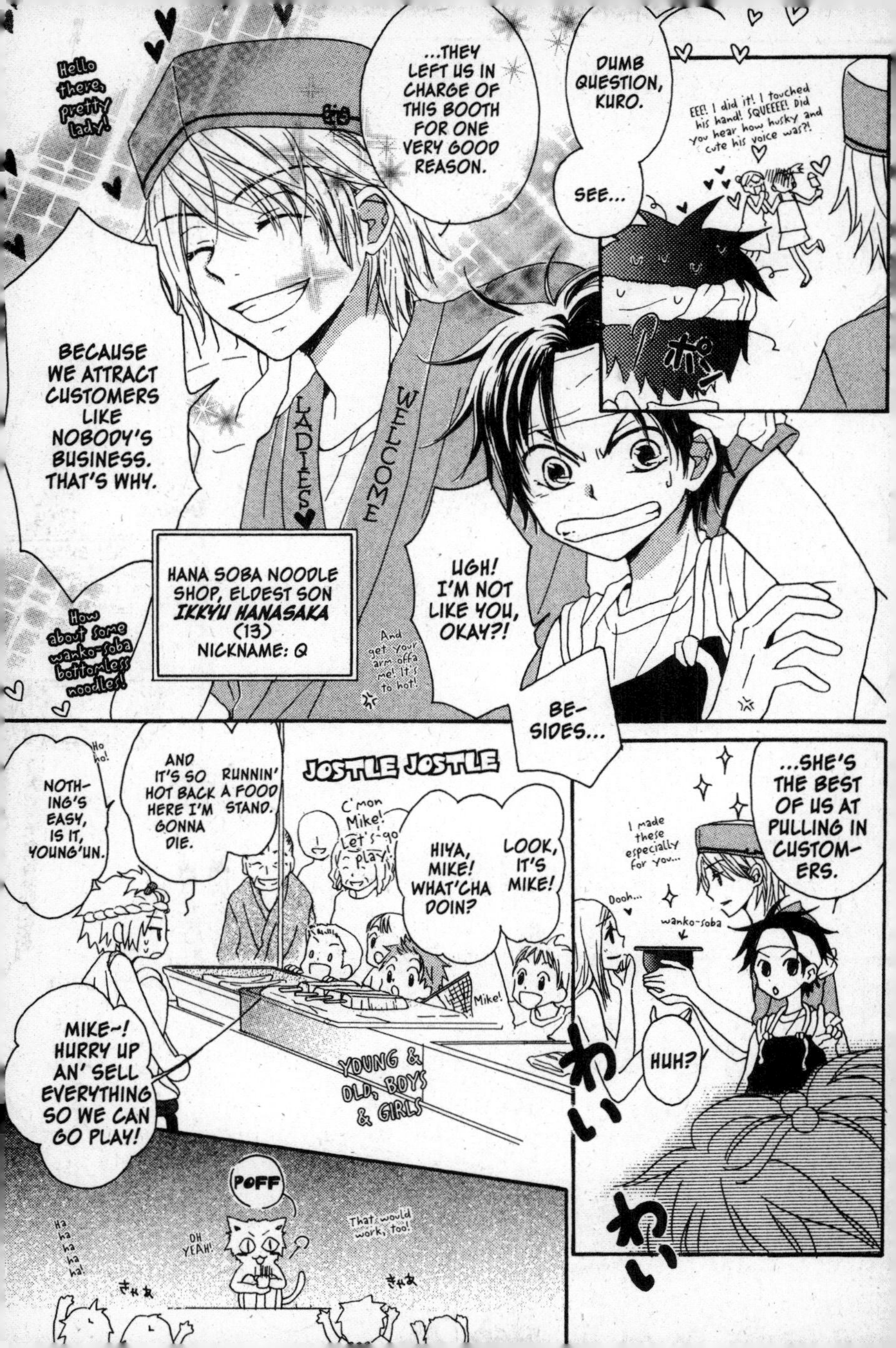

DUMB QUESTION, KURO.
SEE...
EEE! I did it! I touched his hand! SQUEEEE! Did you hear how husky and cute his voice was?!
ポッ
...THEY LEFT US IN CHARGE OF THIS BOOTH FOR ONE VERY GOOD REASON.
Hello there, pretty lady!
BECAUSE WE ATTRACT CUSTOMERS LIKE NOBODY'S BUSINESS. THAT'S WHY.
LADIES WELCOME
HANA SOBA NOODLE SHOP, ELDEST SON
IKKYU HANASAKA (13)
NICKNAME: Q
UGH! I'M NOT LIKE YOU, OKAY?!
And get your arm offa me! It's to hot!
How about some wanko-soba bottomless noodles!
BE-SIDES...
...SHE'S THE BEST OF US AT PULLING IN CUSTOMERS.
I made these especially for you...
Oooh...
wanko-soba
HUH?
わい
わい
JOSTLE JOSTLE
LOOK, IT'S MIKE!
HIYA, MIKE! WHAT'CHA DOIN?
C'mon Mike! Let's go play!
RUNNIN' A FOOD STAND.
AND IT'S SO HOT BACK HERE I'M GONNA DIE.
Ho ho!
NOTHING'S EASY, IS IT, YOUNG'UN.
Mike!
YOUNG & OLD, BOYS & GIRLS
MIKE~! HURRY UP AN' SELL EVERYTHING SO WE CAN GO PLAY!
POFF
That would work, too!
OH YEAH!
Ha ha ha ha ha!
きゃあ
きゃあ

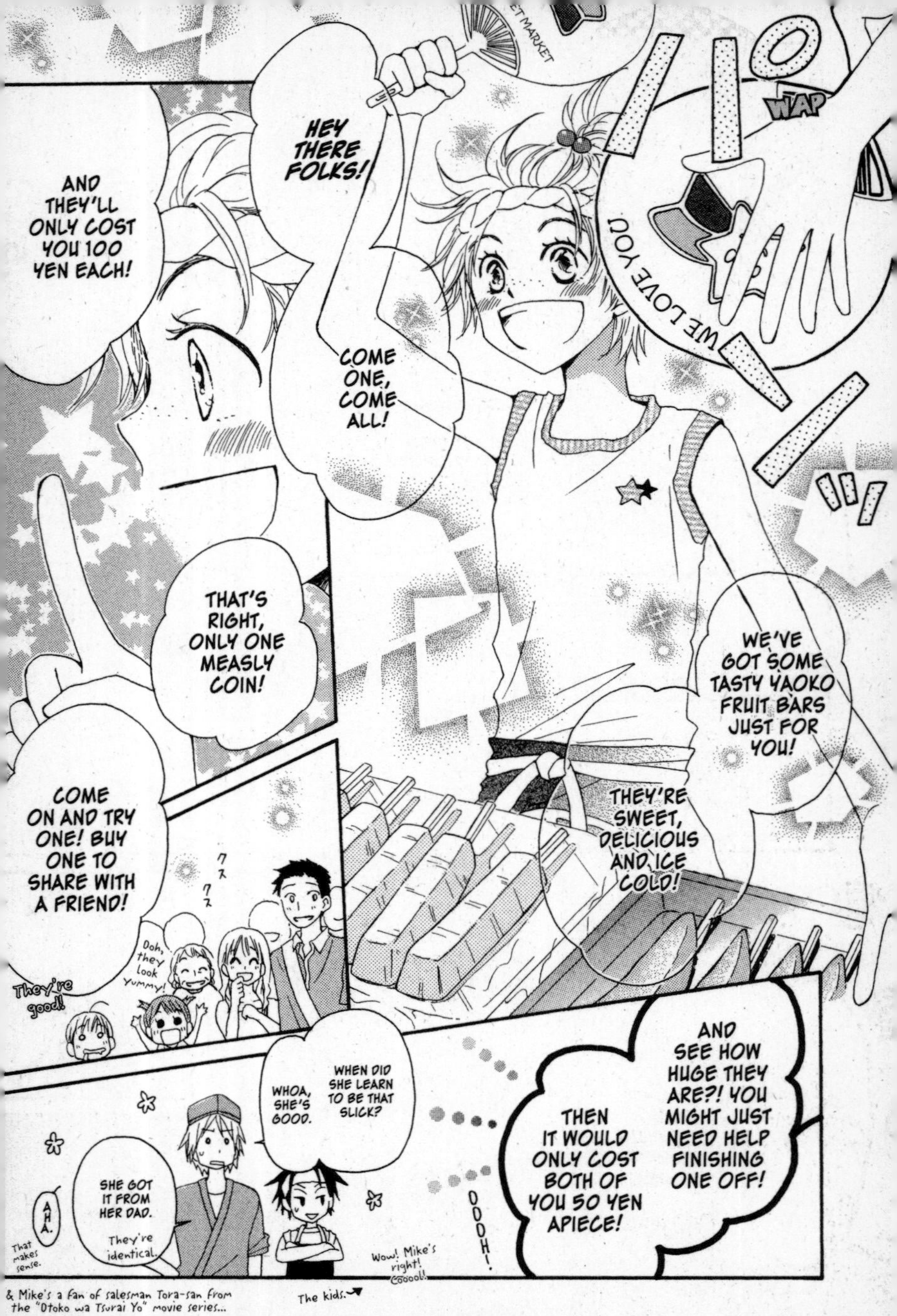
WAP
WE LOVE YOU
HEY THERE FOLKS!
COME ONE, COME ALL!
WE'VE GOT SOME TASTY YAOKO FRUIT BARS JUST FOR YOU!
THEY'RE SWEET, DELICIOUS AND ICE COLD!
AND THEY'LL ONLY COST YOU 100 YEN EACH!
THAT'S RIGHT, ONLY ONE MEASLY COIN!
COME ON AND TRY ONE! BUY ONE TO SHARE WITH A FRIEND!
クス クス
Ooh, they look yummy!
They're good!
AND SEE HOW HUGE THEY ARE?! YOU MIGHT JUST NEED HELP FINISHING ONE OFF!
THEN IT WOULD ONLY COST BOTH OF YOU 50 YEN APIECE!
OOOH!
Wow! Mike's right! Coooool!
The kids.
WHEN DID SHE LEARN TO BE THAT SLICK?
WHOA, SHE'S GOOD.
SHE GOT IT FROM HER DAD.
They're identical.
AHA.
That makes sense.

& Mike's a fan of salesman Tora-san from the "Otoko wa Tsurai Yo" movie series...

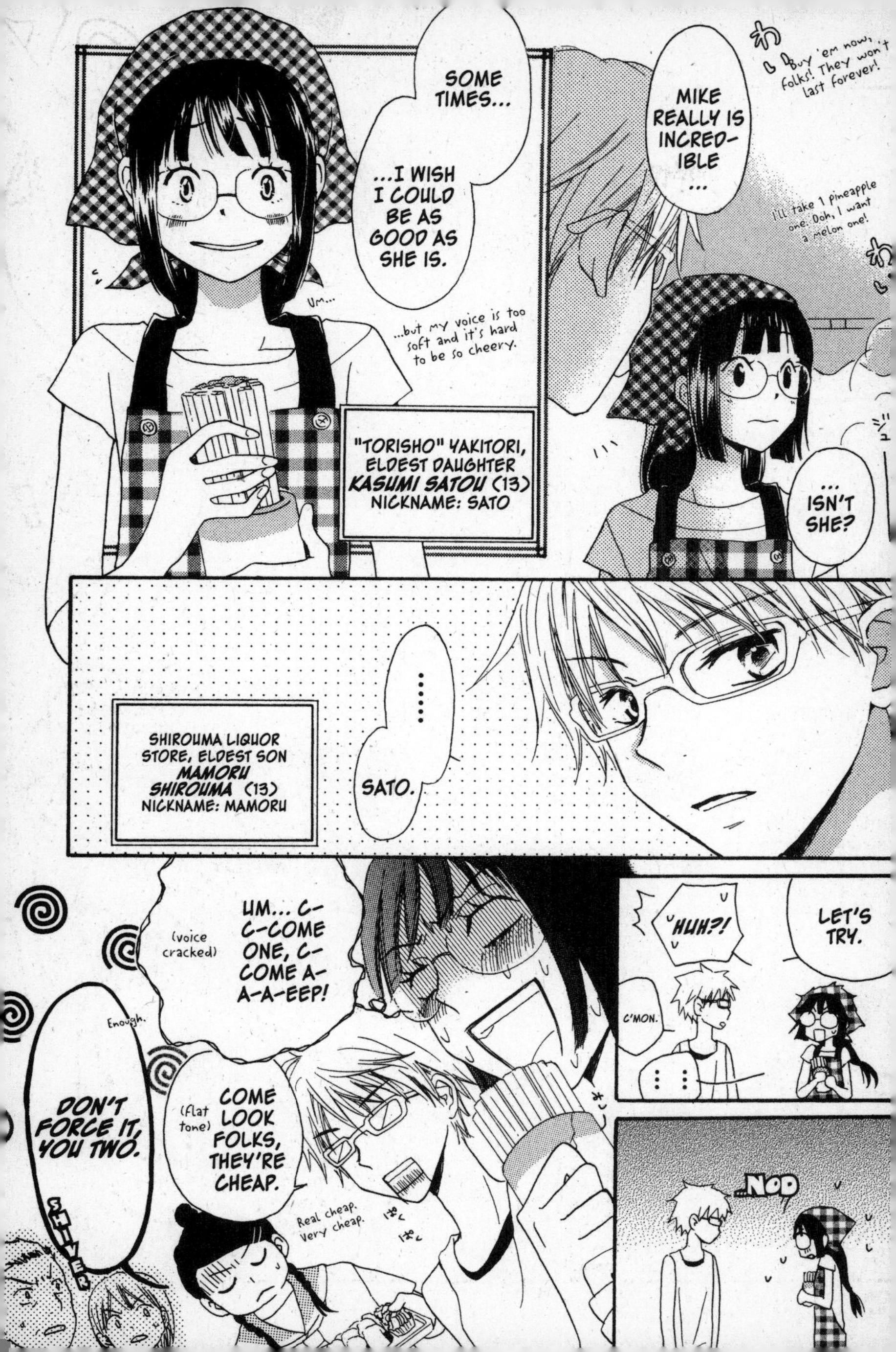
Buy 'em now, folks! They won't last forever!
MIKE REALLY IS INCREDIBLE...
I'll take 1 pineapple one. Ooh, I want a melon one!
...ISN'T SHE?
SOME TIMES...
...I WISH I COULD BE AS GOOD AS SHE IS.
Um...
...but my voice is too soft and it's hard to be so cheery.
"TORISHO" YAKITORI, ELDEST DAUGHTER KASUMI SATOU (13) NICKNAME: SATO
......
SATO.
SHIROUMA LIQUOR STORE, ELDEST SON MAMORU SHIROUMA (13) NICKNAME: MAMORU
LET'S TRY.
HUH?!
C'MON.
...
...NOD
UM... C-C-COME ONE, C-COME A-A-A-EEP!
(voice cracked)
COME LOOK FOLKS, THEY'RE CHEAP.
(Flat tone)
Real cheap. Very cheap.
Enough.
DON'T FORCE IT, YOU TWO.
SHIVER

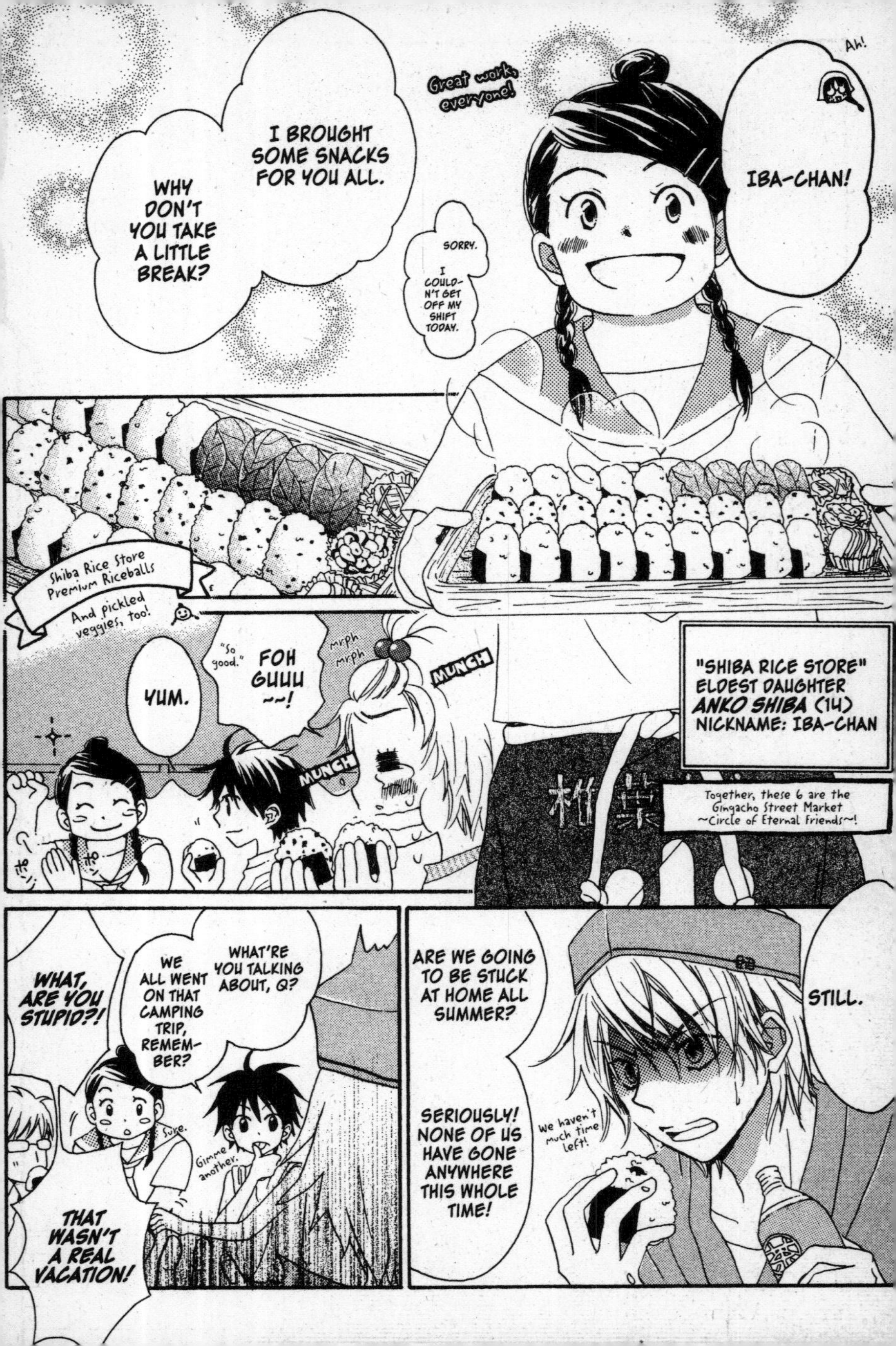
Ah!
IBA-CHAN!
Great work, everyone!
SORRY. I COULDN'T GET OFF MY SHIFT TODAY.
I BROUGHT SOME SNACKS FOR YOU ALL.
WHY DON'T YOU TAKE A LITTLE BREAK?
Shiba Rice Store Premium Riceballs
And pickled veggies, too!
"SHIBA RICE STORE" ELDEST DAUGHTER ANKO SHIBA (14) NICKNAME: IBA-CHAN
Together, these 6 are the Gingacho Street Market ~Circle of Eternal Friends~!
MUNCH
mrph mrph
FOH GUUU ~~!
"So good."
YUM.
MUNCH
STILL.
ARE WE GOING TO BE STUCK AT HOME ALL SUMMER?
SERIOUSLY! NONE OF US HAVE GONE ANYWHERE THIS WHOLE TIME!
We haven't much time left!
WHAT'RE YOU TALKING ABOUT, Q?
WE ALL WENT ON THAT CAMPING TRIP, REMEMBER?
Sure.
Gimme another.
WHAT, ARE YOU STUPID?!
THAT WASN'T A REAL VACATION!

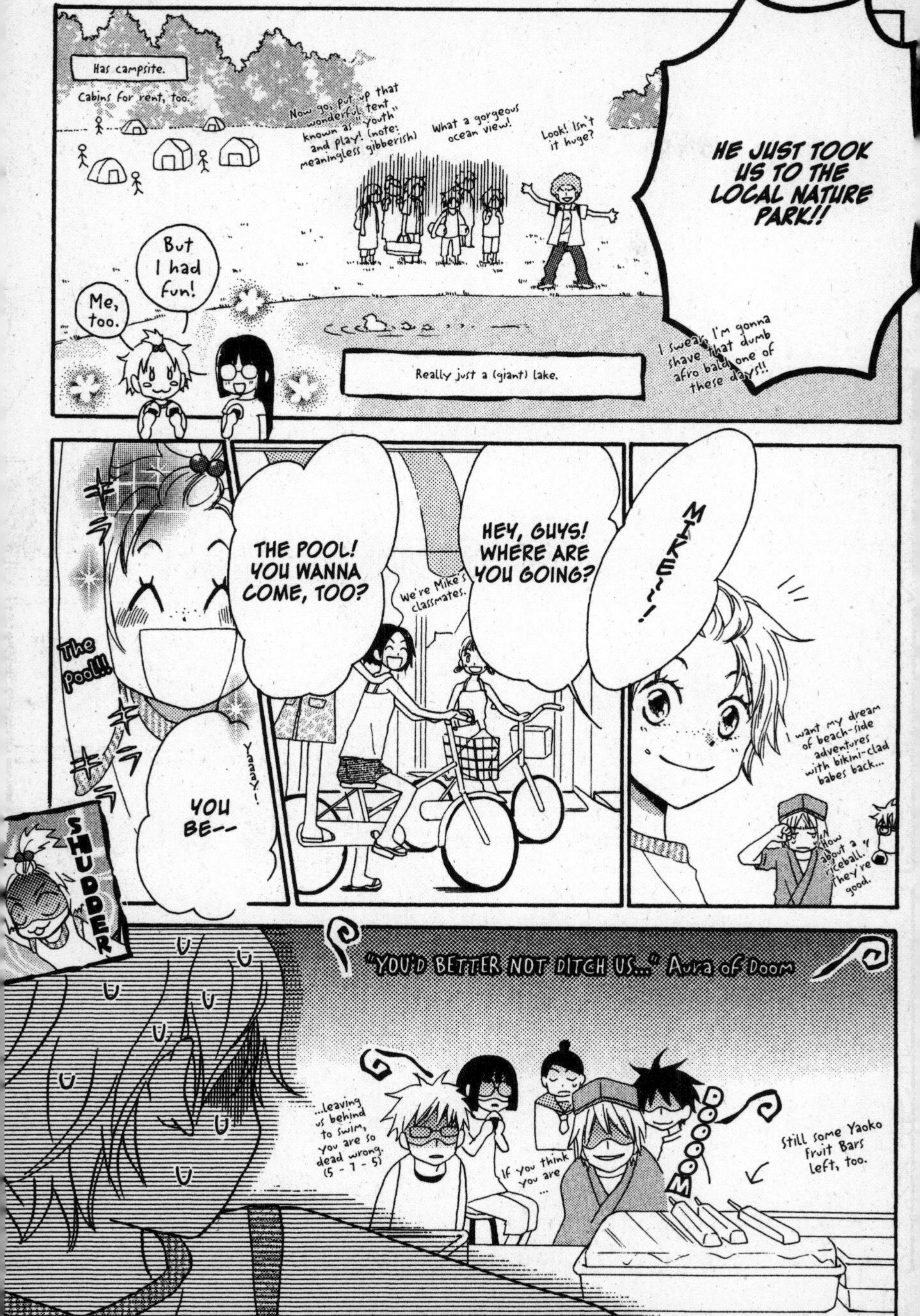
HE JUST TOOK US TO THE LOCAL NATURE PARK!!
I swear, I'm gonna shave that dumb afro bald one of these days!!
Look! Isn't it huge?
What a gorgeous ocean view!
Now go, put up that wonderful tent known as "youth" and play! (note: meaningless gibberish)
Has campsite.
Cabins for rent, too.
But I had fun!
Me, too.
Really just a (giant) lake.
MIKE~~!
I want my dream of beach-side adventures with bikini-clad babes back...
How about a riceball. They're good.
HEY, GUYS! WHERE ARE YOU GOING?
We're Mike's classmates.
THE POOL! YOU WANNA COME, TOO?
The pool!!
YOU BE--
Yaaaay!
SHUDDER
"YOU'D BETTER NOT DITCH US..." Aura of Doom
DOOOOOM
Still some Yaoko Fruit Bars left, too.
If you think you are ...
...leaving us behind to swim, you are so dead wrong. (5 - 7 - 5)

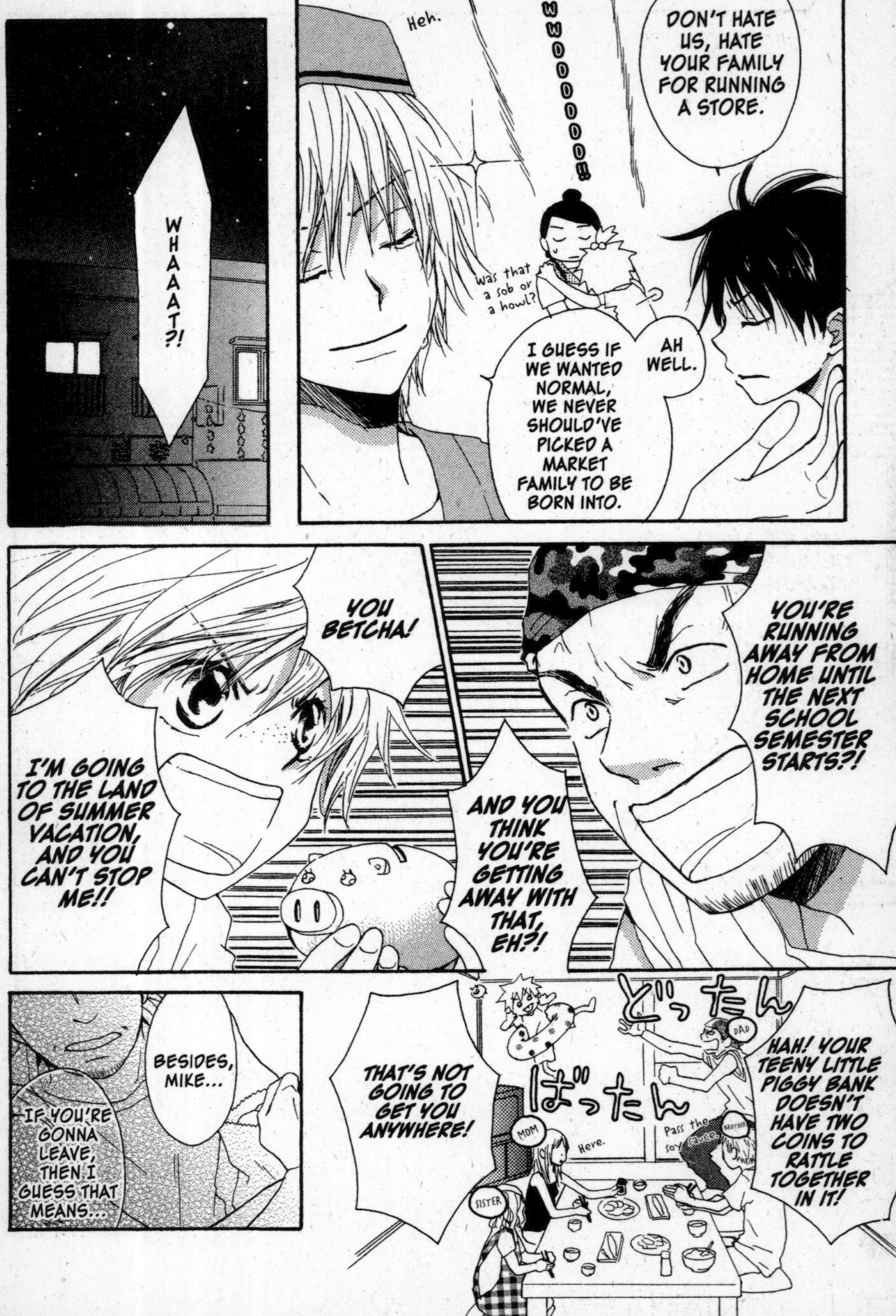
DON'T HATE US, HATE YOUR FAMILY FOR RUNNING A STORE.
AWWOOOOOOOOO!!
Heh.
Was that a sob or a howl?
AH WELL.
I GUESS IF WE WANTED NORMAL, WE NEVER SHOULD'VE PICKED A MARKET FAMILY TO BE BORN INTO.
WHAAAT?!
YOU'RE RUNNING AWAY FROM HOME UNTIL THE NEXT SCHOOL SEMESTER STARTS?!
AND YOU THINK YOU'RE GETTING AWAY WITH THAT, EH?!
YOU BETCHA!
I'M GOING TO THE LAND OF SUMMER VACATION, AND YOU CAN'T STOP ME!!
HAH! YOUR TEENY LITTLE PIGGY BANK DOESN'T HAVE TWO COINS TO RATTLE TOGETHER IN IT!
どったん
DAD
ばったん
BROTHER
Pass the soy sauce.
MOM
Here.
SISTER
THAT'S NOT GOING TO GET YOU ANYWHERE!
BESIDES, MIKE...
IF YOU'RE GONNA LEAVE, THEN I GUESS THAT MEANS...

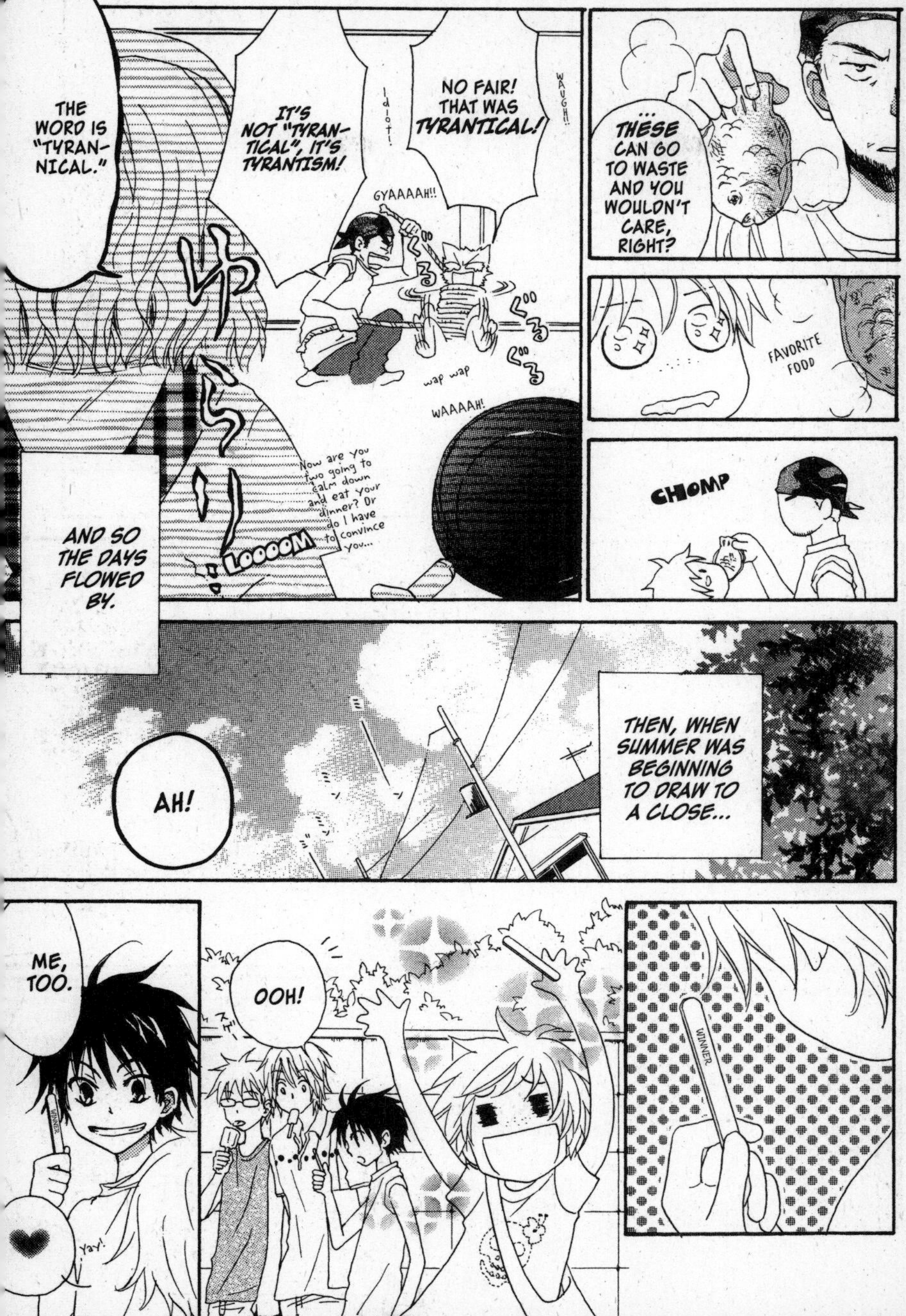
... THESE CAN GO TO WASTE AND YOU WOULDN'T CARE, RIGHT?
FAVORITE FOOD
CHOMP
NO FAIR! THAT WAS TYRANTICAL!
WAUGH!!
IT'S NOT "TYRANTICAL", IT'S TYRANTISM!
Idiot!
THE WORD IS "TYRANNICAL."
GYAAAAH!!
wap wap
WAAAAH!
Now are you two going to calm down and eat your dinner? Or do I have to convince you...
LOOOOM
AND SO THE DAYS FLOWED BY.
THEN, WHEN SUMMER WAS BEGINNING TO DRAW TO A CLOSE...
AH!
WINNER
OOH!
ME, TOO.
WINNER
Yay!

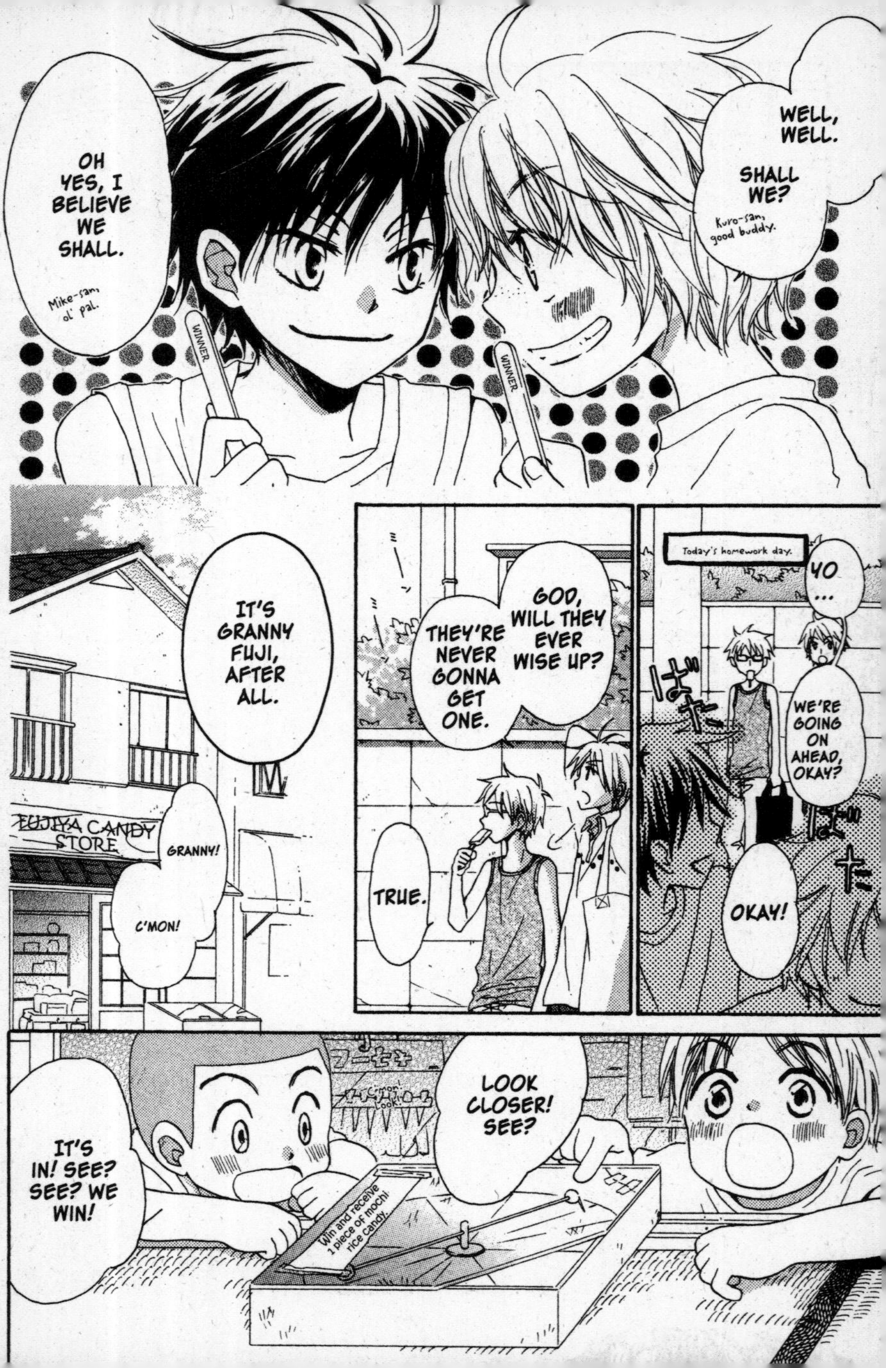
WELL, WELL.
SHALL WE?
Kuro-san, good buddy.
OH YES, I BELIEVE WE SHALL.
Mike-san, ol' pal.
WINNER.
WINNER.
Today's homework day.
YO...
WE'RE GOING ON AHEAD, OKAY?
OKAY!
GOD, WILL THEY EVER WISE UP?
THEY'RE NEVER GONNA GET ONE.
TRUE.
IT'S GRANNY FUJI, AFTER ALL.
FUJIYA CANDY STORE
GRANNY!
C'MON!
LOOK CLOSER! SEE?
C'mon! Look!
IT'S IN! SEE? SEE? WE WIN!
Win and receive 1 piece of mochi rice candy.

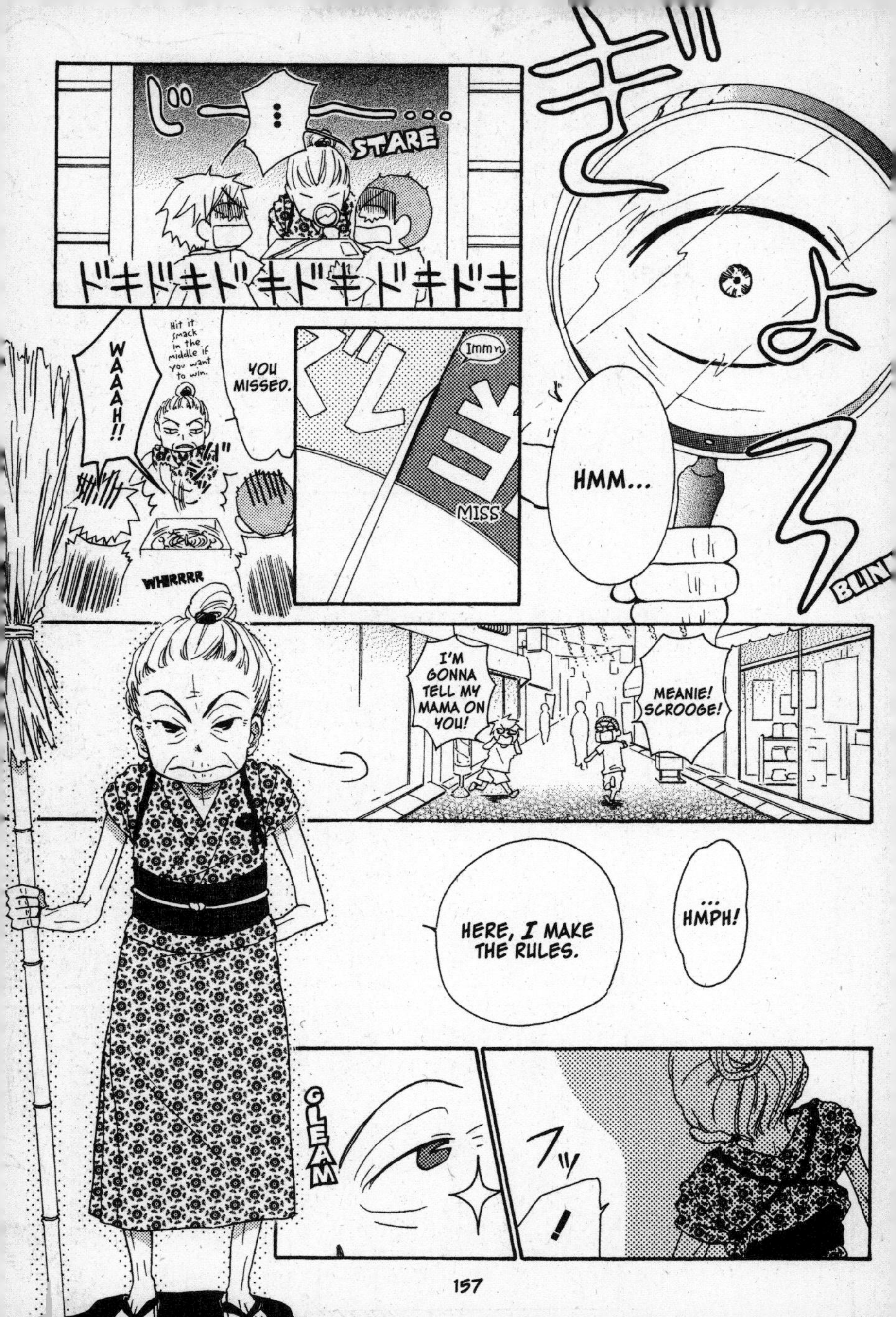
ぎょろ
HMM...
BLIN
じーー…
STARE
...
ドキドキドキドキドキドキ
Immn
MISS
YOU MISSED.
Hit it smack in the middle if you want to win.
WAAAH!!
WHIRRRR
MEANIE! SCROOGE!
I'M GONNA TELL MY MAMA ON YOU!
...HMPH!
HERE, I MAKE THE RULES.
フッ
!
GLEAM

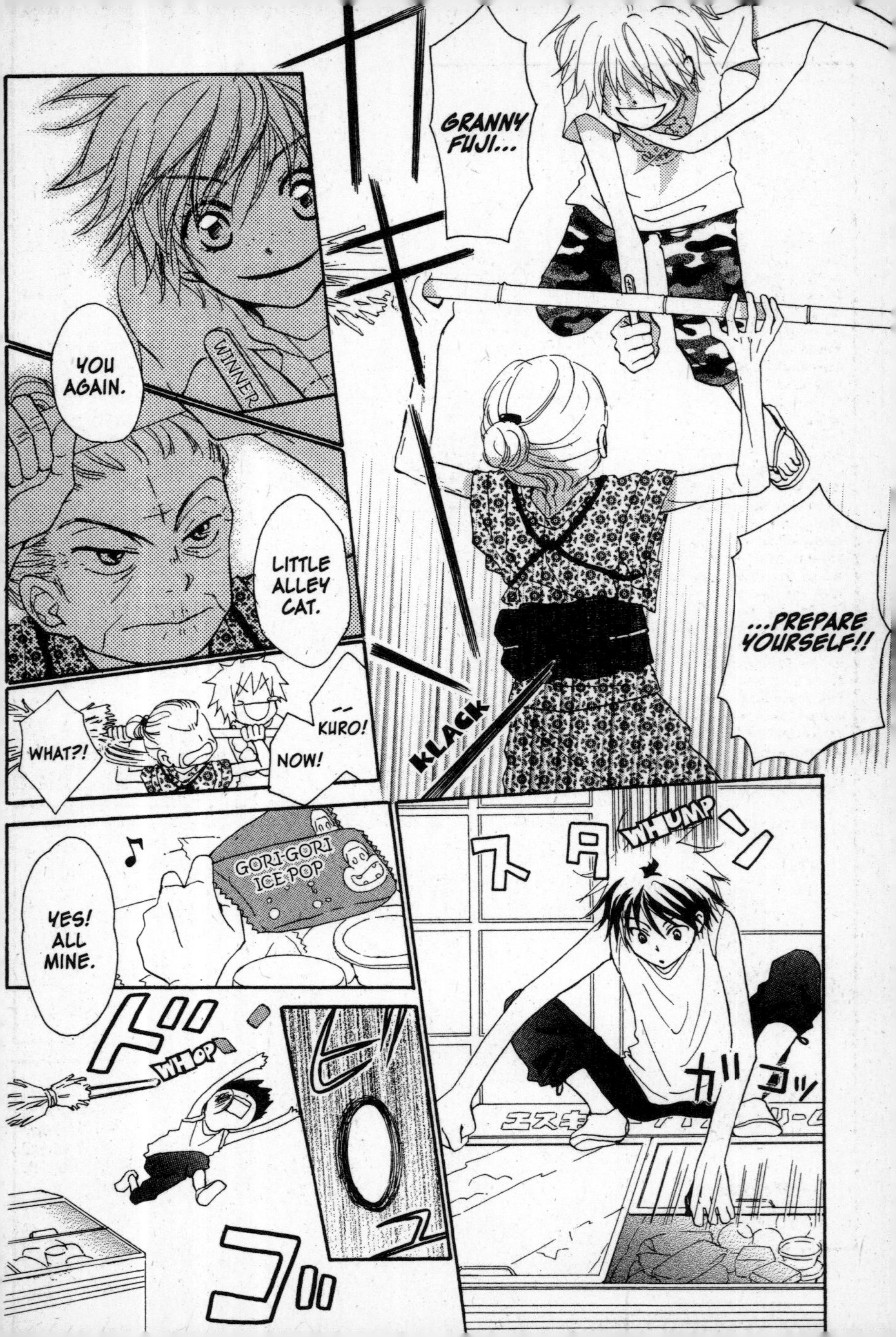
GRANNY FUJI...
...PREPARE YOURSELF!!
KLACK
WINNER
YOU AGAIN.
LITTLE ALLEY CAT.
--KURO! NOW!
WHAT?!
WHUMP
GORI-GORI ICE POP
YES! ALL MINE.
WHOP

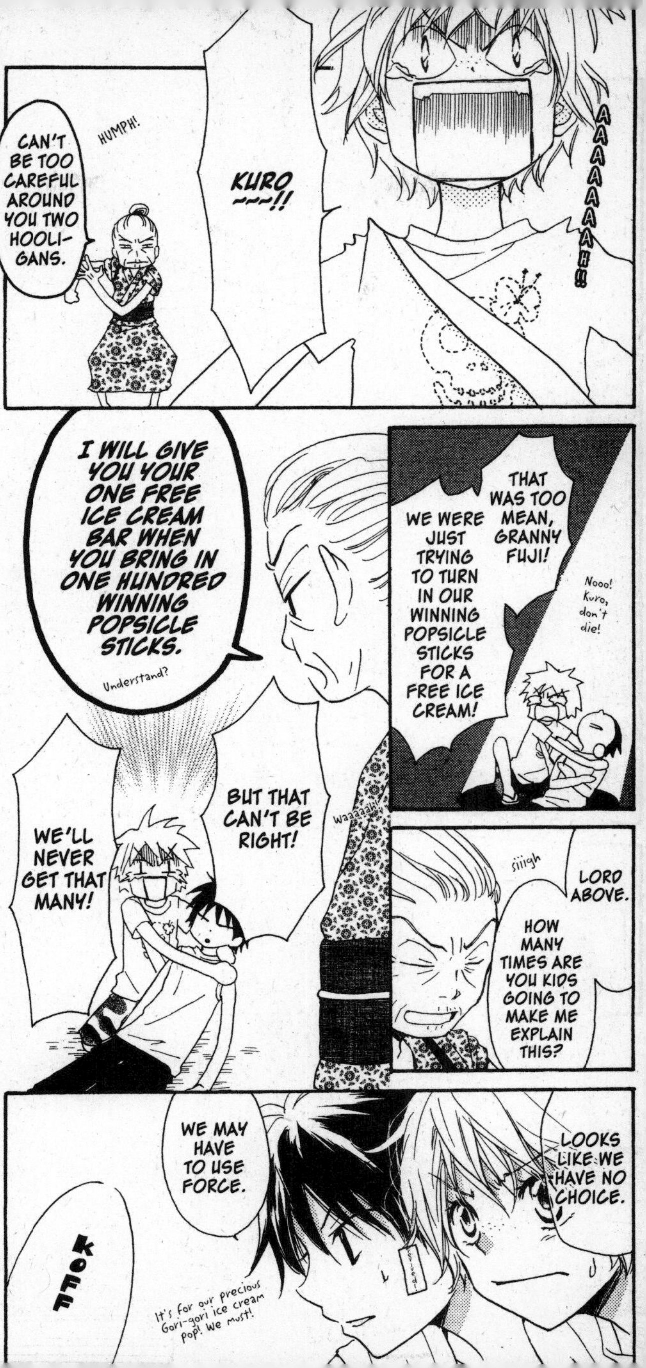
AAAAAAAAH!!
KURO~~~!!
HUMPH!
CAN'T BE TOO CAREFUL AROUND YOU TWO HOOLIGANS.
THAT WAS TOO MEAN, GRANNY FUJI!
WE WERE JUST TRYING TO TURN IN OUR WINNING POPSICLE STICKS FOR A FREE ICE CREAM!
Nooo! Kuro, don't die!
siiigh
LORD ABOVE.
HOW MANY TIMES ARE YOU KIDS GOING TO MAKE ME EXPLAIN THIS?
I WILL GIVE YOU YOUR ONE FREE ICE CREAM BAR WHEN YOU BRING IN ONE HUNDRED WINNING POPSICLE STICKS.
Understand?
Waaaaah!
BUT THAT CAN'T BE RIGHT!
WE'LL NEVER GET THAT MANY!
LOOKS LIKE WE HAVE NO CHOICE.
WE MAY HAVE TO USE FORCE.
KOFF
It's for our precious Gori-gori ice cream pop! We must!

4

So there is something that I would like to apologize to all of you about. Back when I had an interview with Hakusensha, I said my hometown was in Miyazaki Prefecture. I'm sorry, that's not actually correct. I was only born in Miyazaki Prefecture, I didn't grow up there at all. You can't really call that my "hometown" then, can you? I didn't even notice until my parents told me. So to all of you readers who sent me fan mail saying "I grew up there, too!", I'm so sorry! But if you ask where my most of my family lives, then yes, that'd be Miyazaki. Both my parents are from there, so we visited it a lot when I was little. I'd love to go swimming by Aoshima again...

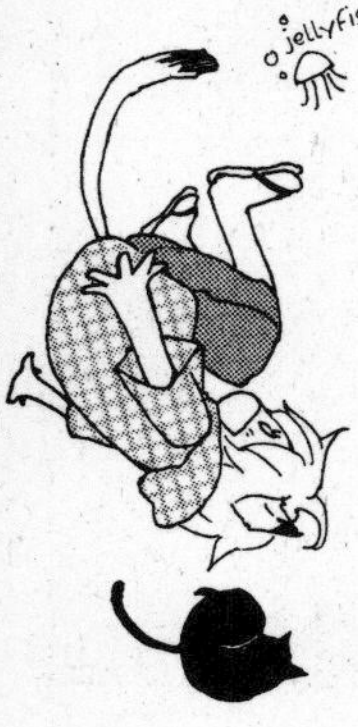
jellyfish!

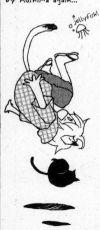

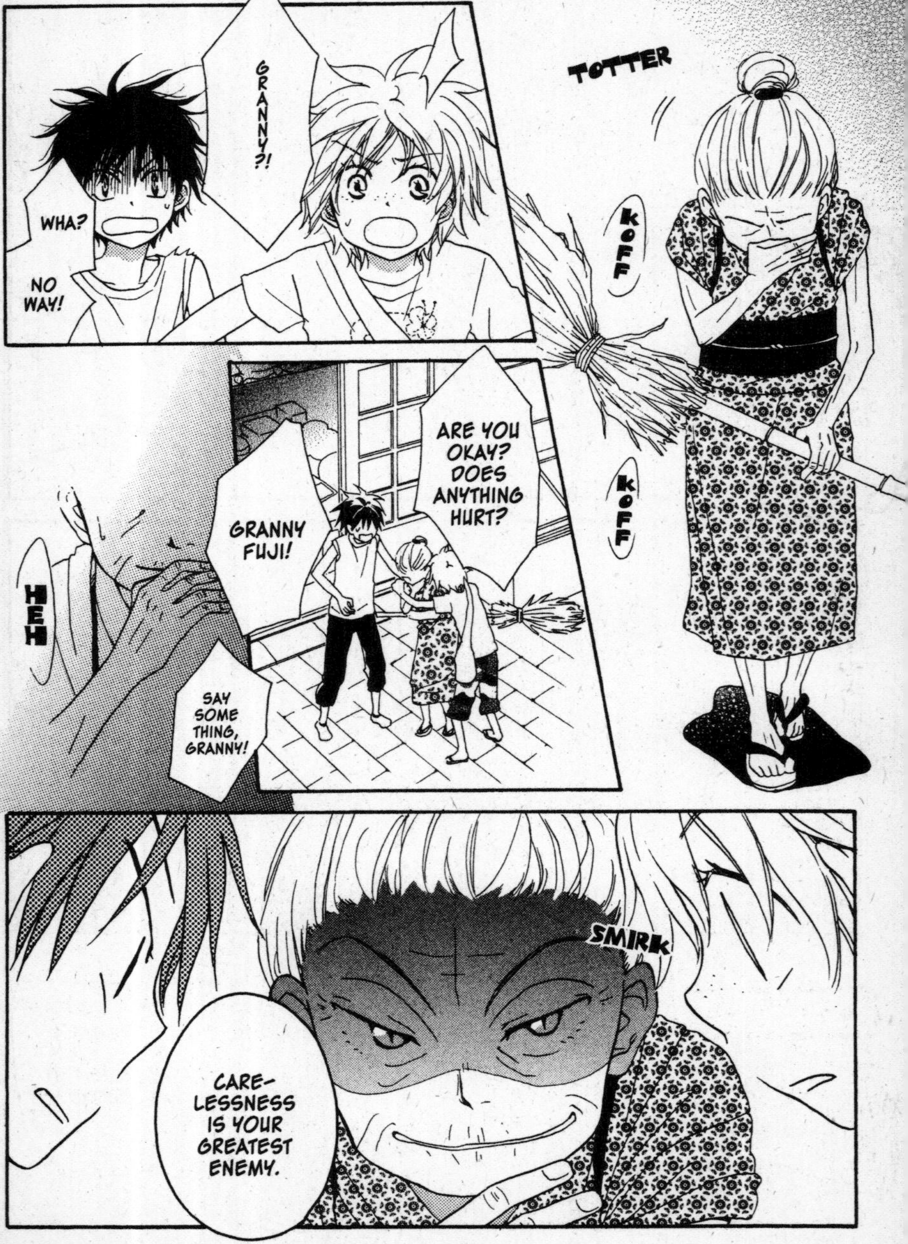
TOTTER
KOFF
KOFF
GRANNY?!
WHA?
NO WAY!
ARE YOU OKAY? DOES ANYTHING HURT?
GRANNY FUJI!
SAY SOME THING, GRANNY!
HEH
SMIRK
CARE-LESSNESS IS YOUR GREATEST ENEMY.

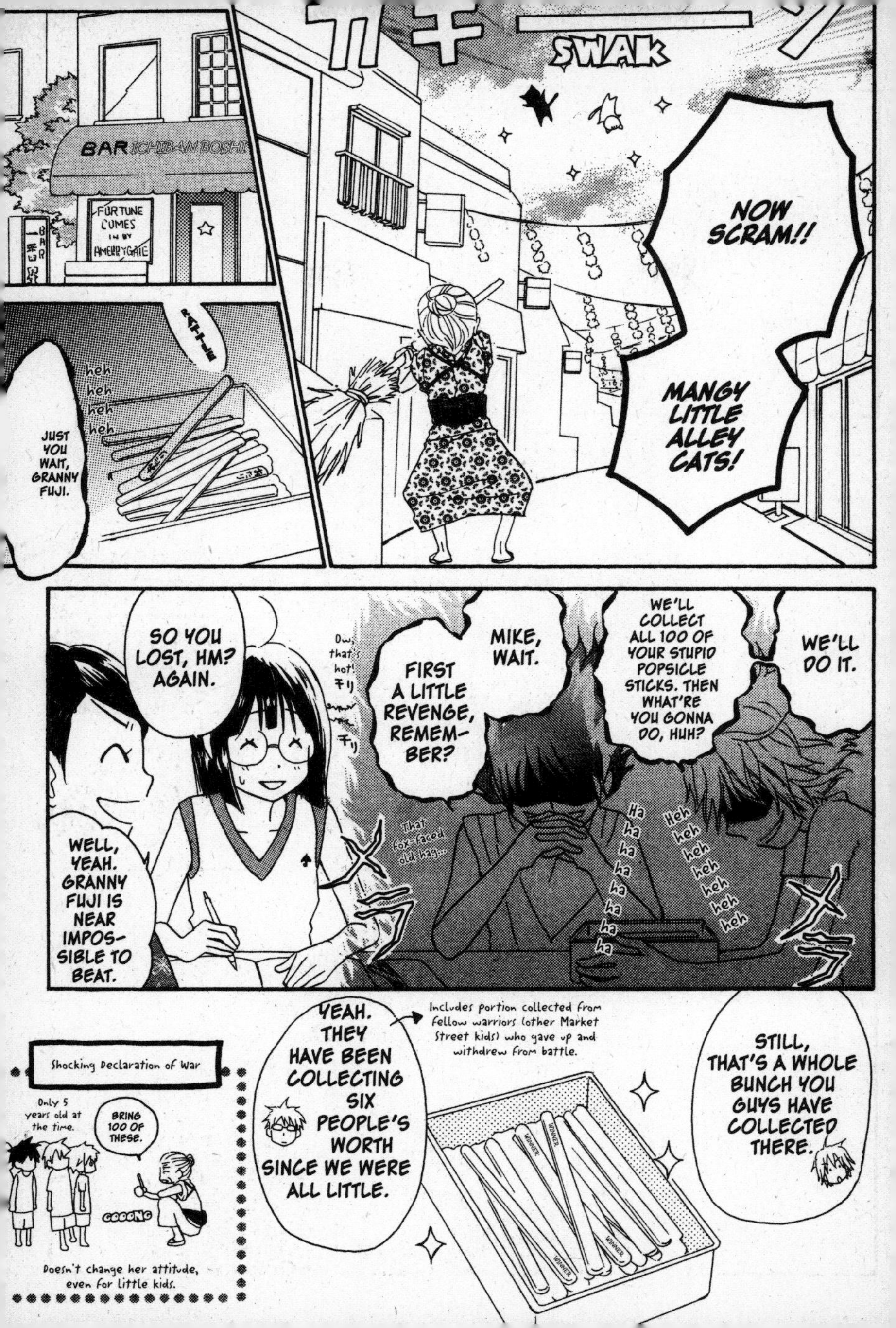
SWAK
NOW SCRAM!!
MANGY LITTLE ALLEY CATS!
BAR ICHIBAN BOSHI
FORTUNE COMES IN BY A MERRY GATE
RATTLE
heh heh heh heh
JUST YOU WAIT, GRANNY FUJI.
WE'LL DO IT.
WE'LL COLLECT ALL 100 OF YOUR STUPID POPSICLE STICKS. THEN WHAT'RE YOU GONNA DO, HUH?
MIKE, WAIT.
FIRST A LITTLE REVENGE, REMEMBER?
Ow, that's hot!
SO YOU LOST, HM? AGAIN.
Heh heh heh heh heh heh heh
Ha ha ha ha ha ha ha ha
That fox-faced old hag...
WELL, YEAH. GRANNY FUJI IS NEAR IMPOSSIBLE TO BEAT.
STILL, THAT'S A WHOLE BUNCH YOU GUYS HAVE COLLECTED THERE.
YEAH. THEY HAVE BEEN COLLECTING SIX PEOPLE'S WORTH SINCE WE WERE ALL LITTLE.
Includes portion collected from fellow warriors (other Market Street kids) who gave up and withdrew from battle.
WINNER
Shocking Declaration of War
Only 5 years old at the time.
BRING 100 OF THESE.
GOOONG
Doesn't change her attitude, even for little kids.

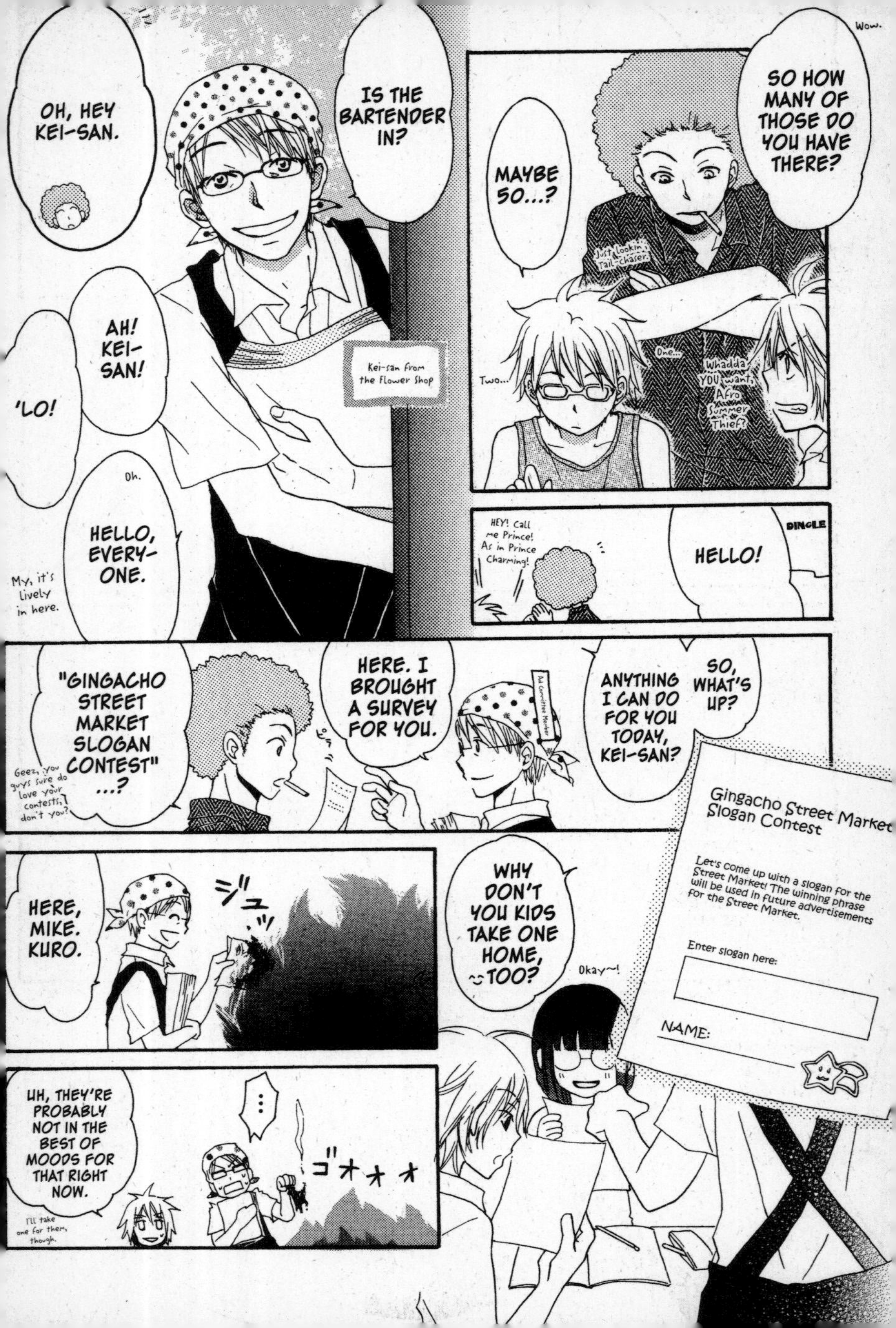
Wow.
SO HOW MANY OF THOSE DO YOU HAVE THERE?
MAYBE SO...?
Just lookin, Tail-chaser.
One...
Whadda YOU want, Afro Summer Thief?
Two...
DINGLE
HELLO!
HEY! Call me Prince! As in Prince Charming!
IS THE BARTENDER IN?
OH, HEY KEI-SAN.
Kei-san from the Flower Shop
AH! KEI-SAN!
'LO!
Oh.
HELLO, EVERY-ONE.
My, it's lively in here.
SO, WHAT'S UP?
ANYTHING I CAN DO FOR YOU TODAY, KEI-SAN?
HERE. I BROUGHT A SURVEY FOR YOU.
Ad Committee Member
"GINGACHO STREET MARKET SLOGAN CONTEST"...?
Geez, you guys sure do love your contests, don't you?
Gingacho Street Market Slogan Contest
Let's come up with a slogan for the Street Market! The winning phrase will be used in future advertisements for the Street Market.
Enter slogan here:
NAME:
WHY DON'T YOU KIDS TAKE ONE HOME, TOO?
Okay~!
HERE, MIKE. KURO.
ジュッ
UH, THEY'RE PROBABLY NOT IN THE BEST OF MOODS FOR THAT RIGHT NOW.
...
ゴオオオ
I'll take one for them, though.

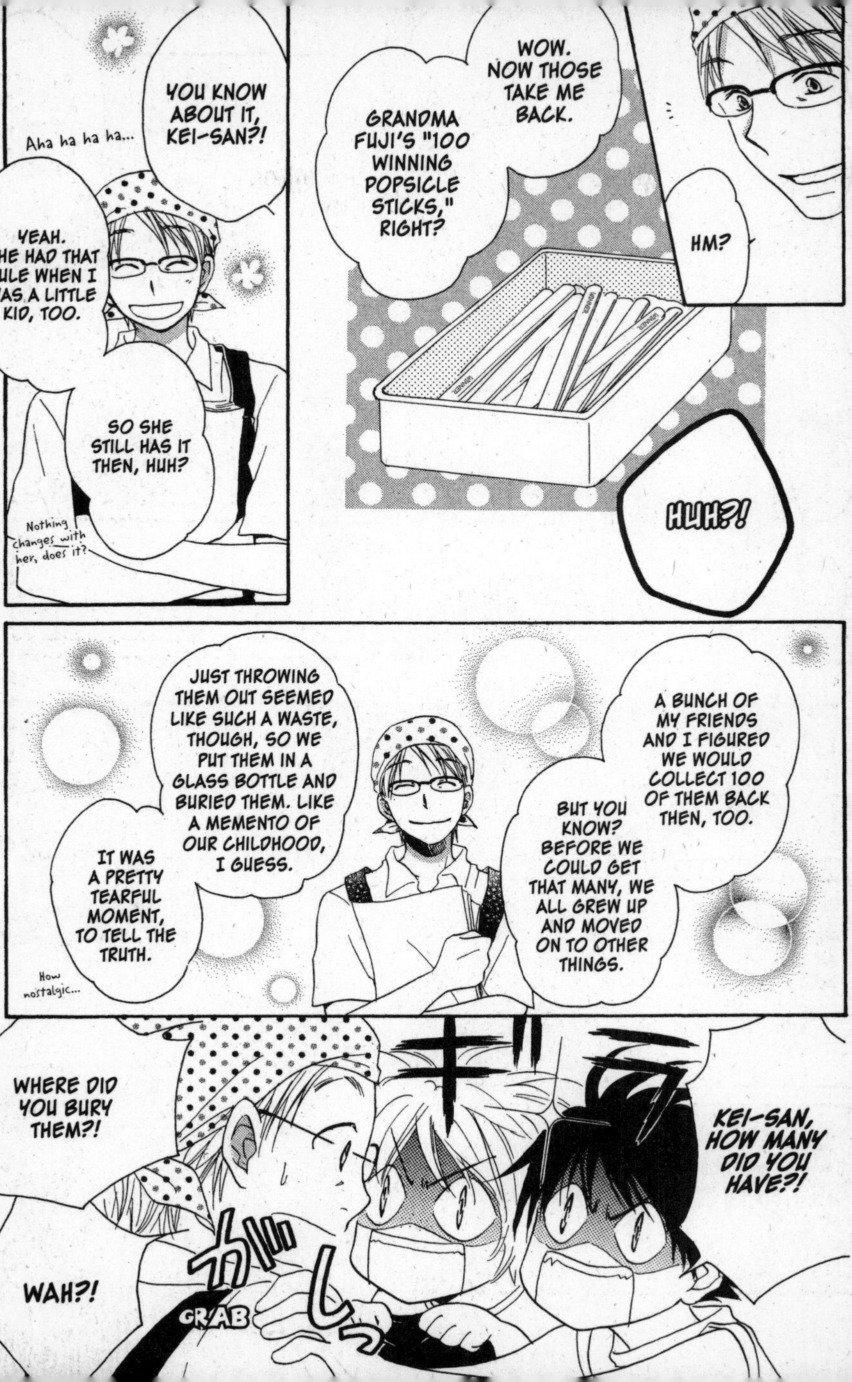
HM?
WOW. NOW THOSE TAKE ME BACK.
GRANDMA FUJI'S "100 WINNING POPSICLE STICKS," RIGHT?
HUH?!
YOU KNOW ABOUT IT, KEI-SAN?!
Aha ha ha ha...
YEAH. SHE HAD THAT RULE WHEN I WAS A LITTLE KID, TOO.
SO SHE STILL HAS IT THEN, HUH?
Nothing changes with her, does it?
A BUNCH OF MY FRIENDS AND I FIGURED WE WOULD COLLECT 100 OF THEM BACK THEN, TOO.
BUT YOU KNOW? BEFORE WE COULD GET THAT MANY, WE ALL GREW UP AND MOVED ON TO OTHER THINGS.
JUST THROWING THEM OUT SEEMED LIKE SUCH A WASTE, THOUGH, SO WE PUT THEM IN A GLASS BOTTLE AND BURIED THEM. LIKE A MEMENTO OF OUR CHILDHOOD, I GUESS.
IT WAS A PRETTY TEARFUL MOMENT, TO TELL THE TRUTH.
How nostalgic...
KEI-SAN, HOW MANY DID YOU HAVE?!
WHERE DID YOU BURY THEM?!
WAH?!
GRAB

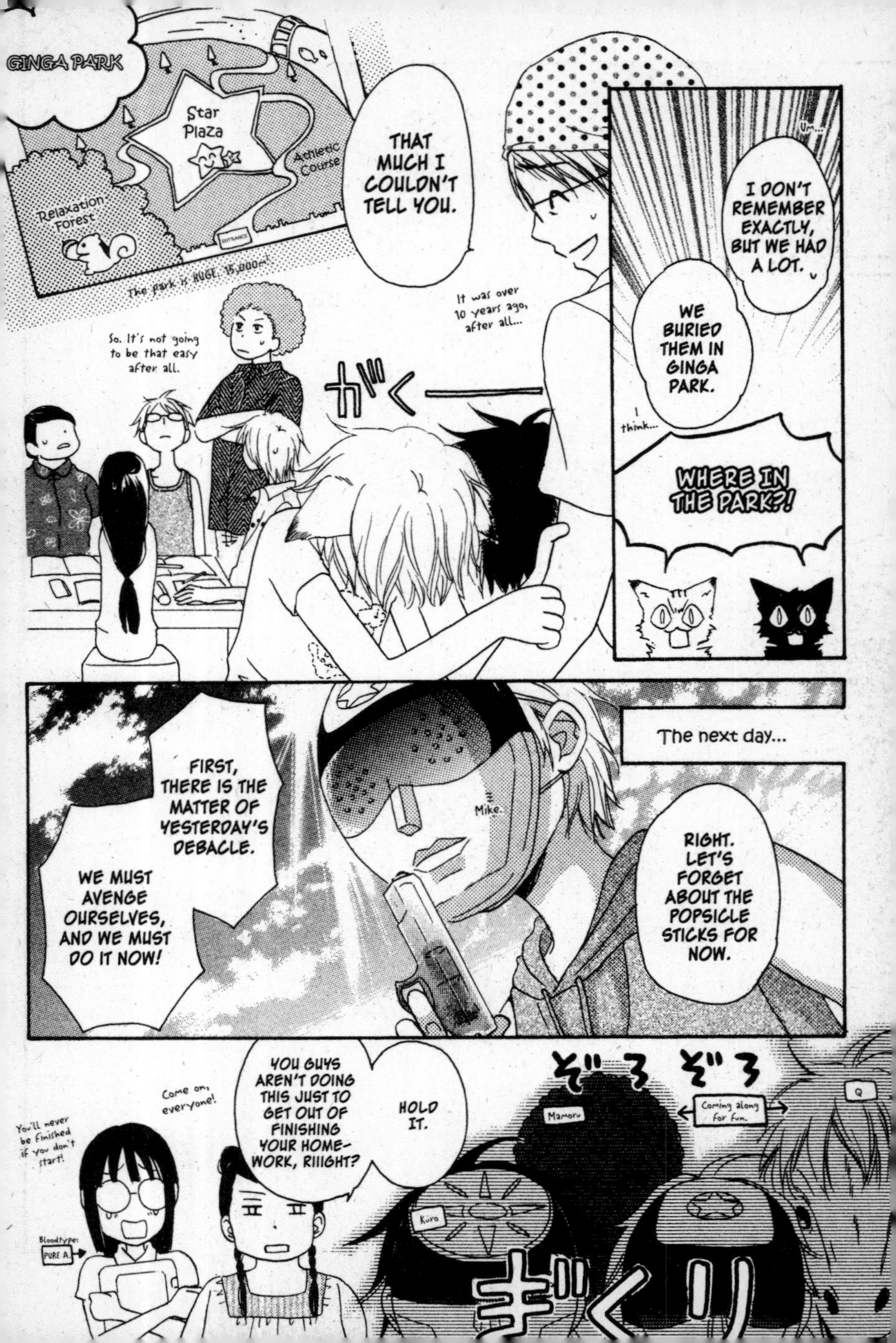

Um...
I DON'T REMEMBER EXACTLY, BUT WE HAD A LOT.
WE BURIED THEM IN GINGA PARK.
I think...
WHERE IN THE PARK?!
THAT MUCH I COULDN'T TELL YOU.
GINGA PARK
Star Plaza
Athletic Course
Relaxation Forest
ENTRANCE
The park is HUGE. 15,000m
It was over 10 years ago, after all...
がく——
So. It's not going to be that easy after all.
The next day...
RIGHT. LET'S FORGET ABOUT THE POPSICLE STICKS FOR NOW.
Mike.
FIRST, THERE IS THE MATTER OF YESTERDAY'S DEBACLE.
WE MUST AVENGE OURSELVES, AND WE MUST DO IT NOW!
ぞろぞろ
Q
Coming along for fun.
Mamoru
Kuro
ぎくり
HOLD IT.
YOU GUYS AREN'T DOING THIS JUST TO GET OUT OF FINISHING YOUR HOME-WORK, RIIIGHT?
Come on, everyone!
You'll never be finished if you don't start!
Bloodtype: PURE A.

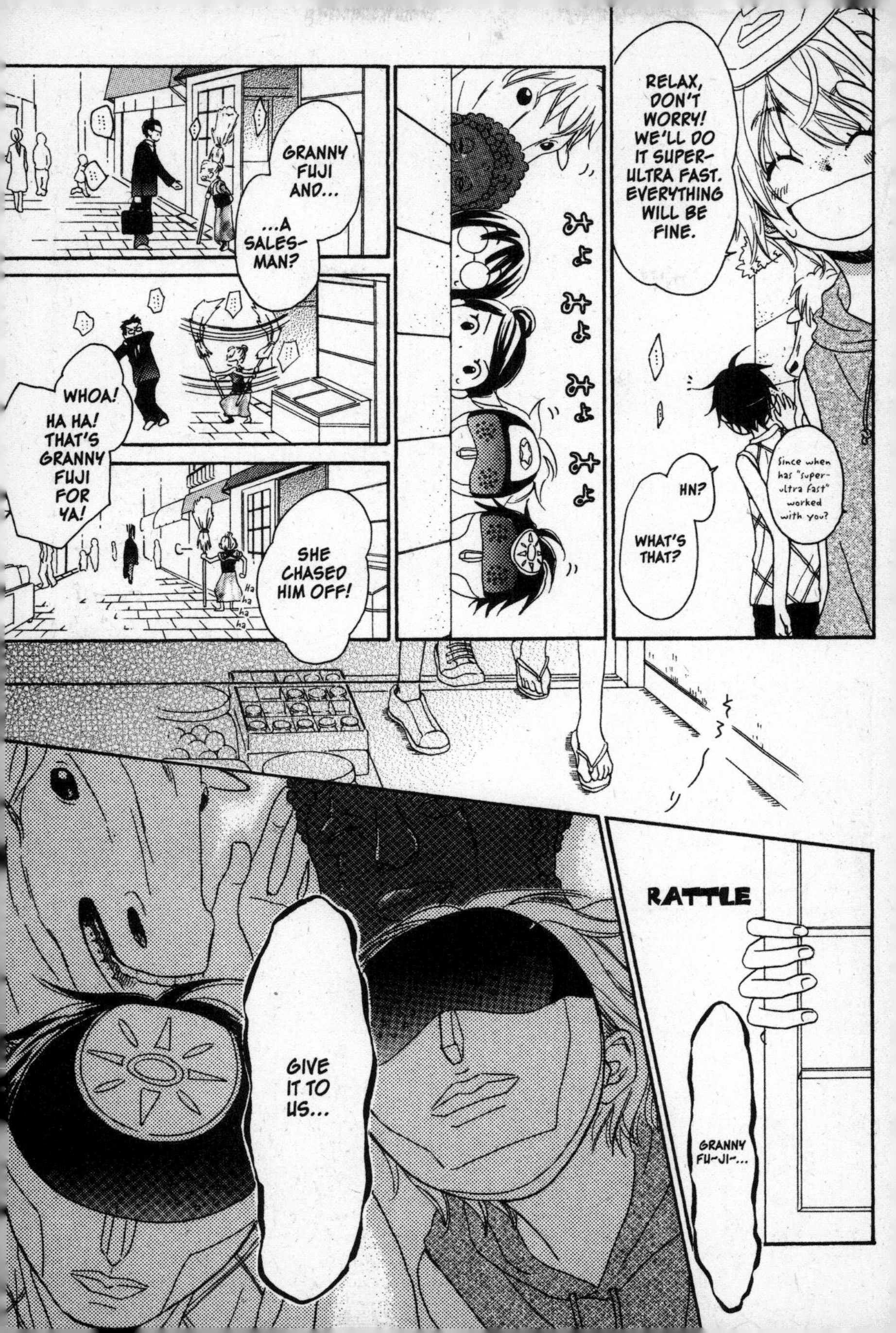
RELAX, DON'T WORRY! WE'LL DO IT SUPER-ULTRA FAST. EVERYTHING WILL BE FINE.
Since when has "super-ultra fast" worked with you?
HN?
WHAT'S THAT?
GRANNY FUJI AND...
...A SALES-MAN?
WHOA!
HA HA! THAT'S GRANNY FUJI FOR YA!
SHE CHASED HIM OFF!
Ha ha ha ha
RATTLE
GRANNY FU-JI-...
GIVE IT TO US...

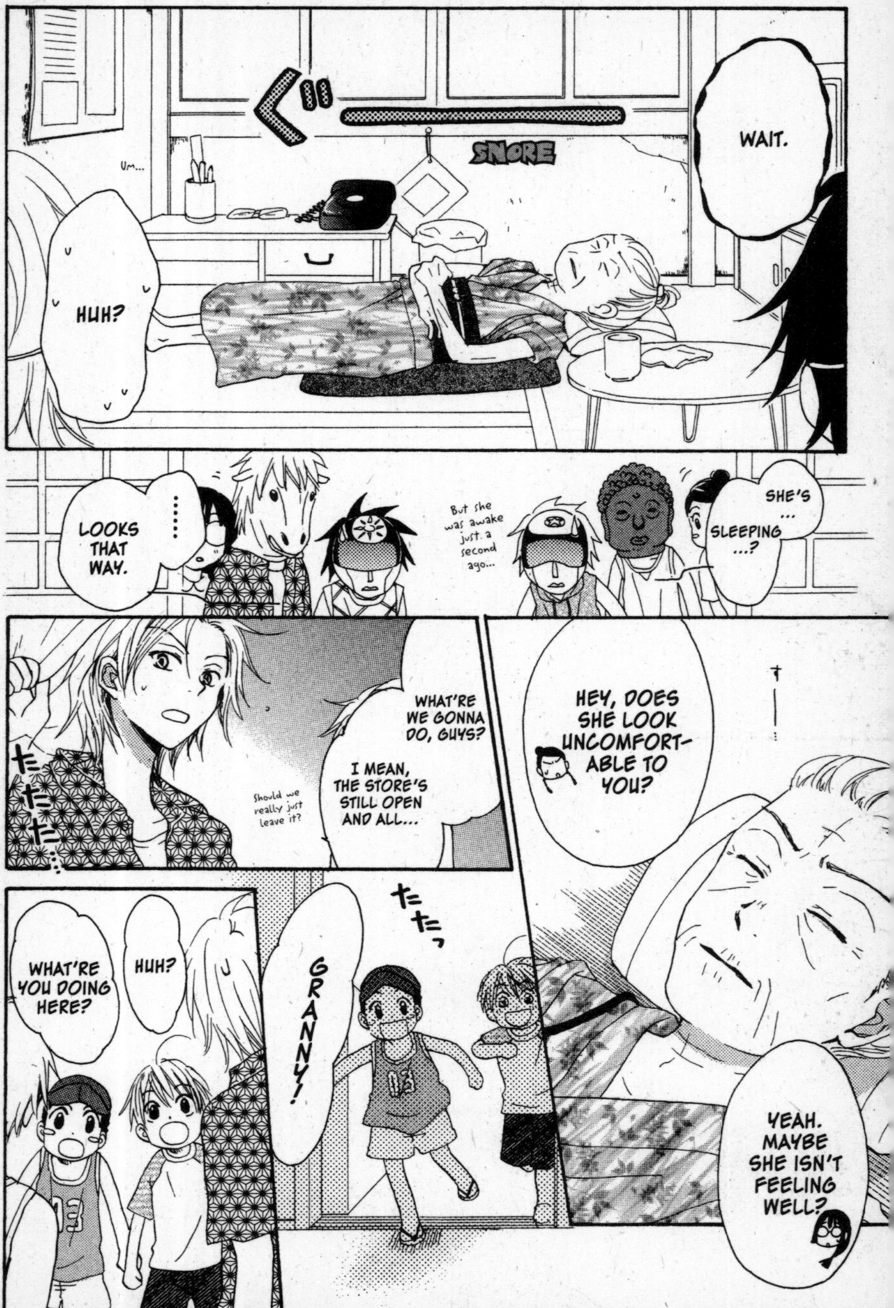

WAIT.
SNORE
Um...
HUH?
SHE'S ... SLEEPING ...?
But she was awake just a second ago...
......
LOOKS THAT WAY.
HEY, DOES SHE LOOK UNCOMFORTABLE TO YOU?
YEAH. MAYBE SHE ISN'T FEELING WELL?
WHAT'RE WE GONNA DO, GUYS?
I MEAN, THE STORE'S STILL OPEN AND ALL...
Should we really just leave it?
たたた...
たたっ
GRANNY!
HUH?
WHAT'RE YOU DOING HERE?

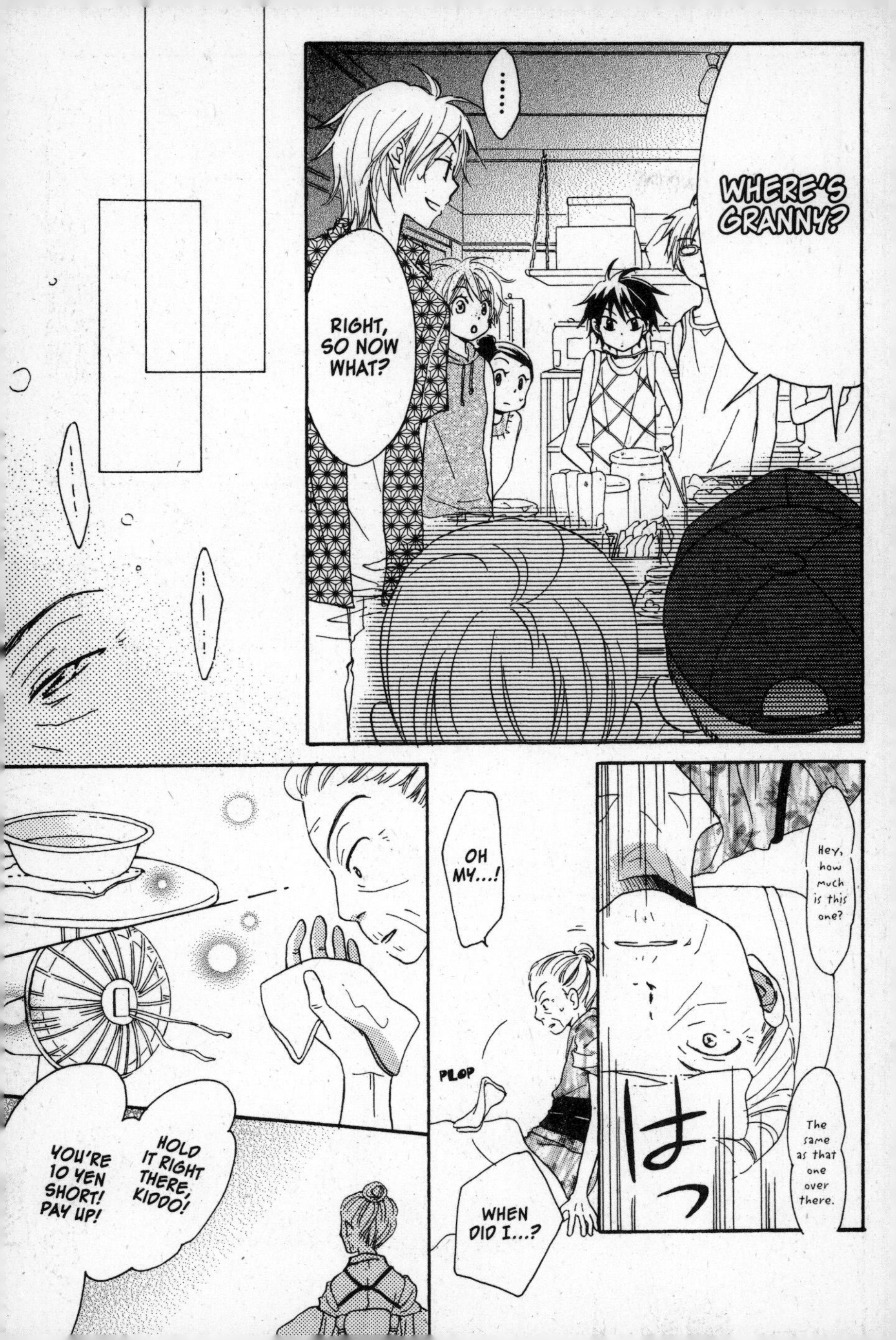
WHERE'S GRANNY?
......
RIGHT, SO NOW WHAT?
Hey, how much is this one?
The same as that one over there.
はっ
OH MY...!
PLOP
WHEN DID I...?
HOLD IT RIGHT THERE, KIDDO!
YOU'RE 10 YEN SHORT! PAY UP!

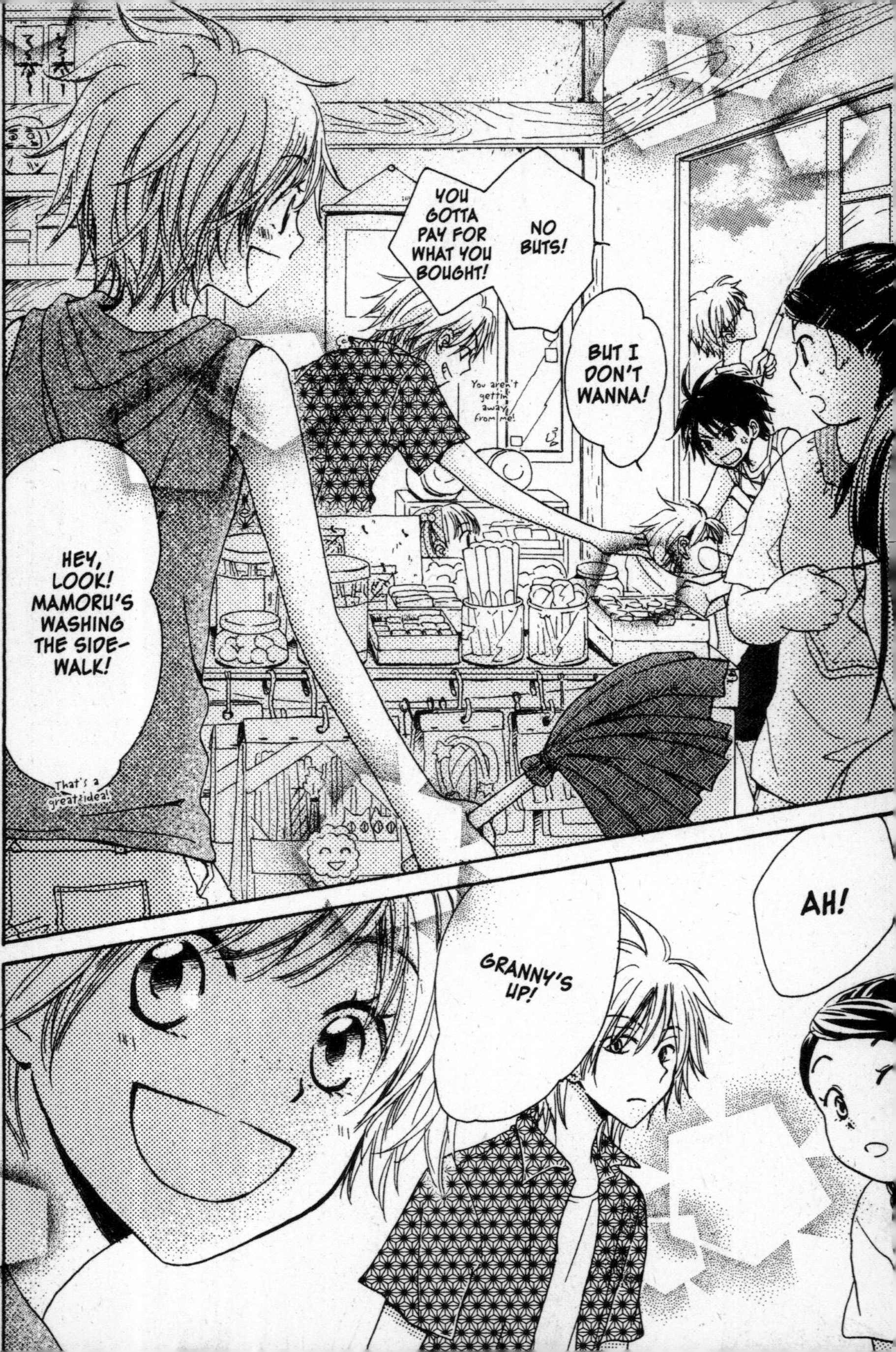
YOU GOTTA PAY FOR WHAT YOU BOUGHT!
NO BUTS!
BUT I DON'T WANNA!
You aren't gettin' away from me!
HEY, LOOK! MAMORU'S WASHING THE SIDE-WALK!
That's a great idea!
AH!
GRANNY'S UP!

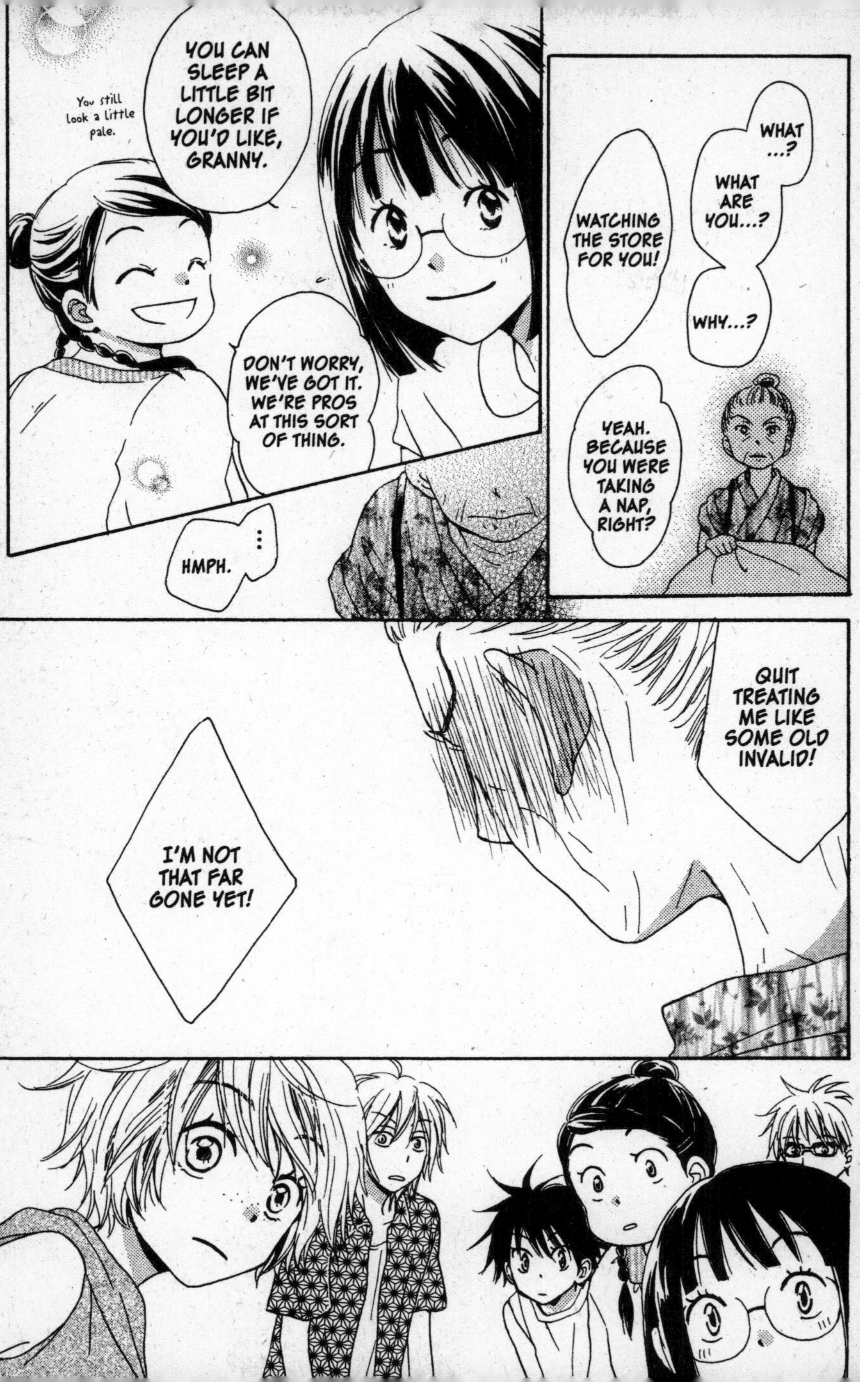
WHAT ...?
WHAT ARE YOU...?
WHY...?
WATCHING THE STORE FOR YOU!
YEAH. BECAUSE YOU WERE TAKING A NAP, RIGHT?
YOU CAN SLEEP A LITTLE BIT LONGER IF YOU'D LIKE, GRANNY.
You still look a little pale.
DON'T WORRY, WE'VE GOT IT. WE'RE PROS AT THIS SORT OF THING.
... HMPH.
QUIT TREATING ME LIKE SOME OLD INVALID!
I'M NOT THAT FAR GONE YET!

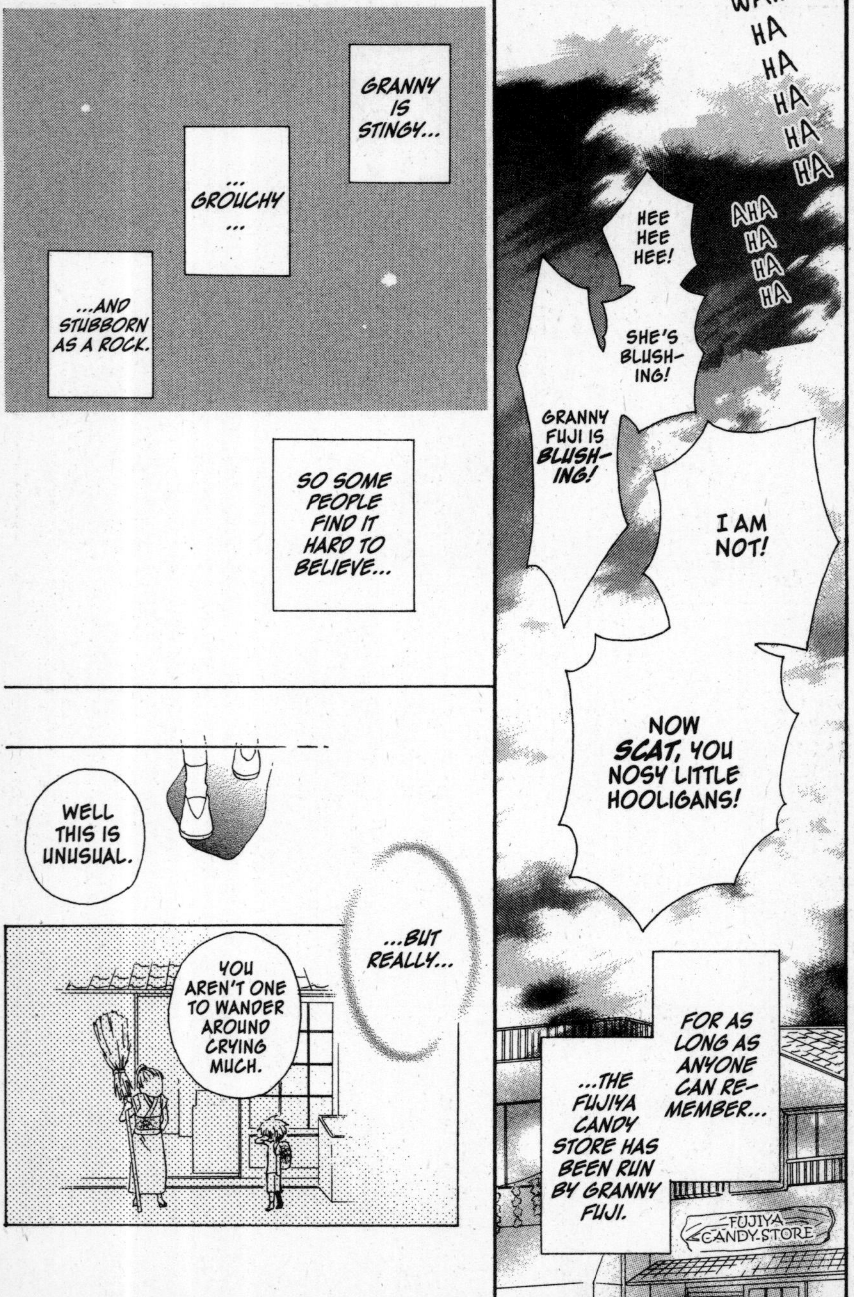
WAH HA HA HA HA HA
AHA HA HA HA
HEE HEE HEE!
SHE'S BLUSH-ING!
GRANNY FUJI IS BLUSH-ING!
I AM NOT!
NOW SCAT, YOU NOSY LITTLE HOOLIGANS!
FOR AS LONG AS ANYONE CAN RE-MEMBER...
...THE FUJIYA CANDY STORE HAS BEEN RUN BY GRANNY FUJI.
FUJIYA CANDY STORE
GRANNY IS STINGY...
...GROUCHY...
...AND STUBBORN AS A ROCK.
SO SOME PEOPLE FIND IT HARD TO BELIEVE...
WELL THIS IS UNUSUAL.
...BUT REALLY...
YOU AREN'T ONE TO WANDER AROUND CRYING MUCH.

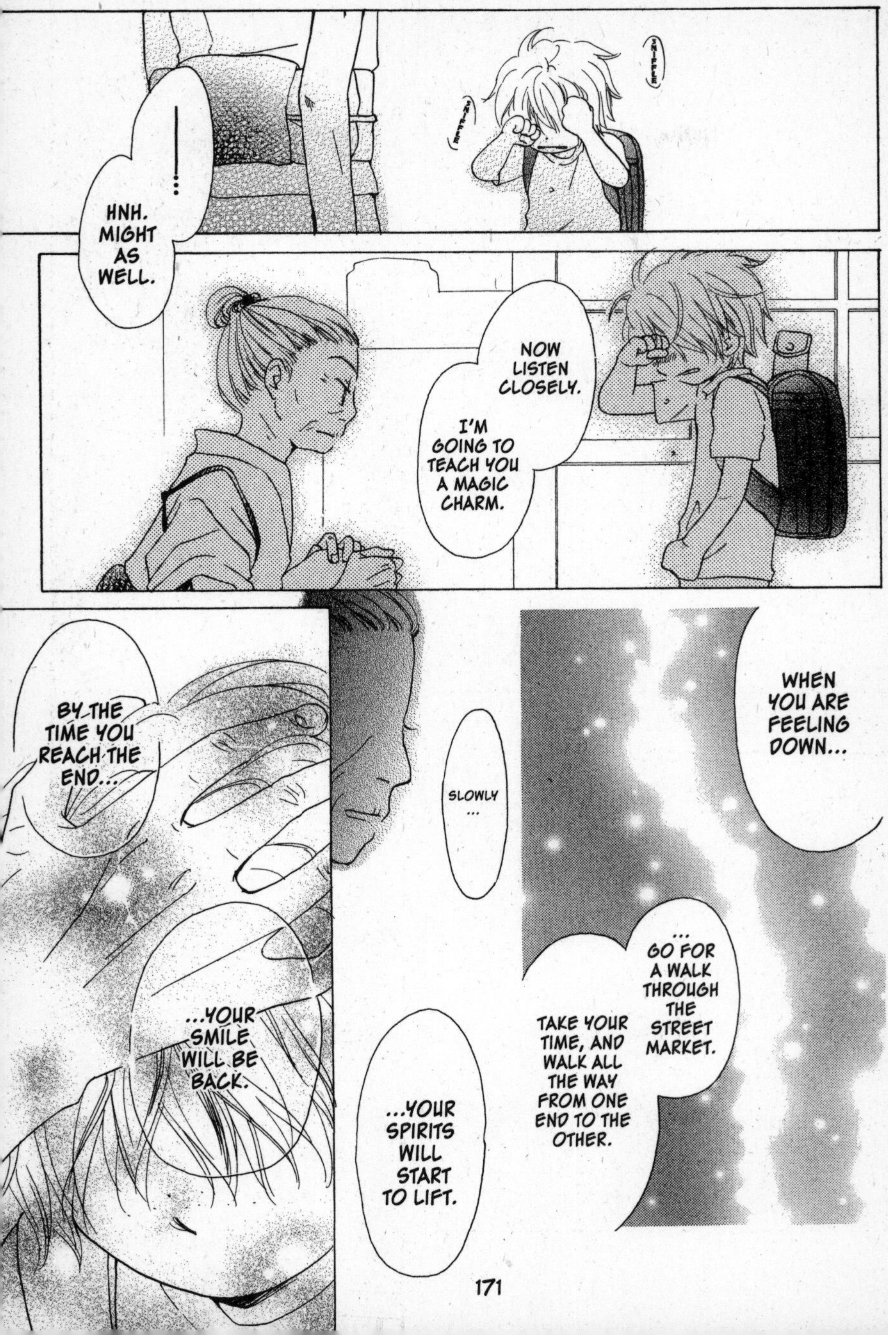
SNIFFLE
SNIFFLE
HNH. MIGHT AS WELL.
NOW LISTEN CLOSELY.
I'M GOING TO TEACH YOU A MAGIC CHARM.
WHEN YOU ARE FEELING DOWN...
...GO FOR A WALK THROUGH THE STREET MARKET.
TAKE YOUR TIME, AND WALK ALL THE WAY FROM ONE END TO THE OTHER.
SLOWLY...
...YOUR SPIRITS WILL START TO LIFT.
BY THE TIME YOU REACH THE END...
...YOUR SMILE WILL BE BACK.

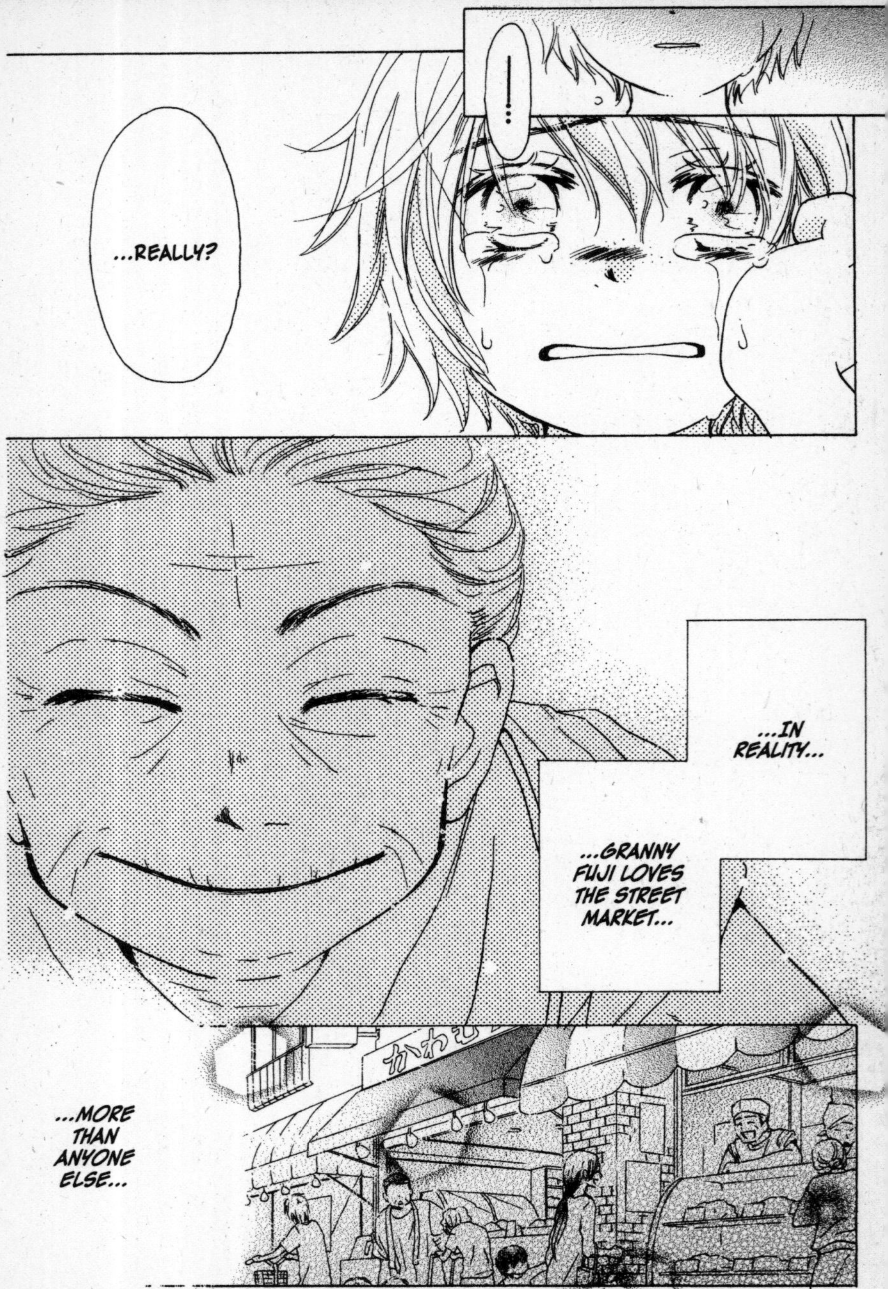
!...
...REALLY?
...IN REALITY...
...GRANNY FUJI LOVES THE STREET MARKET...
...MORE THAN ANYONE ELSE...

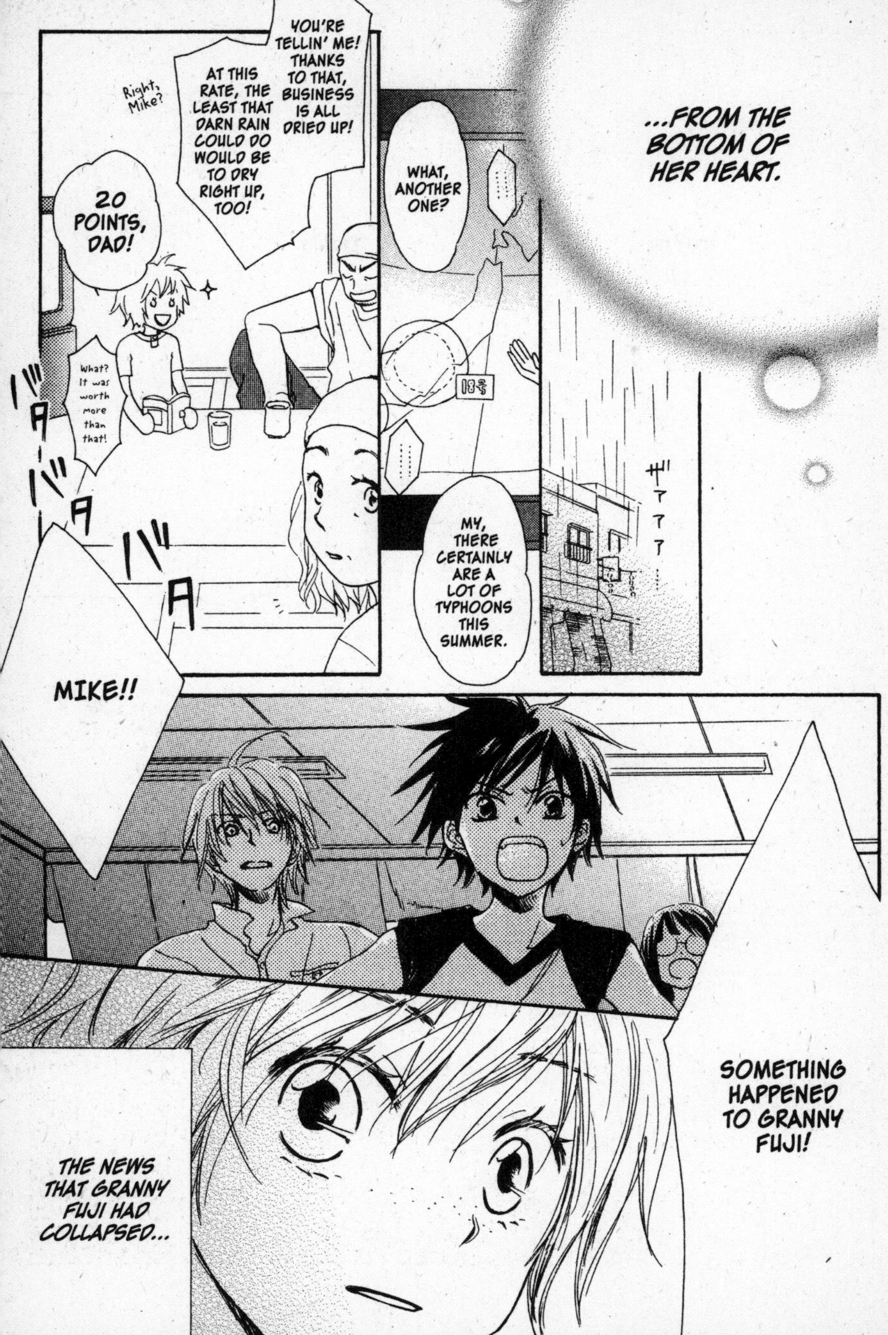
...FROM THE BOTTOM OF HER HEART.
ザァァァ…
WHAT, ANOTHER ONE?
……
18号
……
MY, THERE CERTAINLY ARE A LOT OF TYPHOONS THIS SUMMER.
YOU'RE TELLIN' ME! THANKS TO THAT, BUSINESS IS ALL DRIED UP!
AT THIS RATE, THE LEAST THAT DARN RAIN COULD DO WOULD BE TO DRY RIGHT UP, TOO!
Right, Mike?
20 POINTS, DAD!
What? It was worth more than that!
バタバタバタ
MIKE!!
SOMETHING HAPPENED TO GRANNY FUJI!
THE NEWS THAT GRANNY FUJI HAD COLLAPSED...

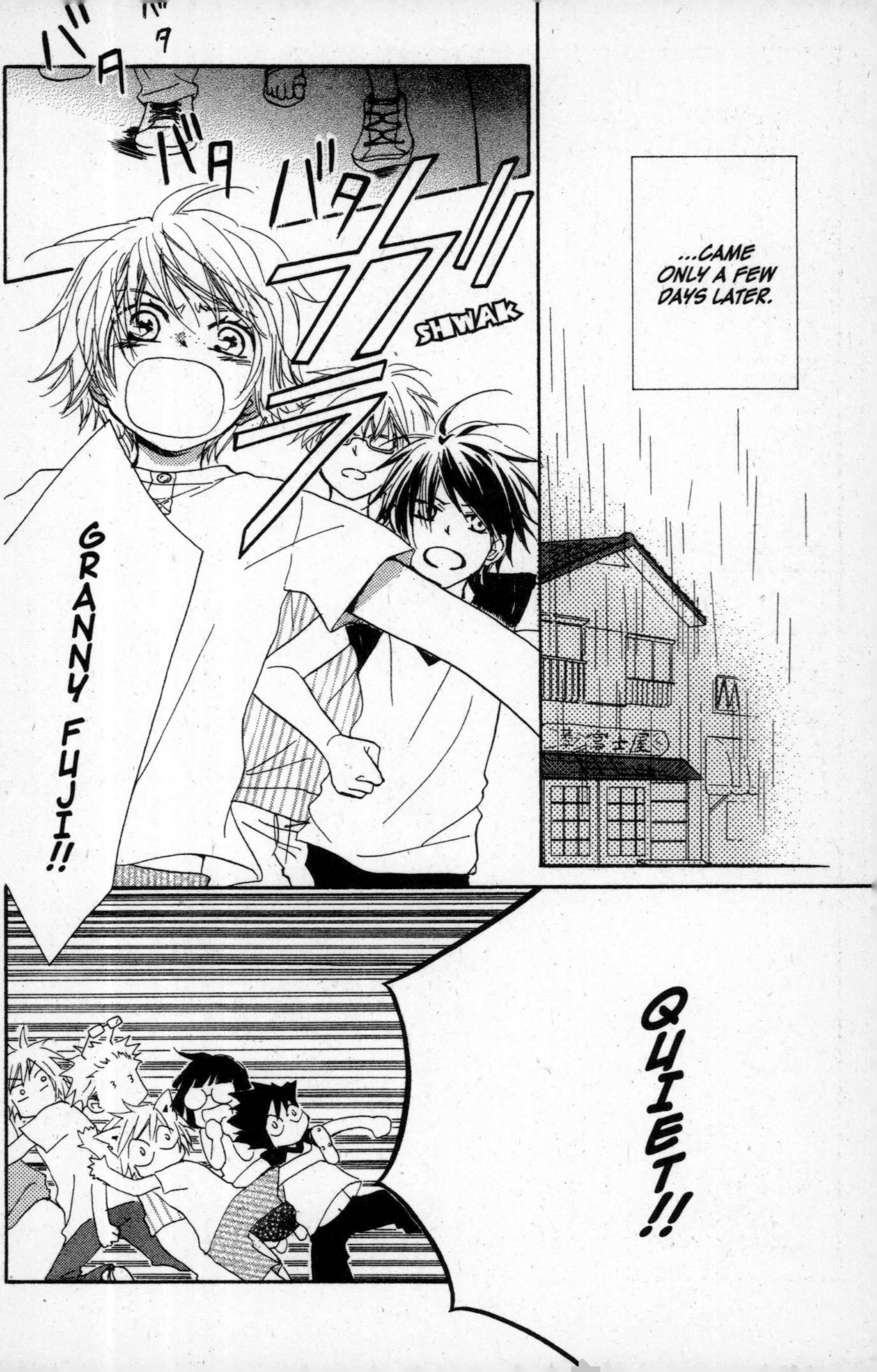
...CAME ONLY A FEW DAYS LATER.
バタ バタ
バタ
バタ
ガラッ
SHWAK
GRANNY FUJII!!
QUIET!!

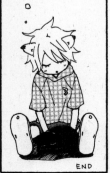

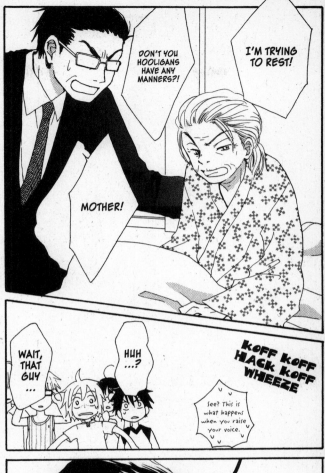

DON'T YOU HOOLIGANS HAVE ANY MANNERS?!
I'M TRYING TO REST!
MOTHER!
KOFF KOFF HACK KOFF WHEEZE
See? This is what happens when you raise your voice.
HUH ...?
WAIT, THAT GUY ...
HE'S THE SALESMAN FROM BEFORE!
HUH?
"Sales-man"...?
Before
Whoa! That's Granny Fuji for ya!

5

Hello! So this is the last freetalk for this volume. Thanks for sticking with it this far! You know, the whole time I've been writing these, it feels like I've been holding a one-sided conversation. Kind of like a radio show! This is Fujimoto, signing off! (Man, what a sad excuse for a radio show!)

If you have any questions or comments, please direct them to the following...

Fan-mail makes me so happy I could cry.

TOKYOPOP
Editorial Department
5900 Wilshire Blvd.
Suite 2000
Los Angeles, CA 90036

See? Crying already.

See you at the end of the volume...!

END

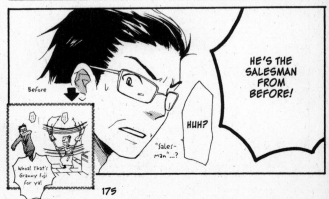

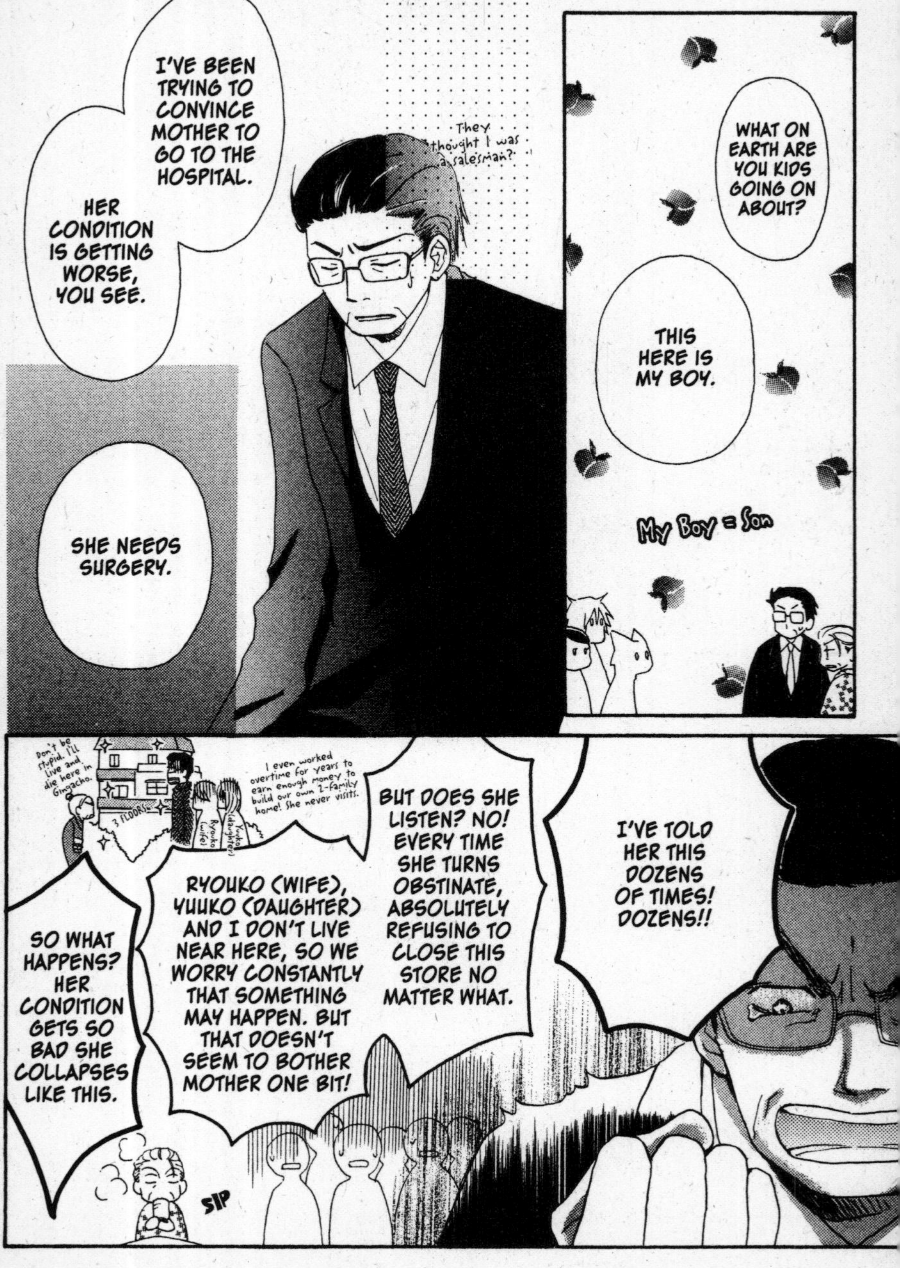
WHAT ON EARTH ARE YOU KIDS GOING ON ABOUT?
THIS HERE IS MY BOY.
My Boy = Son
I'VE BEEN TRYING TO CONVINCE MOTHER TO GO TO THE HOSPITAL.
HER CONDITION IS GETTING WORSE, YOU SEE.
They thought I was a salesman?
SHE NEEDS SURGERY.
I'VE TOLD HER THIS DOZENS OF TIMES! DOZENS!!
BUT DOES SHE LISTEN? NO! EVERY TIME SHE TURNS OBSTINATE, ABSOLUTELY REFUSING TO CLOSE THIS STORE NO MATTER WHAT.
I even worked overtime for years to earn enough money to build our own 2-family home! She never visits.
RYOUKO (WIFE), YUUKO (DAUGHTER) AND I DON'T LIVE NEAR HERE, SO WE WORRY CONSTANTLY THAT SOMETHING MAY HAPPEN. BUT THAT DOESN'T SEEM TO BOTHER MOTHER ONE BIT!
Don't be stupid. I'll live and die here in Gingacho.
3 FLOORS
Ryouko (wife)
Yuuko (daughter)
SO WHAT HAPPENS? HER CONDITION GETS SO BAD SHE COLLAPSES LIKE THIS.
SIP

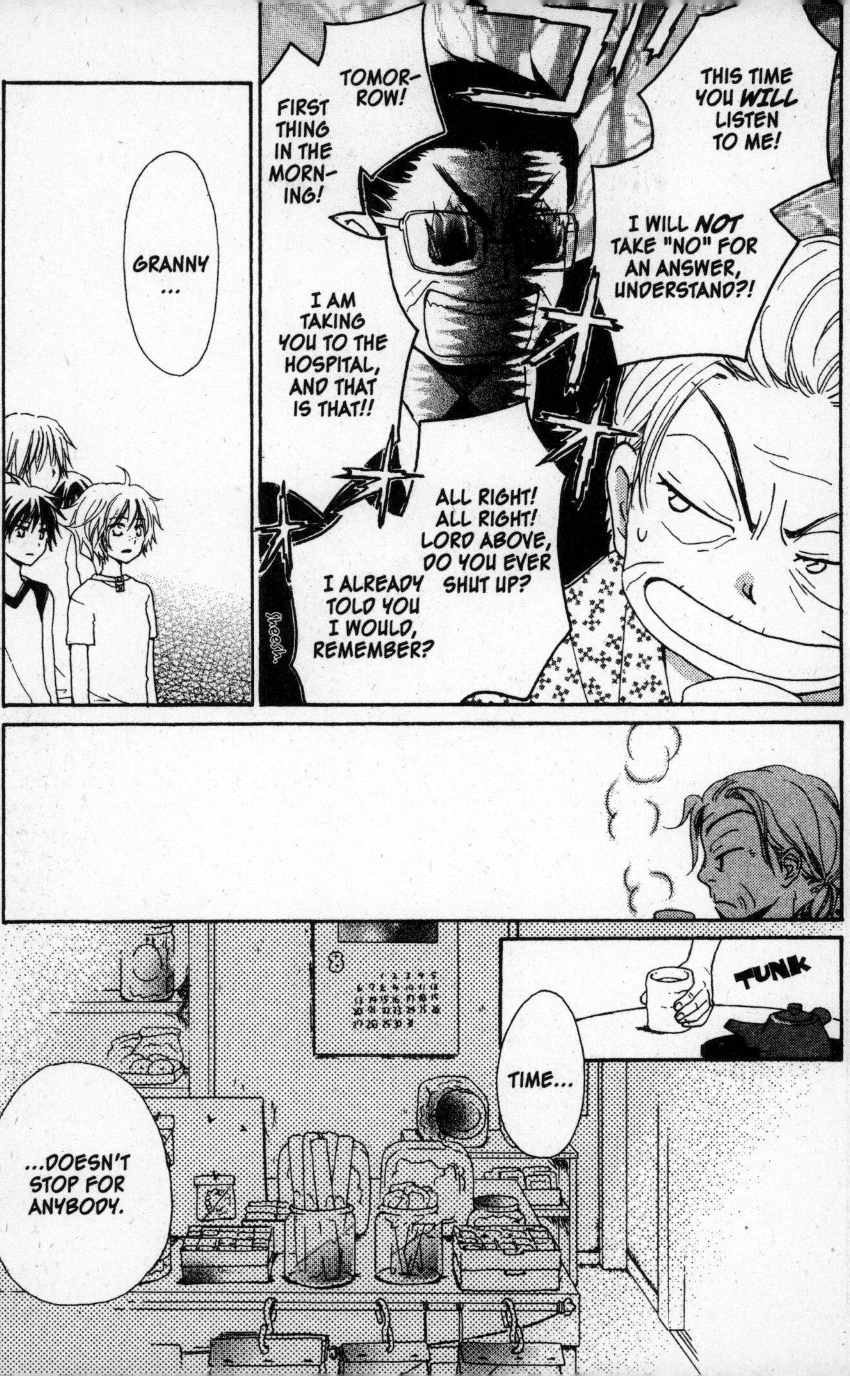
THIS TIME YOU WILL LISTEN TO ME!
TOMORROW!
FIRST THING IN THE MORNING!
I WILL NOT TAKE "NO" FOR AN ANSWER, UNDERSTAND?!
I AM TAKING YOU TO THE HOSPITAL, AND THAT IS THAT!!
ALL RIGHT! ALL RIGHT! LORD ABOVE, DO YOU EVER SHUT UP?
I ALREADY TOLD YOU I WOULD, REMEMBER?
Sheesh..
GRANNY ...
TUNK
TIME...
...DOESN'T STOP FOR ANYBODY.

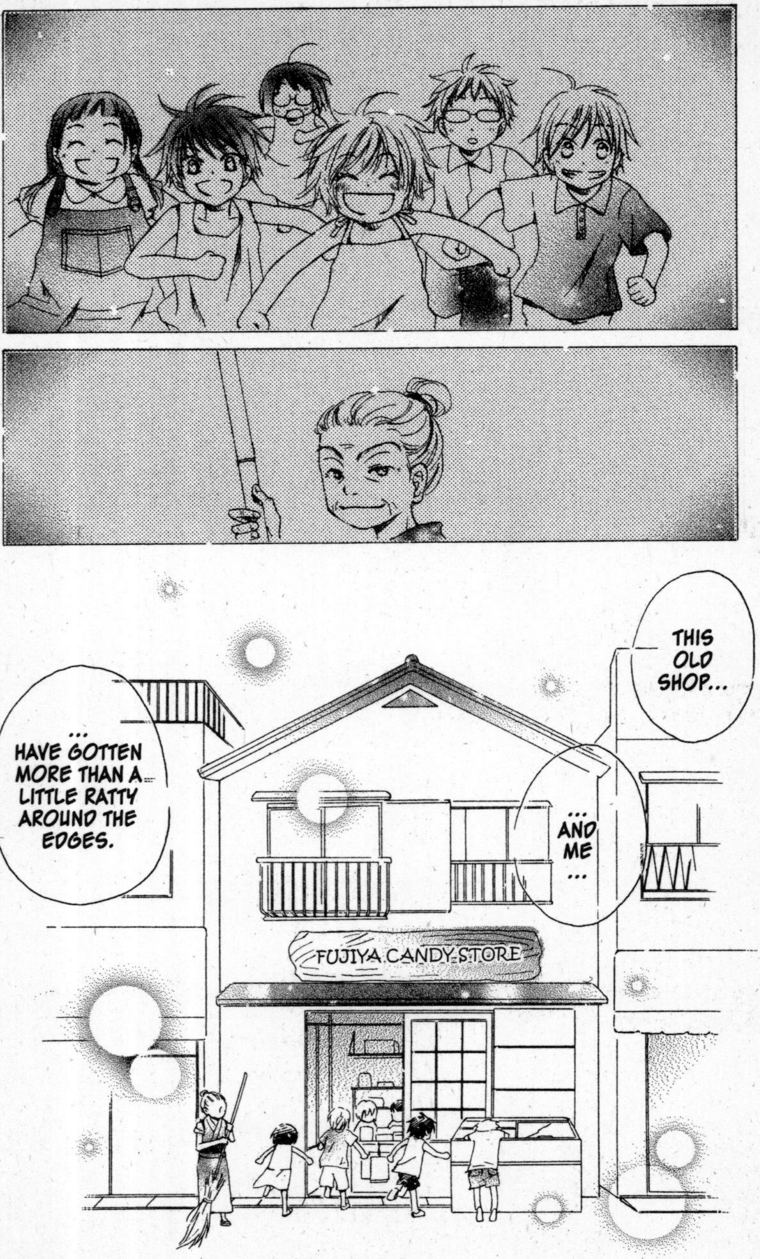
THIS OLD SHOP...
...AND ME...
...HAVE GOTTEN MORE THAN A LITTLE RATTY AROUND THE EDGES.
FUJIYA CANDY STORE

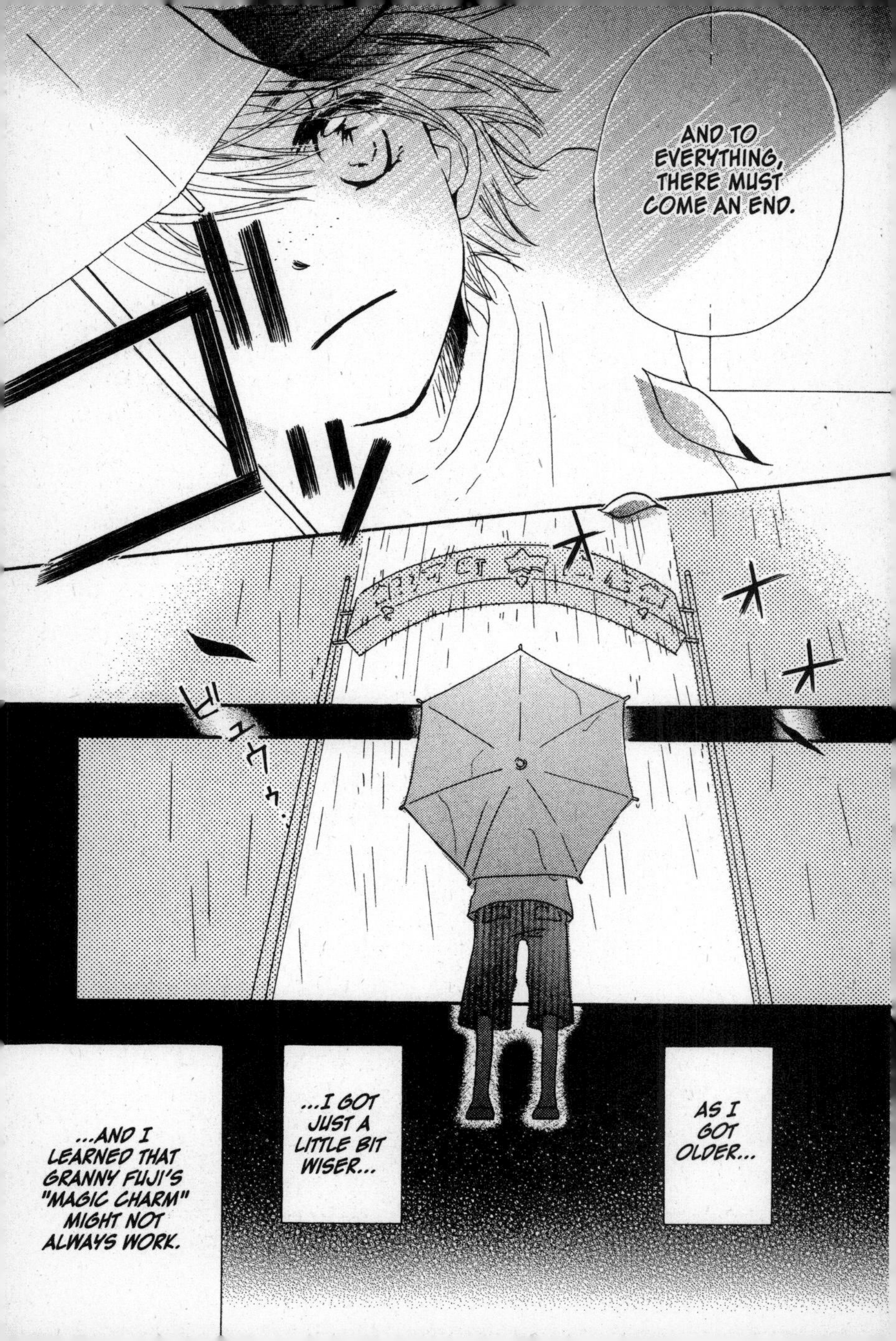
AND TO EVERYTHING, THERE MUST COME AN END.
AS I GOT OLDER...
...I GOT JUST A LITTLE BIT WISER...
...AND I LEARNED THAT GRANNY FUJI'S "MAGIC CHARM" MIGHT NOT ALWAYS WORK.

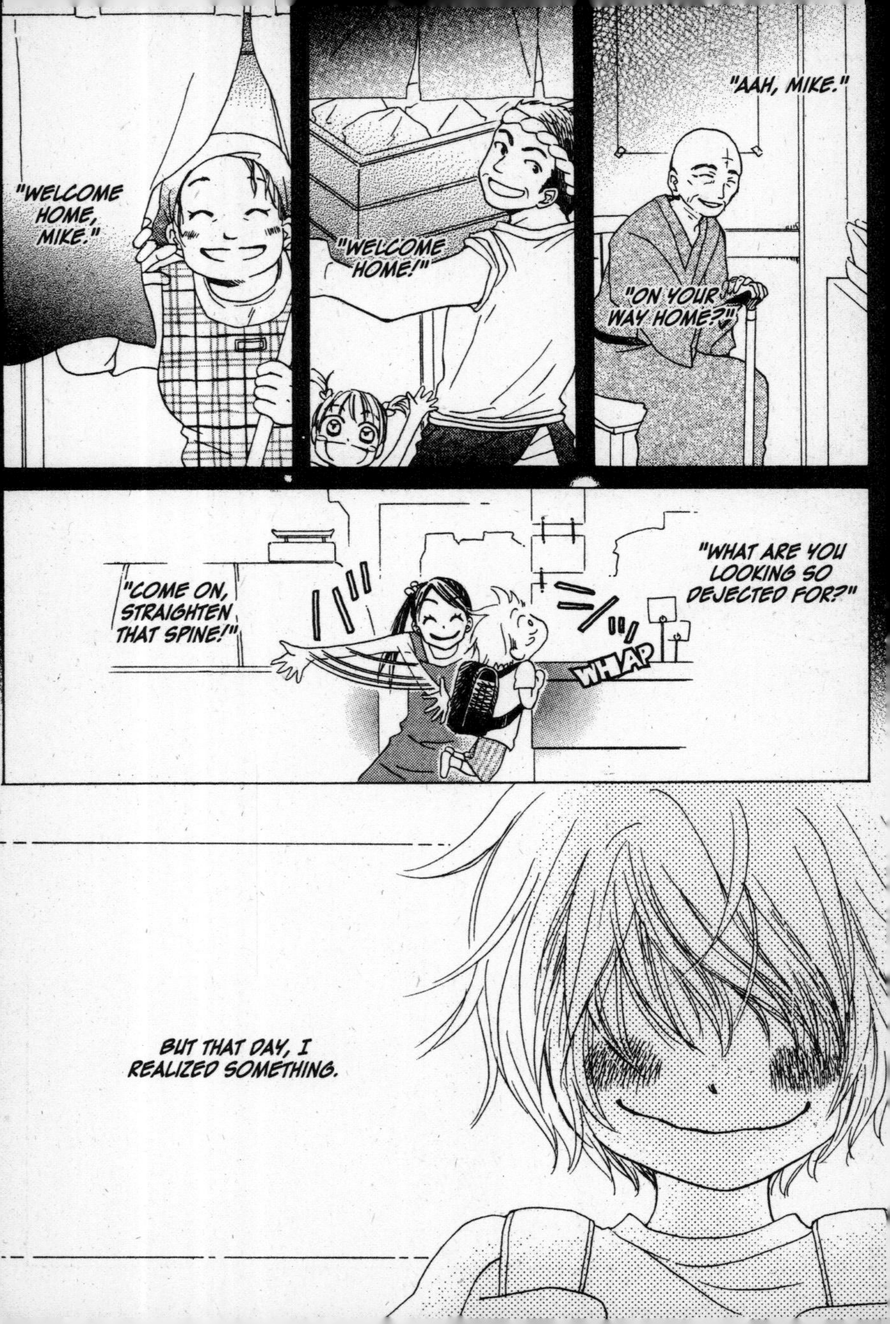
"AAH, MIKE."
"ON YOUR WAY HOME?"
"WELCOME HOME!"
"WELCOME HOME, MIKE."
"WHAT ARE YOU LOOKING SO DEJECTED FOR?"
WHAP
"COME ON, STRAIGHTEN THAT SPINE!"
BUT THAT DAY, I REALIZED SOMETHING.

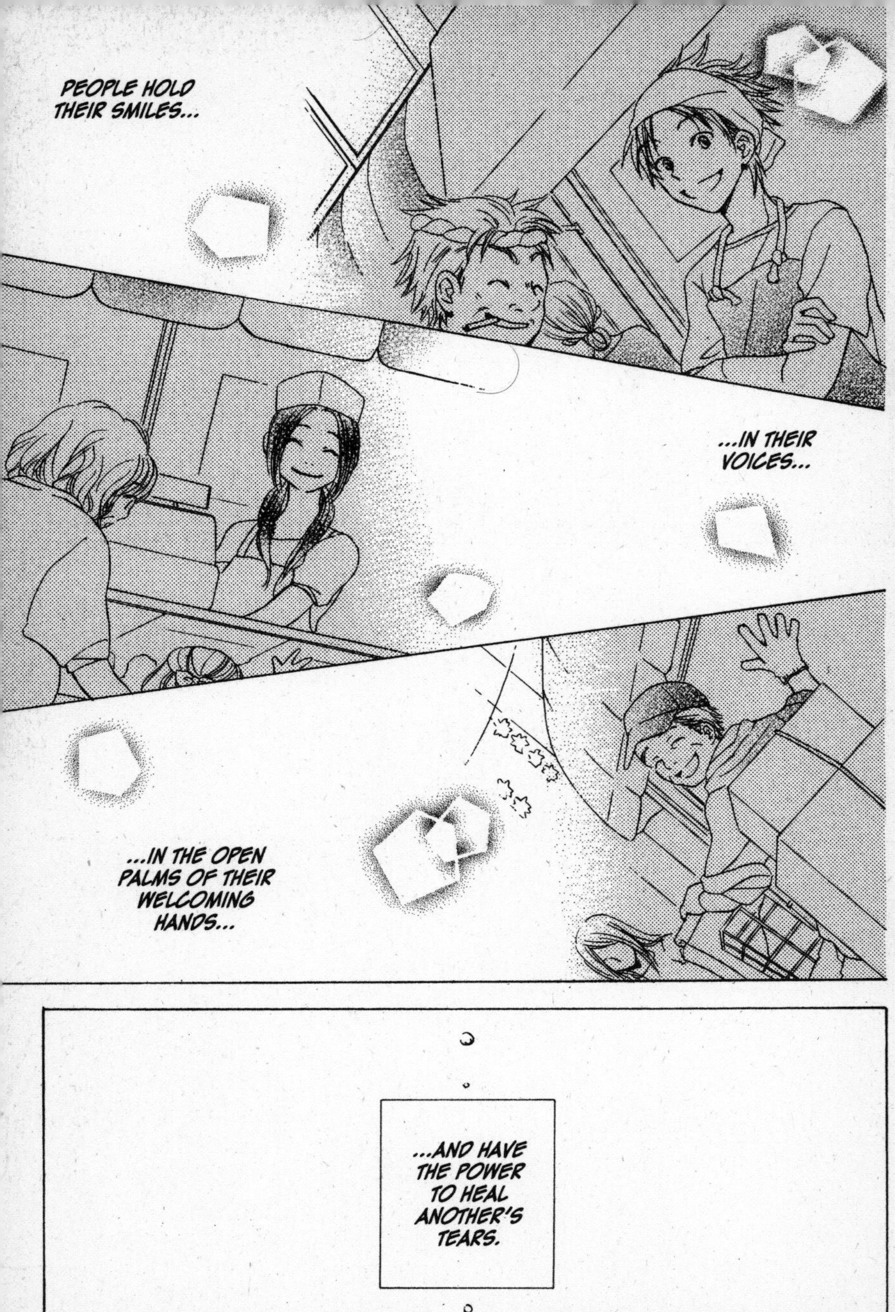
PEOPLE HOLD THEIR SMILES...
...IN THEIR VOICES...
...IN THE OPEN PALMS OF THEIR WELCOMING HANDS...
...AND HAVE THE POWER TO HEAL ANOTHER'S TEARS.

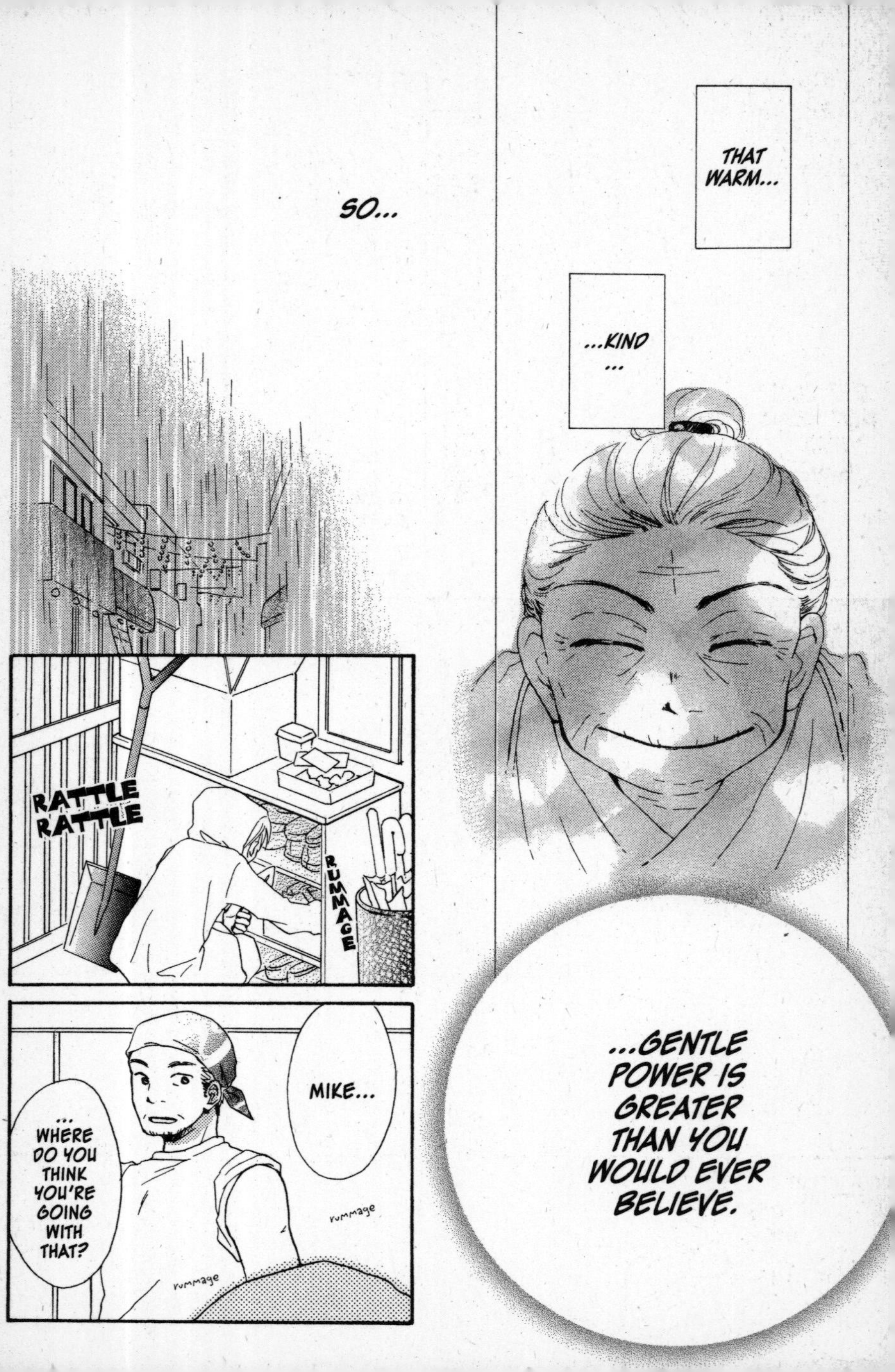
THAT WARM...
...KIND ...
...GENTLE POWER IS GREATER THAN YOU WOULD EVER BELIEVE.
SO...
RATTLE RATTLE
RUMMAGE
MIKE...
... WHERE DO YOU THINK YOU'RE GOING WITH THAT?
rummage
rummage

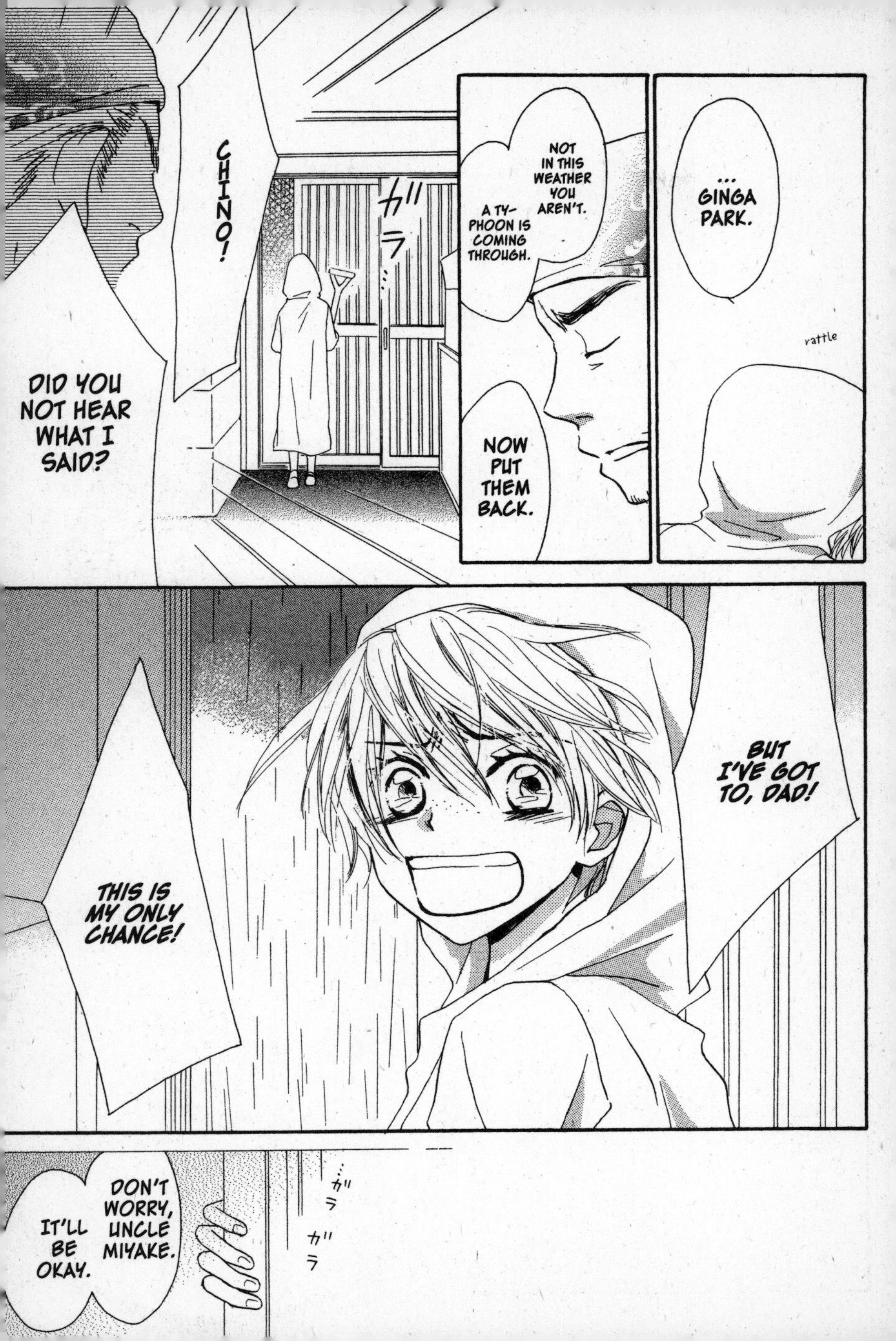
...GINGA PARK.
rattle
NOT IN THIS WEATHER YOU AREN'T.
A TY-PHOON IS COMING THROUGH.
NOW PUT THEM BACK.
ガラ...
CHINO!
DID YOU NOT HEAR WHAT I SAID?
BUT I'VE GOT TO, DAD!
THIS IS MY ONLY CHANCE!
...ガラ
ガラ
DON'T WORRY, UNCLE MIYAKE.
IT'LL BE OKAY.

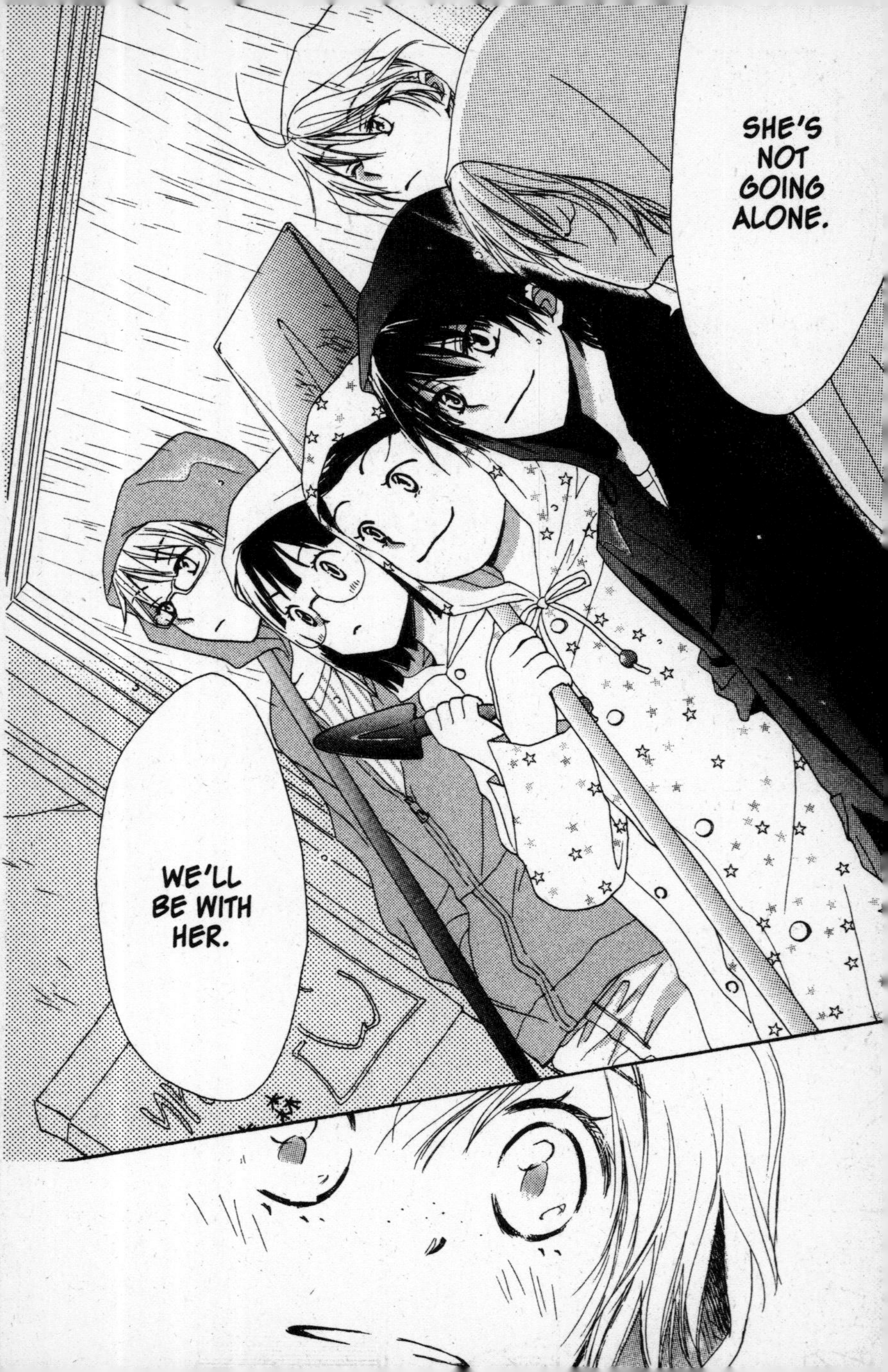
SHE'S NOT GOING ALONE.
WE'LL BE WITH HER.

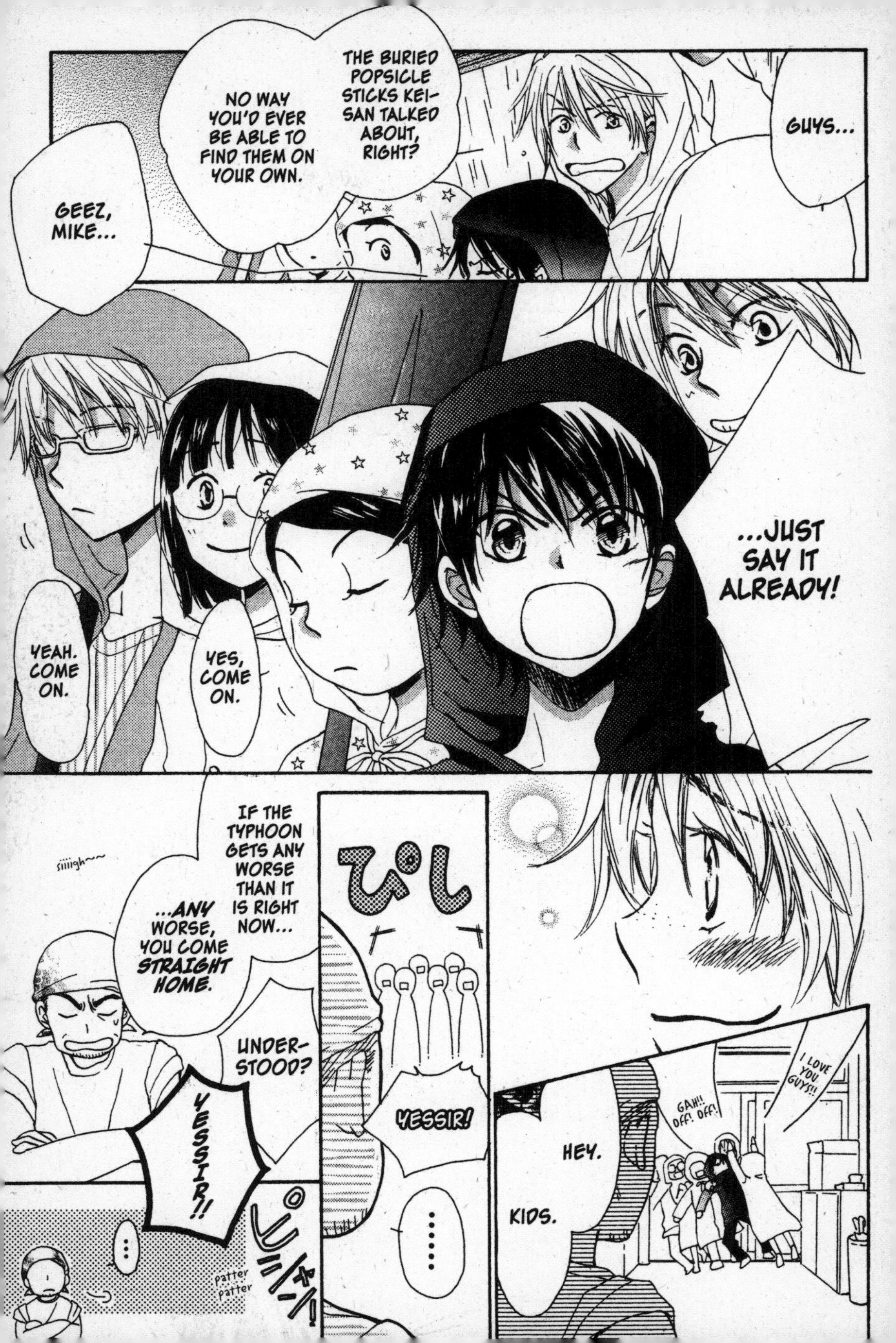
GUYS...
THE BURIED POPSICLE STICKS KEI-SAN TALKED ABOUT, RIGHT?
NO WAY YOU'D EVER BE ABLE TO FIND THEM ON YOUR OWN.
GEEZ, MIKE...
...JUST SAY IT ALREADY!
YES, COME ON.
YEAH. COME ON.
I LOVE YOU GUYS!!
GAH!! OFF! OFF!
HEY.
KIDS.
ぴし
YESSIR!
......
IF THE TYPHOON GETS ANY WORSE THAN IT IS RIGHT NOW...
siiiigh~~
...ANY WORSE, YOU COME STRAIGHT HOME.
UNDER-STOOD?
YESSIR!!
...
patter patter

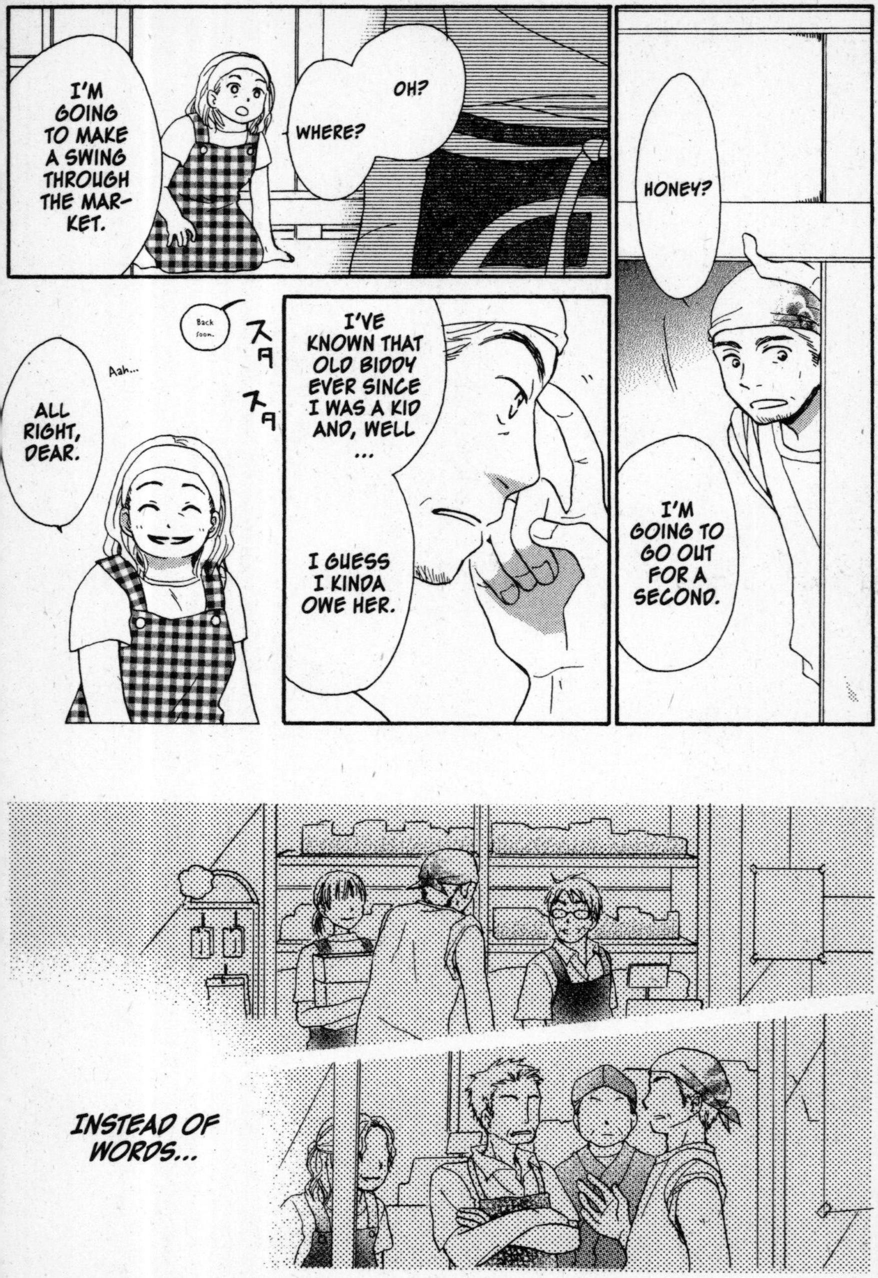
HONEY?
I'M GOING TO GO OUT FOR A SECOND.
OH? WHERE?
I'M GOING TO MAKE A SWING THROUGH THE MARKET.
I'VE KNOWN THAT OLD BIDDY EVER SINCE I WAS A KID AND, WELL ...
I GUESS I KINDA OWE HER.
Back soon.
スタ スタ
Aah...
ALL RIGHT, DEAR.
INSTEAD OF WORDS...

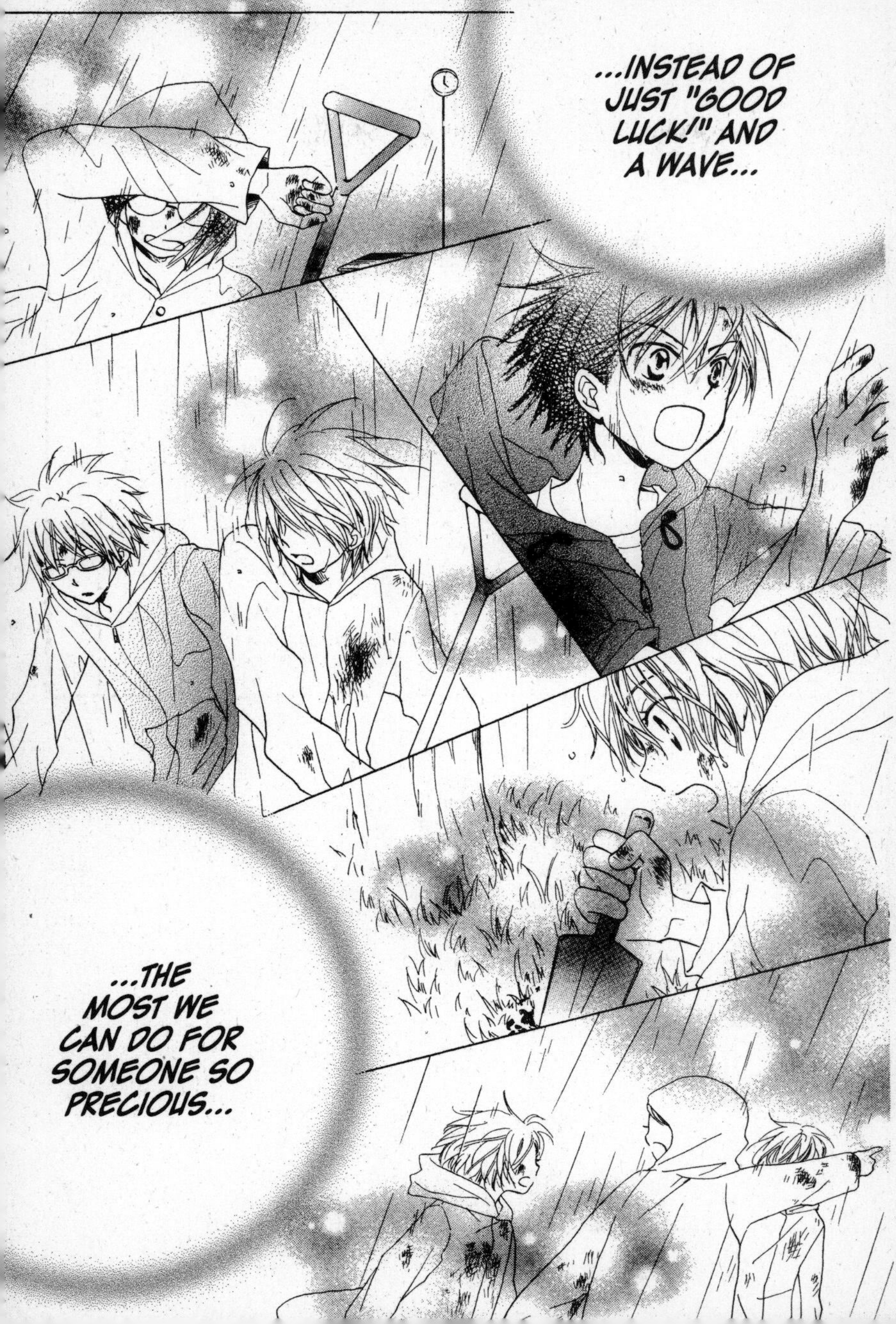
...INSTEAD OF JUST "GOOD LUCK!" AND A WAVE...
...THE MOST WE CAN DO FOR SOMEONE SO PRECIOUS...

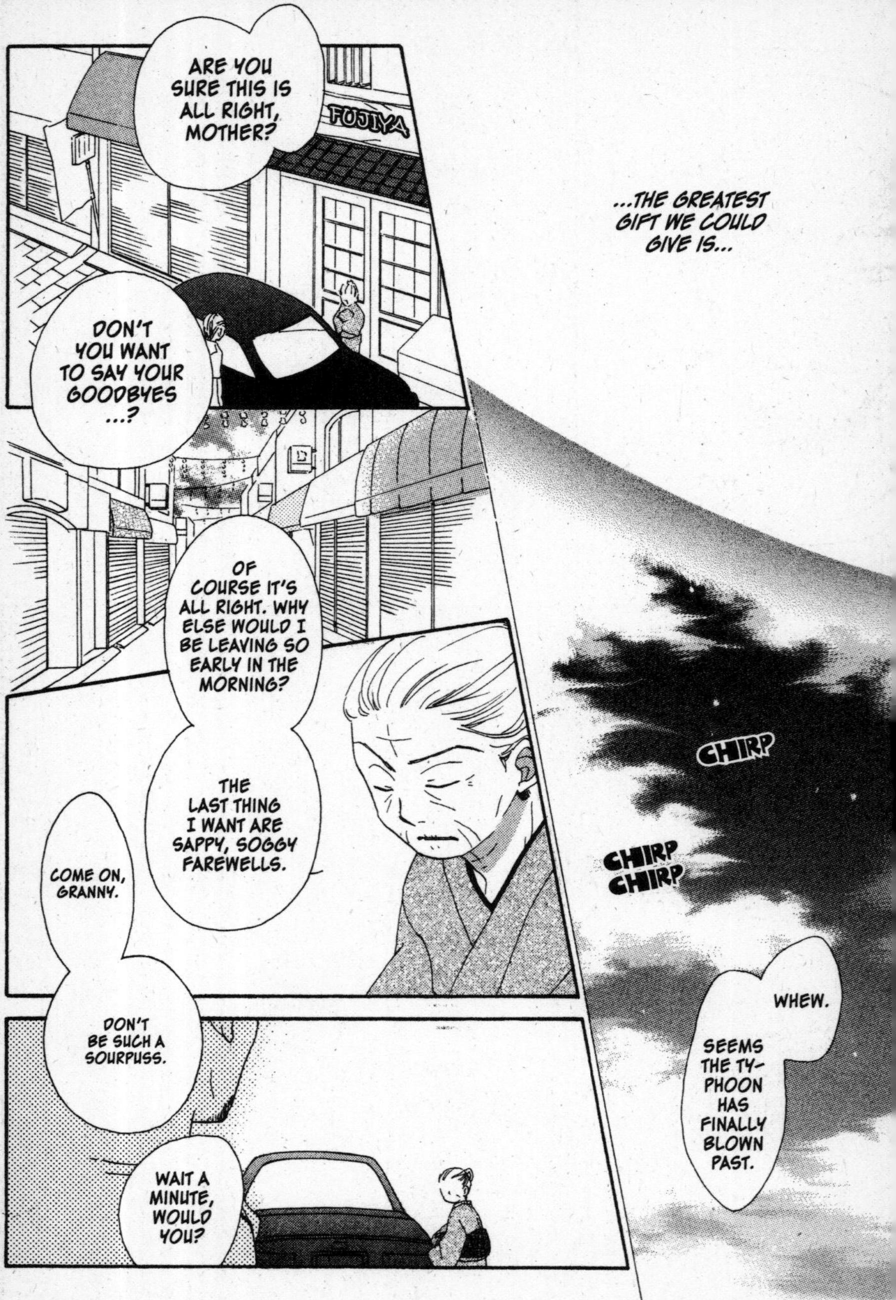
...THE GREATEST GIFT WE COULD GIVE IS...
CHIRP
CHIRP CHIRP
WHEW.
SEEMS THE TY-PHOON HAS FINALLY BLOWN PAST.
ARE YOU SURE THIS IS ALL RIGHT, MOTHER?
FUJIYA
DON'T YOU WANT TO SAY YOUR GOODBYES ...?
OF COURSE IT'S ALL RIGHT. WHY ELSE WOULD I BE LEAVING SO EARLY IN THE MORNING?
THE LAST THING I WANT ARE SAPPY, SOGGY FAREWELLS.
COME ON, GRANNY.
DON'T BE SUCH A SOURPUSS.
WAIT A MINUTE, WOULD YOU?

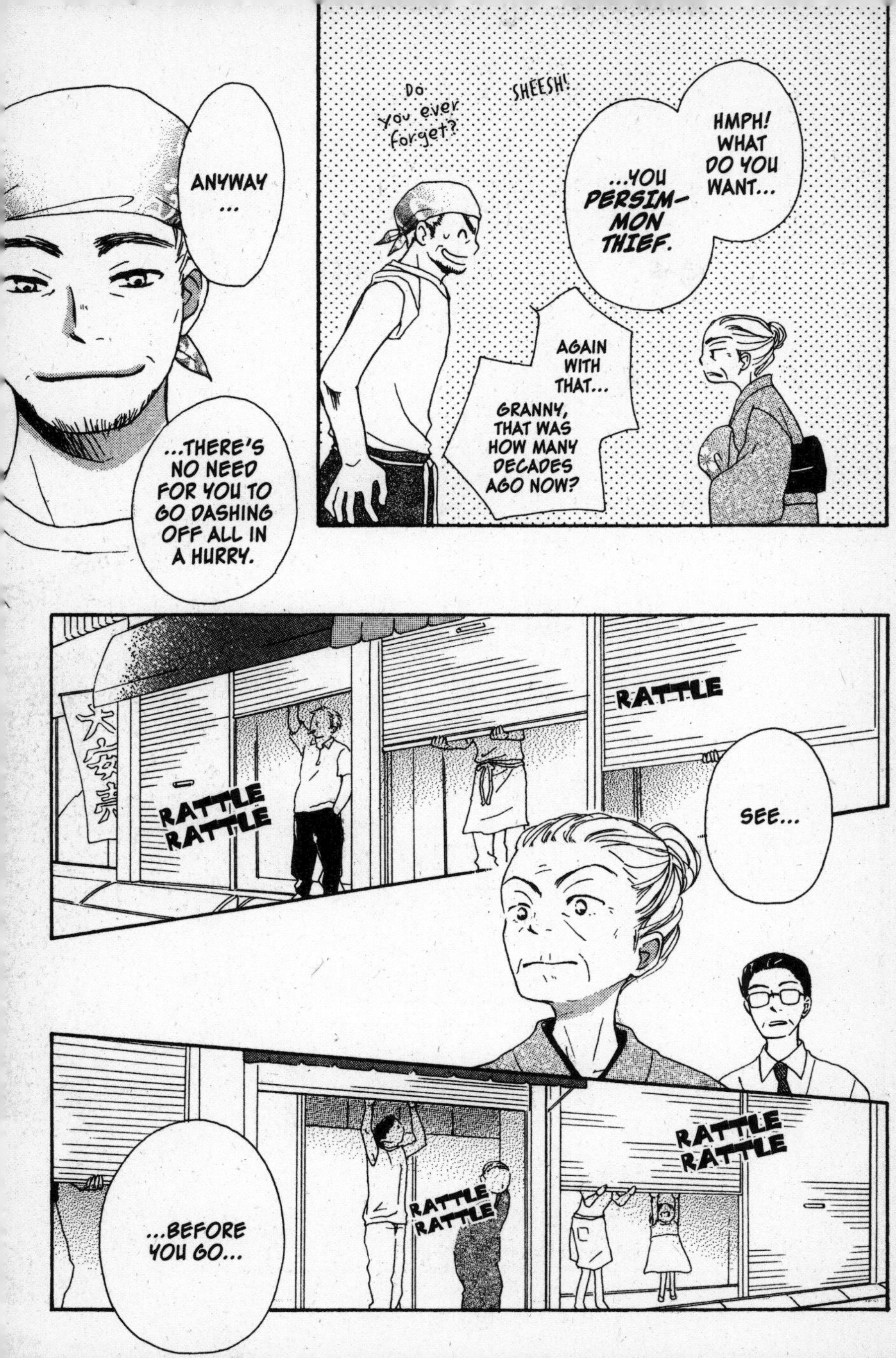
HMPH! WHAT DO YOU WANT...
...YOU PERSIMMON THIEF.
SHEESH!
Do you ever forget?
AGAIN WITH THAT...
GRANNY, THAT WAS HOW MANY DECADES AGO NOW?
ANYWAY...
...THERE'S NO NEED FOR YOU TO GO DASHING OFF ALL IN A HURRY.
RATTLE
SEE...
RATTLE RATTLE
大安売
RATTLE RATTLE
RATTLE RATTLE
...BEFORE YOU GO...

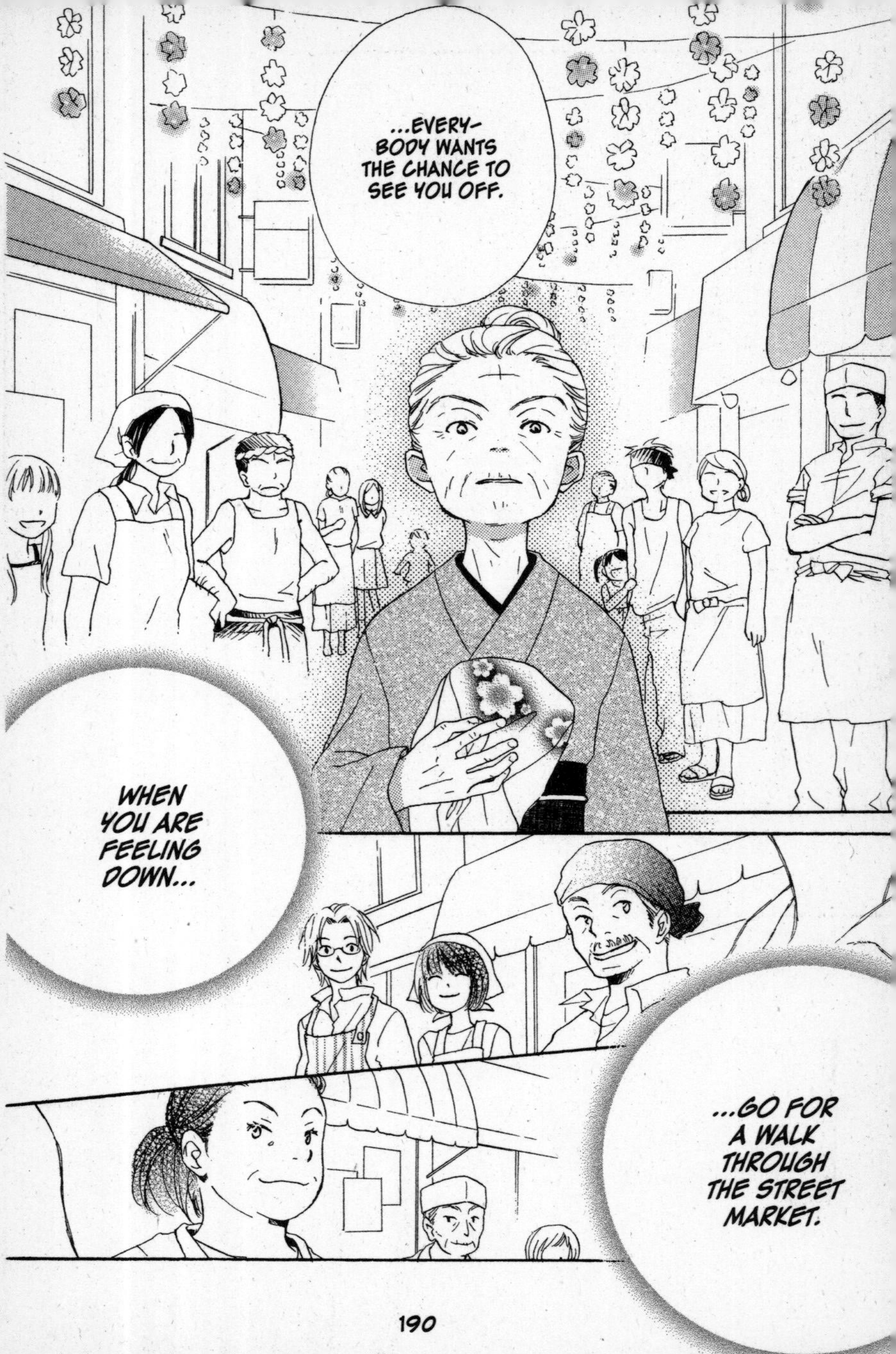
...EVERY-BODY WANTS THE CHANCE TO SEE YOU OFF.
WHEN YOU ARE FEELING DOWN...
...GO FOR A WALK THROUGH THE STREET MARKET.

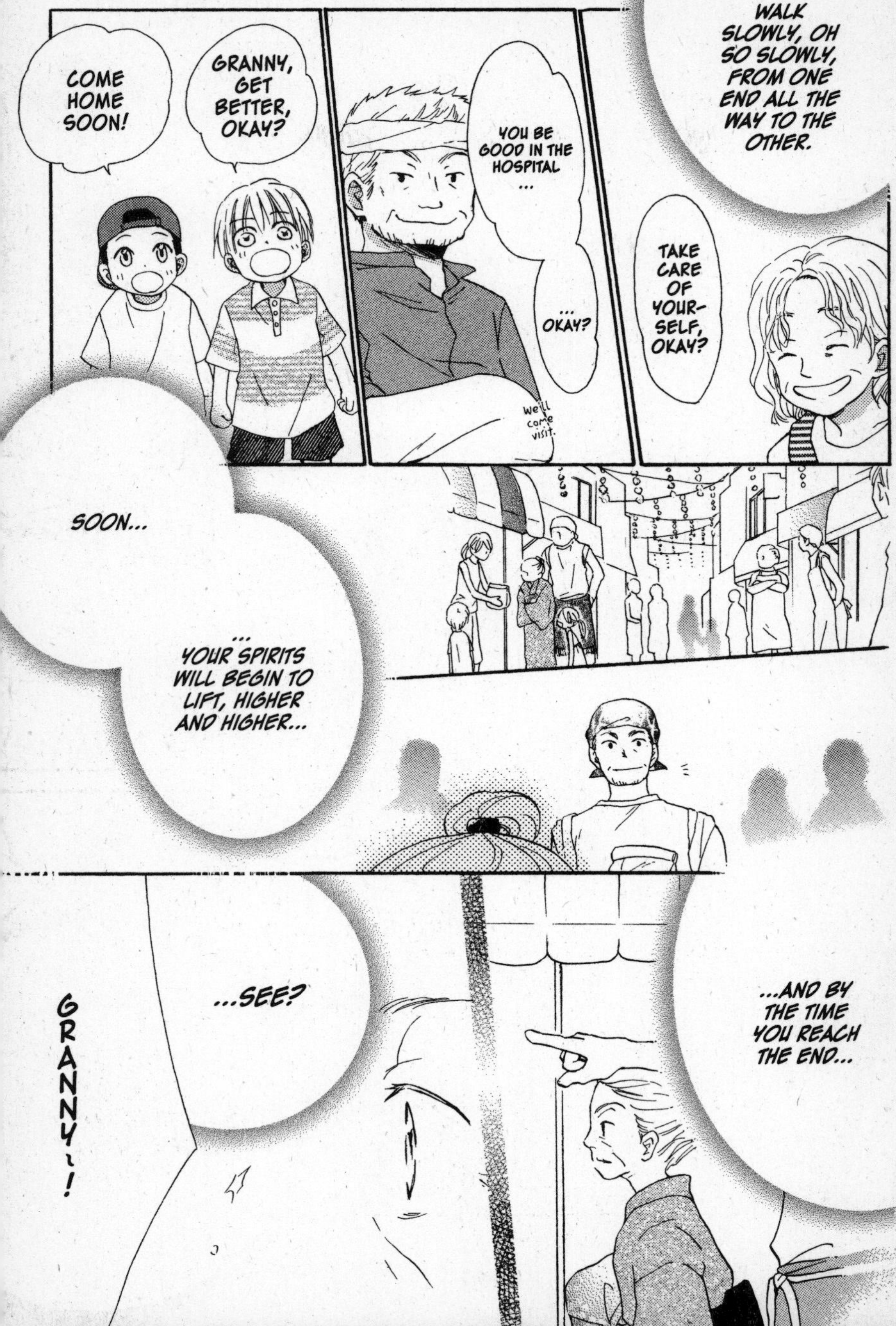
WALK SLOWLY, OH SO SLOWLY, FROM ONE END ALL THE WAY TO THE OTHER.
TAKE CARE OF YOUR-SELF, OKAY?
YOU BE GOOD IN THE HOSPITAL ...
... OKAY?
We'll come visit.
GRANNY, GET BETTER, OKAY?
COME HOME SOON!
SOON...
... YOUR SPIRITS WILL BEGIN TO LIFT, HIGHER AND HIGHER...
...AND BY THE TIME YOU REACH THE END...
...SEE?
GRANNY~!

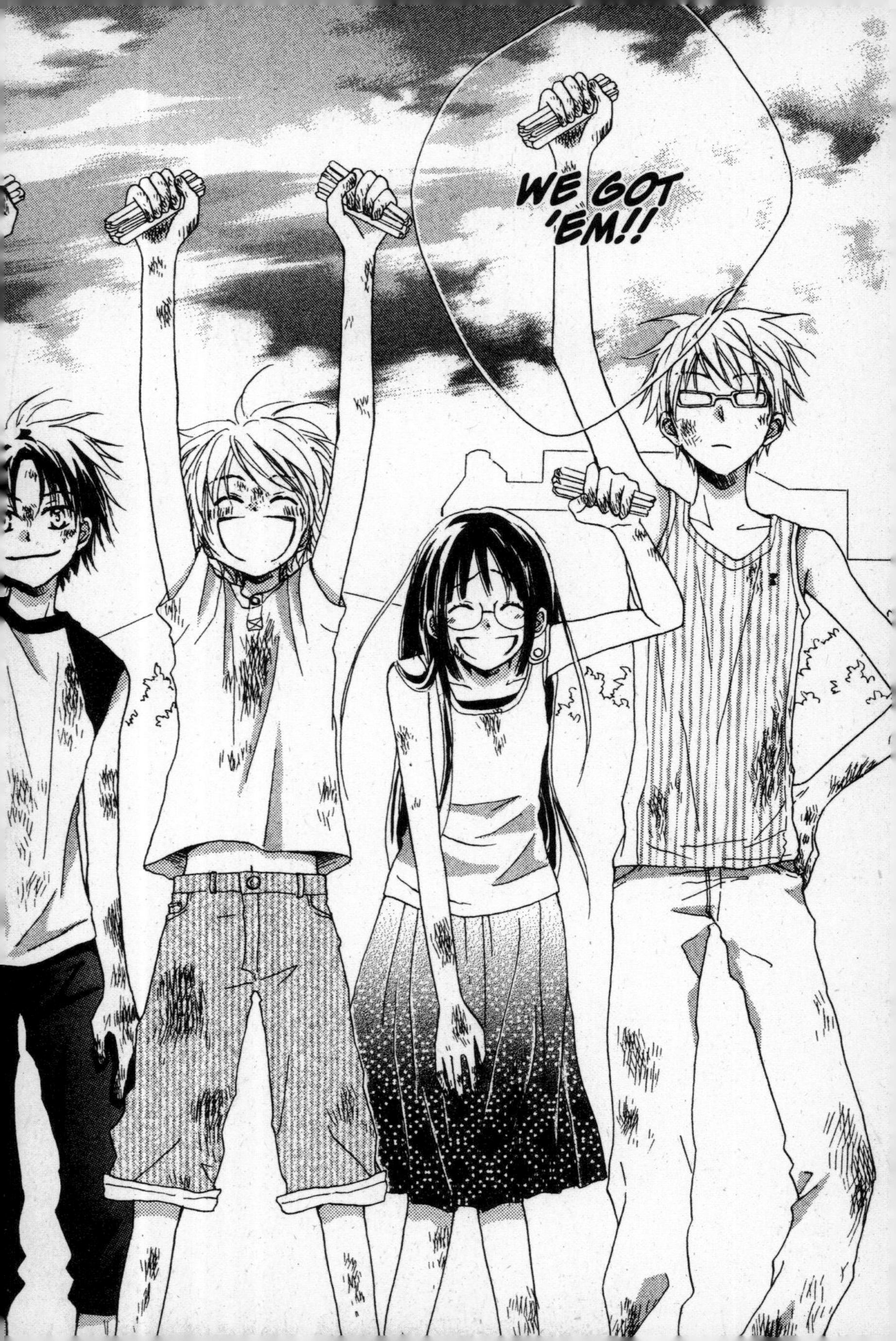
WE GOT 'EM!!

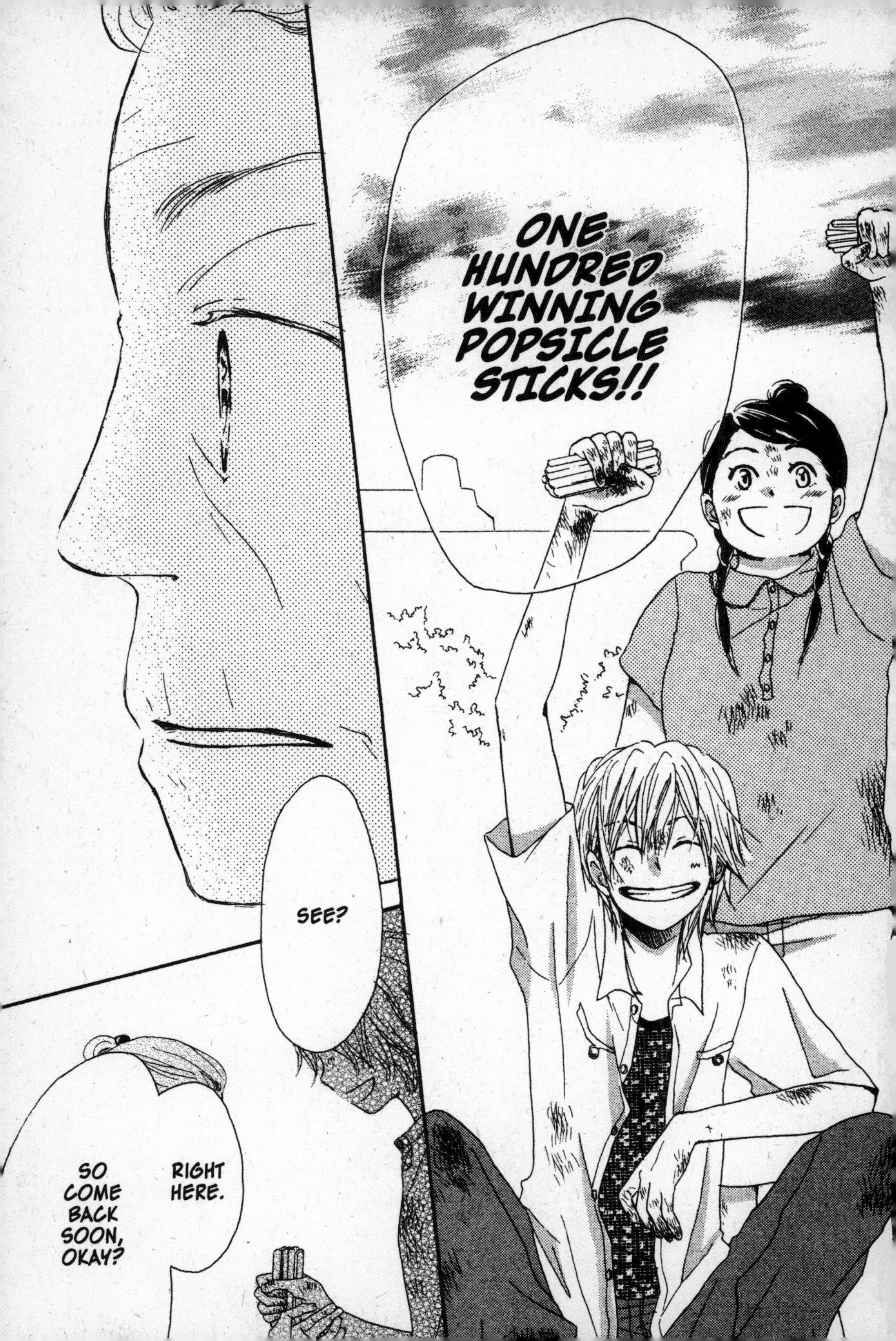
ONE HUNDRED WINNING POPSICLE STICKS!!
SEE?
RIGHT HERE.
SO COME BACK SOON, OKAY?

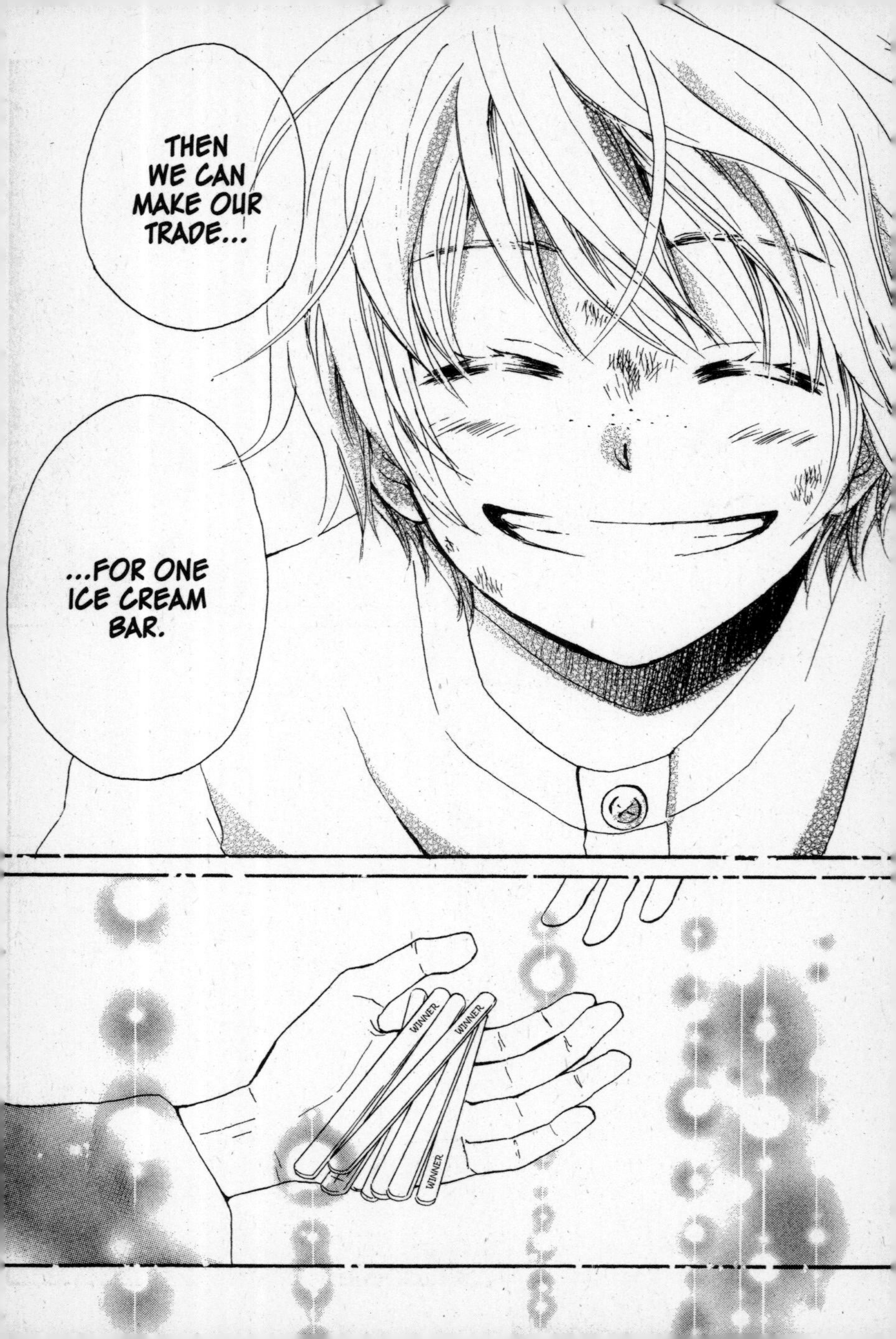
THEN WE CAN MAKE OUR TRADE...
...FOR ONE ICE CREAM BAR.
WINNER
WINNER
WINNER
WINNER

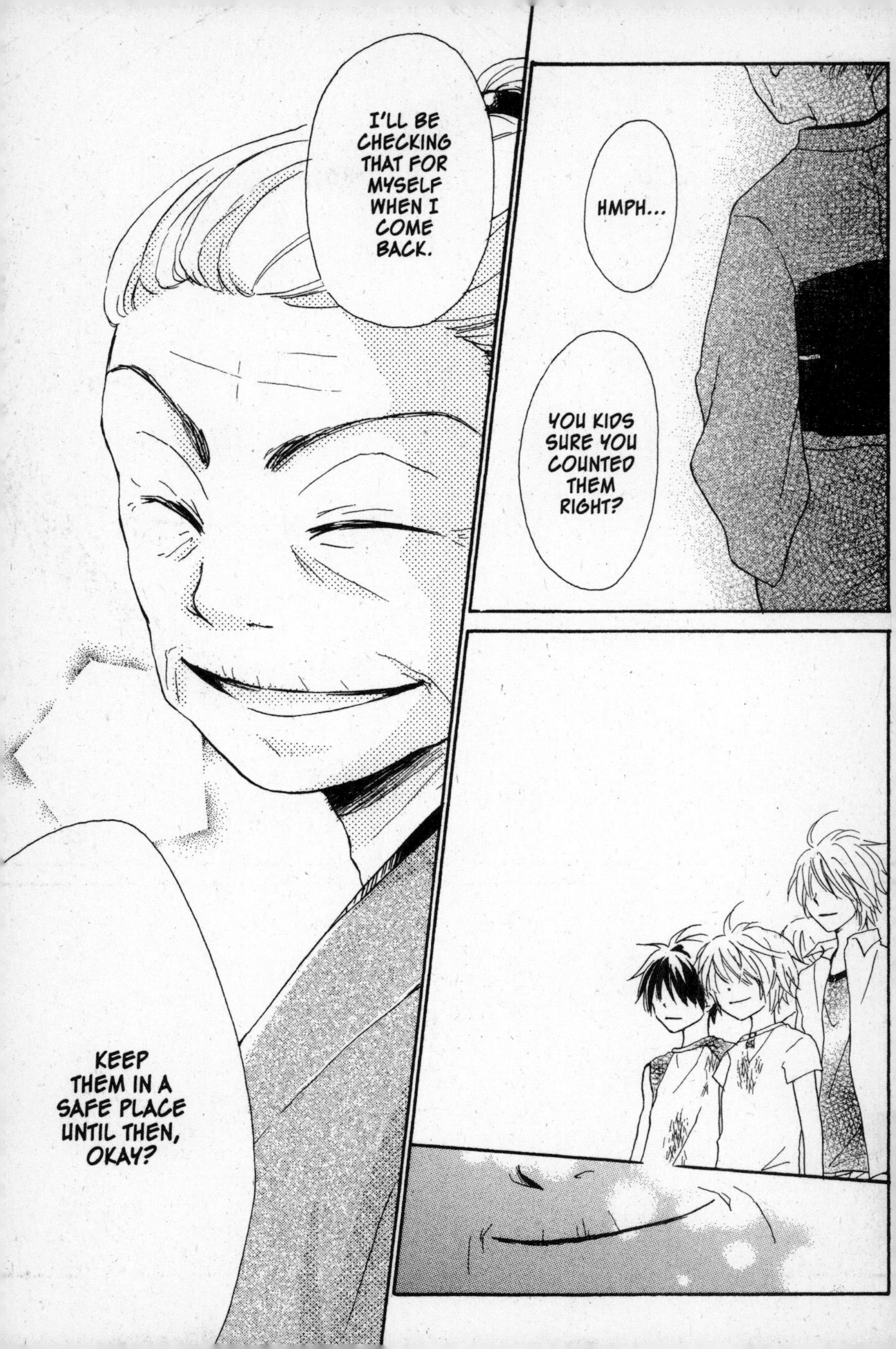
HMPH...
YOU KIDS SURE YOU COUNTED THEM RIGHT?
I'LL BE CHECKING THAT FOR MYSELF WHEN I COME BACK.
KEEP THEM IN A SAFE PLACE UNTIL THEN, OKAY?

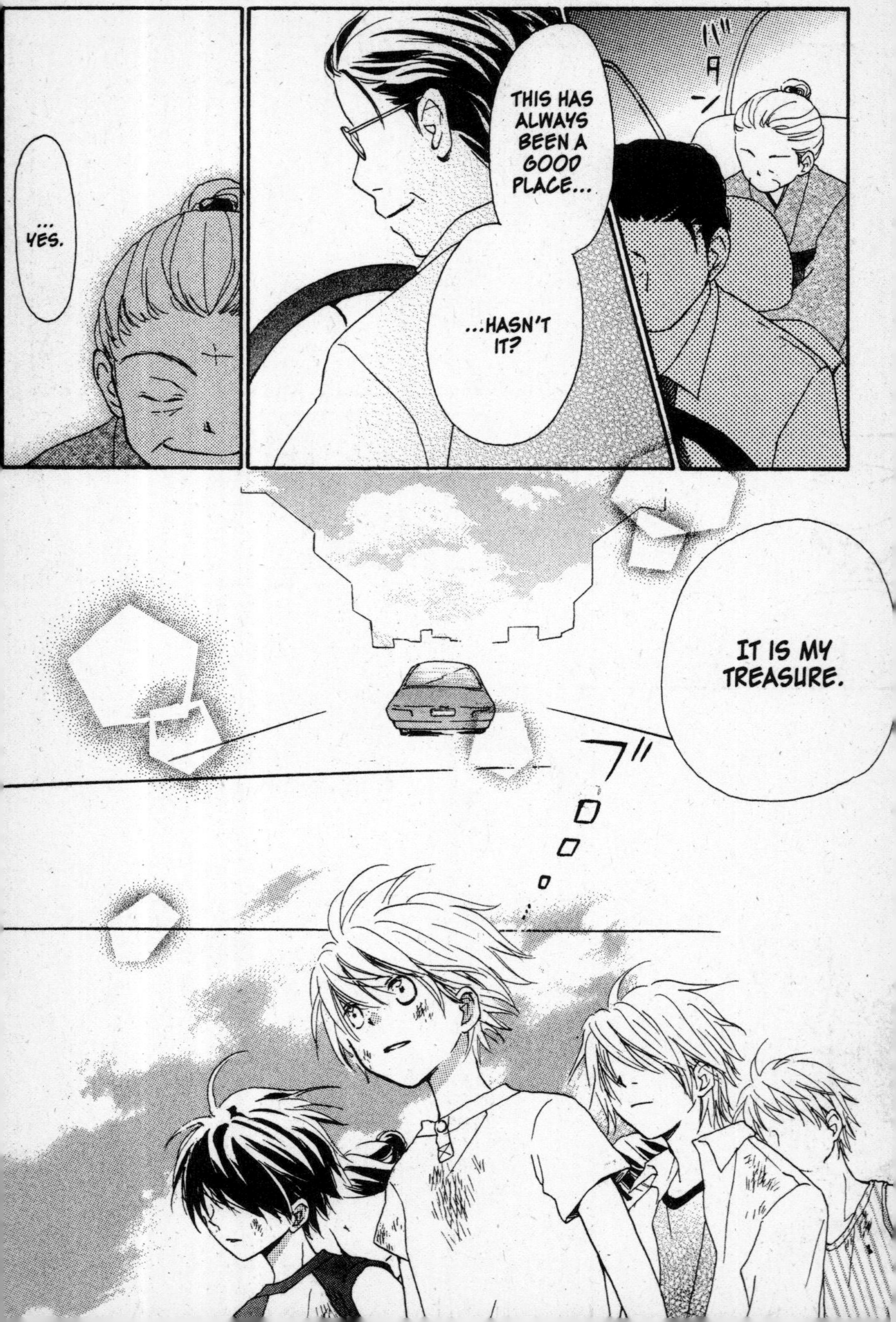
THIS HAS ALWAYS BEEN A GOOD PLACE...
...HASN'T IT?
... YES.
IT IS MY TREASURE.

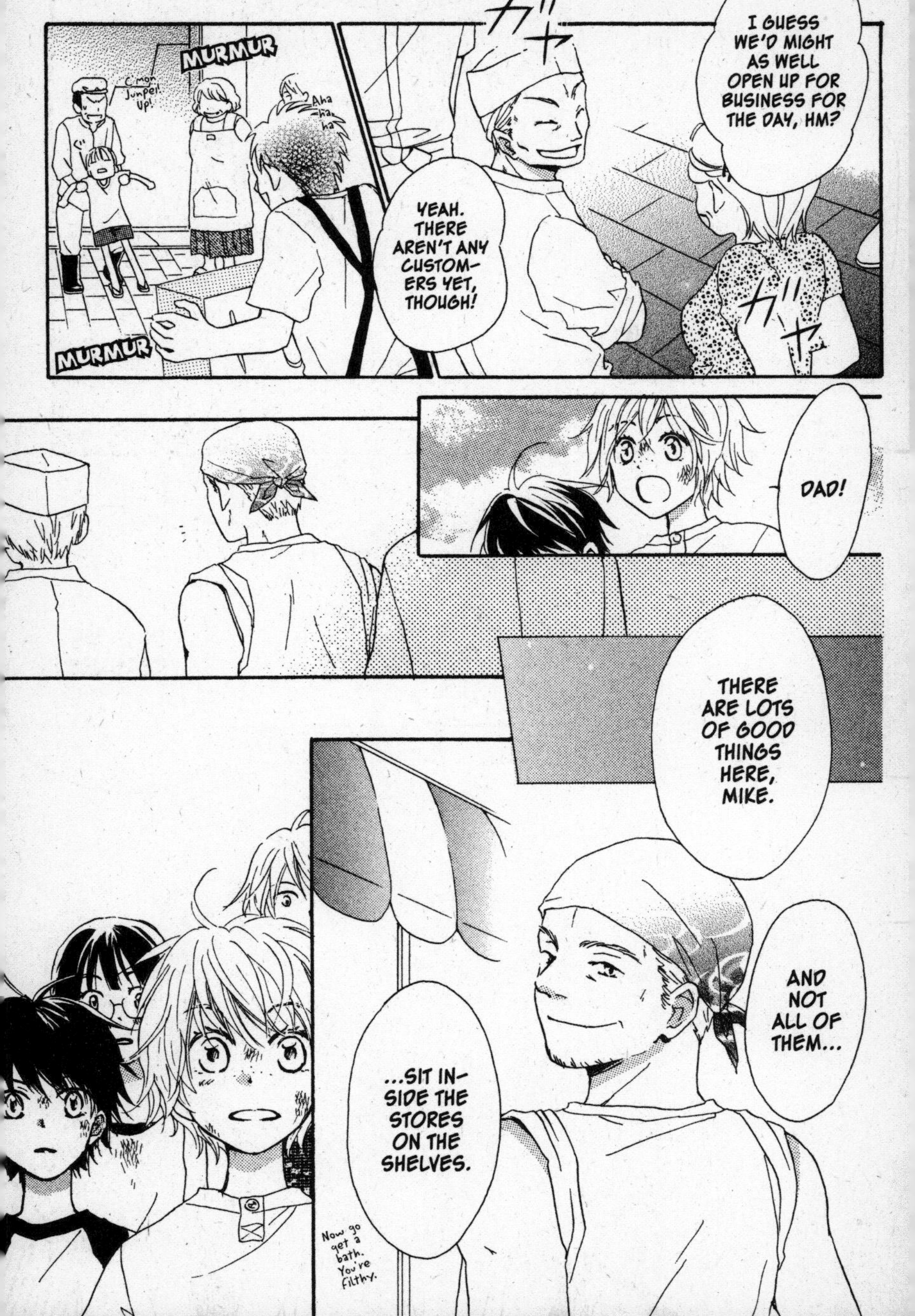
ガヤ
I GUESS WE'D MIGHT AS WELL OPEN UP FOR BUSINESS FOR THE DAY, HM?
ガヤ
YEAH. THERE AREN'T ANY CUSTOMERS YET, THOUGH!
MURMUR
C'mon Junpei! Up!
Aha ha ha
MURMUR
DAD!
THERE ARE LOTS OF GOOD THINGS HERE, MIKE.
AND NOT ALL OF THEM...
...SIT INSIDE THE STORES ON THE SHELVES.
Now go get a bath. You're filthy.

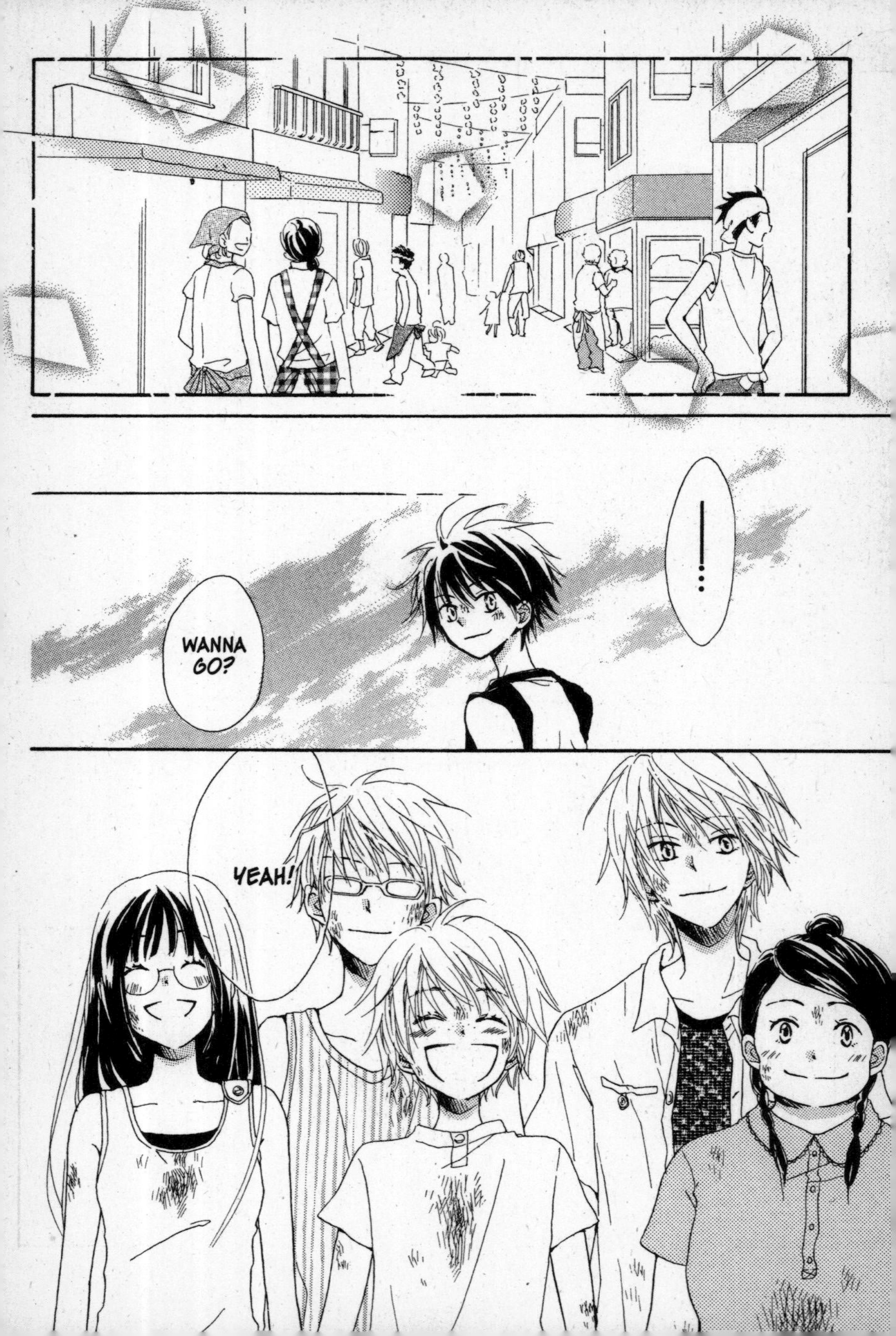
!
...
WANNA GO?
YEAH!

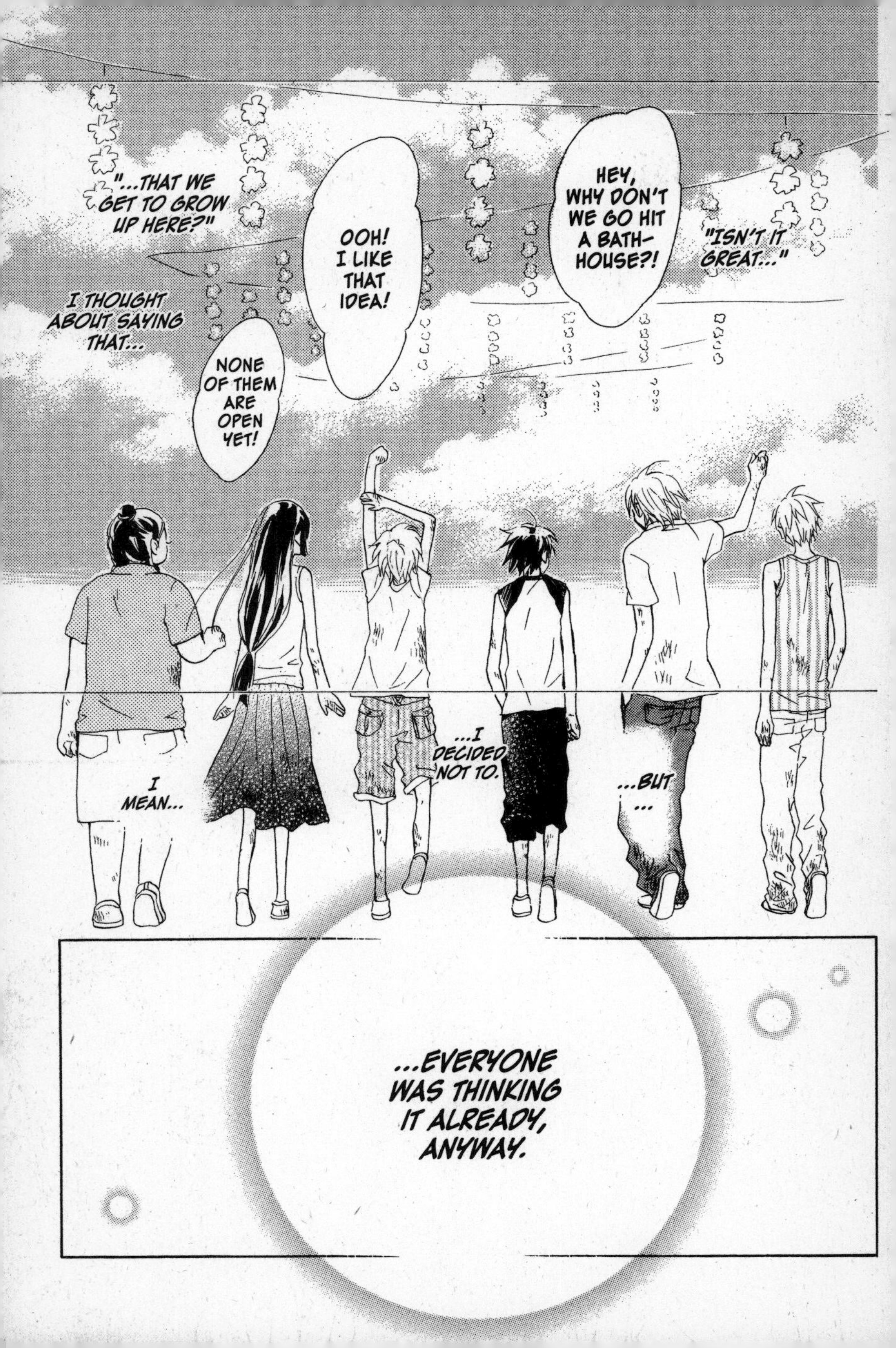
"ISN'T IT GREAT..."
HEY, WHY DON'T WE GO HIT A BATH-HOUSE?!
OOH! I LIKE THAT IDEA!
"...THAT WE GET TO GROW UP HERE?"
NONE OF THEM ARE OPEN YET!
I THOUGHT ABOUT SAYING THAT...
...BUT ...
...I DECIDED NOT TO.
I MEAN...
...EVERYONE WAS THINKING IT ALREADY, ANYWAY.

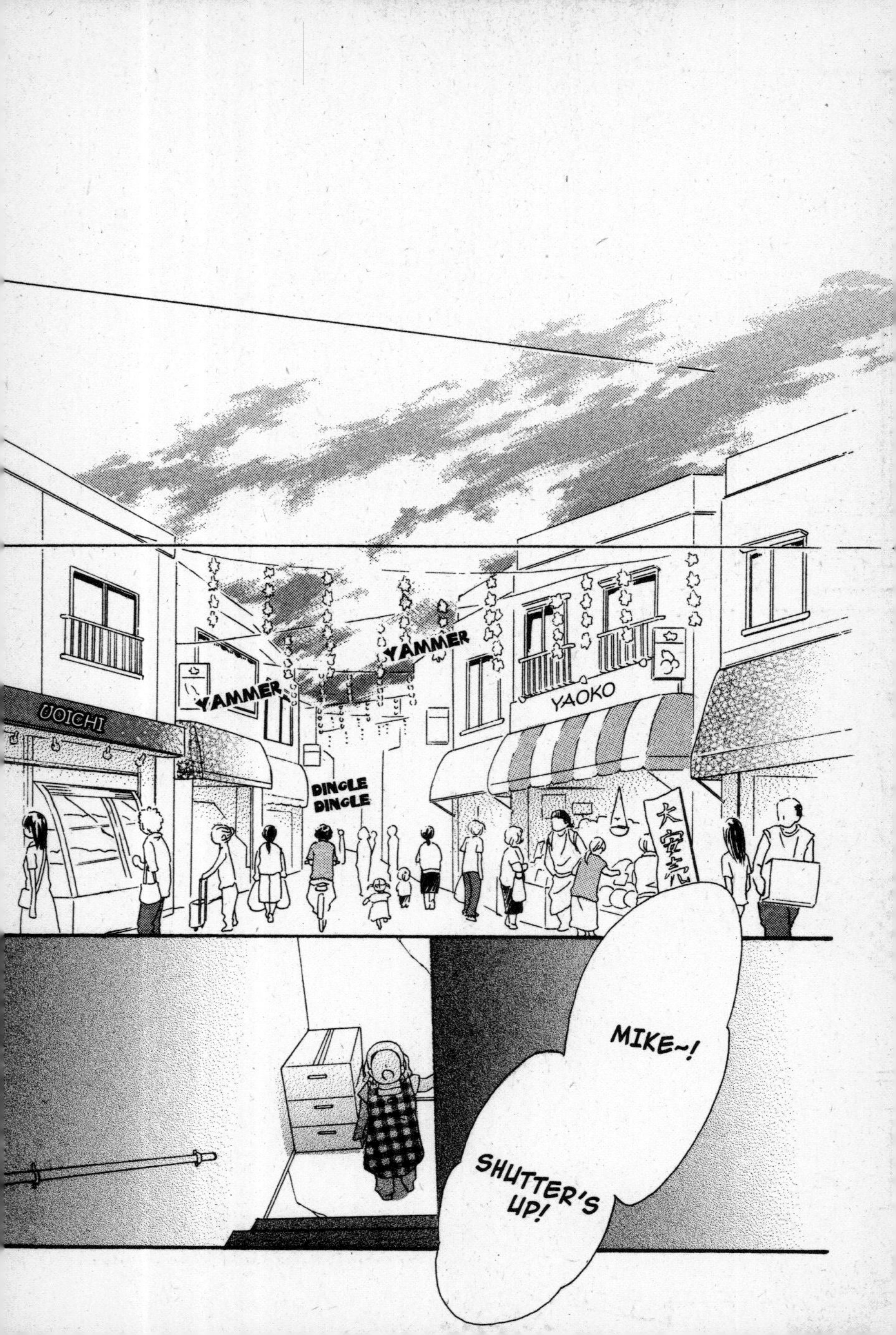
YAMMER
YAOKO
大安売
YAMMER
UOICHI
DINGLE DINGLE
MIKE~!
SHUTTER'S UP!

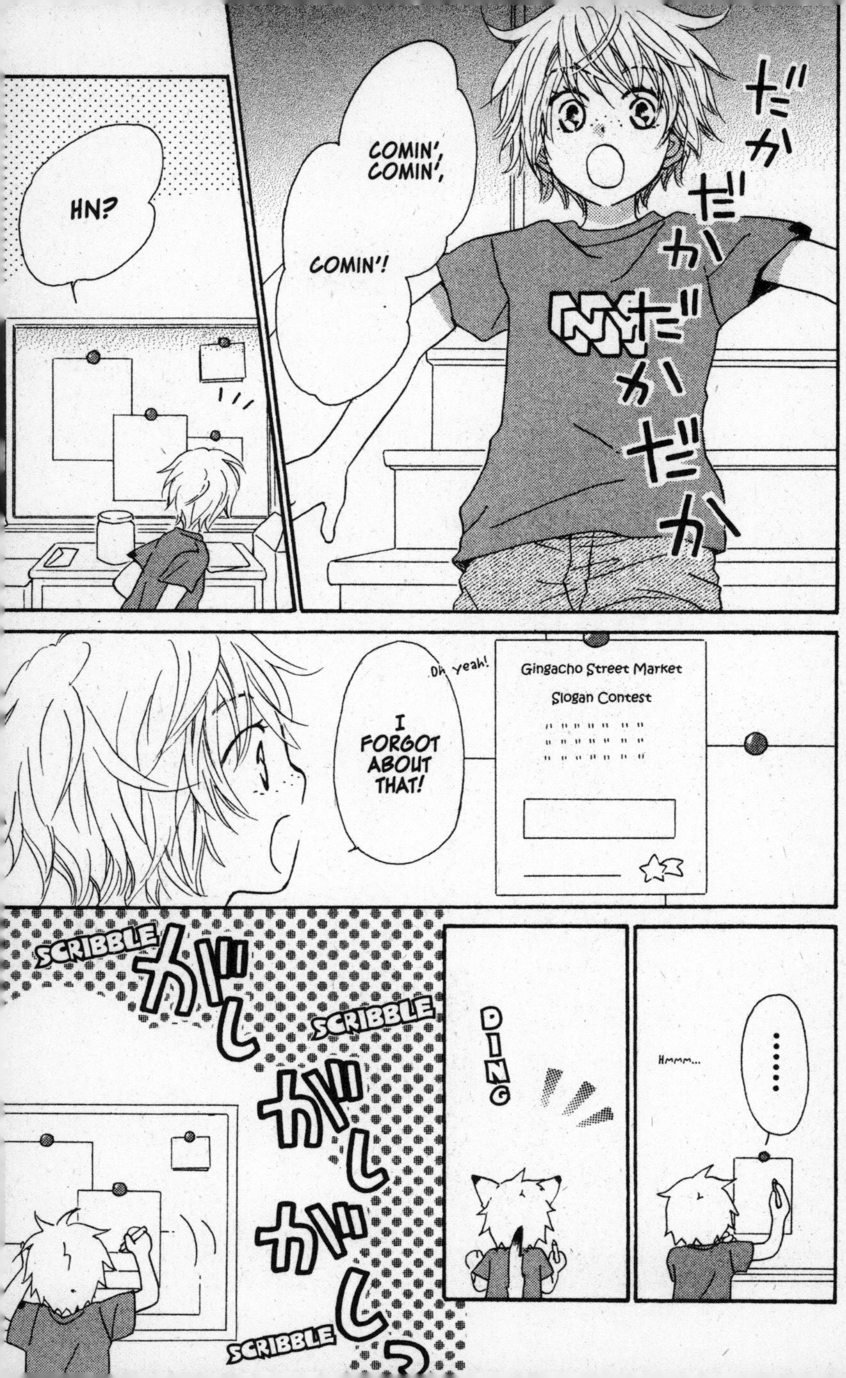

COMIN', COMIN', COMIN'!
だかだかだかだか
HN?
Oh yeah!
I FORGOT ABOUT THAT!
Gingacho Street Market
Slogan Contest
Hmmm...
......
DING
SCRIBBLE
がしがしがしっ
SCRIBBLE
SCRIBBLE

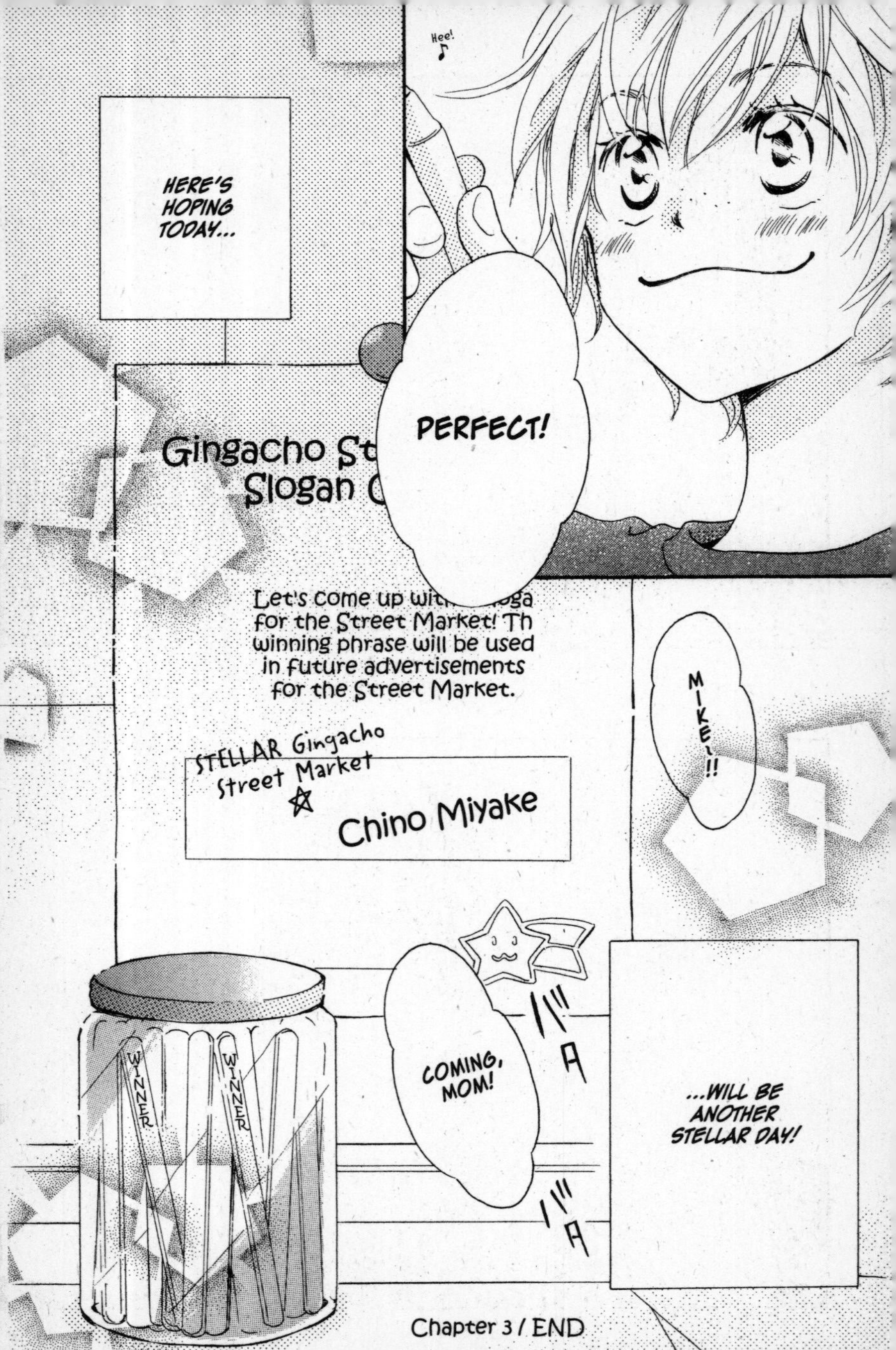
Hee! ♪
PERFECT!
HERE'S HOPING TODAY...
Gingacho St
Slogan C
Let's come up wit sloga for the Street Market! Th winning phrase will be used in future advertisements for the Street Market.
STELLAR Gingacho Street Market ☆
Chino Miyake
WINNER
WINNER
MIKE~!!
COMING, MOM!
バ
バ
...WILL BE ANOTHER STELLAR DAY!

Chapter 3 / END

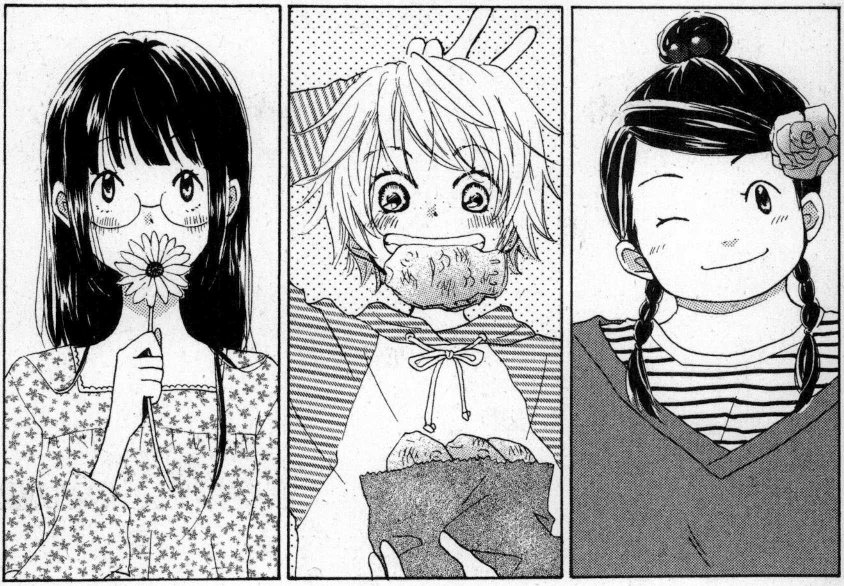

BONUS PAGES

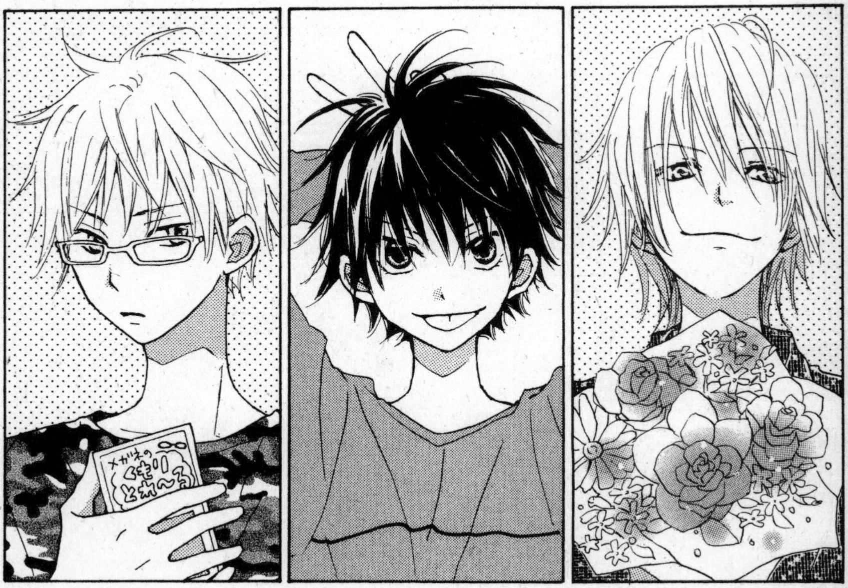
メガネの
くもり
とれ〜る

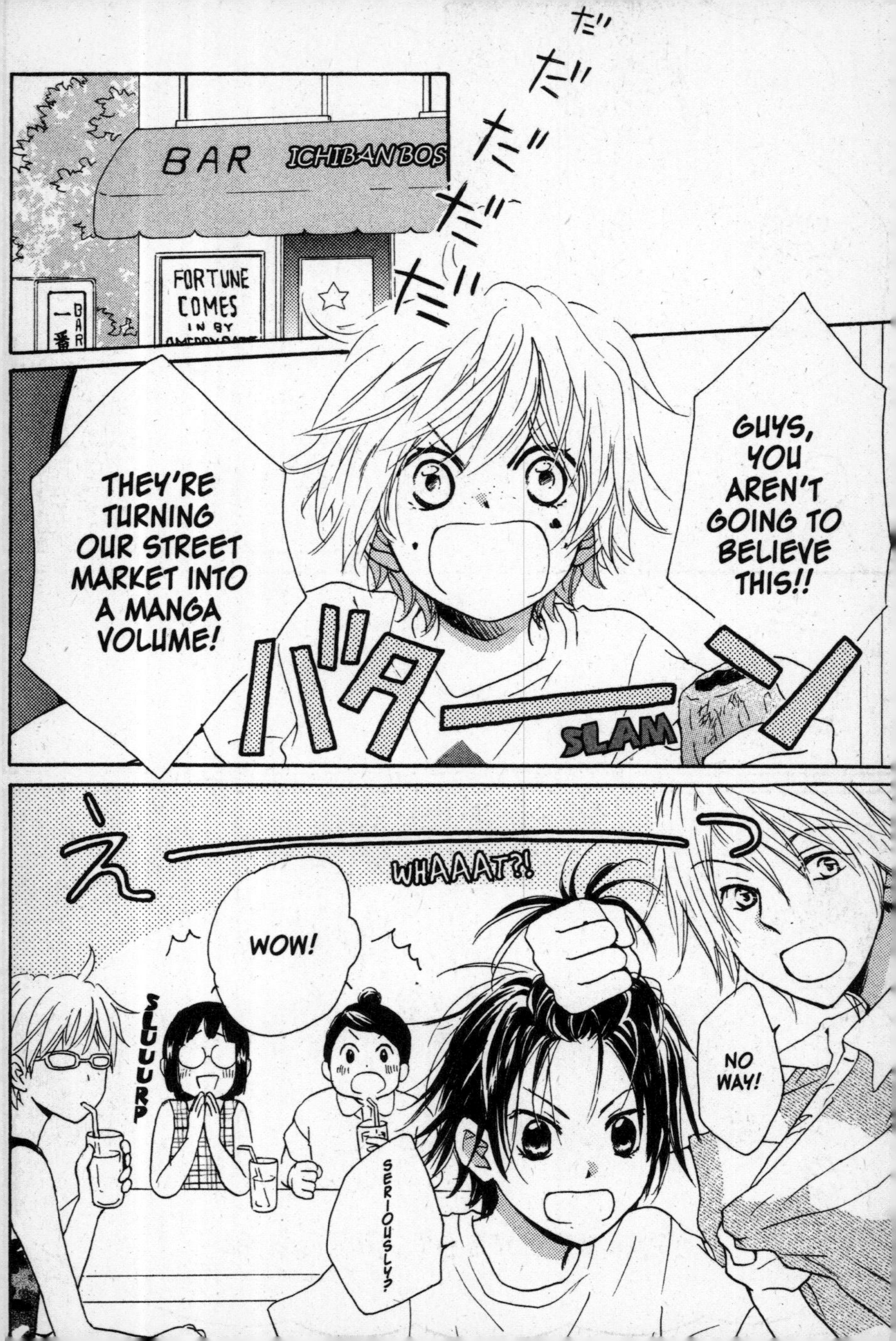
だだだだだ
BAR
ICHIBANBOS
FORTUNE COMES IN BY
BAR 一番
GUYS, YOU AREN'T GOING TO BELIEVE THIS!!
THEY'RE TURNING OUR STREET MARKET INTO A MANGA VOLUME!
バターン
SLAM
えーーっ
WHAAAT?!
NO WAY!
SERIOUSLY?
WOW!
SLUUURP

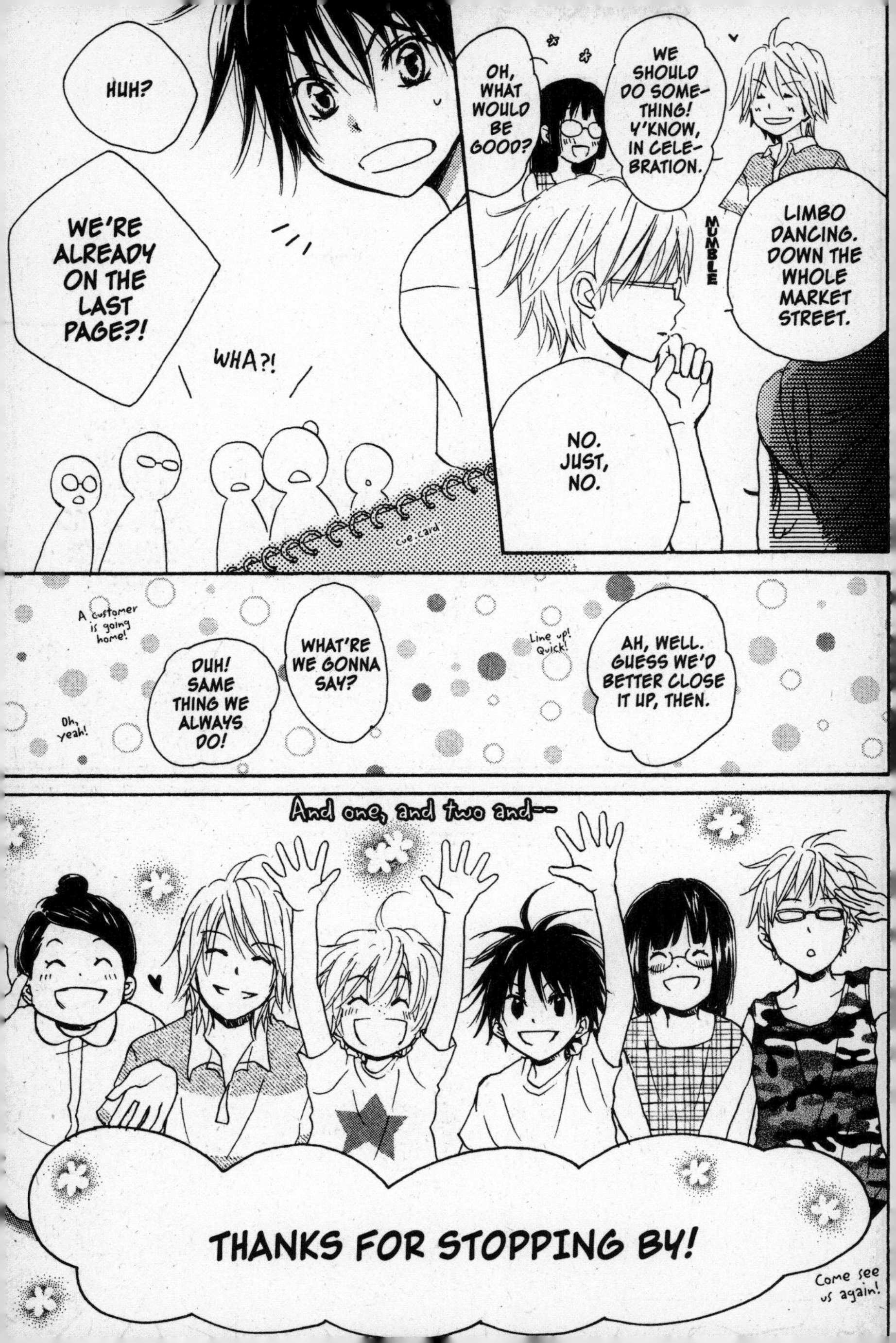
WE SHOULD DO SOME-THING! Y'KNOW, IN CELE-BRATION.
OH, WHAT WOULD BE GOOD?
LIMBO DANCING. DOWN THE WHOLE MARKET STREET.
MUMBLE
NO. JUST, NO.
HUH?
WE'RE ALREADY ON THE LAST PAGE?!
WHA?!
Cue card
AH, WELL. GUESS WE'D BETTER CLOSE IT UP, THEN.
Line up! Quick!
WHAT'RE WE GONNA SAY?
A customer is going home!
DUH! SAME THING WE ALWAYS DO!
Oh, yeah!
And one, and two and--
THANKS FOR STOPPING BY!
Come see us again!

Thank you

very much.
2006.3 Fujimoto

Special Thanks!!

Yuzucchi	Everyone at Kitasenju-marui's Kinokuniya Bookstore
Kasshi	Hoven Kikaku-sama
Daidai-san	The market family who let me visit them for research.
Yagi	My family.
Nagi-san	My friends.
Hisako	
Sakuma-san	And you, who are reading this.

I hope we meet again! ☺

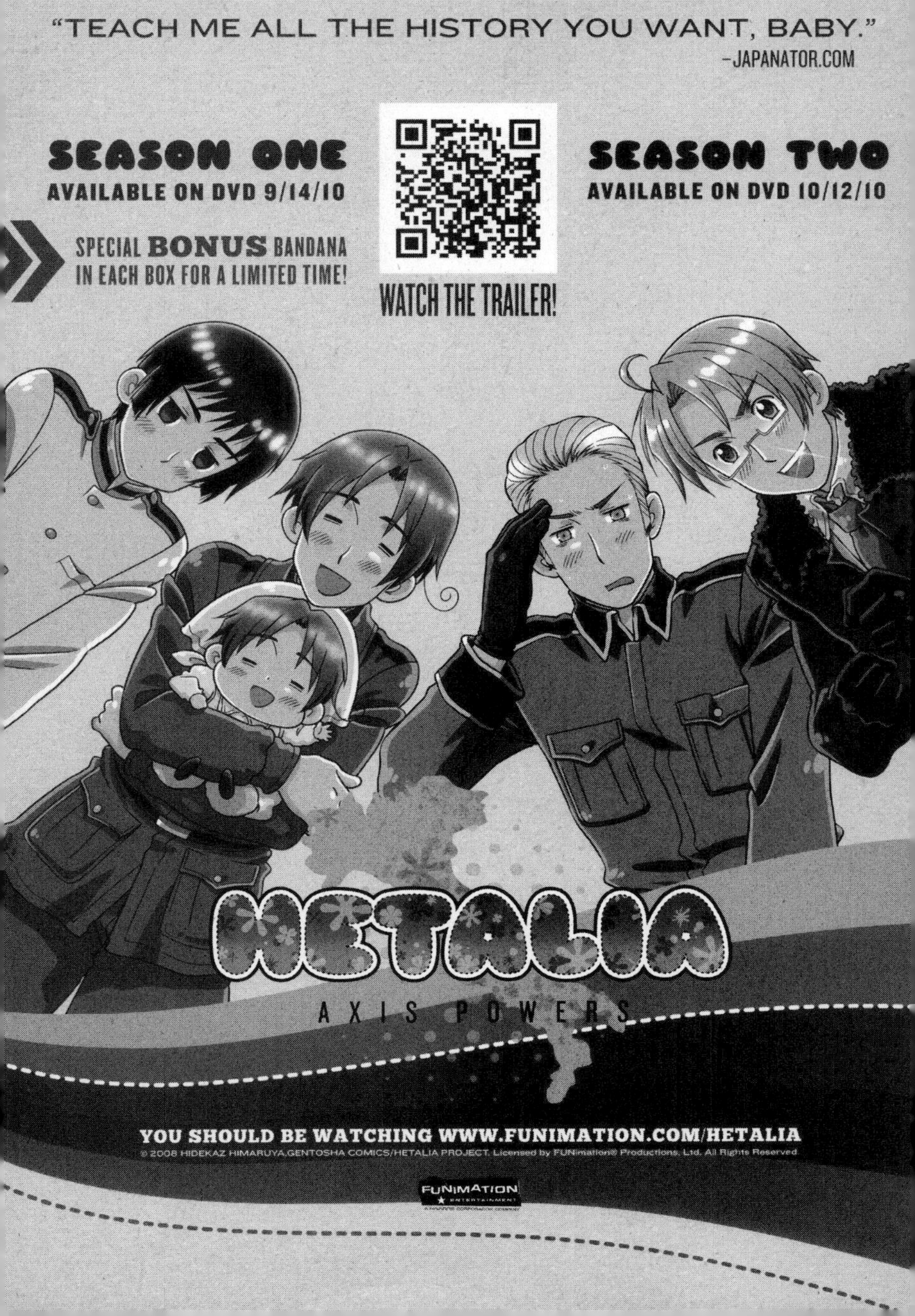

STOP!

This is the back of the book.
You wouldn't want to spoil a great ending!

This book is printed "manga-style," in the authentic Japanese right-to-left format. Since none of the artwork has been flipped or altered, readers get to experience the story just as the creator intended. You've been asking for it, so TOKYOPOP® delivered: authentic, hot-off-the-press, and far more fun!

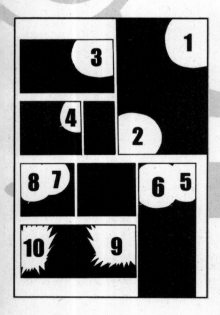

DIRECTIONS

If this is your first time reading manga-style, here's a quick guide to help you understand how it works.

It's easy... just start in the top right panel and follow the numbers. Have fun, and look for more 100% authentic manga from TOKYOPOP®!